THE GREAT PLATEAU
OF NORTHERN RHODESIA

F. H Melland, phot.

LUITIKILA RIVER.

THE GREAT PLATEAU
OF NORTHERN RHODESIA

Being Some Impressions of the
Tanganyika Plateau

BY

CULLEN GOULDSBURY

AND

HUBERT SHEANE, F.R.A.I., F.R.G.S.
OF THE BRITISH SOUTH AFRICA COMPANY'S SERVICE

With an Introduction by
SIR ALFRED SHARPE, K.C.M.G., C.B.

ILLUSTRATED

NEGRO UNIVERSITIES PRESS
NEW YORK

Originally published in 1911
by Edward Arnold, London

Reprinted 1969 by
Negro Universities Press
A DIVISION OF GREENWOOD PUBLISHING CORP.
NEW YORK

SBN 8371-1289-3

TO

THE MEMORY OF THE LATE

R O B E R T   C O D R I N G T O N,   C. M. G.

ADMINISTRATOR OF NORTH-EASTERN RHODESIA, 1898-1907,

TO WHOSE MASTERFUL ENERGY AND TIRELESS DEVOTION

NORTH-EASTERN RHODESIA OWES SO MUCH,

THE HUMBLE TRIBUTE OF THIS BOOK

IS RESPECTFULLY DEDICATED

NOTE BY SIR ALFRED SHARPE

I HAVE been asked by the Authors to write a short introduction to their work—which deals with one of the most fascinating districts of Tropical Africa. We read in these days many books on Africa, most of which contain the impressions gathered by travellers passing through on fleeting visits. Their opinions are the result of information hastily gleaned from others, and are in many cases quite unreliable. To get at the bottom of things in Africa there is only one method—long continued residence —backed by a proper sympathy with native ideas. The Authors of this book have spent a considerable portion of their lives in the land and among the peoples they write of, and no one could be better qualified than they to deal with the subjects they have taken in hand.

I knew the Tanganyika Plateau well twenty years ago : it is a charming land, cut off, as the Authors state, from all that we understand as 'civilisation,' where everything is peaceful, the natives kindly and willing, the climate delightful and fairly healthy.

How long will this remain so ?

The Plateau lies on the backbone of Africa, along which the existence of valuable minerals is being every year more clearly proved. The Rand, Southern Rhodesia, and Katanga all lie on this continental watershed, and even the distant Kilo gold-mines (Albert Nyanza). It will probably not be long before the scheme outlined by the Authors on page 328, of a line of rail and water communication from the sea-coast (Beira) to Tanganyika is carried out, thus giving an outlet with cheap transport for the Tanganyika Plateau and Northern Katanga.

Meantime, the Authors of this volume give a description of native life on the Tanganyika Plateau—as it now exists—minute, reliable, and deeply interesting.

ALFRED SHARPE.

12th September 1911.

AUTHORS' PREFACE

Year by year the glamour of the Outer Fringe is fading, and it is becoming more difficult to enlist the sympathies of the stay-at-home upon the side of the Silent Places. European Royalties and vivacious journalists, Republican Presidents, and lady travellers are contracting a habit of invading the immemorial vastness, of disturbing the immemorial silence of tropical Africa.

And, in inverse ratio to this depreciation of glamour, the output of literature dealing with the sub-continent increases. Every month witnesses many additions to the bibliography of Africa—almost every year some new society springs into being, avowedly constituted to drag from the unfortunate land whatever rags may yet remain of its mantle of pristine mystery. As a natural consequence, almost every new volume bearing upon African affairs opens with an apology.

Let us, at least, be original upon this point if upon no other, and, waiving apology, preface our work with the statement that an urgent need exists for some exposition of the conditions which govern life upon the Southern Tanganyika Plateau at the present day.

Our aim is to give some impression, however blurred or imperfect, of an almost unique, and hitherto unrecorded, phase of colonial isolation. Alone among other British African dependencies, we possess neither coast ports nor railway termini to connect us with the Empire at large. Consequently, the Plateau native, preserved from the perils of progress, has maintained his distinctive characteristics. His folklore and customs are still intact ; his country is still a happy hunting-ground for the ethnologist. And, also, the existence which is led by the few Europeans now in the country differs very materially from the stereotyped exile prevailing in other dependencies or possessions. In many ways our lives resemble those of dwellers in the

Indian Empire; yet our luxuries and our hardships are quite other than theirs.

But all this is, pre-eminently, a passing phase. Slowly, but none the less surely, the Cape to Cairo Railway is penetrating to the fringes of our territory, to be followed inevitably by a wave of European immigration. While the German railway, forging ahead to the shores of Lake Tanganyika, is bringing in its train the influence of the Arab and of the East Coast native.

And yet, although existing conditions would appear to be threatened on every side, although we are upon the verge of amalgamation with the sister territory of North-western Rhodesia, when it is probable that the individuality of this sphere will be submerged, no book has, hitherto, been written upon this tract of country—more than fifty thousand square miles in extent—with which we propose to deal. The meagre papers upon North-Eastern Rhodesia which have, so far, appeared, are scattered through the ephemeral files of magazines, or buried in the journals of the learned societies. Bearing this in mind, it may, perhaps, be held not too presumptuous an aim to endeavour to depict the conditions of a country, and the manners and customs of a people, while, for the moment, they still remain primitive —before they fade and are forever obliterated by the corrosive contact of civilisation.

It may here be necessary to define with some exactitude the precise sphere of which these pages treat. A glance at the map will serve to show the area dealt with. That area lies, for the purposes of general definition, between the 8th and 12th parallels of south latitude, and between the 30th and 34th parallels of east longitude. And its claim to be considered as a concrete whole, to the exclusion of other portions of the territory, is based upon the fact that this area was, until quite recently, the sphere of influence of one of the most interesting, virile, and warlike tribes of Central Africa—the Awemba, or subjects of the Crocodile Kings.

There is, moreover, an important topographical reason for the selection of this particular tract of country for treatment, which is that the major part of it consists of a plateau, varying in height from four to six thousand feet above sea-level, bounded on the south by the Muchinga Highlands, and begirt by the four great lakes of southern Central Africa.[1] Of this territory Sir Lewis Michell has said : ' The fact of its being high plateau land is, I think, of enormous importance. It would be criminal to tempt people from this country to go to the malarial swamps and rivers of some portions of Africa. But a country that possesses thousands of square miles of high plateau land in the heart of Africa is a very valuable possession indeed, and the day will come when the inhabitants of these crowded isles may be glad to go to a country like that and make it their home. That was the dream of Mr. Rhodes's life. . . .'

This book is in no sense a history of the whole of North-Eastern Rhodesia. Neither is it intended as a guide-book upon the country ; such a task would lie beyond the powers of the writers, who have, unfortunately, no intimate knowledge of the southern portion of the territory.

Naturally the treatment of such a subject offers many difficulties. It obtrudes the temptation to neglect matters of general interest in favour of sheer anthropology. It demands a fine sense of proportion in balancing the claims to consideration of many lesser peoples, whose customs and beliefs resemble in all essentials those of the dominant Awemba, and yet present many interesting divergences upon minor points. While, in so young a country, where all are groping individually for the truth amid the shifting sands of unstable native record and tradition, an attempt to enshrine any definite facts in print is a dangerous offering of hostages to fortune in the person of the critics. But perhaps the crowning difficulty of all is the effort to present, in terms which shall be intelligible to the stay-at-home, a picture of the life which is led by a mere handful of white men and women scattered through a tract of country at

---

[1] Those who are interested in the natural configuration of this Plateau country cannot do better than read the paper by Mr. L. A. Wallace, C.M.G., on North-Eastern Rhodesia (*Geographical Journal*, vol. xxix. pp. 369-400), which contains a clear and most interesting account of its main physical and geological features, illustrated by an excellent map. Roughly speaking, the whole of North-Eastern Rhodesia is composed of a series of plateaus, of which the Tanganyika Plateau is the greatest.

least as large as England ; a tract which, from our view-point, is still in its infancy, and which has behind it only a quarter of a century of civilisation.

Again, upon the Tanganyika Plateau there are, at present, no vital questions of policy at issue. Our exports do not swell the markets of the world ; our views upon international subjects have for the moment not the slightest weight. We float in a peaceful backwater, where no ripple disturbs the quiet of our daily existence, where neither wars nor rumours of wars may serve to quicken our pulses or thrust us out upon the swirling flood of public notice.

Later—it may be in ten, or it may be in fifty years—we shall arise and step into our allotted place in the policies of the nations. One day the railway will reach us ; one day prosperity, long denied, will come to us like the Prince in the story-book, and kiss us into life. But that day is not yet.

Meanwhile, in quiet, unobtrusive fashion, the work goes on. Day by day the grim shadow of pristine barbarity fades and pales—imperceptibly, it may be, yet none the less surely. And thus, living as we do in a land which, if little known, yet bears within its womb germs which may one day blossom into greatness, it is, perhaps, no presumption in us to take up our pens and to endeavour to depict this unique aspect of Imperial expansion.

In conclusion, we must express our thanks to all those who have so generously assisted us by information, suggestion, and advice. Our special thanks are due to H. H. Mr. Justice Beaufort, Acting Administrator ; Mr. H. C. Marshall, Magistrate at Abercorn ; Dr. J. A. Chisholm, Livingstonia Mission, Mwenzo ; Mr. F. H. Melland, Assistant Magistrate, Mpika ; and Mr. David Ross, Kasama. Our obligations to others will be found noted in the text.

C. G.
H. S.

North-Eastern Rhodesia,
July 1911.

AUTHORS' NOTE

Chapters I., III., V., VII., X., XIII., XIV., XV., XIX., XX.—comprising the European and General section—have been dealt with by Cullen Gouldsbury.

Chapters II., IV., VI., VIII., IX., XI., XII., XVI., XVII., XVIII.—comprising the Ethnographic section—have been dealt with by Hubert Sheane.

Each section has, however, been jointly revised, though no attempt has been made to achieve uniformity of style. The matter, as thus divided, falls naturally into two parts, European and Native, and the collaborators, while realising that this method is open to criticism, consider that its advantages outweigh its defects.

CONTENTS

xv

PAGE

LIST OF ILLUSTRATIONS

xx

LIST OF ILLUSTRATIONS

BIBLIOGRAPHY

OF THE PRINCIPAL WORKS MADE USE OF IN THIS VOLUME

Official Papers of the British South Africa Company, by permission of H. H. the Acting Administrator.

Bemba Grammar, . . .	W. G. R.
British Central Africa, . .	Sir HARRY JOHNSTON.
Native Life in East Africa, .	Dr. KARL WEULE.
Dawn in the Dark Continent, .	Dr. JAMES STEWART.
With Stairs to Katanga, .	D. MOLONEY.
Studies in Ancient History, .	McLELLAN.
Nyasaland under the Foreign Office, ...	H. C. DUFF.
The Rise and Fall of our British East African Empire,	Sir FREDERIC LUGARD.
Ancient Law, . . .	Sir HENRY MAINE.
Kafir Socialism, . . .	DUDLEY KIDD.
The Essential Kafir, . .	DUDLEY KIDD.
Head Hunters—Black, White, and Brown, . . .	Dr. HADDON.
British Central Africa, . .	ALICE WERNER.
Primitive Culture, . . .	Professor TYLOR.
Last Journals, . . .	DAVID LIVINGSTONE.
Station Studies, . . .	LIONEL PORTMAN.

And various papers from *Journal of the African Society, Aurora, Folk-Lore Journal, Journal of the Geographical Society, Journal of the Anthropological Society,* etc.

THE GREAT PLATEAU OF NORTHERN RHODESIA

CHAPTER I

THE PLATEAU IN PERSPECTIVE

THE world at large is, perhaps, too apt to regard Rhodesia in the lump ; to judge it as a whole by the application, for comparative purposes, of the standards of the south ; to invest it, in short, with all the attributes of a South African dependency.

As usual, the world at large is wrong. North-Eastern Rhodesia, indeed, belongs far more definitely to Central than to Southern Africa. Her traditions, her general atmosphere partake infinitely more of the nature of those lands which lie about the equator than of those which breed mining magnates, rejoice in networks of railways and comprehensive telephone systems, revel, in short, in the variegated luxuries of Europe in Africa.

North-Eastern Rhodesia—of which our Plateau is an integral part—is, like her southern sister, administered by the British South Africa Company, the Imperial Government exercising its supervision through Pretoria. The peculiar *cachet* of the country is considerably more in keeping with that of Zanzibar or Mombasa than with the utilitarian civilisation of Salisbury or Bulawayo ; and, for some occult reason, we regard any connection with South Africa with a comical mixture of irritation and dismay.

Here on the Plateau—rimmed about by the encircling lakes, overshadowed by the hills of old ; exempt, the gods be praised! from the boisterous commercialism of twentieth-century civilisation—we lead a lotus-life of our own. Away in the dim distance, within hearing of those tourist hordes that flock to view the Victoria Falls, lie Broken Hill and the railway. But, between us and that outpost of modernity there are many many miles of dim bushland, and swamps, and rugged hills. It is a six-weeks' walk from Tanganyika to the Zambesi, and, in a month and a half, one finds ample scope for a change of viewpoint.

North-Eastern Rhodesia indeed—and more especially that northern central portion of it which constitutes the Plateau proper—ranks unique among the countries of the world. Twenty years ago maybe, Bulawayo represented, for many people, the Ultima Thule of African travel. Half a century back a glamour lay upon the Gold Coast and the banks of the Niger—even British Central Africa, which is now the Nyasaland Protectorate, was decked about with the glories of romance. But nowadays there is electric light at Zomba, and a photographer at Blantyre ; Bulawayo possesses a Grand Hotel and a roller-skating rink, while the West Coast is hardly less frequented than Piccadilly.

But here upon the Plateau we still tread the old, primitive paths. Our mails and stores must reach us, if at all, through the channel of the native carrier—who is, by the way, by no means to be despised. Mailrunners are four weeks on the road between Abercorn and Broken Hill. Our European population, dispersed over fifty thousand square miles, numbers considerably under one hundred. We have neither part nor parcel in the turmoil of European politics ; our international relations consist in an interchange of courtesies and cooling drinks with Germany on the north and Belgium on the west. Postally, we are outside the Union ; geographically we inhabit the region between the 8th and 12th degrees of south latitude, and between the 30th and 34th parallels of longitude east of Greenwich. Philosophically, we are ' quite nicely, thank you,' and not in the least disturbed at our remoteness from civilisation.

It is scarcely possible for the untravelled epicure to picture a life which is lived, now and again, without flour— or sugar—or Egyptian cigarettes, or a *petit verre* after dinner. Nevertheless, on occasion, one can eke out a cheerful and praiseworthy existence upon four-inch nails, kitchen soap, and a modicum of paraffin, which, beyond calico and native blankets, is about all that the local stores can sometimes quote as available.

Quinine, perhaps, should be mentioned. That, as an article of diet, ranks high. The accepted dose is forty-five grains a week; five a day with ten on Thursdays and Sundays. Whether or not it is really necessary is a moot point—the climate, in most parts of the Plateau, is absurdly healthy for Central Africa—but it lends a zest to existence to imagine that one would promptly succumb without the drug. And, incidentally, it gives point to the evening peg.

It has become the fashion—Heaven alone knows why !— to depict the white man in Africa as a gin- or whisky-sodden individual, whose life is spent in the pursuit of imaginary spiders, whose death occurs to the accompaniment of snakes and sulphur in a rat-riddled native hut. Reality, of course, differs totally. For one thing, a large proportion of the officials, and the bulk of the missionaries, are married, and have their wives with them. Never was there so much-married a community in a young country as are we. For another, there is not a single liquor-licence in force upon the Plateau. And so, although the evening whisky-and-soda becomes a ceremony on no account to be omitted save when the gods are evilly enough disposed to decree a shortage in the land, yet two or three drinks a night is usually the outside limit except at seasons of unwonted jubilation. Bear in mind that wine, beer, liqueurs are practically unknown. Yet we survive—though, now and again, we may sigh for the early days of immigration, with their cheerful orgies, their jubilant laxity of life.

There is no Dutch element here. We have said good-bye to the ox-waggon, the ' span,' the *Voorlooper*, and—thank heaven !—to the town ' boy,' that exotic in a ragged shirt and a dirty tweed cap, with the vices of both black and white and the virtues of neither. Our ' vleis ' have become *nyika* —which is surely a prettier word ?—our ' sluits,' and ' spruits,' and ' drifts ' are merged in canoe ferries, presided over by ancient heathen, who have the air of having walked out of some early book of travel. We call things, more or less, by their right names—a man is a man, not a 'boy,' and the 'nigger' has given place to the 'native.' There are no bars and no race-meetings, no small shopkeepers, with their everlasting little bills, neither town councils nor sanitary boards. And it is, perhaps, for these reasons more than for others that the country is, in verity, a lotus land.

As yet, too, the necessity has not arisen for the Plateau to bewail a fearful past. No other African dependency or possession can show so clean a record. Hitherto there has been no shadow of rebellion to stain the annals of the country ; nor is it easy to see why such a contretemps should ever arise. For here your native lives in the lap of luxury, and, making allowances for small divergences between his point of view and that of the white man upon such minor points as sanitation and human sacrifices, exists in far greater peace and safety than of yore, being freed from the dread, once ever present, of Angoni or Wemba raids and their attendant barbarities.

The country is, essentially, his own. White settlers—farmers, traders, and the like—are welcomed, but on the understanding that their interests shall not conflict with those of the native to whom the land belongs. And, indeed, the savage self-interest of the settler, so deplorably to the fore in many other African dependencies, is here conspicuous by its absence. Missionaries there are, in plenty, but they work, for the most part, upon common-sense lines, and preserve excellent relations with the tribes. The native is administered, in so far as is possible, through his chiefs and headmen—whom he himself elects. It is not, perhaps, a system which encourages the money-grubber ; but at least it makes for the peace of the people.

Meanwhile, on the other hand, we have no particular industries, if cattle-ranching be excepted. In the far south of the territory, and outside the scope of this book, there is a gold-mine. A little farther north cotton—excellent cotton—is grown. Here on the Plateau, owing to excessive cost and transport difficulties, cotton and rubber, though pregnant of promise, have only reached the experimental

F. H. Melland, phot.

MAGISTRATE'S OFFICE, FIFE.

F. A. Usher, phot.

POST OFFICE, ABERCORN.

stage. Whence it follows that, save for a cattle-farmer or two, the white population consists almost entirely of missionaries and administrative officials.

As a natural consequence the life is a lonely one. Stations are few and far between—anything, indeed, from forty to a hundred miles apart, and, in most cases, the only method of intercommunication is by native runner. Certain favoured stations—Abercorn and Fife—are served by the African Transcontinental Telegraph line ; the others keep in touch with the outer world by means of a remarkably well-organised weekly postal service.

That postal service is a marvellous thing. Wet or fine, storm or rain, letters and papers arrive each week from Broken Hill, six hundred miles away, within an hour of scheduled time. Perhaps once a year a stray lion may play havoc with a bag or two (*teste* Postal Notice, No. 8 of 1907); and in the wet season it is no uncommon thing for magazines and periodicals, more especially such as are printed upon glossy paper, to arrive in an undecipherable condition owing to the bags having been saturated *en route*. But they arrive—which is the main thing—with the regularity of clockwork.

Needless to say, such a system costs money in the upkeep —and, even so, is run at a loss. It is intensely aggravating to receive budgets from home, which have travelled, immune from the tax-stamp of the postal official, under the ægis of a penny King's head, when, with us, half an ounce costs twopence-halfpenny.[1]

Our stations are funny little places. The blatant cosmopolitan would probably look upon them with scorn. Picture a congeries of buildings, thatched or tin-roofed, comprising three or four dwelling-houses, a *boma* or office (palatial enough to one accustomed to the south), a surgery, a gaol like the toy forts which, in our youth, we received as Christmas presents, and a brick sentry-box roofed with slabs of iron. That is Abercorn—which, you will be pleased to note, is *the* city of the Plateau, the metropolis of the north. And yet, in many ways, we rise superior to our less

[1] This disability has now been removed from April 1, 1911.

fortunate brethren 'down below.' For our buildings are, at least, of well-made bricks—the roofs, whether of grass or tin, are substantially constructed and moderately water-proof. Timber, well-grained and of a good colour, is a feature of the country ; were it not for the cost of trans-port it would, undoubtedly, form a lucrative article of export. Nor is the native *fundi*, or carpenter, to be despised. For seven pounds a year, plus a yard of calico a week wherewith to purchase rations, you may buy, body and soul, a personage who, with a little white supervision, will turn out work that would not discredit a London cabinetmaker. In the majority of cases these men have been educated at one or other of the mission stations which are scattered throughout the territory.

Here, where the cost of transport is the *bête noire* of the average man's existence, a housewife makes excellent glue from the hoofs of buck, zebra, or domestic cattle. From cassava-root most serviceable starch can be concocted. It is quite within the bounds of possibility to turn out remarkably good home-cured bacon, pork-pies, potted meat, cocoanut ice, iced cakes, and a variety of other comestibles for which, in Europe, you would be forced to send round the corner. Bricks, of course, are made on the premises —where the right clay is available, houses are frequently tiled—there is nothing like native mats, at four for a shilling, or two for a yard of calico, both for ceiling and for carpeting purposes ; a dye called *nkula* (camwood), properly prepared, yields a dark, red fluid equal to the best distemper for mural decoration ; local chalk makes good lime for white-washing, and, for a small quantity of salt, one can purchase peas, potatoes, eggs, onions, or fowls in quite respectable quantities.

Market rates among the natives are ridiculously low— but none the less quite high enough for the present stage of the development of the country. A full-grown sheep fetches three shillings, a goat half-a-crown ; eggs vary, but, generally speaking, a teaspoonful of salt per egg is a fair price. Needles, matches, a hunk of meat or an old hat will purchase most things which are for sale. And the average rate of a man's wages per month—excepting domestic servants or highly-skilled specialists, such as carpenters or bricklayers, is three shillings, which is also the amount of the yearly tax upon each hut. Nevertheless, this cheapness is more than counterbalanced by the exorbitant price of necessaries imported from overseas.

It would be the task of a genius to point out the one definite factor in the charm of the country. And yet this definite charm, though intangible, undoubtedly exists. Maybe it is to be traced in the long, undulating lines of purple hills that bound one's view ; or in the dense *musitos* —clumps of tall, cool trees, interlaced with creepers—that line the banks of the innumerable streams. Perchance it is in these very streams themselves, rippling peacefully through sleepy valleys where the slender buck stalk, shadow-like and dim.

Or is it, rather, in the wide tracts of woodland, where the trees, with their silvery bark, recall the dream-forests of Alice in Wonderland ? Almost, in these woodland spaces, one looks for the White Knight to come galloping furiously down the silent glades ; fantastic, madly equipped, he would, at least, be in keeping with the picture.

Maybe, again, the charm lies in the sense of infinite space, of utter, vast loneliness. So far as the eye can reach there is naught but the exuberance of vegetation : tall, tangled grasses—tufted trees—fantastic antheaps, the primeval rock—these and nothing more. Here and there, a pin-point in the wilderness, lie little clusters of thatched huts, wreathed in a mist of smoke—tiny patches of human life and human thought hedged about with gardens, wrested from the void. And, outside, the dim, inscrutable silence of the virgin land, where great beasts move noiselessly in the twilight, and where every twig and blade teems with insect life.

But it is mere presumption to seek to analyse the attributes of such a land ; the presumption of the pigmy who should essay to paint a giant. In the cities, perhaps —in London, Paris, New York—man is in his own domain. There he may classify, schedule, arrange to his heart's content.   Here, in the bosom of the wonderful wilderness, he can only pause, humble or terrified according to his nature—can only live tentatively, as it were, with the knowledge that the elemental forces have him in their grip.

And so, to one who knows the land and its majesty, what might otherwise appear mere pagan superstition becomes natural, necessary, inevitable.   The religion of the people—if, by such a term, one may designate the network of custom and belief with which their lives are ensnared—has been evolved under this stupendous weight of Nature's influence.   Man, here, has no false views as to his capabilities.   He is a mere atom in the everlasting scheme—a pawn in the game of the great gods.   What wonder, then, that he should seek, by any means that may occur to him, to propitiate these unknown forces which rule the air and the land and the deeps beneath ?   Fetishes, spirit-worship, the propitiation of ancestors—what are they but the natural instinct to stand well with the powers that hold him in their hands ?

It has become traditional to invest the native of Africa with the attributes of a good-natured, happy child.   Smiles, laughter, neglectfulness, carelessness of what the morrow may bring—these are, it would seem, the signs by which we may know him.   But is it really so ?

Watch the face of the adult native in repose.   Surely in the dark eyes there is a kind of unconscious sadness ? Are there not lines upon the forehead and about the mouth that seem to argue an incessant anxiety, unrecognised, perhaps unfelt, yet none the less existent ?   May it not be that he, too, feels that pressure of the illimitable spaces —knows that Nature rules, and that it is futile to kick against the pricks ?

The white man, on the other hand, has interests which serve to distract his thoughts from such primitive pessimism.   Upon the Plateau the European population falls, naturally, into four distinct classes—the administrative official, the missionary, the settler, and the trader.

Within the first two classes are comprised seventy per cent. at least of the total.   And both administrative and

LAKE CHILA NEAR ABERCORN.

missionary work—which have a common basis, though different methods—are fascinating enough. On the other hand, the settler and the trader are, one presumes, making money—which is surely sufficient to tinge any man's outlook with *couleur de rose*?

Again, for all alike, there is the fascination of sport, the joy of head-hunting, the glamour of a life made up of cool, fresh dawnings and camp-fire nights. For this Plateau of ours is the hunter's paradise, fully equal, if not superior, to British East Africa or Uganda.

There are but few horses on the Plateau as yet—two that belong to ancient history, having been brought up via the East Coast route in the days of the telegraph construction, and three more that have been imported since this chapter was first drafted. A plenitude of horses would, indeed, put the coping-stone upon our happiness. As yet, situated many hundred miles from railhead, hemmed in by belts of fly, the importation seems a dangerous speculation. Yet with great care and infinite precautions all difficulties can be surmounted ; there is, indeed, no reason to assume that, once suitable breeding stock arrived, horses would not increase and multiply. Meanwhile the solution of the problem might be found in the crossing of grey donkeys with half-muscats from German East Africa.

At present, with the exception of bicycles, the only means of locomotion for the European is the *machila*—a canvas litter slung upon a pole, and carried upon the shoulders of two natives. It is a lethargic, somewhat effeminate method of travel—more suited, perhaps, to a southern or eastern race than to Englishmen—but, for the time, we accept it thankfully.

Indeed, in machila-travelling, we stumble upon the most outstanding feature of the white man's life. Existence for all is compact of touring—by the official of his district, by the missionary of his schools, by the trader of his outlying stores. A fortunate circumstance—since the monotony of perpetual station-life would, in a very short time, become unbearable.

Casting around for a pendant feature, characteristic of

the country, one seems to light, instinctively, upon calico. Calico here is the staff of life—for most purposes it takes the place of hard cash.   Men draw their rations in calico—they are buried in calico, marriage-dowries are often paid in calico.   The headman who brings you presents is recompensed with a yard of two, and retires wreathed in smiles. In brief, calico is to the Plateau what cowrie-shells are to the South Sea Islanders—and, were it not that lotus-land expresses more or less aptly the mental attitude of both white and black, one would be tempted to christen the plateau, Calico Country.

Yet, for all that, coinage is every day becoming more common than it was.   Currency must come with civilisation—a trader named De Mattos once remarked, aptly enough, that it was just as ridiculous to pay a native in calico as to pay a white man in dress clothes.   Copper was at first received with abhorrence—nowadays it is becoming popular enough, and even farthings have been recently introduced by a missionary.   At the present day, in Johannesburg, the 'Tyranny of the Ticky' has become a byword ;   we ourselves are within measurable distance of feeling the tyranny of the sixpenny piece.   Not so long ago an amateur financier found that a new penny served as well as a shilling in one of the western districts—but those days are past, and the rawest native realises in this year of grace that coinage is a useful thing, and one which merits mastering.

In conclusion of this chapter a brief sketch of the tribes which inhabit the area with which we are dealing may serve to introduce the native to the general reader.   It may be said that, except for slight differences in language and customs, these tribes bear, without exception, the well-known stamp of the Bantu, and, in selecting as our theme the habits, customs, manners, and individuality of the Awemba, we are, it is hoped, affording a general insight into the principal characteristics of the remaining Plateau peoples.   For the information which follows, the writers are principally indebted to a report by the late Mr. Robert

Codrington (Administrator of N.E. Rhodesia) for the two
years ending 31st March 1900, and to notes by Mr. Robert
Young, Native Commissioner at Chinsali, who has made
an exhaustive study of many of the eastern tribes.

The AWEMBA.—Of this tribe it will be unnecessary to
say much, since they will be dealt with at length in the
following chapters. They are a strong, intelligent, and
adventurous race, fond of travelling, and especially adapted
to machila and load carrying. Formerly turbulent and
a menace to all the weaker tribes, they have long since
shown that, wisely administered, they are amenable to
discipline. They constitute the aristocracy of the country,
and there is a striking similarity of feature among the
members of their royal family, while the dignity of the men
and the grace of the women are remarkable, even among
the commoners.

The WATAWA, living to the north-west of the Awemba,
appear in almost every respect, except some slight dialectic
differences, to resemble the Awemba, though by some
authorities they are grouped with the Amambwe and
Alungu.

The AMAMBWE inhabit a large portion to the north-east
of the Plateau. Pre-eminently peaceable agriculturalists
and husbandmen, they suffered very severely from the
depredations of the Awemba previous to the coming of the
European, and, indeed, were only saved from extermina-
tion by the advent, in the first place of the London Missionary Society, and later of the Administration. They possess
considerable intelligence, and make good station workers,
but their physique is not of the first order, and their character somewhat unstable.

The WALUNGU, whose original home was around the
southern shores of Lake Tanganyika, can hardly be distinguished from the Amambwe. Indeed, in the opinion of some
competent judges, the very names of the two are interchangeable. They also suffered very severely from the incursions
of the Awemba—as, indeed, did all the tribes in the vicinity

—and, now that the authority of the white man is paramount, are apt to assume a somewhat irritating air of equality towards their former conquerors and masters. They, perhaps more than other tribes, are split up into a number of sub-tribes, or rather family groups, the petty overlord of each assuming almost the airs of a paramount. In the words of Mr. J. G. Hall (a Native Commissioner, resident in their territory), ' they have been unfortunate in their chiefs, and the chiefs have been unfortunate in their people,' with the result that, at the present day, there is no recognised paramount chief of the tribe, while constant bickering still continues between them and the Awemba. They probably possess a higher intelligence than the latter, owing to their more constant intercourse in the early days with Arab traders and the resultant intermarriage with the Alungwana, or bastard Swahili—and, as is often the case with a more intellectual race, physical courage would not appear to be one of their predominant characteristics.

The WINAMWANGA reside in the Fife division. They are quiet and fairly industrious, and grow tobacco largely. They have very few cattle, probably owing to the combined effects of Awemba raids and rinderpest. Since the advent of Europeans, they have shown themselves most loyal, peaceful, and law-abiding, crime being almost unknown among them, while they are most reserved, and do not easily make friends with outsiders. Their chief is in German territory, and they still continue to acknowledge him : whether the coming generation will continue to do so seems doubtful.

The AWIWA are also very loyal and peaceable. Formerly they lived in large stockaded villages, but these have now been broken up. They are industrious husbandmen, and cultivate tobacco on a large scale, but are not partial to other work, though they were, formerly, noted iron-workers.

The WATAMBO.—This is a small tribe which, some few years ago, was estimated to consist of about five hundred people, occupying a narrow strip of land between the Wiwa conntry and the Luangwa river. Until fairly recently they were nomadic, but are now more settled, and appear quite willing to work. Owing to the mountainous nature of their country, they are necessarily poor.

The WALAMBIA.—A small tribe of industrious and willing people, under two chiefs, Muyereka and Mwiniwisi.

The NYIKA.—These people are of fine physique, independent, but very loyal. They are good workers, and exceptionally intelligent. Their country is situated high up among the Namitawa mountains.

The WAYOMBE are a branch of the Kamanga nation. They have, during the last ten years, made a considerable advance from their once furtive and nomadic state, and many go down to the mines for work. They are industrious and good agriculturists.

The WAFUNGWI, probably connected with the Walambia, are quiet and industrious, and have at all times been friendly to the European. It may be noted here that all these small tribes obviously retain their independence from being isolated each from each by mountain ranges.

The WABISA form a large section of the Mirongo district, and are also found in the Kasama district and around Lake Bangweolo. They suffered severely from Wemba raids, and many were sold into slavery among the Arabs and Swahili. Many were driven to the swamps and islands of Lake Bangweolo, while others took refuge east of the Luangwa. They were formerly—and may be again, now that security is assured—an industrial people, great weavers of cotton cloths and workers in iron, and bartered these articles, besides salt and dressed skins, with the surrounding tribes, becoming, in consequence, rich in flocks of sheep and goats. The standard of morality of the Lake Bisa tribe is, perhaps, lower than that of any other Plateau people, but their general intelligence is high.

The WAUNGA.—Probably less is known of these people than of any other tribe in N.E. Rhodesia. For a long time they resisted any form of government; indeed, as is a common trait among lake tribes, they are very independent, and their tribal organisation appears to be very loose.   The young men are constantly moving about and building hovels by fresh fishing-grounds, or are engaged in hunting lechwe and otters, and consequently are very impatient even of the control of their own chiefs.   There is still a great deal of lawlessness in the Waunga country ; fights in the swamps, and raiding of women in canoes, and even murders are far too frequent and thought little of.   The Waunga are skilled hunters.   They organise large tribal battues for lechwe, and are constantly engaged in fishing or otter-hunting.

The WASENGA.—This tribe inhabits the Luangwa Valley, and cultivates a large area.   Mr. Young states that the villages are the filthiest that he has seen in his travels ! Formerly, living as they did in terror of the Arabs, Awemba, and Angoni, they built their villages in the midst of almost impenetrable thickets.   The water supply is exceptionally bad : in the rains, the country is flooded, and the water merely liquid mud ; in the dry weather the people are obliged to dig for water in the sand.   They seem willing and industrious, and their tobacco is widely known, but they are nervous and easily scared—which, considering their past history, is hardly to be wondered at.   The cotton bush grows well in their country.

The WANYAMWEZI came to this country with the Arab and Swahili traders.   They cultivate largely, and are more intelligent than the surrounding tribes.   Their habitat is in what was formerly the Mirongo division.   They keep plenty of sheep and goats, and build good huts, both square and round, while they are all skilled traders, and many have had much experience as elephant hunters.   They carry heavy loads excellently, but are slow travellers.

SWAHILI-SPEAKING NATIVES. — These can hardly be termed Swahili, as they are mostly natives of this country, though some of them have made journeys to the coast. Others are the offspring of Swahili men and Wemba, Bisa, Senga, or other local women.   They are industrious in their

THE CHAMBESHI RIVER.

F. H. Melland, phot.

THE MUNCKASHI RIVER.

F. H. Melland, phot.

own way, and are fond of elephant hunting, mat-weaving, making wooden boxes, etc., but as a general rule they do not like transport work. A few of them are really expert at repairing guns, even making new parts, stocks, etc. They cultivate largely, and are great traders.

From the above it will be seen that the native population of the Tanganyika Plateau is a somewhat heterogeneous mixture of tribes, each possessing its salient characteristics, its good and bad points. Day by day—or at least year by year—the increased inter-tribal communication (which comes from security and peace, and the presence of the white man, who is continually travelling from one end of the country to the other, shuffling the natives of the various localities like the cards in a pack) is tending to break down the barriers of tribal reserve and hostility. Such fusion of tribes must necessarily accompany any attempt at civilisation, and its advantages undoubtedly exceed its defects. But there are dangers in the breaking down of barriers, not the least of which is the idea of ultimate combination against the white man which it might, conceivably, awake in the native mind. There are no signs of such cohesion at present ; the country is more peaceable and prosperous than it has ever been, and there seems every reason to suppose that it will remain so. None the less, the factor is one which should not be lost sight of.

CHAPTER II

THE CROCODILE KINGS

' O MIGHTY Chiti, son of the Crocodile, thy flame is fierce in the land. Thou art above all, and ever present, and encirclest thy people like the river Chosi. Awake, O mighty Chiti Mukulu ! '

So, through the grey shades before the dawn, the chant of the blind court singer would awaken, with its eerie cadences and abrupt intervals, the slumbering king of the Wemba nation. Nor was his vaunting song conjured up by any vain vision of kingly power. Had not he himself felt the cruel thumb turn in his eyeballs, so that he might never escape, nor his cunning minstrelsy grace the court of another chieftain ?

The Wenang'andu, chiefs of the Crocodile totem, had extended their dominion outwards from the Luwemba and Ituna provinces, until their suzerainty was acknowledged, roughly speaking, from Chosi river to Lake Bangweolo, and their sphere of influence extended almost from Lake Nyasa to the shores of Lake Mweru.

Those central provinces, Luwemba and Ituna, were fenced about by a ring of barrier outposts, and long after the Nyasa-Tanganyika trade route was open to all comers, the Wemba country was closed and impenetrable to Europeans. The grim barrier of severed heads staked on poles on the Stevenson Road, near Zoche village, was left by Chitimukulu, as the natives say, to terrorise European pioneers, and to warn them not to trespass within the Wemba domain.

And yet, previous to this, the traveller passing through the country was welcomed, and Livingstone, in his *Last Journals*, describes his courteous reception in 1867, and the

pomp and circumstance surrounding Chitimukulu Chitapankwa, the seventeenth king of the line.

'We passed through the inner stockade, and then on to
an enormous hut, where sat Chitapankwa with three
drummers, and ten or more men with rattles in their hands.
The drummers beat furiously, and the rattlers kept time to
the drums, two of them advancing and receding in a stooping posture, with rattles near the ground, as if doing the
chief obeisance, but still keeping time with the others. I
declined to sit on the ground, and an enormous tusk was
brought 'for me. The chief saluted courteously.' Livingstone adds later that the tusk on which he sat was sent
after him, in addition to his present of a cow, ' because he
had sat' on it.'

Again, the French lieutenant, Giraud, passing through
the Wemba country nearly twenty years later, waxes
eloquent as to his splendid reception by Chitimukulu.
When Giraud mentioned his inability, through lack of
sufficient goods, to make a worthy return for the munificent
presents of the king, the interpreter came back with the
following message : ' Chitimukulu is a great chief, and
gives of his bounty without thought of recompense,' which
words, so unique from the lips of an African chief—' are
worthy,' says the enthusiastic Giraud, ' of being inscribed
in letters of gold.'

The reason of this sudden change of attitude and subsequent opposition to the intrusion of the white men, was,
according to tradition, because Giraud was suspected of
having poisoned or bewitched the reigning Chitimukulu,
who died shortly after the Frenchman reached Bangweolo.

As will be seen from the map, the Wemba kingdom was
a very extensive one, and the Wemba sphere of influence
extended still farther, including nearly all the territory
between the four great lakes, Nyasa, Tanganyika, Mweru,
and Bangweolo.

From the moment of their accession to their burial, the
kings were hedged in by a ring-fence of sinister ceremonies
and ruthless ritual, undoubtedly devised to strike terror into
the hearts of the common people, and to pave the way for

and render possible the stern and rigorous administrative system with which we are about to deal.

The main principle of the succession was matriarchal. The heir must be the son of a princess of the royal blood, though the status of his father was immaterial. It followed that only the brothers or nephews of the reigning king could succeed, the brother having the first claim. But if the brother were a *fainéant*, or 'kept silent in the land,' the nephew would appeal to Chief Mwamba, head of the lesser branch of the Wenang'andu royal race. So tradition relates that Mutale, the nephew of the reigning Bwembia, protested to Mwamba against his uncle's weak and power-less rule, suggesting that Mwamba should dispossess him and amalgamate the two branches. Mwamba, however, declined the task, but bade Mutale succeed himself, which he promptly did.

The reigning king would never nominate his successor. Thus, when in 1902 the magistrate of the Wemba district convened an assembly at Chitimukulu's village, the old king, though cross-questioned, would only mention Ponde and Chikwanda, his nephews, as possible successors, absolutely refusing to indicate his own preference, and stating that the matter would be settled after his death. In the older days, however, since one of the two kings of the sister houses of Chitimukulu and Mwamba was always alive, he was asked to point out the successor for the defunct ruler. Thus, when the last Chitimukulu died, the late Mwamba designated the present holder, Makumba.

There were no strict laws of primogeniture; an ambitious *Nanfumu*—mother of a potential heir—would often, like Rebecca of old, secure the accession of her favourite son.

And here the respect in which these 'mothers of kings' were held, and their peculiar privileges, are deserving of a passing note.

These *Nanfumu* must be of the direct royal line, being themselves the daughters of a previous royal princess. As soon as they had passed the initiation ceremonies upon attaining puberty, they had the right to seize any comely man whom they wished to espouse, and bring him before

Bernard Turner, phot.

CHIEF CHUNGU AND HIS WIVES.

Bernard Turner, phot.

THE LATE CHIEF MPOLOKOSÒ.

the king. No reluctance was tolerated from the chosen
Lumbwe, or consort, who, if already married, had to re-
linquish his wife. The same evening the bridal party
seated themselves in front of the assembled villagers on
carved stools, and finally, amidst gun-play, dancing, and
marriage songs, the *Nanfumu* would proudly lead away
the *Lumbwe* to her own hut within the king's harem.

Shortly after the *Nanfumu* was thus espoused she was
given a separate village to rule, and retired there until a
child was born. If, however, after a year's time she bore
no children, the luckless *Lumbwe* was dismissed, and the
chieftainess selected another. The *Lumbwe* had no share
in the government, and his position was always a precari-
ous one ; if, for instance, one of his children died, the angry
mother would promptly accuse him of infidelity, and
straightway cause him to be blinded. The *Nanfumu*,
though a stern moralist on such occasions, was no mirror
of virtue herself ; in fact, it is related that the older women
of the royal blood took advantage of their position as
chieftainesses to enjoy the privileges of secret polyandry,
despatching their consorts on bootless errands, and summoning to their huts from time to time more fascinating youths.

Yet their infidelities were winked at so long as they bore
strong children ; and, indeed, this selection of the most
handsome and powerful men as parents seems to have
produced a hardy, stubborn, and virile race of kings. When
these ' royal mothers ' had done their duty to the state,
the hereditary titles of Chandamukulu and Mukukamfumu
were, in the fulness of time, accorded to them, and if fit to
rule, a group of villages was entrusted to their care.

To return to the question of the succession. When the
king was sick, none of the royal blood were allowed to visit
him, only his sons, who could not succeed, being permitted
to attend their father. It may be noticed that even when
the king was well, entry to the capital was tabooed to any
scion of the direct line. Even when making a visit of respect,
a Wenang'andu had to camp at some distance from the
village, and the meeting was arranged outside the stockade.
But the instant Chitimukulu died, there was a race for the

slaves and ivory now left masterless at the capital, which often became the scene of a fierce fight between rival uncles and nephews. This was, however, considered as ' stealing,' though the practice was customary, and gave no right to the succession. When Chitimukulu died, the reigning Mwamba would canvass the other chiefs, and finally point out an heir. Furthermore, the actual enthronement only took place after a year had elapsed, and the burial rites had been consummated. Meantime, the heir, though designate, was not allowed to enter the deceased chieftain's village, nor even to light a fire or cook food close by ; the wives of the dead king were also forbidden to him, since he could only take the slave wives or concubines during this interregnum.

But when the *masaka* (millet) was ripe, and the old king had been safely buried at Mwaruli (as described in Chapter XII.), a great concourse of Awemba gathered together in his village, including the Wakabiro, or chief councillors, the Walashi, or district officers, the medicine-men, and the priestesses of the rites of the ancestral spirits.

That same evening the heir entered one of the huts of the inner harem courtyard, and, with his head wife, slept ' within the fence.' Before the dawn of the next day, it was Chief Chimba's special duty to carry secretly into their hut the ceremonial bowl, used at all the consecrations of the Wemba kings. A fire was then lit, and the bowl—filled with water which was, it is said, mingled with herbs of sanctifying potency—was held thereon by the chief, who joined hands with his wife. When the water boiled, Chimba spoke the customary sentences, saying that now ' the country was hot ' as the fire again ' flamed in the land,' and anointed the limbs of the chief and his wife. Chimba then departed, and, after carefully secreting the mystic bowl, sent his son to call the Wakabiro together.

All the people were marshalled together outside while the five principal Wakabiro entered the hut, and anointed the heir and his wife with oil, arraying him in gorgeous cloths, while Chimba handed him the ancient bow of war and the spear. While thus preparing him, they gave him the customary advice : ' Now that thou art the Navel of the Land, and hast duly inherited the Capital, harden thy heart like a stone, and bestir thyself. If thou noddest or reclinest for a moment, others will take thy place, and thy country will fall away from thee ! '

Finally, the king and his wife, adorned and suitably admonished, emerged from the hut, stepping over the carcase of a bullock newly slain for the sacrifice, and were received with the shouts and acclamations of the people, who all prostrated themselves on their backs, clapping their hands (*kutota*) in the royal salutation. Drums were beaten, and matchlocks blazed off, and, in the midst of all the king made merry, singing the succession song of self-praise, and whirling round in an improvised war-dance, brandishing the coveted bow and spear. This ceremony ended, the king would consult the various councillors and district headmen, probably projecting some immediate expedition, so that he should show his mettle, and dismissing them, after a few days feasting and drinking, to their various villages.

Having thus settled the king safely on his throne, let us turn to a brief sketch of his system of administration.

This system was upheld with the utmost rigour, and enforced a scale of punishments and mutilations so ferocious that it is, perhaps, unparalleled except by the monstrous cruelties of King Chaka. Like that of Chaka, it was extremely well organised, and disobedience to the orders of the king's deputies in the provinces, or refusal to supply men to do the king's work, or to contribute the customary dues, was checked by mutilation, devastation of gardens, seizure of cattle, and, finally—for the contumacious—enslavery of the whole village to the Arab merchants who flocked around the capital.

The following sketch is mainly derived from notes given by Simumbi (Zapaira), mentioned by Livingstone, the uncle of the present Mwamba, and of royal birth, who called one of the writers in shortly before his death to speak of the succession of other chiefs in the West Awemba district (see Chapter III.). The old chief, whose age Bishop Dupont puts at well over ninety, was absolutely bedridden, and could not bear the light, but was, none the less, in full possession of his faculties. It seems truly astonishing that the Awemba themselves, to say nothing of the other conquered tribes, endured such a rigorous administration. But though the writer asked Zapaira, and, later, some of the older men of the common people, why they remained passive when they could easily have escaped, the reply always was, ' Where could we flee to ? If we reached the village of a foreign tribe, such as the Washinga, they would say, " Here are the Awemba, with the *mtoso* neck-mark ! " and fall upon us, and slay us ! A Shinga or Winamwanga chief would fear to harbour us, and, if they did not kill us in revenge, would simply send us back under escort to Chitimukulu.' The statement in the report of the late Administrator, Mr. Robert Codrington (p. 66, *British South Africa Co.'s Annual Report*, 1902), that the Awemba were tired of the barbarities of their chiefs, and gladly welcomed British rule, is not hard to understand.

To deal first with the headquarters officials.

Over the huge village of Chitimukulu, divided into thirty-three quarters, were set the Wachilolo, or, literally, overseers, each in charge of a quarter, or *chitente*. These worthies were usually middle-aged men, selected by the chief for their proved valour in war, and for their position in the village as parents of large families. They marshalled before the king, when the great war drum boomed, the young men of their quarter, and led them to battle ; theirs, too, was the grim privilege, on return, of driving the sharpened stakes into the ground prepared outside the village, and setting thereon, before the admiring gaze of the village women, the heads of the victims slain in war.

Major Wissmann states that among the Awemba there existed, in 1887-88, a perfectly developed rank, determined by the number of heads of the enemies each man had killed.

The Wachilolo may be termed town councillors, and generally acted as aediles over their group. All persons suffering from communicable disease were banished by them into the bush. They saw that refuse was cleared up, and kept the stockades in repair. As will be seen later, they further acted as a petty court, and as no one could take his case to the king direct, discharged the duties of a court of first instance, referring all serious matters to the king.

The second, smaller, but more august body of officers were called the Wakabiro, who formed, as it were, the inner privy council of the king. Though some Wakabiro were stationed in the provinces, the main body were retained at the capital as a permanent advisory council. These men were also called the *Weningala*, or plume-bearers, since, by the king's permission, they were allowed to flaunt the carmine feathers of the calling bird (*mkuta*), and to bedizen themselves with jangling anklets of grotesque little iron bells.

All the more serious state affairs, the making of wars, or the declaration of peace, grave criminal offences, propitiatory sacrifices, came under their cognisance, and were settled by them in council, presided over by the king. Together with the medicine-man, and the priestesses of the departed chiefs (*Ba Muka Benye*), they decreed the slaughter of cattle necessary to obtain rain. The ordering of the *Lupupo* midnight ceremonies in honour of the souls of the departed fell partly under their care. In company with the medicine-men, the older Wakabiro shared the reputation of being the repositories of traditional law and custom. Even to the present day, when headmen who have been Wakabiro are called into court as native assessors, one cannot but feel impressed with their sententious delivery of past precedents, their grave demeanour, their marvellous memory, and their mastery of the most minute details of native law and custom.

As has been stated, the other Wakabiro were often placed over important villages in the provinces, but were always summoned to deal with their fellows in the village concerning the more important questions of war, peace, rainmaking, and the like.

The Wakabiro had no need to be men of such good

lineage as the Walashi ; so long as they were freemen it sufficed.

Turning from these officials, whose functions were central-ised in the capital, to those set over the provincial divisions, we find the same careful organisation.

Foremost among the latter ranked the Wasimupelo, or Lords of the Barriers, who controlled the remote provinces and the lines of boundary villages. The Wasimupelo were picked men : either ambitious brothers or nephews of the reigning king, who considered it wise to keep them at a distance, and to give them some outlet for their energies in border raids ; or else they were men who had distinguished themselves by their ' composition and fierce quality ' in war, chosen from the sons and more distant relatives of the king.   We find that the villages occupied by these ' Lords of the Marches ' were stockaded across a main trade route, or else controlled an important ferry, being flanked by a line of minor stockaded villages along the frontier.

It was necessary that the border should be constantly patrolled, and the chief ready to withstand and repel any sudden incursion from outlying tribes.   Further, it was the duty of the Wasimupelo to see that the tribute was regularly brought in by such subject tribes as were within his sphere of influence. As may be imagined, the office was a lucrative one, since the Wasimupelo exacted a heavy toll from all who wished to enter and trade in peace in the Luwemba and Ituna provinces.   Thus a Winamwanga trader would have to pay his toll of a woman slave or a cow to Chipakula and Makasa before being allowed to enter. The tribute was rigorously exacted from the border tribes ; it is still the boast of the Awemba that they do not know how to hoe, that their only trade was war, and that the subject tribes supplied their various wants, the Wasenga bringing in tobacco, the Wabisa fish and salt, the Wiwa and Winam-wanga hoes, livestock, and grain.

If, for instance, the Wasimupelo reported that Kafwimbi, the Wiwa chief, was in arrear, a sharp reminder was sent to him by Chitimukulu in the shape of a messenger carrying a spear, in token of war unless the dues were instantly paid.

MUSHOTA, A WEMBA CHIEF.

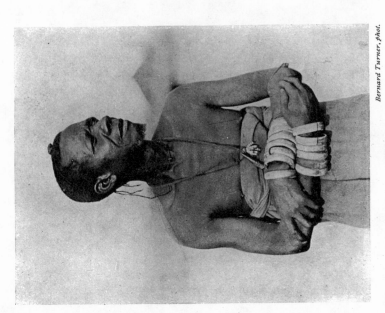

MUTUTU, A LUNGU CHIEF.

Kafwimbi—who, in spite of his title of the 'Were Lion,' was a man of peace—would hurriedly despatch the most beautiful of his daughters with a hoe on her head in sign of submission, following this up by a file of carriers to the Wasimupelo carrying beer, hoes, and foodstuffs. And if the girl found favour in Chitimukulu's sight, Kafwimbi would be graciously informed that, for that year, his people might live in peace.

Next in importance to the Wasimupelo came the Walashi, or district officers, to each of whom was allotted a division with definite hill and river boundaries. The king's sons and relatives were usually drafted into this office, and were held responsible for the good order and tribute payment of their sections, and for supplying men to perform the *mulasa* or statute labour of the chief, his garden-cutting and so forth, and a contingent for war.

The main dues collected were : the tusks of ivory found in the bush, or cut out by the various *fundis* (hunters whom the Walashi kept supplied with powder) ; two legs, the heart and the liver of every animal killed. The Walashi were active men, and constantly travelled in their divisions, taking dues and living on their subjects *en route*, much in the fashion of an old-time royal progress. Neighbouring Walashi often quarrelled about their boundaries, but such disputes were settled by the king and his Wakabiro.

Last came the Wasichalo, who were the heads of large families, chosen by the king for their loyalty, and given charge of minor villages, but responsible to the Walashi. These men were of low birth, but by intermarrying their children with the conquered inhabitants, soon produced a 'Wemba' village, since Bisa children despised their mother's race, and eagerly adopted that of the more powerful tribe.

It must not be supposed that the Wasimupelo and Walashi were independent petty chieftains ; on the contrary, they were always receiving instructions through the king's messengers, who were well-known men, and who carried guns and a large horn of powder, besides being decked, on important occasions, in fine raiment (*miala*) and a headdress.

Another check upon the authority of these remote officials was the spy system. These spies, or 'Walengesya,' would disguise themselves, often pretending to be men in search of wives, or to have been banished from the capital by the king ; they would prowl about at night, eaves-dropping over the fires at the central village hut. If the chief spoke too boastfully, or kept back part of the dues, these spies would immediately report it, nosing out old scraps of elephant meat, and bringing them in as proof positive against villagers who had not recently paid tribute ivory. The king would, moreover, send out one of his sons or near relatives on a tour of inspection, which also served as a check on the conduct of the divisional chieftains. The ceremonies and methods of travelling observed by members of the royal family were most interesting.

Before the *ulendo* started, the chief would gather together his medicine-men and the priestesses. They prayed in the dusk before the little god-huts (*mafuba*) of their ancestors, and made libations of beer, so that their journey might be prosperous. Early the next morning the chief, having selected one or two medicine-men and priestesses to accompany him, marshalled the motley crowd of his ' young men ' and servants, his slaves, and the usual *Mung'omba* or court singer, who acted as his bugler at dawn. Then the cortège set forth in long, single file. The chief, having again prayed, mounted on the shoulders of one of his men, who relieved each other in turn. When any considerable river was crossed the bearers would set down the chief, *lulliloo*, as Livingstone puts it, and clap their hands. Provided no ill omens were encountered *en route*—such as a python gliding into the bush, which meant that the party might encounter war by the way—the destination would be reached about midday. A messenger had been sent ahead with a warning, and, on arrival, the chief would be shown into a newly plastered hut, surrounded with a grass shelter for privacy.

As he approached, all the villagers would meet him on the path, bending on their knees and clapping their hands, and, with the usual din of salutation, the old women would perform an uncouth dance, singing his praises. Water would then be drawn by the women, and the headman would bring his presents of a sheep or goat and flour. Meanwhile the medicine-man, or one of the chief's attendants, would retire into the bush, and, with a firestick, make a flame and carry the lighted tinder into the village, since no village fire might be used for the chief's cooking.

After the chief had rested and eaten, he would see the headmen again, act as arbiter in any cases brought before him, and generally discuss village questions, communicating any orders he might have received from Chitimukulu. In case there had been many unaccountable deaths, he would inspect the village god-huts, and the medicine-man would examine the roan's horn stuck in the ground—the ' foundation-stone ' of the village, and, after consultation with the local elders and witch-doctors, decree the necessary propitiatory sacrifices. When evening drew nigh he would distribute the presents of flour to his followers, since he himself would eat only flour prepared by his wives : pipes were filled with tobacco and bhang over the camp-fires, and, with the customary liturgy for further health and safety on the journey, the day was ended.

CHAPTER III

THE OLD ORDER AND THE NEW

In dealing with the early history of the Tanganyika Plateau, the first authentic date available is, perhaps, the year 1730, about which time the first Kazembe Kanyimbe came from Lunda, and invaded the country then occupied by the Senga and Bisa tribes.

From then until 1867—in which year Livingstone visited Kazembe—but little is known of the internal affairs of the Plateau ; history being confined to the records of visits made by various Portuguese, which may be generally summarised as follows (see résumé of history in W. G. R.'s *Introductory Handbook to the Language of the Awemba*) :—

1796.—Pereira visted Kazembe. An easterly movement among the Awemba was then in progress.

1798.—Lacerda visited. Kazembe-Lekwisa was then ruling ; he subdued the Sira of Muchinga country, and banished Kapaka to Kassange. Probably about this time Chiti settled with the title of Chitimukulu.

1802.—Pombeiros visited the then Kazembe, Cireka.

1831-32.—Monteiro and Gamitto visited Kazembe. About this time there was a considerable tribal movement among the Awemba. The Fipa and also, probably, the Alungu and Amambwe began to advance into their respective countries. The reigning Kazembe was then Kapumba, the son of Cireka.

1853.—Freitas visited Kazembe, and, about this time, Chitimukulu Chitinta was driven out by Chitimukulu Chilesie.

1856 (about).—The Arab, bin Saleh, came to Kazembe's.

The reigning Kazembe was then Chinyanta, son of Cireka. About this time the Angoni reached the country. Chileshie and Chewe quarrelled, and Chewe was defeated and fled, first to Kafwimbi's in Wiwa country, thence to Chikana-muliro in Nyamwanga. The reigning Kazembe was Lekwisa, the son of Cireka.

1862.—Kazembe (Muongo), the son of Cireka by a slave woman, expelled Lekwisa.

1867.—Livingstone visited Kazembe. He found Mper-embe, the son of Katere, still living, but very old. At this time Kasonso was ' chief of the lake and of a very large country all round it ' (Livingstone, *Last Journals*, vol. i. p. 202). The lake is, of course, Tanganyika. The Alungu chief, Chitimbwa, had just died. Tiputipu was already at Ponde in Itawa, and was raiding Nsama. The Awemba seem to be settled where they are now.

About 1868 Tiputipu appeared. The reigning Chiti-mukulu was Bwembia. The Arabs Kalonga and Kum-bakumba now arrived. With the help of the Arabs, Chitimukulu Mutali fought and defeated the Angoni. Chewe settled in the Kanyala district.[1]

To understand the origin of the Awemba and kindred peoples, it will now be as well to quote the history of one Simumbi, now dead, who at the time that he proffered the following information was the oldest chief of the Awemba, and brother of Mwamba wa Milengi. Simumbi, hearing that one of the writers, who was then in charge of the Luena division, was leaving, expressed a wish to see him, so that he might give a proper account of the Wemba immigration. Only ' youths,' as he put it, were left, and he wished that his words might be written down so that boundaries could henceforth be observed.

His information is especially useful as confirming what, on linguistic grounds, has already been held plausible, that the Wemba and Bisa heads of the present houses came originally from Lubaland, probably in successive waves of

[1] For further details of the Awemba conquest of surrounding tribes, see paper by one of the writers (*Journal African Society*, Oct. 1911), entitled ' Wemba Warpaths.'

immigration. Thus the Wemba and Lake Bisa peoples, in the Luena division at least, acknowledge as their chiefs men who all claim to have come from the Lualaba. While the Wemba and Bisa aristocracy are undoubtedly of Congolese (or of Lubaic) origin, the proletariat may be held to approximate—especially in the case of the Lake Bisa and the Waunga—physically to the aboriginal inhabitants, though, in point of customs, religion, and language, the Lubaic origin is distinctly indicated throughout.

' Our ancestors,' said Simumbi, ' came from Kola, in the country of the Luban King Makasa. Chitimukulu was one of the sons of Makasa Mulopwe, and was found sleeping with one of his father's young wives. He gathered his men together, and tried to lead them against his father, but without success, the old men refusing to do so base a deed. However, many escaped with him.

' Chitimukulu took with him the future heads of the houses of Matipa, Chyavula, and Chungu. On the way he left behind him Kazembe, who gained ascendancy in the court of the old Muato, and, inheriting his head wife Kafuto, eventually became the Muato. Mwansakawamba was left by Chitimukulu when he went forward from the Shinga country towards what is now Chinsali division. His brother Kolimfumu crossed the Luangwa, and penetrated to the Senga country, where he caused a fight by abducting the wife of a friendly chief Mwase. Kolimfumu was wounded by a poisoned arrow, from which he died. Mwase fled, but a woman showed where he was hiding, so they killed him, and made a belt of his skin, which is used to this day at Chitimukulu's as a charm to fertilise the *masaka* (millet).

' The Mweni-mwansa were the original inhabitants [of the country subsequently occupied by Simumbi], and their title of honour is that they hid the paramount chief Chinyimba in a huge cooking-pot when he was pursued by his enemies. Mwamba told me that I was never to interfere with their elephant hunting, and that they need not bring in lion skins, as is the custom. As regards Chitimkubwe and Matipa, they were always closely related, even in the olden times, and, during the reign of Mwamba-wa-Kabwe, a sister of Matipa was head wife of Chitimkubwe Musinka.

' I myself am the brother of Mwamba wa Milengi, and was, when a boy, given rights over the Lubemba. At first I lived near Kabwibwi in the Kasama division, and then I had to run away from Chitimukulu when he was a young man.' (This is the Chitimukulu mentioned by Giraud, 1883, p. 270 of his book.)

' I lived successively at Tondo, Luitikishya, and Mwala, where Chitimukulu came to fight me, thinking that I was growing too strong for him to manage. We fought for six days, and both sides were about equal. I then moved to the Chyantika, thence to the Chimbwe, thence to Sofwe, and finally to within six miles of Luena station.'

Simumbi then gave a list of the eighteen kings of the Chitimukulu dynasty, which tallies with that compiled by Mr. R. A. Young in the Mirongo district note-book.

Simumbi's account may at least be considered as trust-worthy as any other source. Other old chiefs were questioned at the time (1903), and their stories corroborate his. A parallel account is to be found in the *Journal of the African Society* for October 1906, p. 146. Mr. Pirie (writing in 1906) deals at length with the legends describing the immigration to the influence of the white man, the movement into the Senga country, the fatal amour of Kolimfumu with Mwase's wife, the departure of the white man, and the establishment of the dynastic line of eighteen kings.

A writer in the above journal in January 1904, p. 186, states that it is difficult to reconcile these traditions with the history as handed down by European observers, and adds, ' The natural tendency of a people to augment the importance of their own tribe, and to increase its antiquity, is particularly apparent when we find lists of chiefs sufficient to cover a period of three hundred and fifty years.'

Any one who has read M'Lellan's *Studies in Ancient History* (Second Series), in which he devotes a chapter to demonstrating the readiness of men of all ages to fabricate genealogies, and gives African examples, will, naturally, regard such evidence with great care. At the same time, the evidence of the European travellers would not seem of sufficient strength or importance to discredit the traditional accounts of a line of kings compiled from so many sources.

The above quoted writer apparently fixes the coming of the Awemba from west by identifying the traditional white leaders as being Pereira's party in 1796. It is peculiar that the book of ' O Muata Cazembe ' gives no such particulars as recorded by the Portuguese themselves, who would, surely, have emphasised the fact of their leadership. Nor does Lacerda, in his book, refer to their leadership. In fact, when close to the Chambeshi himself, he writes two years later (21st September 1798) : ' They—the natives— also assured me that north-west was the Wemba nation, between the Muisas and Mussacuma (the Fipa), who reached the banks of Shire or Nyanja. Also they assure me that the Uemba and the Mussacuma are mortal enemies, never sparing the Kazembe people, but they are equally so with the Muisas, whom they know by their combed heads ' (Burton's translation, p. 99). Livingstone writes that Pereira told Lacerda he was known as the ' Terror,' perhaps foolish vanity, as Livingstone surmises, but hardly in keeping with the Wemba traditions, which ascribed the most kindly qualities to their white leaders. Burton, in his note, says that Monteiro in 1831 mentions the Awemba as a nomad tribe from the west-north-west of the Kazembe country, and as having seized part of the land of the Wabisa. Yet, according to Lacerda, they were established as a *nation* [1] in 1798. Again, though a line of eighteen kings might cover a period of three hundred and fifty years, it might also, in such turbulent times, have been easily compressed into a much shorter period. Moreover, such chiefs are subject to deposition—witness the case of Bwembia—and it must be remembered that the average reign of African chiefs is comparatively short. Again, the Bisa and Shinga people mention the Wemba list of kings as contemporaneous with the long lists of their own chieftains. The statement that white men were their original leaders in migration, is found so frequently in

[1] *Nação* in the original. See *Annaes Maritimos e Coloniaes*, 1845, p. 115.

Central African tribes, that the Wemba story seems rather more of a tribal variant of a great Bantu folk-legend, and there seems to be no good reason for postponing the Wemba migration until the first known appearance of Portuguese half-castes in 1796. Witness the Luban legend quoted by Mr. Crawford in the *Aurora*, of the great white Captain Kara ya Rove. ' All men marched from the south in his caravan,' says the legend, ' but various Bantu tribes deserted this "great humanity caravan" (*chendo cha bumuntu*); the Europeans, however, stuck to God's captain, and so reached wonderful Europe.'

Finally, it seems safer to presume—in the absence of more definite evidence—that there were successive waves of Wemba migration which possibly covered a period of over a hundred years, and this theory seems more in harmony with the general course of primitive migratory movements.

In compiling the following résumé of the history of the Alungu tribe, the writers are indebted to Mr. J. Gibson Hall, who has kindly placed at their disposal his copious notes upon the Alungu royal family.

Probably over two hundred years ago a tribe arrived in what was till lately the Sumbu division, from the north-west. They were called the Asao, and over them was a chieftainess named Mwenya, who married one Chomba, and to him bore five daughters with, possibly, other children. These five daughters were destined to become the heads of the five families which are to-day recognised as those of Tafuna, Chitimbwa, Moluo (Watawa) in Belgian territory, Nsama (Watawa) and the Malaila Alungu living south of the Luangwa river.

The history of the Moluo and Nsama families may, for the purposes of this book, be disregarded. Into its scope there enter only the fortunes of the descendants of Mwenya and Namukali, both daughters of the original chieftainess Mwenya, from whom sprang the Tafuna and Chitimbwa families.

Tafuna the First was the son of Chilombo, and grandson of Mwenya Chiteo, the chieftainess. He was absolute paramount, and to him Chitimbwa was subject. It would appear that his power was great, and that he enjoyed the confidence of his people, but, as his date must be placed at over one hundred years ago, it is difficult to speak with accuracy. What at least is certain is that the number of his wives ran into hundreds, that his family was enormous, and that he built villages in different parts of the country at the south end of Tanganyika to house them, his seat of government being at Isoko, midway between what are now known as Kasakalawe and Abercorn.

As Tafuna's sons grew to manhood, he chose five of them to whom he gave distinct districts—and Chitimbwa having his own district, which had been given to him by Kambole, uncle of Tafuna, there were in all six of these divisions, which were known by the names of Pumpe (Chitimbwa), Kasanga (now in German East Africa), Ntala (the country around Abercorn, now occupied by Zombe), Mwela (on the summit of the Mwenda Hills, overlooking Lake Tanganyika), Isunga, which is now embodied in that of the Awemba chief Kalimilwa, and Kakonde on the Lovu, at present under Yamutenga.

Of the sons mentioned, Kasonso—or Tinda, as he was also called—who was the first in authority over Ntala division, plays by far the most important rôle in the history of the Tafunas.

From the day of the death of the first Tafuna, either the chiefs were unfortunate in their people, or the people in their chiefs—for, with one exception, neither a regent nor a Tafuna has ruled at peace with his subjects.

Upon the death of Tafuna the First, his younger ' brother ' Kafumbo became chief ; a cruel and unscrupulous tyrant. During his reign the Angoni first made their appearance—and, probably, at their approach he fled to Niamkolo, while Kasonso went on to Isoko. The proximity of Kasonso annoyed Kafumbo, who attempted to murder him—but the plot was discovered, and in the ensuing hostilities Kafumbo received an arrow wound which, shortly afterwards, proved fatal. Upon his death Kasonso once more played the part of kingmaker, and summoned

Chungu, grandson of the fourth daughter of Mwenya, from Kasakalawe, to assume chieftainship as Tafuna the Third. With what smacks somewhat of ingratitude, Chungu's first aim upon attaining his dignity seems to have been to punish Kasonso for his hostility to the former Tafuna, Kafumbo. Fighting, alternated with brief periods of unstable peace, continued for some little time, until, eventually, Chungu, whose followers were leaving him when they found that he could no longer provide them with food, realised the futility of remaining at Isoko the capital, and retired to Chilimba on the Lofu River, having visited *en route* Chitimukulu, paramount of the Awemba.

From Tafuna the Second, Chungu inherited the various royal insignia—The Stool, Bow and Arrows, Wand, Food Baskets of the God, and the original Hoe of Tafuna the First; but, though he was undoubtedly asked to take up his residence at Isoko the capital, he refused to do so, as the country was by now constantly exposed to the attacks of the Awemba, and a retreat from the Lofu would have meant the loss of that part of the country. Then followed a period of regency, a time of storm and stress, in which Kakungu, whom Chungu looked upon as his own brother, turned against his own people, and, invoking the aid of Chilangwa, the Wemba chief, made incessant war upon his own tribe. He defeated Chitimbwa and Chikusela—but was, in turn, driven from Isoko by Zombe. Since that day no Tafuna has lived at the capital—and there has been no paramount Tafuna.

In May 1904 it was admitted, at an indaba held in Abercorn, that Chungu was the *Mweni* or paramount of the country; but, owing to the superstitious beliefs of Chinakila, who had heard that the god Kapembwa was wroth at the proposal that Chungu should be brought to Isoko, and the fact that a further claimant, Wantekwi, had been produced—it was held to be desirable to allow Wantekwi to build at the capital. On the understanding that Wantekwi would be subject to him, Chungu consented; thus, to-day, there is no Tafuna.

The more recent history of the Alungu is one of constant

fighting with the Awemba. Ponde, a well-known Wemba chief, took a large share in these hostilities. He defeated Nyente, the fourth Chitimbwa, and slew him in his village ; somewhat earlier Chitimukulu Chitapankwa had attacked Zombe, but was repulsed. However, in the following year, Chitimukulu returned, and Zombe was defeated, his body being taken and burned in the Wemba country. Had it not been for the advent of the Administration, there can be no doubt that the Awemba would have completely conquered the country. In fact, the only man who made any stand against them (beside Zombe) was the present Chungu—and such was his bravery and determination that the Awemba respected him, and Mporokoso, a minor chief, entered into an alliance with him which is to this day preserved.

The history of the Awemba and the Alungu obviously does not represent the history of all the tribes on the Plateau, but these are given as examples, it being impossible to summarise the history of the Amambwe, the Wabisa, the Senga, and other important tribes in one chapter.

So much for the vaguer and less well-substantiated history of the olden days. To understand the subsequent development of the Plateau, it is now necessary to turn to the contemporary history of what was at first British Central Africa, and is now known as the Nyasaland Protectorate. Detailed accounts are to be found in Captain Lugard's *Rise of our British East African Empire, The Shire Highlands* by John Buchanan, at one time H.M. Consul at Zomba, and *British Central Africa* by Sir Harry Johnston. We, however, are merely concerned with the history of a missionary-trading association known as the African Lakes Company, which, at the present day, still controls the commerce of both Nyasaland and North-Eastern Rhodesia.

This company had been founded by a body of philanthropists of Glasgow, for the purpose of opening up this part of Africa to trade, and, incidentally, to the propagation of the Gospel. The brothers Moir were managers. Early in its history a small trading outpost had been opened

Dr. J. B. Davey, ph t.

ANGONI WARRIORS.

Gibson Hall, phot.

CHIEF MAKASA'S BAND.

(SHEWING MAN MUTILATED IN THE OLD DAYS.)

at Karonga, on the north-west end of Lake Nyasa, and in 1888-89 the company found itself in conflict with Arab slavers from the north. Eventually Mlozi, who, under a commission from Tippoo Tib (Tiputipu), had overrun the country to the very gates of Karonga, proclaimed himself Sultan of the Wankonde country, and demanded payment of tribute from Mr. L. Monteith Fotheringham, then the agent in charge at Karonga, who has since written a book entitled *Adventures in Nyasaland*, which gives the history of the time in detail. Karonga was attacked, and for some time the little garrison was in considerable danger, but it was eventually relieved by the appearance of a Mr. Nicol with five thousand Wankonde.

Matters had reached this stage when Sir Frederic (then Captain) Lugard—who was at the time on temporary half-pay from his regiment, the Norfolk, his health having broken down from service in India and Burmah—arrived in the country. The situation appeared critical, it being generally considered that decisive steps should be taken to vanquish the Arabs, both to maintain the safety of the small European population, mostly missionaries or A.L.C. agents, and also to suppress, once and for all, the Arab slavers. Captain Lugard applied to Mr. John Buchanan for permission to take command of an expedition against these slavers, and this permission was granted on certain conditions. The movement was crowned with success, after which Lugard sailed for England.

At this time no proclamation had been made with regard to the country which is now Nyasaland—the country was the property of the chiefs, and, in reality, it is surmised, the whole difficulty arose out of a mere traders' quarrel, though quoted as a determined effort to suppress slavery. None the less, the heroic efforts of Captain Lugard and of the white men under his command were, no doubt, the basis of our supremacy in this part of Africa, from the Zambesi to Tanganyika, and from the Indian Ocean to Lake Mweru.

The troubles of the African Lakes Company near Karonga, Lake Nyasa, were concluded in 1889. In that year Mr.

(now Sir Harry) Johnston arrived in the country, charged with a mission from the Foreign Office to put a stop to the fighting between the African Lakes Company and the Arabs, and to make treaties in the north and north-west for Mr. Rhodes.

To understand this step on the part of Mr. Rhodes, it must be remembered that the war, necessitating, as it did, the importation of white men from the south, and the expenditure of vast quantities of ammunition and supplies, had pressed very heavily upon the shoulders of the African Lakes Company from a financial point of view, and many of their shares had been bought by the British South Africa Company, which thus ultimately found itself in a position to dictate a policy to the smaller concern.

Mr. Johnston was equipped with authority from the Foreign Office, and also had letters from the Sultan of Zanzibar. On his way up the Zambesi and Shire he passed a Portuguese expedition under Serpa Pinto, which, under guise of exploration, intended to obtain possession of Nyasaland. Mr. Johnston talked to them very diplomatically (for a fuller account of this meeting see *British Central Africa*, p. 83 *et seq.*), but he failed to induce the expedition to retrace its steps. On arriving at Chiromo, at the mouth of the Ruo River, Mr. Johnston obtained from Mr. Buchanan full information as to the state of affairs then existing. They were forced to act entirely on their own initiative, no communication with the Home Government being possible, since the nearest cables were at Zanzibar to the north and Delagoa Bay to the south. Under the circumstances they agreed to proclaim the country a Protectorate—and this was done at once, the proclamation being subsequently ratified by the Imperial Government.

Meanwhile Mr. Johnston visited Blantyre, Karonga, and Abercorn, which latter was not yet an administrative station, engaged in the task of obtaining the signatures of chiefs to various treaties. Upon arrival at Tanganyika he received assistance from the captain of the L.M.S. steamer the *Good News*, which was then at Niamkolo. The

London Missionary Society had penetrated into the Mambwe country, and opened a station at Fwambo in 1887. At that time the Belgian frontier was not yet fixed, and the Germans had not arrived in what is now German East Africa. Mr. Johnston sent Captain Swann to the north of Tanganyika to obtain the signatures of chiefs as far north as Lake Victoria Nyanza. In June 1890 Mr. Johnston returned to England, hearing from Mr. Buchanan on his way down that the Imperial Government had decided to ratify their proclamation of the Protectorate.

Previous to this, Mr. Johnston had sent Mr. (now Sir Alfred) Sharpe to Msiri in the Congo to obtain treaties. The latter was unfortunate in his mission. Upon arrival he found the chief unwilling to treat—and, consequently, left the papers with a Plymouth Brother who happened to be there, asking him to submit them to the potentate when a more favourable opportunity should occur. A few days after Mr. Sharpe left, Msiri signed the treaties and sent them after him, but they never arrived at their destination.[1] Meanwhile Captain Stairs, of Stanley's Emin Pasha Relief Expedition, arrived with a commission from the Belgian Government to treat with Msiri.

In July 1891 Mr. Johnston returned as H.M. Commissioner, and instituted a Civil Service in the newly formed Protectorate (B.C.A.). Previous to this the Portuguese had put three gunboats on the Zambesi, and were imposing heavy customs dues upon goods of the African Lakes Company passing up and down the river. This practice, however, was stopped by Lord Salisbury's action in sending out two gunboats, which ultimately secured the right of free trade upon Zambesi waters.

Between 1891 and until June 1895, what is now North-Eastern Rhodesia was administered from Zomba, the head-quarters of Mr. Johnston, who, as H.M. Commissioner, acted as administrator of all the British South Africa Company's territory north of the Zambesi. The British South Africa Company defrayed expenses of administering the whole sphere by annual subsidies ranging from £10,000

[1] Since Captain Stairs intercepted the letter and kept it.

to £17,500, and, in addition, various grants were made for specific purposes, such as £10,000 for the suppression of the power of Makanjira, a slaver. But when, in 1894, the British South Africa Company's total expenditure had reached £750,000, a new arrangement was made, by which that company undertook the whole administration of their own territory, and, in the summer of 1895, Major P. W. Forbes went up as first Deputy Administrator.

Previous to this, Kalungwisi had been established in North-Eastern Rhodesia itself, with a sub-station at Choma, in 1892.[1] The next year, 1893, Abercorn was established as headquarters of the Tanganyika District, with a sub-station at Sumbu, near the Congo border. To this latter station Mr. H. C. Marshall was sent as Consular Judicial Officer. His force consisted of six Sikhs and some Atonga from Lake Nyasa, and his duty lay in pursuing a waiting policy, gradually obtaining the friendship of the Mambwe and Lungu tribes, while watching his opportunity to enter into negotiations with the hitherto wholly uncivilised and much-dreaded Awemba to the south. By diplomatic measures open friction, both with the Arabs and the Awemba, was averted, though, for some time, there was every prospect of serious trouble, which would have been most difficult to suppress, as Mr. Johnston had definitely stated that no reinforcements could, under any circumstances, be sent from Nyasaland.

In 1894 the White Fathers—Les Pères Blancs d'Algers—who had established themselves at Mambwe, between Abercorn and Karonga, in 1890, commenced negotiations with Makasa. The credit of thus first penetrating into the country of the dreaded Awemba belongs to Père Van Oost, who went down in person ; but there is no doubt that the presence of the Company's officials with an armed force at Abercorn greatly facilitated his undertaking.

In the province—then known as the Chambeshi District,

[1] The first station to be established was Chienji, by Captain Crawshay. Sir Alfred Sharpe chose the site in 1892 in his journey to Mweru, in which he concluded the treaties with Kazembe, Mkula, and other chiefs, under which this portion of North-Eastern Rhodesia is now held.

but now divided into the two districts of North Luangwa and Awemba—the only station which existed up to the year 1895 for any Government purpose was that of the African Lakes Corporation. This station was called Fife, and was subsidised by the Government with a view to establishing friendly relations with the neighbouring chiefs. The agent was, however, more successful in peaceful negotiations with the chiefs on the German than on the British side, and, moreover, his trading business did not permit of much travelling. At this time a great traffic in slaves was carried on, and large caravans used to pass through the Chambeshi District from the Wemba country into German territory. Accordingly, Major Forbes established in 1895 the station of Ikawa, now known as Fife, about nine miles east of the original African Lakes Corporation Station, now abandoned. A Collector was placed in charge at Ikawa, and a substation was founded at Nyala under charge of an Assistant Collector, close to where the famous Stevenson Road terminated.

During the year 1896 several large caravans of slaves were captured by the Collector and his assistant. Though this certainly prevented slave caravans from passing through the district, yet the slave trade, though checked, was not stopped, since the Arabs resorted to the more southerly route through the Senga country, entering the sphere of what is now known as Nyasaland near the Lufira River, whence the journey lay open to Mirambo in German territory. This year the Stevenson Road was continued from Nyala to Mambwe, and a good brick house was built at Ikawa.

In December Mr. Bell, the Collector, resigned, and Mr. Charles M'Kinnon assumed charge of the district. During 1896 Major Forbes reported that the Arab slave raids were practically at an end, but that the Awemba were still a menace to the country, since they were raiding other tribes. In order to protect the Senga people, who were still suffering from those incursions of the Awemba, Mr. R. A. Young was sent as Assistant Collector to open a station called Mirongo, as near as possible to the village of Chiwali, a friendly Senga chief. The station was hardly occupied before Chiwali appealed for European aid, reporting that Kapandansaru, the head of the Arabs after Mulozi died, had built a *tembe* close to his village in concert with Wemba headmen and warriors, and had ordered him, on pain of death, to go with them to Mwamba and explain why he had encouraged the white men to build a station so near his village. Mr. Young, though his force consisted of only ten police, promptly went to aid Chiwali, entered the village, and assisted in the defence. A graphic account of the brave resistance made by Mr. Young is given in Mr. Pirie's paper published by the African Society, to which we have already referred. Suffice it to say that, after holding out for five days, Chiwali's village was relieved by Mr. M'Kinnon and Mr. Drysdale, the assistant at Nyala. The Arab besiegers fled, and were promptly followed up; village after village was taken, and slaves were liberated. Kapandansaru was captured, but died before the sentence of death passed upon him could be carried into effect. The expedition then pursued the Awemba, who had retreated by another route, ousted them from a large village where they made a brave stand, and drove them in flight across the Chambeshi. This little war had far-reaching results. External raids by the Awemba upon the surrounding tribes were checked, and the power of the Arab slavers was broken. Only three Arab chiefs responsible for these raids now remain in the country; they have no influence, and are on good terms with the Administration. The Wemba kings, being now confined within their own boundaries, turned, as if in rage, upon their own people, and inflicted upon them atrocious mutilations and other horrors, which previously they had reserved for their enemies alone. Dissension naturally followed, but the most cruel punishments were meted out to the rebels, and many of the Awemba were sold into slavery by their own chiefs.

All this obviously paved the way for the acceptance of European domination.

In May 1898 Mr. Robert Codrington was appointed Deputy Administrator for North-Eastern Rhodesia, in place of Major Forbes, the first Administrator, who had been invalided home in 1897. Mr. Codrington came north in October 1898, and sent Messrs. M'Kinnon and Young to visit Chitimukulu, the Wemba king, who had made friendly overtures. When they were at Chitimukulu's village news arrived of the death of Mwamba, the chieftain of the second branch of the Wemba royal houses, whose influence at the time overshadowed even that of Chitimukulu. The Collectors went on and found the people massed in great numbers round the French missionaries, who had been called in by Mwamba to doctor him (see Chapter XV.). The people welcomed the officials, and requested them to remain and build a *boma*. They were, in truth, very much afraid of the coming of Ponde, the heir to Mwamba, lest they themselves should play too prominent a part in the human sacrifices and massacres, which would inevitably take place upon his accession.

While Mr. Young was absent, moving his belongings from Mirongo, Mr. M'Kinnon built a *boma* close to the present Kasama. Mr. Young was then left in charge, and a warning was sent to Ponde that he must not enter the country—which, however, he disregarded, establishing himself within the borders in a strong natural site. However, the combined forces of the Collectors of Fife and Kasama rushed and carried his village by assault at day-break, and Ponde, with a small following, found safety in flight. This was the end of the Wemba resistance.

In 1899 the headquarters of the British South Africa Company's Administration was removed from Blantyre to Fort Jameson. During the transition stage the administration was for three months carried on from Fife and Abercorn. In April of the same year Mr. Codrington paid another visit to Kasama, and there established Kalonganjofu, the nominee of Chitimukulu, as successor to the chieftainship of Mwamba. In 1900 Mr. Codrington was made Administrator of North-Eastern Rhodesia.

From that date onwards history takes on a more peaceable and modern aspect. During 1900 the foundations of a

Civil Service were laid, by the promulgation of the North-Eastern Rhodesia Order in Council, which provided for magisterial and district officers. By Government Notice, No. 1 of 1900, nine fiscal and magisterial districts were defined, of which three only come within the scope of the present work—*North Luangwa*, with sub-stations of Fife, Koka, Nyala, and Mirongo ; *Awemba*, with sub-stations at Kasama, Mpika, and Luena ; and *Tanganyika*, with sub-stations at Abercorn, Sumbu, Katwe, and Mporokoso.

During this year smallpox, which had long been endemic, became almost universally epidemic. Vaccination was carried out on an extensive scale, and lymph distributed, with considerable success.

In 1901 the Hut Tax was first imposed, and was well received, more especially in the north, where authority had been longer enforced, and by the stronger tribes, such as the Awemba and Angoni. The people in the vicinity of Bangweolo were, however, practically unapproachable, and many of the swamp dwellers continued to evade their obligations, assisted by the difficult nature of the country which they inhabit.[1]

In the north, the anticipations of a general commercial development were not realised, partly because the Shire Highlands Railway, which would have secured the permanency of the Nyasa route to Tanganyika, was not carried through, and partly because very little development took place in the Tanganyika regions, except the construction of the Transcontinental Telegraph. In 1902, however, importation of material for this purpose by the Nyasa-Tanganyika route through German territory began to be made, and a valuable outlet for local labour was thus lost to the country.

The steamship *Cecil Rhodes*, the property of the Tanganyika Concessions Limited, was launched on Lake Tanganyika in October 1901, while in August 1900 the steam launch *Scotia*, the property of the African Lakes Company, had been placed on Lake Mweru. Small townships were

---

[1] Nowadays, however, both Waunga and Wabisa have fallen into line, having paid their taxes in otter skins.

laid out at Kasakalawe and Sumbu on Tanganyika, and at Abercorn and Fife on the Plateau. The London Missionary Society and the mission of the White Fathers slightly extended their operations; the African Lakes Company established themselves at Sakontwi, Sumbu, and Kasama; and a Government farm was started at Ikomba, to preserve and improve the cattle of the country, which, in native hands, were fast disappearing. Ox-waggons were at this time plying along the Stevenson Road, and were proving satisfactory; pack-donkeys also, which had been tried for the first time, were doing well. Most of the telegraph material went through in 1900. In 1901 the Flotilla Company established a station at Chienji, on Lake Mweru, and in 1902 Fife township was moved to higher ground.

From 1900 to 1902 the Plateau was at the zenith of its prosperity. There was, at that time, a larger European population than at the present day; loads were plentiful, and wealth circulated briskly. But with the completion of the telegraph construction commercial activity dwindled, and no further developments arose to replace it. One by one the trading firms—the Tanganyika Concessions, the Flotilla Company, the African Lakes—drew in their horns; one by one the Europeans, their various tasks completed, withdrew to other spheres, until only the missionaries and the administrative officials remained. One by one, too, administration stations were closed down as unnecessary, and in this way Nyala, Mirongo, Koka, Sumbu, being merged into the headquarters' stations, passed into oblivion. And then, when commercial depression was at its height, came the Sleeping Sickness, which—though only temporarily, let us hope—has rung the knell of Plateau progress. During 1908 it was decided to move all natives away from the shore of Tanganyika, and this measure was promptly carried into effect, thus invalidating the one great waterway of the country, and destroying the *raison d'être* of all the coastal settlements, which are now but heaps of ruined huts. A cordon was drawn round the northern part of the Plateau bordering upon the lake, and strict surveillance instituted to prevent natives moving in or out of the area so enclosed. And, for the moment, progress is in abeyance.

Yet, although commercial development was arrested, the period from 1903 to the present date has been no mere empty lacuna, but full of quiet consolidation, improvement of the country and of the native administration. Of the establishment and development of law and order fuller details are given in a subsequent chapter. Let it suffice to quote the opinion of an independent and experienced southern observer. Mr. P. L. Jenkins, who travelled over some two thousand miles, and remained eight months in the country, records his impressions in a most interesting paper read before the Rhodesia Scientific Association, and though this paper was written before the advent of the Sleeping Sickness, it is not without value in exhibiting the possibilities of the country under happier auspices. Mr. Jenkins writes :

'Good government has been established by a handful of officials, and nothing is more striking than the apparent ease with which everything has been accomplished and is now carried on . . . the amount of work so quietly done in a few years is surprising, when you consider the vastness of the country and the slowness of communication. There are good roads from end to end of the territory connecting the Government stations with one another. Swamps are drained, and bridges of poles constructed over rivers. The good brick houses at the Native Commissioners' stations are a pleasing contrast to the wattle-and-daub camps which are still seen in Southern Rhodesia as residencies for the principal officials of large districts. Gardens are laid out and trees planted in all stations. . . . Cotton is grown in small quantities, and the Government shows commendable energy in experimenting with rubber, grape vines, and other plants. . . . In fact, the efforts of the Company appear to have been directed towards quietly perfecting the machinery of administration and exploring the possibilities of the country.'

So, although this chapter may close in gloom, although it may seem that we are dealing merely with the history of a colossal Might-Have-Been, it must be remembered that there are other chapters yet to come. The records of this territory are not yet closed, even if for the moment we are passing through a phase of gloomy unproductiveness. And in Africa—indeed throughout the British Empire—territories which have been won in the very jaws of disease and at the point of the sword are not lightly cast aside.

CHAPTER IV

NATIVE LEGAL NOTIONS

No part of the white man's administration is perhaps more keenly criticised among the natives themselves than that which concerns the hearing of *milandu*, or law suits and palavers, and the dispensation of justice. They are prompt to mark where the old precedents have been followed, or where they have been discarded and superseded by new principles of jurisdiction. The procedure of tribal and customary law still holds the native mind with a grip that is not easily shaken off, and this is clearly seen in the bizarre and eccentric cases which they bring into the native court-house as fit subjects for its cognisance. One day an angry father will rush before the Native Commissioner with an obvious case for divorce on behalf of his daughter, and a criminal charge for manifest witchcraft. Did not his son-in-law take his wife's apron into the bush and force it into the cleft fork of a tree, wherein he had previously wedged a live snake ? And was not the tortured reptile using so personal a garment as a connecting link, able to project its angry and vindictive soul into the body of the girl, and wreak her destruction by its evil influence ?

Another day a woman will sue for damages and divorce because ' the death was not taken off her body ' at the proper time and with the proper ceremonies ; or, again, it is a claim for damages for loss of stock preferred by the headman and villagers against neglectful parents who have failed to perform the purification demanded by customary law after the birth of twins, and so have clearly caused this loss of livestock. Other more strictly criminal accusations of witchcraft and poisoning are continually brought up. Thus, from the point of view of the Native Commissioner, the whole subject of native law and its precedents is of such paramount importance, and deserves such close and exhaustive study, with reference to each tribe, that it is manifestly impossible to deal adequately with its problems in the limits of a single chapter. Hence our scope is confined to the examination in a merely general way of some of the more prominent native legal notions and conceptions, illustrated by the customary law of one tribe, that of the dominant Awemba.

The origins of Plateau tribal law are shrouded in a veil of truly African mystery, impenetrable yet alluring. Nor have vaunted modern theories gone far towards the rending of that veil. The theory of the development of customary native law through the obligations of either patriarchal, matriarchal, or totemistic systems is of doubtful application here. When one considers how, at every point, native life touches the religious and the supernatural, much evidence might be adduced to show that customary law may be merely an ethical and political development of the superstitious fears and magical beliefs of primitive religion.

Taking native law, however, as we find it, we can clearly perceive that the fount of justice is the king, supported by his Council of Elders, the repositories of the ancient wisdom. How the king attained his position as the recognised and unquestioned authority in legal matters it is extremely difficult to say. Doubtless such authority rests ultimately upon the sanctions of ancestor worship. The king was ' the Son of God ' and of his deified ancestors. Like his Homeric prototype, his judgments were probably ' assumed to be the result of direct inspiration from these sacred sources.' The king in his person held together the bonds of law and order ; when he died, they were loosened. For instance, on the death of the king all the villagers dispersed, and a form of anarchy manifested itself. Any man could reap his neighbour's garden, or take and kill his sheep and goats (this practice being known as *chisondo* or *kulya chilyelye*), ' and there was no *mulandu*, because this was during the sleeping time of the king.'

And, indeed, the quality of the Wemba justice showed

that the kings were by no means blind to the responsibilities of this inherited trust. Tradition states that they assiduously attended to their judicial duties, one king, it is said, dying upon the seat of justice itself, from an obstinate determination, in spite of his severe illness, to conclude a case.

Livingstone appears to have been much impressed with the way in which justice was administered, and describes a scene which he witnessed at Mwamba's village as follows : ' One old man spoke for an hour on end, the chief listening all the time, with the gravity of a judge, then delivered his decision in about five minutes, the successful litigant going off lullilooing. Each person before addressing him turns his back to him and lies on the ground clapping his hands. We had a little talk with the chief, but it was a little late before the case was ended.' Indeed, the statement made by a writer in the *Journal of the African Society*, p. 46, Oct. 1906, that the trial of offences was conducted by a chief, whose ' decision was given to the party who could pay the highest price,' is quite at variance not only with accounts given by travellers, but also with the present procedure of chiefs hearing cases at their own villages, far away from any European station. As in all countries, certain kings were venal and unjust. But such injustice was held in check by the council of old men, who were by no means shy of ' straightening the king's word,' in accordance with precedents which they remembered, or said they remembered. Moreover, the medicine men would have their say as to what would be pleasing or unpleasing to the ancestral spirits. It is true, as the writer above quoted states, that all members of the royal family were considered to be above the law ; but even to this there were limits. Younger scions of the blood royal, who had overstepped the bounds in their ill-treatment of commoners, would be admonished by the king in the words of the proverb—' I shall veil my eyes with a goatskin '—as a hint that he would punish his offending relative with blind equity of justice. And, accordingly, there are many cases of banishment on record. It may be said on the whole, with greater truth, that severe but substantial justice was the outcome. This, in fact, is the opinion of a magistrate of very long standing, who stated that, even immediately after the country had been taken over, very few cases were brought up to him for revision, the decisions of the chiefs having been sound in the main.

Before dealing in detail with the Wemba code, some phases of the attitude of the common people to the customary law of the land deserve to be mentioned. First and foremost, every Central African is a born lawyer. From childhood upward he has been familiarised with the procedure in innumerable cases heard in the open village courtyard. or has listened to the accounts of old time decisions, rounded off by some neat proverb or epigram, and accordingly, when he has attained to man's estate, the mind of the average native is a veritable storehouse of past precedents. Should the need arise, he can act as his own pleader, and set forth his case with fluency and lawyer-like adroitness. It is doubtless from this early-acquired knowledge and legal bias that the natives derive the great respect for constituted authority shown in their singularly law-abiding nature.

Nor was law or its action regarded, as through the more matter-of-fact focus of modern thought, in the light of a somewhat ponderous and slow-moving mechanism essential to the maintenance of social order, but devoid of intrinsic interest. By our Central African it was considered more in the light of some living, sentient organism, as a mystical, sacred, and all-powerful creation lurking in the recesses of religion and superstition, and protecting its mysteries from profanation. As will be shown in the chapter upon Religion, the influence of the medicine man or village priest cannot be over-estimated. He would never lose any opportunity of pointing out misfortunes as the result of a breach of customary observance, until the people began to regard such lapses with dread and detestation, and as pregnant with calamity in the future. Some time ago a full-grown native had to fly to the *boma* for protection, since his fellow-villagers, incited by the witch-doctor, were determined to drown him, and so correct the breach of customary law in the past committed by his parents, in having suffered him to live though *chinkula*—an ill-omened child.   (See p. 180.)

The accepted doctrine of corporate responsibility for illegal acts enhanced the prestige of customary law in the eyes of the natives.   Its inconsistencies and injustices were regarded in the more mellow light of family and collective standards, not thrown into jagged relief by the fierce and unkindly flare of modern individualism.   As Maine points out, in the case of ancient law the family not the individual was the legal unit, and, from the native viewpoint, customary law may be considered as ' filling the interstices ' between such family units, and adjusting their external relations. As later, according to the well-known law, the ties of family were superseded by those of local contiguity, each village became corporately responsible for the acts of its individual residents.   Native law, considered, as it undoubtedly was by the natives themselves, as a system of class legislation, stands unabashed and unassailed in many points which would not pass unquestioned if brought before the bar of latter-day jurisprudence.   To the Plateau native it seems natural enough that any one of royal lineage should be above the law, as being a member of the aristocratic corporation which dispensed it.   Nor was there any apparent inconsistency in the fact that many ordinances which made for fair dealing and equity only applied in the case of blood relations, connections by marriage, or by blood brotherhood.

Mutilations and the cruellest punishments, which from modern standpoints may seem merely ' wild spasms of justice, half punishment, half outrage,' were regarded by the native as imperative for the maintenance of order in turbulent times.   The idea of lengthy imprisonment as a punishment for serious crime is entirely foreign to native conceptions.   In several cases, witnesses have openly alleged their preference for the short and sharp sanctions of the older régime.   ' Why should we take this big *mulandu* to the white man, who will only put an iron round the prisoner's neck, and give him good food and clothing ? ' was the argument used by the avenger in one case, who promptly took the guilty man to the stream, and drowned

CHIEF KATIETE HEARING A CASE. THE HANDS ARE CLASPED IN THE
CORRECT POSTURE FOR A TAMBO CHIEF WHEN HEARING A CASE.

A NATIVE CASE IN PROGRESS.

him without more ado. Selling into slavery or domestic servitude was the nearest approach to the idea of long service as equivalent to expiation.

Finally, their sense of injustice is abnormally vivid. Many a man in the olden time would so take to heart what he considered the unjust decision of the chief in depriving him of his wives, or causing some other injury to his family, that he would go straightway from the tribunal and hang himself from the nearest tree. It may perhaps be mentioned here that, in native law, the accused was invariably considered guilty until proved innocent, and, to the present day, natives cannot understand the assumption of innocence in English justice. Again, they cannot understand the warning, before taking the evidence of the accused in serious cases, that, if he wishes, he need make no defence to the charge, so as to avoid incriminating himself; and it is impossible to recall any case of the accused having taken advantage of such warning by standing mute.

Having dealt with some aspects of the mental attitude of the common people, we may now turn to the actual procedure in vogue among the dominant tribe.

The Awemba had distinct tribunals, according to the nature of the offence. The most serious cases were, as we have mentioned elsewhere, heard *in camera* by the Wakabiro, presided over by the king. After secret consultations, the king would finally deliver as his own the decision of the elders, the Wakabiro listening in silent approval.

Certain civil cases and less important criminal offences were heard in the open courtyard by the king himself, surrounded by his Wakabiro and his Wakilolo, who, however, unless specially called upon, were not supposed to give their opinions.

The third court, which dealt with the bulk of petty criminal and the ordinary civil cases was that of the Wakilolo, who, assisted by other village elders, settled such cases and decreed the fines to be paid, reserving all *mulandu* in which they thought punishment advisable for the higher court.

The District Courts, moreover, in the various villages were conducted on the same lines ; the judge, who must be of the king's family, unless special powers had been granted to him to decide cases, sitting with the elders in the more serious cases, but trying lesser offences unaided.

These various courts were, however, not the only resources for litigants. Those who preferred physical pangs to the ' intellectual pleasure of legal procedure ' would appeal to the *mwavi* (poison) ordeal, and to various other methods, which, being a form of evidence, may be discussed more conveniently later under that head.

The distinction between criminal and civil law was not clear to the native mind, except in so far that offences against the king were placed in an entirely different category and assigned different punishments from those meted out to similar offences of the common people against each other. The latter classification is the more convenient in presenting the following outline of the ordinary penal offences. We may here recall the dictum that the penal law of ancient communities is not the law of crimes, but the law of wrongs and of sins against religion and morality.

I. CRIMES AGAINST THE KING

High Treason.—A spy might report that one of the district headmen was meditating sedition against Chitimukulu. In case the culprit were of royal blood, more finesse than usual would be required, and the king would be compelled to call in the medicine man and the ' Possessed Chieftainesses of the Spirit,' who were as useful politically as the Delphic prophetesses of old. A *séance* would be held, and these *Mfumu ya mipashi* would writhe on the ground, groaning forth dark hints against the suspect, but not mentioning him by name. Backed by the interpretation of the medicine man, the king would send for the accused, who would be at once arraigned before the Wakabiro as having plotted and woven enchantments against the ' Son of God ' Chitimukulu. The king would then see that the *mwavi* was prepared for him. If he swelled up shortly afterwards, the king's servants immediately surrounded and killed him ; his body being cut into small pieces and burnt by the medicine men. Even if the *mwavi* test failed, the chief supporters of this erring headman would be arrested and sold into slavery, the culprit himself being deprived of all power, and kept under strict surveillance at the capital.

Adultery with the King's Wives.—Though careful watch was kept over the king's harem by the *wakalume*, or royal servants, both male and female, yet infidelity was by no means uncommon. In the cases where the adulterer was caught *flagrante delicto*, the guilty pair were dispatched by a spear-thrust through the back. The blood-stained spear was sent to the father of the frail one, his duty being to find without delay a more faithful partner for his royal son-in-law. Where mere undue intimacy was proved, adultery was nevertheless taken to have occurred, and Chitimukulu would have the luckless Lothario executed at the principal gate of the village by gunshot. Women were subjected to the most atrocious mutilations, but rarely survived when their breasts had been cut off. In the Wemba country it is a common sight to see handless women with their noses cut off and their ears slit. The adulterers, if not killed outright, were shockingly mutilated. In one case it is related that the late Mwamba burned the adulterer and his partner in shame alive, watching their tortures from a raised seat. Shortly after this, however, he would seem to have been stricken with remorse and the dread of Nemesis. The presiding witch-doctor was therefore ordered to collect the ashes of the twain, and decoct therefrom a potion, which was administered to the king, to avert the avenging furies of evil spirits of the murdered pair, which might otherwise have hounded him into a fit of madness.

Murder of a King.—Only one instance, and that not well authenticated, is given of this. In case of the murder of one of royal blood, the murderer was taken to the principal gate of the village and there smitten between the eyes with a knobkerrie, his body being subsequently cut piece-meal and burned.

II. OFFENCES BETWEEN EQUALS AND AMONG THE COMMON
PEOPLE

Murder.—Usually the injured clan pursued the murderer,
killing him out of hand, unless he gained sanctuary with the
district headman.

More commercially-minded avengers would bind him and
hold him to ransom, with threats of torture and mutilation,
unless he paid sufficient *wer-gild* in slaves or calico. If the
crime occurred near the head village, before putting the
murderer to death they would hale him before the chief,
who was, as a general rule, nothing loth to order his execution. The Wakabiro, if the guilty man were rich, or had
many relatives, would interpose, and the brother of the
deceased would be suitably recompensed, taking as his slave,
in addition, the wife of the murderer. However, if the
murderer were poor, and no extenuating circumstances
appeared, he and all his household were handed over as
slaves to the head of the accusing clan. Where a murder
was committed in a large village, the king would hold the
headman responsible, and the latter would frequently pay
a woman slave or a tusk of ivory to the injured relatives,
recouping himself later by enslaving the murderer's whole
family.

It may here be noted that many extenuating circumstances
were allowed as an excuse for homicide. The statement by
a murderer that he had slain his victim because the latter
had appeared to and cursed him in a dream was taken into
consideration, though a drunken man, or one intoxicated
with *bhang*, might not plead this in self-defence. On the
other hand, an insane man who killed another in a mad fit
was not held responsible, the relatives ingeniously arguing
that the murdered man must have been a wizard all the
time, else the spirit tenant of the insane body would not
have inspired it to do the deed. But though the madman
personally escaped scot-free, his relatives had to pay for him.
No allowance was made for homicide by accident—*e.g.* by
gunshot—but the brother of the deceased would spear the
careless owner of the gun without compunction.

Assaults and Grievous Bodily Harm.—These offences were atoned by payment.

Adultery.—In cases of adultery between persons of equal status the adulterer was flogged by the chief and fined in live-stock and goods to compensate the husband, but the wife was not put away for the first offence. If, however, she again misbehaved, she was sent back in disgrace to her own village, and her parents were in duty bound to replace her.

When the adulterous pair were taken in the act the husband slew both. There were no proceedings for murder or manslaughter against him. He would merely return the blood-stained spear to his father-in-law, who, by his words in the ' marriage ceremony,' ' You shall spear the man who lusts after your wife,' was estopped from taking vengeance for the death of his daughter, and was compelled either to find another daughter or to return the dowry. In cases where the husband spared the guilty pair, and the wife was again taken in adultery, the villagers themselves decreed the punishment. The incontinent wife and her partner in sin were dragged outside the village and impaled on sharp stakes, amid the taunts and jeers of the bystanders, who only desisted when death had stilled their writhing agonies. If a woman gave birth to a still-born child, she was asked to name the adulterer, who was held guilty without further proof, and was called the *musoka*, or murderer of the child ; in the same way, if the woman died in childbirth, the man she named as her lover was called the murderer until he had satisfied the husband by payment of heavy damages.

Theft and Robbery.—Robbery from strangers was a time-honoured custom, and the phrase, *Kutapatapa chya Wawemba chyene*—' Stealing is the *métier* of the Awemba ' —became quite a proverb. Theft of the goods of the king was usually punished by cutting off the offender's ears. The evidence as to the punishment for theft of the crops or of food among persons of equal rank in the same village is somewhat contradictory. Some of the older men assert that, as a general rule, such thefts were never punished, but others give instances where a fine was inflicted. Again, accounts are conflicting as to the punishments awarded for theft from the gardens of the chief. One woman appealed to the Native Commissioner at Luena to free her from the domestic slavery which she had undergone for years, because, when a little child, she had stolen monkey nuts from the chief's garden. But there can be no doubt that some chiefs would ignore such thefts ; and among the Amambwe it is certainly held that the crops of the chief are the food of the people, since it is his duty to see that his ' children ' do not starve.

Other forms of theft were punished by flogging, and the thief had to restore the stolen property or to make it good. In native law the appropriation of goods found was neither theft nor larceny, since, as the saying ran, ' What is in the path belongs to all men.'

Perjury.—To speak falsely before the king himself was a serious offence if touching an important case, but it is obvious that much latitude was allowed, and the crime was by no means so heinous as it is considered at the present day. Those who continually reported their fellow-villagers to the chief were detested by all, and were sometimes poisoned for their perjury. ' 'Tis but a jackal howling whenever he sits on his haunches,' was the scornful taunt at the informer who was continually squatting before the chief with some story of outrage. Sometimes such a spy would overreach himself with false denunciations of innocent people. The king would then secretly call for the parties, and if he could catch the spy tripping in details on confrontation, would tie him up with the words, ' I shall do a thing to you to-morrow.' The thing so euphemistically referred to would, when done, leave the unfortunate spy sightless, or with his hands cut off as a warning.

We may note that, in the case of murderers or other serious offenders, the Awemba seem to have had some kind of arrangement for extradition with the surrounding tribes. Thus Mukoma, the Winamwanga chief, would send back murderers to Chitimukulu. Again, when the murderer of Chief Kaoma, a Lungu chieftain, fled to Mwamba's court, Mwamba, though at war with the tribe, nevertheless handed him over to the Alungu envoys without demur, since he had killed a reigning chieftain.

Let us pass on to what may, for convenience' sake, be termed Civil Law.

Inheritance and Family Succession.—The questions of the inheritance of wives will be dealt with in Chapter XI.

The method of succession to other family property varies considerably among the different tribes. Among the Awemba any undue haste in the settlement of the succession is deemed ill-advised, and likely to be distasteful to the spirit of the deceased. After a period varying from a few months to as much as a year, the elders of the family gather together, and, after much beer drinking, decide as to the distribution of the goods and chattels. Where the inheritance is a substantial one, the cattle, goats, sheep, hoes, and other household effects are handed over to the heir in the presence of the headman and the assembled villagers as witnesses. A dying man can set aside the claims of his brother, if the latter has not treated him well during his lifetime. Regard is paid to such wishes when uttered in the presence of reliable witnesses, and the brother is occasionally disinherited in favour of a son. When cattle are abundant, the heir, as a concession and not in fulfilment of a righteous demand, apportions part of the live-stock to his younger brothers. Sisters or daughters of the deceased do not inherit anything from the father in their own right, though, on the death of an elder sister, they would inherit her ' belt,' and succeed to her position.

Land Laws and the System of Tenure.—The problem of native land tenure is a complex and vexed question all over Africa. Into the dispute as to whether native tenure can be described as communal or individualistic we obviously cannot inquire in the present chapter. In theory the whole of the land belongs to the paramount chief, presumably by right of conquest. This ownership is not absolute, and, in fact, it is safer to assert that the chief formerly held the land, as it were, in communal trust for the people.   The king, for instance, could not sequestrate the village lands nor hand them over to an alien owner.   He could induct his sons as landlords over large provinces, which they administered, and from which they collected the customary dues as described in a previous chapter.   But, technically, the whole country was still his own.   Nor could his overseers, even though of royal blood, dispossess a village of its corporate rights to the surrounding land.   All such questions of productive land between different villages and all boundary disputes could be settled only by the king himself.

Each village group possessed common rights of grazing on all the unreclaimed land near the village.   In the olden times the headman divided the land suitable for gardens, which was, of necessity, close to the village, owing to the fear of raids, among the various heads of families, and saw that their respective boundaries were strictly observed. On the coming of peace and security, as we have seen, this valuable land-allotment system was discontinued, and family heads chose their own sites for garden-cutting, which gave rise to the pernicious system of *mitanda*.   The idea of individual tenure extending to peculiar rights over property or any kind of freehold title was foreign to the native mind. By cutting down a few boughs, or by various other signs, each cultivator could bespeak a plot of unallotted land for himself.   By subsequently cultivating it he acquired the right to till it, which was respected only so long as he continued to work it.   No man could sell his plot of ground, though he could dispose of its standing crops.   Under the common system of cultivation, each owner changed the position of his garden every year, so that it was unlikely that such temporary occupation should ever ripen into true ownership.   Moreover, it is clear that, with a population averaging about two to each square mile, there was no excessive land greed to strengthen the principle of absolute ownership.

In dealing with the question of evidence before native

tribunals, it is almost impossible to ascertain the exact truth. Both plaintiff and defendant would be supported by the evidence of their respective families. The value of independent witnesses was fully realised, and cases would sometimes be delayed several days to allow of their appearance. The old men, however, gave their decisions in the main from intuitive reasoning and comparison with past cases. To the native mind mere verbal evidence was insufficient as proof, at least in serious cases. Hence, as Professor Tylor says, ' Barbaric law early began to call on magic and divine powers to help in the difficult task of discovering the guilty and getting the truth out of witnesses.' From this arises the practice of the *mwavi* ordeal, common among all Central African tribes. The Awemba ceremony of the ordeal is very typical of the procedure observed among the various Plateau races. Though sometimes other poisonous barks are used, *mwavi* is usually made from the bark of a tree the scientific name of which is *Erythroplœum guineense*. It is a true poison, and fatal unless vomiting occurs shortly after the dose.

In the serious *mwavi* cases the chief sent some of his people into the bush with the medicine man, carrying a young child stripped of all his clothing. On arrival at the *mwavi* tree (*Wikalampungu*), they prayed, and laid before the tree an offering of small white beads—presumably to the spirit residing in the tree. With a stout log they proceeded to beat the tree until the bark fell off in strips. Only those flakes of bark which fell flat down were used for the poison. They were tied up in a bundle of grass placed in the hands of the naked child. The people then returned to the village, the boy being carried on the shoulders of an old man, as his feet must touch neither water nor mud ; moreover, the carrier himself must avoid molehills and fallen logs on the way. The bundle of *mwavi* was not taken into the village, but deposited outside, and guarded by a *mushika* of· the chief, and the medicine man who mixed it. The accused was compelled to sleep that night outside the village under close guard. As he was taken thither, the villagers would intone the ' Song of Witchcraft '—' The Mwavi Tree desires the father of sorcery '—and repeat the usual formula, ' If you have not done this thing, may you survive—but, if you are guilty, may you die ! ' Early next morning the suspect was stripped, retaining only a girdle of leaves. If he still protested his innocence he was given the poisoned cup, which was sometimes handed to him by a young child. Swelling up without vomiting was considered proof positive of guilt, and unless the chief relented, the suspect would die with all the symptoms of violent poisoning. In the more serious cases, such as witchcraft, the poison was almost invariably allowed to take its course. The body would then be burned by the medicine man, lest the deceased should arise again as an evil spirit to plague the village. The children, and sometimes the whole family of the accused, were sold by the chief as slaves to the Arabs.

If, however, the accused vomited, the chief would give him the ' Prayer of Absolution,' and declare him innocent. The accusers of the innocent man were then fined heavily in slaves, live-stock or goods, which reverted to the chief, who would give part, as compensation, to the injured man. A good deal of trickery crept into the ordeal procedure. The accused would, if possible, take an emetic just before the draught. Instances are also related of the medicine man being induced by secret gifts to mix an emetic with the pounded *mwavi* to cause instant vomiting. Among some tribes, such as the Senga, wholesale *mwavi* drinkings took place. In a village where witchcraft had occurred, each head of a family was constrained to drink the potion until the inquiry narrowed down and the guilty party was discovered. Where the charge involved an important man or a relative of the king, the *mwavi* was given to a cock which was held to represent the accused.

The Boiling-Water Test, in which the accused was made to plunge his hand into a pot of boiling water and take therefrom a stone, was more in vogue among the Wabisa and the tribes to the west. The Trial by Hunting is described in Chapter XII. In case of theft, the guilty man was supposed to be discovered by the little ' speaking gourd ' (*kalubi*), by the axehead rubbed against a block of wood, or by other methods of divination (see Chapter VI.)

In conclusion, we may raise the question, How does the coming of European law affect native customary law and procedure ?

In civil cases, the North - Eastern Rhodesia Order in Council lays down that the Magistrates' Courts ' . . . . shall be guided by native law so far as that law is not repugnant to natural justice and morality,' and the King's Regulations of 1909 contain other directions as to the administration of justice by Native Commissioners. Year by year, Native Commissioners, while retaining and assimilating many of the better features of native law, gradually modify and extend the native code, relying to a great extent upon native assessors in unravelling the complex civil cases. The influence of the justice of the European spreads slowly and almost imperceptibly, but, nevertheless, along sure and sound lines. Scientific jurisprudence may quarrel with this system, and point out that, since so much latitude is allowed to Native Commissioners, widely different precedents may possibly be created in each division. Such scientists might advocate that the law applied in this fashion to natives should be codified, to ensure uniformity. Against this must be considered the fact that each district is inhabited by different tribes, among whom the essential ideas both of criminal and civil law are conflicting. For instance, among some Plateau tribes, infanticide, the procuring of abortion, etc., are enjoined by custom, though regarded by neighbouring races as serious offences. Again, the civil law varies in every tribe. And, as records of all criminal sentences are forwarded each month, by Magistrates to the Judge, by Native Commissioners to the Secretary to the Administrator for Native Affairs, anomalies, at least, in the penalties imposed for various offences are, to a certain extent, controlled. It is highly probable that whatever might be gained in regularity, precision, and uniformity by codification would be lost by cramping the present sympathetic flexibility of native courts under a rigid code.

This question, however, can of course only be indicated here, as it is purely a principle of policy. One may, however, quote, as broadly applicable, the opinion of a ' Colonial Administrator,' who, when dealing with such problems of native administration, writes as follows in the *Journal of the African Society* : ' The answer to this—the kernel of the nut—is to govern the natives in accordance with their own laws and customs and their own councils and courts under supervision . . . except in so far as where certain customs, such as human sacrifice, death for witchcraft, the killing of twins, and slave dealing, are entirely at variance with the laws of humanity and civilisation.'

CHAPTER V

THE ADVENT OF WHITE MAN'S LAW

THERE are, upon the Plateau, about twenty administrative officials, divided into Magistrates or Assistant Magistrates, Native Commissioners or Assistant Native Commissioners, and probationers in the Native Department. There are also three District Surgeons, detailed mainly for Sleeping Sickness duties, and one Postmaster. With this staff a native population of roughly 150,000, spread over an area of fifty thousand square miles, is controlled.

There are neither white troops nor white police. Among the administrative stations or *bomas* are distributed about one hundred men of the North Eastern Rhodesia (native) Constabulary, in detachments ranging from ten to twenty-five, each detachment being in charge of a native sergeant or corporal, under the direct control of the senior official of the station. There is also a bugler to discourse sweet music.

These *askari*, as they are called, are well armed with Martini-Enfield rifles ; they are smartly uniformed in blue serge ' jumpers ' and ' shorts ' with khaki tunics, and the usual Mackenzie equipment for full dress ; their headgear consists of a black fez with a tassel, and they drill with the precision of machines. In the Somaliland campaign of 1902-1904, several Awemba of this corps served with the King's African Rifles, and won the golden opinions of their officers for their pluck and discipline. But, none the less, it is permissible to doubt whether, in the event of a local native rising, they would be of much assistance.

In the first place—possibly from motives of policy—they receive but little training in shooting. This is well enough, regarded from the viewpoint of their being unable to turn their arms against the white man, but obviously a man who cannot shoot straight enough to injure his superior will fail to inflict much damage upon that superior's enemy, should occasion arise. The matter is one which has received much attention in Southern Rhodesia, and it would be unprofitable to discuss the ethics of it here. As a matter of fact, volley firing into dense masses of natives at close quarters, which would probably be the class of fighting that the native policeman would be called upon to perform, does not require much accuracy of aim. Besides which, the N.E.R.C. is essentially a civil force.[1]

There is, however, a sensible disadvantage in the fact that the corps is recruited, in many cases, from the very tribes against which, in the event of trouble, its members would be arrayed. In Somaliland this was all very well. The Mullah and his followers were, for all practical purposes, beings from another planet; our men had nothing in common with them, and spitted them as gaily and with just as little compunction as they would the domestic goat. But in warfare *à outrance* traitors would undoubtedly arise; indeed, treason would in such a case be a harsh word to use, seeing that blood is admittedly thicker than water. Perhaps at least two-thirds of the civil force could be composed of men not belonging to local tribes; thus the Awemba district might be policed with Yaos, Atonga, or Washinga, who would in wartime be staunch to Europeans.

For the rest, these police of ours have their failings, like the remainder of mankind. The abuse of power is, doubtless, a very human characteristic; more especially when to that power, supervised though it be, there is linked the glamour of a tasteful uniform, free rations (or ration allowance), and 5s. per month. Womenkind are apt, in Africa as elsewhere, to follow the drum, and it is to be feared that the responsibility for many a domestic tragedy lies at the door of the gallant *askari*.

None the less a Magistrate of long standing has given it

[1] For many years the British South Africa Company has paid an annual subsidy of over £7000 to the Government of Nyasaland, for defence by the soldiers of the King's African Rifles.

as his opinion that, considering their extensive powers, the civil force of North-Eastern Rhodesia compares favourably with that of any other country.

The native messenger, if his numbers were increased, would become a most useful asset in the administration of the country. Clad in a serviceable uniform of blue canvas with red facings and a red fez, he is a civilian pure and simple—the black counterpart of the genial Robert of the London streets. Now and again, no doubt, he may abuse his position ; but, for the most part, he discharges his duties with a faithful conscientiousness that would do credit to any white man.

However, fortunately for us all, there is at present no cloud upon the horizon. The native has no cause for complaint ; his condition, compared with that of his brethren in the south, is the condition of an angel in paradise.

The all-pervading difference lies, no doubt, in the question of the white population. In many parts of South Africa the native plays a secondary part. His land has been wrested from him ; he is penned in reserves which, owing to the policy of taking the cash and letting the credit go— in other words, renting out the land to farmers and large land compaines, who, in many cases, look to the taxation of the squatting native as their main source of revenue— are year by year becoming too small to hold him. And, in the south, the inferior class of European is much in evidence. The native is at the mercy of uneducated shop-keepers, boilermakers, railway-gangers, and the like ; as a natural result he acquires a meretricious veneer of civilisa-tion, but at heart becomes more debased than his ancestors ever were. Moreover, this class of employer takes no pains to understand him, is at no trouble to learn his tongue, regards him simply as a labour machine.

It may be doubted whether the mines exercise an entirely salutary influence upon the north-country native. All sorts and conditions are there herded together ; vice of every kind flourishes exceedingly, even to unnatural crimes which, says Duff in *Nyasaland under the Foreign Office*, are held in detestation by the native of British Central Africa. Mining centres are usually the scenes of hard drinking among the Europeans.   And yet, granting the foregoing, it cannot be gainsaid that the average north-country native returns, after a year on the mines, more of a *man* than he was before.

Upon the Plateau, indeed, conditions are very different. There are no mines, no big gangs of organised labour.   The country, as a whole, is an abstemious one, so far as the whites are concerned ;   partly, no doubt, because spirits are not only expensive, but often impossible to obtain without considerable delay.   The majority of the white population consists of missionaries and officials, to the interest of both which classes it is to show the native a good example.   Trade is practically in the hands of the African Lakes Corporation, who are involved root and branch with early missionary enterprise, and who insist upon a high standard of sobriety being observed by their employees. The general condition of the native is higher, not because he has risen above that of his southern brother, but because he has never sunk below the savage level ;   while the practice of instructing native clerks and artisans at mission schools, and training them in the Government workshops and departmental offices at Fort Jameson, provides the country with a class of skilled labourers and clerks which, farther south, is filled almost entirely by alien natives from the Cape, Portuguese Territory, or the Transvaal.

The policy, too, of leaving responsibility for good government to a great extent in the hands of tribal chiefs is followed.   Once the native has paid his yearly Hut Tax, his duty as a citizen is discharged.   All work which he does is paid for at a fixed rate, which, in the case of transport, may perhaps even be termed excessive—inflated probably by early ' booms,' from which the country is slowly and thankfully recovering.   He realises that he can, if he wish, attend school and rise in the social scale, or that he can continue in the simple rut along which his father moved before him.   For the most part, at present he prefers to live in his village ;   but even here his wants are on a more ample scale than those of his fellows in Southern Rhodesia.

CHIEF MPOLOKOSO ENTERING THE 'BOMA.'

Gibson Hall, phot.

KOPA, PARAMOUNT BISA CHIEF.

F. H. Melland, phot.

His crops include sweet potatoes, beans, peas, pumpkins, millet, Indian corn—and this higher scale of necessities is bound in the end to produce a higher scale of civilisation. This civilisation to come is being fostered in the right way— by patient leading rather than by unsympathetic driving. The *boma* is his friend, his family solicitor ; he comes to it in trouble and perplexity, sure of help, advice, and redress. And every *Bwana* ranks as a friend, not as a master pure and simple, not only as the fountain-head of money wherefrom to screw out a month's wages with a minimum of work.

The proof of the pudding is in the eating. Though North-Eastern Rhodesia has hitherto been under the supervision of the Governor of the Nyasaland Protectorate, his duties, in our regard, were not very arduous. The Colonial Office scarcely interferes in our concerns, for the simple reason that there is no necessity to do so. Since the occupation of the country, more than a decade and a half ago, with the exception of one or two trivial affairs, not a shot has been fired in enmity. Each year the Administrator tours the country, visiting every station ; chiefs, headmen, commoners are then given ample opportunity to air whatever grievances they may possess, and high-handedness or oppression on the part of district officers would be promptly dealt with.

None the less, it may perhaps be possible to overstep the mark in the matter of paternal administration. As an instance of this, it may be that more might be garnered from the country in the shape of taxation than is actually received. Indeed, in the Order in Council provision is made for an increase of the tax, if necessary, to five shillings per hut, and such increase would probably be met without any great hardship to the native.

For he, the native, accepts the theory of taxation as a necessary part of administration. Under his own chiefs he was accustomed to statute labour (*mulasa*), and, as Father Guillemé, the head of the French mission, once wisely remarked, 'A native does not respect an administration to which he does not pay tribute.' So the native pays when he can, and, when it is inconvenient, bows cheerfully to the necessity for completing a term of work for the State as a prisoner.

The lot of the gaol-bird is not excessively hard, though philanthropists in Europe may raise their hands in pious horror at their black brethren being chained by the neck to their fellow-criminals. With us the gang-chain is a necessity. It is lightly constructed, the total weight that is borne by each man (including the collar) being only one and a half pound, and, with the limited police-force at our disposal, it is essential to prevent escapes. That the prisoner himself would welcome its abolition goes without saying, but that point is strongly in favour of its retention, since it undoubtedly acts as a deterrent more than any other factor in gaol discipline. Besides, it must be remembered that neither compulsory silence nor solitary confinement exists in our native prisons.

Unfortunately the gang-chain detracts to an appreciable extent from the capacity of the prisoner to perform complicated work of any description, since the movements of his three brothers of the chain have to be carefully watched and synchronised with his own. But, as the usual work of the hard-labour prisoner consists in such tasks as hoeing, bush-clearing, stone-breaking, carrying mould or water, and jobs of a similar kind, that objection need not be dwelt upon too insistently.

The gaol-prisoner rises at 5.30, cleans the gaol, breakfasts, and is at work at 7 A.M., gangs of twenty or so working under the supervision of an armed *askari*. From 12 to 1.30 he feeds and enjoys a siesta. At 1.30 he resumes work, which continues till within an hour of sunset, when he collects firewood for his own use and that of his guards during the night. Female prisoners, needless to say, are not chained ; they work within the gaol precincts, grinding corn and preparing the food of the males.

A system of daily good conduct marks is in force, whereby every long-sentence prisoner—one, that is, sentenced to any term of more than six months—may earn a remission. And, in the background, is the *chikoti*, or hippopotamus-hide whip, which, like the cane, is nevertheless used but sparingly, and only in cases of gross misconduct.

The diet of the native prisoner is generous enough—quite as generous, indeed, as that to which he has been accustomed. It consists usually of two pounds of meal—which is his own staple food—and the ordinary salt ration, but it is supplemented by potatoes, beans, peas, and even meat. In one particularly bad year, when food was scarce throughout a certain district, beef or buck figured frequently on the gaol *menu*, and more than once a grand *battue* of pigeons was resorted to to eke out the fare.

The crime of prison-breach is sufficiently rare to constitute an event. And this is not so much from lack of opportunity as from a certain philosophic apathy on the part of the native himself. He realises that, even if he effect his escape —which will be at the risk of life or limb—he will be a man proscribed, and his future existence will be barely worth the living. His own village will be barred to him, for every village is visited periodically, and every man's name is known. True, he might, in the northern districts, make for the German or Belgian frontiers, but, more especially since the introduction of the Sleeping Sickness regulations, the chances are all in favour of his being stopped and rearrested by one of the Border Guards. So keenly, indeed, does the native realise that he has but little chance of ultimately evading justice, that in nearly every case of crime the delinquent, if not rearrested, surrenders within a very short space of time. Negrophiles may see in this the workings of a rudimentary conscience—the more cynical official will say that it is due to realisation, on the part of the native, of the many dangers from wild beasts, exposure, and the like which attend the homeless refugee in an uncivilised country. No doubt, too, the native law of village responsibility—which in some ways resembles the old frank pledge, inasmuch as the relatives consider that they are in some sort hostages to the *boma*—is of untold value to the district official who wishes to effect an arrest for some serious crime. In one instance, where a native had murdered a policeman, the whole village spoored him for ten days through the vast swamps that lie around Lake Bangweolo, and finally captured him.

Besides, on the whole, the native prisoner is happy enough. True, he has not his womenkind with him ; but he is housed, fed, and clothed, works only five and a half days a week, and receives medical treatment for the slightest indisposition. Contrasted with the terrors of his own primitive penal code— a code that prescribed mutilation or death for many offences which we punish lightly or not at all—the rigours of imprisonment under the white man's law are not excessive. It is only to be marvelled at that he is as law-abiding as he is.

Capital punishment exists, and, in all cases of murder, the sentence is passed, though of late years it has rarely been carried out, save in cases of exceptional brutality. This method of execution is not unknown to the native ; indeed, the Awemba recognise it as a suitable means of suicide.   But the native fashion is to pull upward, not to drop downward, resulting in strangulation rather than in spinal dislocation.   A case occurred recently in which a condemned criminal, on receiving the warning, instinctively raised himself upon tiptoe.

Capital charges are heard by Magistrates and Assistant Magistrates, who pass sentence, and forward the records to headquarters for the approval of the Judge of the High Court.   He, in turn, if the death penalty appears necessary, again forwards the records for the necessary confirmation, and, should that confirmation be obtained, it becomes the gruesome duty of the Magistrate to see the sentence carried out.   But, as was before indicated, such cases are rare.

Here on the Plateau we live under English law, in distinction to Southern Rhodesia, where Roman Dutch law prevails.   The criminal offences are, therefore, the same as in England, with the addition of such as arise from local conditions, such as smuggling ivory and rubber, the construction of staked game-pits and elephant traps, and the like.

The practice of staking game-pits is a serious one, and, from its very nature, most difficult to suppress.   In the old days, before the advent of the white man, the whole country, except in the immediate vicinity of villages, must have been riddled with these pits—veritable death-traps, six to eight feet deep, covered over with a layer of grass and twigs, and provided with pointed stakes which ensured the certain, if lingering, death of animal—or human—that might chance to blunder into them.

And nowadays—notwithstanding the rigorous prohibition of the Government, the heavy penalties inflicted, the un-ceasing watchfulness of district officials—these pits are still constructed, though, naturally, in more secluded spots. Some years ago an official fell into one, though luckily he escaped injury. Quite recently a friend of one of the writers wandered round such a game-pit, all unwittingly, for half an hour in pursuit of game, until its existence was pointed out to him by his gun-bearer. Cases of death from this cause are of annual occurrence among natives ; but the average native holds human life cheap, and knows that it is difficult, in such cases, to fix the responsibility upon any one individual. Probably, too, he considers that any one who is fool enough to fall into such a pit deserves all he gets, since the sharp eye of the hunter usually detects the difference between the surface of the pit and the surrounding soil, and, moreover, such pits are in nearly every case con-structed at the foot of antheaps, since buck are in the habit of moving round about such heaps in search of cover, or of ascending them to spy out the land. None the less, the practice is one which, both from its callous cruelty and from the perils which it adds to existence, needs suppression with a heavy hand.

Another fertile source of criminal cases lies in the practice of building *mitanda* or temporary huts. In the days before the advent of European government, it was the practice— more especially among the Awemba and kindred tribes— to sally forth with their chiefs from the village, at certain times of the year, and to occupy temporary huts constructed of twigs, branches, and plastered mud. The practice is an integral part of the system of cultivation known as *chitemene*, that is, the lopping of branches over a certain area, hauling them together, firing them, and planting upon the soil, which, rightly or wrongly, was supposed to have been effectually manured by the influence of the early rains upon the resultant ash.   Nowadays such scattered settlements are in conflict with the orderly system of district administration.   It is recognised that old established customs are not to be lightly prohibited.   The system of *chitemene* is not forbidden, unless trees are lopped wastefully, or at unreasonable distances from the villages.   None the less, an effort has been made to bring both *vitemene* and *mitanda* into line with the necessities of district inspection.   The Native Commissioner has his work cut out to visit the villages of his division each year ;   such supervision would be impossible were each family head permitted to construct *mitanda* when and where he pleased, to say nothing of the gradual deforestation of the country which must inevitably result from widely spread *vitemene*.   However, the native still clings to his ancient customs, and notwithstanding the various pains and penalties, which include the confiscation of his game-nets, the burning of his temporary huts, and the like, *mitanda* are still built and *vitemene* still continue.

Indeed, the position of the Native Commissioner is no sinecure.   He is the guide, philosopher, and friend, arbiter and judge of anything from fifteen to fifty thousand primitive persons, who live scattered over perhaps four thousand square miles of almost virgin country, and whose ideas upon practically every subject under the sun are widely divergent from those of the average European.   It is his duty to keep the people of his division quiet, happy, and contented ; equally is it his duty to see that their taxes are punctually paid.   Recently his power to flog was taken from him ; now he may inflict ten lashes, may sentence up to six months' imprisonment, may fine up to ten pounds.   With this meagre equipment of possible penalties he is set down to deal with whatever circumstances may arise ;   the more serious cases going to his superiors.

And he has many difficulties to contend with.   Beer, for one thing ;   bhang for another ;   witchcraft for a third ;   the eternal feminine, perhaps most troublesome of all ;   and fifthly, or millionthly, any possible combination of all four.

So far it has not seemed advisable for Government to legislate especially against bhang, or the breach of marriage laws. Some officials will uproot hemp if they find it ; others consider that it lies outside their jurisdiction. Dissensions regarding marriage, divorce, abduction, and the like constitute nine-tenths of the daily work of a Native Commissioner ; the only consolation being that the native thinks but little of civil justice unless he pays for it, so that every small *mulandu* brings in fees to swell the annual revenue of the division.

But the administration of the country still goes on, and, considering the innumerable difficulties, most creditably. The Native Commissioner, backed by his *capitaos* or station big-wigs, his police, his messengers, his chiefs, and headmen, at least justifies his existence.

Before going further, it may be interesting to study the principal statutes that govern the actions and decisions of district and divisional officials. First in importance, as laying down the broader lines of native policy, come the Native Commissioners' (King's) Regulations of 1908, and the rules made under them by the Administrator of the territory.

Covering as they do several pages, it is impossible to do more than select their more salient points for reference. Briefly, then, they define the magisterial jurisdiction of Native Commissioners, Acting Native Commissioners, and Assistant Native Commissioners. They provide limits of sentences of imprisonment, flogging, and fine. They provide also for civil jurisdiction, and for the keeping of proper case and record books, and empower the Administrator to appoint and prescribe duties for chiefs, headmen, and native messengers.

Under the rules at present in force, the duties of a tribal chief are, mainly, the reporting of misconduct on the part of messengers, the supply of men for defence and the suppression of disorder within the territory, responsibility for the general good conduct of natives in his charge, the prompt notification of crimes, deaths, and epidemics among his people or their stock, due publication of orders and notices, the nomination of district headmen, notification of arrivals of newcomers in his district, and assisting the official in collecting hut tax.

The principal duties of district headmen lie in the direction of assisting their chiefs. They are responsible to those chiefs for the good conduct of the people, and prompt notification of unusual occurrences. They rank as constables within their sub-districts, and may effect arrests in certain cases, and they are required to assist native messengers to the best of their ability.

Native messengers are charged with the duties of conveying messages, of warning natives of collection of hut tax, of summoning parties in civil cases, and of reporting irregularities and crimes. Full provision is made for suitable punishments for neglecting or exceeding their duties.

With regard to the supply of liquor to natives, stringent regulations are in force, a penalty not exceeding five hundred pounds, or, in default, imprisonment with hard labour for not more than six months, being provided for a first offence, and an increased term of imprisonment for each subsequent offence.

Special regulations apply to the illegal removal of cattle, the unauthorised purchase of cattle from natives, possession of firearms by natives, the export of ivory and rubber, and the collection of the latter.

The giving of credit to natives beyond twenty shillings, in regard to the sale of goods, by any person not a native of the territory is prohibited.

Special and exhaustive regulations are in force with regard to the recruiting of natives for service both within and without the territory.

Stringent regulations for the suppression of witchcraft have recently been published (Government Notice 19 of 1910, 17th July 1910), which provide penalties ranging from two hundred and fifty pounds fine, thirty-six lashes, and seven years' imprisonment with hard labour, to imprisonment for six months.

There is but little need to dwell upon the maintenance

H. Sheane, phot.

PRISONERS IN CHAINS—ALL MURDERERS.

S. Stokes, phot.

THE ENGLISH MAIL.

of law and order among the white population. The permanent residents are too few in number to embrace many
of the criminal class ! Now and again a luckless European
may be haled before the powers that be upon a charge of
infringing the game laws, shooting a cow elephant—which
was until lately illegal—or breaking Sleeping Sickness regulations, but these are matters which are usually adjusted by
the payment of a fine. Now and again—very, very rarely—
a D.B.S. or Distressed British Subject may misbehave himself *en passant*. But we do not encourage wanderers of this
class, and, as a result, they are few and far between. In
fact, upon the rare occasions upon which it becomes necessary to imprison a white man, the question of where to put
him, and how to treat him, becomes rather a difficult one
to decide. There is usually a European cell available,
but one is reluctant to degrade a white man to the level of
a native convict for anything less than a very serious crime.
And for the same reason it is practically impossible to put
him to work with the black gangs, except in the capacity of
foreman. So the white prisoner undergoes a period of
enforced inactivity, is provided with literature, and is given
a tot at sundown to keep his spirits up.

Rather an amusing incident occurred recently at a station
in the south—not upon the Plateau, though it might equally
well have happened anywhere north of the Zambesi. A
European was alleged to have stolen some dynamite, was
arrested in a state of hilarious drunkenness, and was bestowed
for the night in a brick store, in the hopes that next morning
he would be in a fit state to be examined. Upon the store
being opened next day, however, the last state of that
prisoner was found to be considerably worse than the first.
The mere word ' drunk ' failed most lamentably to describe
his condition ; and, moreover, there was a distinct aroma
of freshly opened whisky in the air.

The authorities were dumbfounded. For the man had
been carefully searched overnight, and, to the best of their
knowledge, the store had contained only a few cases of station
requisites. The case assumed more aggravating aspects
from the fact that in the official mess there was at the time

a drought of alcohol ; indeed, the prisoner appeared to be the only man who had had anything to drink for some weeks. But a close examination revealed the fact that one of the cases in the store consisted of whisky, under the disguise of ' medical comforts,' and the festive prisoner, having had all night in which to make the discovery, had, naturally enough, broached the case, and knocked off the necks of several bottles.

Upon another occasion a gentleman who had been educated as a locksmith, finding himself behind a door which was secured only by a cheap American padlock, proceeded to pick his way out, and, upon being reincarcerated, repeated the performance at intervals until daybreak.

But, as we have said before, the consideration of white malefactors is merely a 'side issue '; and the native, taking him ' by and large,' is no confirmed criminal.   Possibly this may be due to the sharpness of the contrast between his primitive barbarity and his present security.   Nowadays, though the younger generation may still hanker after the picturesque past, the old men, at least, realise the benefits of European rule.   One has only to listen to camp-fire talk of old wars and mutilations—not so distant, either, in mere point of time—to realise how the attitude has changed. Nowadays, too, they have precedents of white-made law, constituted by the case-books of the various stations, and your native, being a born litigant, is quick to note and to compare.   More especially, perhaps, has the general attitude changed in regard to contract, the whole idea of which was formerly unknown.   As Miss Werner says in the *Natives of British Central Africa,* ' the native has a substantial sense of justice,' and this very sense of justice has led him to assimilate the code of the white man, and to appreciate it, even while he may not invariably act up to its precepts.

To summarise briefly : our advent has been followed by many very definite results, of which the most important are, perhaps, the establishment of peace with such comparative ease, and its maintenance with the minimum of effort ; the lavishing of education upon the native by the

White Fathers, the London Missionary Society, and other missionary bodies ; the almost total absence of crime ; the complete cessation of raids and mutilations ; the quiet consolidation of native administration ; the increase of white population and revenue, more especially in the south-west ; the present security of the natives as contrasted with the grim tragedies of their past history, and the abolition of the Arab slave trade.

Our sojourn in the country has been short, but by no means barren of result ; and, surely, any administration might point with pride to a territory where so many and such vital ameliorations in the lot of the people had been carried out so swiftly and so successfully.

CHAPTER VI

ANIMISM AND WITCHCRAFT

OUR Plateau native is emphatically a man of religiosity rather than a man of religion. How completely his whole life is obsessed by the precedents of superstition, and controlled by ritual observance, is shown in the succeeding chapters on native custom. He is far more of a formalist than a clear, free, and fearless thinker, and hence arises much of that vagueness of thought which is so tantalising to the modern observer.

At the very outset in the native idea of God, we find that mystic formlessness which defies modern analysis.

Throughout the numerous tribes from Tanganyika to the Zambesi, although we find the same word Leza indicating the existence of a Supreme Being, yet this term does not connote any clearly defined idea of God, whose attributes, at least among the Plateau tribes, are still in process of evolution.

In the first stage of thought, Leza seems to be regarded more as a nature force than as a personal deity. Thunder, lightning, earthquakes, rain, and other phenomena of nature are grouped together under this word, as being the manifestations of Leza.

Gradually, however, a second phase of thought appears, in which, owing to the influence of Animism, Leza emerges as a personal deity, the greatest of all the spirits. Now, to the Awemba, the thunder is ' God Himself who is angry,' the lightning is the ' Knife of God.' He is said to be the creator of life and death. According to the well-known Wemba fable, God created two of the common people, who increased and multiplied and replenished the earth. To this first man and woman Leza gave two small bundles, in one

of which was life (*Bumi*), in the other death (*Mfwa*), whereupon the man unfortunately chose 'the little bundle of
death.' Yet, apart from his experiments in creation, Leza
stands aloof. Serene and imperturbable he controls the
heavens, but does not concern himself with the destinies
of mortal men. In keeping with this idea, there is no idea
of God as a moral being, against whom it is possible to sin
by breaches of the moral law, which, however, the lesser
spirits are prompt to mark and avenge. Leza still remains
the 'incomprehensible' (*Leza ni shimwelenganya*). 'How
otherwise,' say the Wemba old men, 'has he caused the
firmament, the sun, moon, and stars to abide over our
heads without any staypoles to uphold them?' 'Were
Leza by himself,' say the Walambia, 'we should never die of
disease, it is the evil spirits and their allies the wizards who
cause swift death.' Leza only brings at the fit and proper
time the gentle delicate death of old age (*Mfwa Leza*).
Among many of the ancient tribes who still dwell in the
mountain fastnesses of the North Luangwa district this
theory of an impassive God still obtains.

But among the more progressive tribes, such as the Wabisa
and Awemba, a further stage of this idea has been reached,
in which Leza takes an interest in human affairs, and though
not yet prayed to, is invoked (*kulumbula*) by his names of
praise, in which his attributes are gradually unfolded, and
he assumes protective and judicial functions over mankind.
The Cunning Craftsman, the Great Fashioner, the Nourisher,
the Unforgetful, the Omniscient, are all to be found as
propitiatory names of Leza. Leza is again the receiver of
the souls of men after death. The soul of men, according
to the Awiwa, goes down to *kuzimu ku Leza*, to the spirit
world to God, who is not only controller of the heavens,
but also acts as judge and arbitrator for the spirits.

Yet, as far as the dominant Wemba tribe is concerned,
the cult of Leza is outside their ordinary religion. There
is no direct access to him by prayer or by sacrifices, which
are made to Mulenga and the other great tribal and ancestral
spirits instead. For upon such Animism is founded the
whole fabric of Wemba religion.

Two distinct names are found, indicating two different classes of spirits, viz., the *Mipashi*, or ancestral spirits, and the *Milungu*, who approximate closely to 'nature spirits.'

Of Awemba *Milungu*, the principal is *Mulenga*, who is approached in euonymous prayers as a benevolent spirit. Mulenga can grant abundant rains and plenteous harvests. But in reality he is chiefly propitiated from dread of his malignant powers, which he exercises at the least offence. In Chapter VIII. we find the great rinderpest of 1894 ascribed to Mulenga, who stalked through the country like an angel of death, and became the father of albino children. Mulenga is usually worshipped through his priest, the *kasesema*, or prophet, through whom offerings are made. In 1909 one of these prophets, called Muchilingwa, caused a good deal of trouble during an epidemic of severe dysentery by asserting that this was a visitation from Mulenga, who had been neglected by Chief Muwanga, and that the disease could alone be stayed by suitable offerings and respect shown to his priest.

The *Milungu*, being nature spirits, are mainly entreated to send rain and to fertilise the crops, and they reside in the hills, mountains, and great rivers.   Mr. Gibson Hall, in notes we have previously referred to, mentions such a nature spirit as existing among the Walungu, called Chisya, dwelling in a mountainous region of the same name.   This god is evidently the spirit of the heights, and is diligently tended by a priest who takes the name of the god, and acts as intercessor between the god and his people.   Kapembwa, another spirit of the rain, worshipped on the shores of Lake Tanganyika, was first visited by Mr. W. R. Johnston (the late Native Commissioner) by boat, when that official and the paddlers narrowly escaped with their lives owing to a storm suddenly arising and capsizing the canoe.   This circumstance added to the fame and power of Kapembwa, who is supposed to have resented the visit.

The *Mipashi*, or ancestral spirits, may be divided into two main classes.   First, the spirits of the departed chiefs *publicly* worshipped by all the tribe, and what may be

ANIMISM AND WITCHCRAFT 83

called the domestic spirits, worshipped *privately* by each
head of the family.

The priestesses of the spirits of the dead chiefs are called
the ' wives of the departed,' and were represented by certain
elderly women who lived a celibate life. At the capital of
Chitimukulu they swept out the ghost huts (*mafuba*) of the
chiefs, and, as we shall see in Chapter XII., attended to the
burial huts at the sepulchre at Mwaruli. The aid of the
departed chiefs was evoked in time of war, in period of
drought, and special offerings were made at their shrines
at harvest time (see Chapter XVIII.).

These royal spirits possessed the power of temporary
possession and of reincarnation.

One form of temporary possession is in the bodies of
men or women. When the spirit comes over a man he
begins ' to roar like a lion,' and the women gather together
and beat the drums, shouting that the chief has come to
visit the village. The possessed person, while the spirit
is in him, will prophesy as to future wars, and warn the
people of approaching visitations by lions. During the
period of possession he eats nothing cooked by fire, but
only unfermented dough. The functions of *mfumu ya
mipashi* (chiefs of the spirits) are usually performed by
women. These women assert that they are possessed by
the soul of some dead chief, and when they feel the ' divine
afflatus,' whiten their faces to attract attention, and anoint
themselves with flour, which has a religious and sanctifying
potency. One of their number beats a drum, and the others
dance, singing at the same time a weird song, with curious
intervals. Finally, when they have arrived at the requisite
pitch of religious exaltation, the possessed woman falls to
the ground, and bursts forth into a low and almost inarticulate chant, which has a most uncanny effect. All are silent
at once, and the *bashing'anga* (medicine men) gather round
to interpret the voice of the spirit. In the old time many
men and women were denounced as *waloshi* (sorcerers) by
these possessed women, whereupon the accused, unless
protected by the king, or willing to undergo the ordeal,
were instantly killed or mutilated.

The spirits of departed chiefs may become reincarnated in animals. The Mambwe paramount chief or the Sokolo becomes reincarnated in the form of a young lion (see Chapter XII.), and Bisa and Wiwa chiefs become reincarnated in pythons. In one of the rest-houses on the Stevenson Road, near Fife, lived a tame python, which waxed fat on the sour beer and fowls offered to it by the Winamwanga, who reverenced in it their ancestral spirit Chief Kachinga. One day, alas ! the deity so far forgot himself as to dispute the ownership of the rest-house with a German cattle-dealer who was passing by ; whereupon his hiss of disapproval was silenced by a charge of S.S.G., and the worshippers of Kachinga saw him no more !

Though the spirits of the chiefs may have ' resting-places ' in hills or rocks, they are quite distinct from the veritable mature spirits, or *Milungu*, since they are not confined to any definite spot, though usually worshipped near their burying-ground. There is no idea of a good spirit being confined to one special spot like the Oread nymphs of classical folklore. Small grass shrines are as a rule placed underneath some shady tree, because it is considered to be a good and convenient resting-place for the spirit to come to and to take the offering and hear the petition or prayer.

To turn to those spirits which may be called *domestic*, as being the subject of private family worship. Such spirits are prayed to by the head of the family, who acts as a priest for the other younger members. Among the Awemba there is no special shrine for these purely family spirits, who are worshipped inside the hut, and to whom family sacrifice of a sheep, a goat, or a fowl is made, the spirit receiving the blood spilt on the ground, while all the members of the family partake of the flesh together. For a religious Wemba man the cult of the spirit of his nearest relations (of his grandparents, or of his deceased father, mother, elder brother, or maternal uncle) is considered quite sufficient. Out of these spirit relatives a man will worship one whom he considers as his special familiar, for various reasons. For instance, the diviner may have told him that his last illness was caused because he had not respected the spirit

of his uncle ; accordingly he will be careful in future to
adopt his uncle as his tutelary spirit. As a mark of such
respect he may devote a cow or a goat to one of the spirits
of his ancestors.   Holding the fowl, for instance, in his hands,
he will dedicate it, asking the spirit to come and abide in
it, upon which the fowl is let go, and is afterwards called
by the name of the spirit. If the necessities, however,
of the larder demand that it should be killed, another animal
is taken, and the spirit is asked to accept it as a substitute !
Before beginning any special task, such as hoeing a new
garden, or going on a journey, Wemba men invoke their
tutelary spirits to be with them and to assist their efforts,
in short ejaculatory prayers usually couched in a set formula.
Among many of the tribes in the North Luangwa district
longer formal prayers are still made to all the deceased
ancestors of the clan at the time of harvest, asking them
to protect the crops and to drive away illnesses and evil
spirits from the family, which honours them with libations of
beer and offerings of the first-fruits.   As we shall see later,[1]
the spirit of an ancestor may enter into a child at birth,
and such possession is considered most auspicious.

   The above spirits, *Milungu* and *Mipashi*, are on the whole
beneficent in their action, and by a species of dualism stand
in contrast with the *Viwanda* or *Viwa* or evil spirits. These
Viwanda are the souls of evil men such as suicides, murderers,
and sorcerers, who die in bitter enmity of the human race,
and retain their malevolence after death.   When a man has
a grievance, and receives no redress, he will as a final resort
go before the wrongdoer and say, ' I shall commit suicide,
and rise up as an evil spirit to torment you.' Those who
have been wizards (*waloshi*) and have practised black magic
during their lifetime become evil spirits after death.   The
wachisanguka, or those men who during their lifetime have
acquired from a wizard the art of changing themselves
temporarily into lions (*kusanguka*, see Chapter XIII.), will
at death permanently become reincarnated in the form of
man-eating lions.   All accidents, diseases, and bad luck in
life are ascribed to their evil influence.   It must be noted

[1] P. 179.

that in the Wemba fables the term *chiwa* often merely designates a fantastic goblin living underneath trees or near an anthill, which vexes mankind with tricks which are more elfish than evil.

Between these divinities and their worshippers stands a kind of hierarchy, composed of various classes of men, who claim to be interpreters of the will of the spirits, and who act accordingly as intermediaries and intercessors betwixt them and the common people. It is true that every man could pray direct to his ancestral spirit, but where sacrifices were necessary, he usually consulted a priest.

The Wemba king, who acted as high priest between the nature and ancestral spirits and his people, sent sacrifices to the shrines of the *Milungu*, and led the tribal prayers to the spirits (*Mipashi*) of departed chiefs, assisted by the priests, to whom he left the management of the sacrifices and other ceremonies of propitiation. The paramount chief of the Wiwa tribe, Kafwimbi, still controls the priests, and at stated times sends messages to the priest and all villages possessing shrines to propitiate the spirits. On receiving such a message the village hereditary priest will kindle a fire with the fire-stick, and order all the villagers to heap upon it faggots of a certain tree called *kalumbwe*, ' so that the spirits may draw near to warm themselves.'

Under the comprehensive term *ng'anga* (or the skilful ones) are included ' doctors,' who act as public and family priests, prophets, and seers, exorcists of evil spirits, diviners, and physicians skilled in the use of herbs and simples. That these *bashing'anga* are divided into guilds, and are bound by various rules, has been indicated in various court cases, but as there is no subject upon which a native is more reticent and evasive in speaking, the evidence is not absolutely reliable. It seems clear, however, at least, that a *shing'anga* cannot practise as such unless he belongs to some guild, and the oldest *shing'anga* in the district ' knows him,' and that a would-be doctor works as assistant to an older practitioner, who gradually imparts his skill in return for money payments, or for work done in his garden.

To take first the priests. Among the Awemba the office

of the priesthood is not hereditary, except in so far that the head of each clan acts as its priest. But among the Winamwanga the priesthood is distinctly hereditary. Only the members of the three clans of Simwanza, Sichalwe, and Simuwaya can act as priests of the departed chiefs. These hereditary priests presided over the sacrifices made at certain seasons, and superintended ceremonies such as those of the first-fruits, described in the chapter on 'Native Husbandry.'

Akin to the priests are the prophets and seers (*ngulu shya kusesema* or *bakusesema*), who are distinct from the *temporarily* ' possessed men and women,' since such prophets are *always* the ' mouths ' of the spirit. Like the *kasesema* of Mulenga, the self-constituted prophet of a great spirit will wander from village to village, even outside the confines of his own tribe, predicting that a great disease is close at hand, and warning the people to abstain from some certain kind of food, lest they be stricken and die of the coming plague. Such *ngulu* have a very wild appearance, as they allow their hair to grow long and shaggy, and are usually addicted to bhang.

Of the exorcists, diviners, and physicians—who may be generally classed as medical practitioners as opposed to priests and prophets—there are many grades.

In pride of place comes the *shing'anga wa kushyula viwanda* (the doctor who digs up the evil spirits), who is often also a *shing'anga wa misaba* (doctor of the bones or diviner), as well. He is a great specialist, who is only consulted in dire extremities when the sick man is on the point of death, or wasting away with continual disease. He only is daring enough to perform the operation of digging up and burning the bones of a dead man whose evil spirit has been proved by divination to be responsible for the sufferings of the patient. To him alone the chief gives the task of burning the bodies of sorcerers and wizards who have died by the poison of the *mwav* ordeal. Inferior to this great doctor is the exorcist (*shing'anga wa kusukula viwanda*), who possesses the necessary medicine to drive away from the village the evil spirit who has been plaguing the sick man. At dawn he goes outside the village with a potsherd containing live embers. Casting his medicine upon the embers till a thick smoke is produced, he repeats the formula : ' Thus we drive you (mentioning the name of the deceased relative) from the village, you are no longer a man of us ' (*i.e.* belonging to our clan). From that time forward the name will never again be mentioned in the village.

The line between the diviner and the physician is not always clearly drawn, as both functions are frequently combined in the same person. But speaking broadly, the physicians differ from the diviners because they attack the disease spiritually as well as physically by the use of certain drugs and simples, whereas the diviners confine themselves to diagnosis of the disease, and decree the necessary rules to avert it without attempting actual cure. Details of the treatment given by native physicians and surgeons are given in Chapter VIII., so there is no need here to enlarge upon their methods. Certain physicians are in great request as knowing the remedies for sterility. The husband will approach, saying, ' Why I have come to you is because in my house it is black (*i.e.* there are no children), hence I approach you to make things more befitting in my house.' The doctor gives the woman two horns to wear on her breast, and both husband and wife are given medicine with which they must bathe themselves.

Methods of divination among the various Plateau tribes are legion. Diviners are called after the name of the special form of divination in which they are experts.

The *shing'anga wa chikumbe*, for instance, divines with an axe and a block of wood, slowly rubbing the axehead to and fro on the face of the block, while the patient repeats all the names of the ancestral spirits of his clan that he can remember. At the name of one particular spirit the axehead sticks fast to the wood, whereupon the diviner proclaims that it has caused the illness, and after giving directions as to its propitiation, departs, assuring the patient that he will feel better in the morning.

The Diviner of the Beans (*shing'anga wa lukusu*) is another well-known expert, who produces a large bean rendered potent by the inclusion of certain medicines and charms from

Bernard Turner, phot.

KALIALIA, A MUCH FEARED WITCH DOCTOR
AND MEDICINE MAN.

A DIVINER AND HIS BONES.

G. Stokes, phot.

his magic basket. The bean is then placed in a gourd, which the diviner gyrates so that the bean rattles inside while the names of various spirits are slowly intoned. As soon as the bean sticks fast to the inside of the gourd and refuses to rattle, all know that the last-named spirit is the author of the sickness or other misfortune.

The *shing'anga wa mukwa* employs a long tortoise-shell which is filled with medicine, and sewn up into a little oval packet representing a tortoise or some crawling insect. The diviner inserts a feather into the tail of the ' tortoise,' and holds the other end. In case of divination for theft, the suspected people are placed around in a circle ; if the thief is present, the ' tortoise ' will move about in a swift and uncanny wriggling motion until it touches the real thief.

The *shing'anga wa chipungu* fills a small duiker horn with medicine and places it underneath a basket, while the names of suspected persons or of spirits who have caused the mischief are called out ; when the culprit—be he individual or spirit—is mentioned, the basket jumps up.

The divination with the bones, which are dealt out in twos while the names of suspects are repeated, until finally an odd bone is dealt out by sleight of hand at the name of the erring spirit, has been so frequently described among Central African tribes as to require no further notice. A kind of haruspication is still in vogue in which the gall-bladders of duiker, netted for purposes of divination, are inspected, and the entrails of fowls are scrutinised by the diviner.

So far we have only described such ' doctors ' as work for the good of the tribe, and endeavour to combat the black magic of their opponents the sorcerers and wizards, whose sinister influence has now to be considered. Secret societies of the *basichiloshi* (or sorcerers) are said to exist among the Awemba people, but such evidence as has been collected is not absolutely conclusive. Moreover, the writer knows of no corroborative evidence of similar societies amongst the neighbouring tribes, though in one case there was evidence to show that a man of the Winamwanga tribe had for a considerable period paid a wizard to acquire his arts of sorcery, and more especially his knowledge of poison as well.

Many causes will drive a man to appeal to a sorcerer. For instance, he may have a serious grievance against one family who has deprived him of his wife, and will accordingly go to a sorcerer to bewitch them in revenge. One of the commonest forms of enchantment is known as *Lupekeso* or *Lupembe*, which is used when a man who has been denounced by a woman in childbirth as an adulterer refuses to pay heavy damages on the death of the child. The husband will consult a sorcerer in revenge for being defrauded of his just damages. The sorcerer will proceed outside the village, hang upon a tree the horn of a roan antelope, in the core of which medicine has been placed, and cause the husband to repeat the formula or *ntembo* as follows :—' You Lupekeso ' (referring to the medicine in the horn), ' I am not calling you up without due cause. It is because this evil man has treated me in this fashion. Go you into his hut and walk with his folk and their children.' It is said that if the adultery was really committed, the relatives of the adulterer will begin to die because of this sorcery, but if not, the spirit of the Lupekeso, being deceived, may fall upon the man who invoked it, and kill his son or his wife. If, however, the evil fetish works, and several relatives of the adulterer die, the injured husband is satisfied, and will see that the sorcerer removes his evil medicine.

In another form of sorcery the wizard (called *ng'anga ya lupembe*) is said to hold a séance inside his hut by burning certain herbs which cause a thick cloud of smoke to ascend to the rafters while he invokes various evil spirits. The smoke, by the assistance of these demons, is supposed to filter through the roof and enter the hut of the person who is to be bewitched, and finally to cause not only his death, but also that of any other relative who may live in the hut.

In another form of enchantment the sorcerer secretly procures part of the clothing of the man to be bewitched, or a clod of mud which has fallen from his feet. Such articles are considered to be a connecting link with the victim, so, after the wizard has submitted them to his sorceries, the unfortunate owner is similarly affected.

Another method of wizardry is by hanging up at night

a horn containing noxious medicine by the door, so that those coming out may brush against it; or by smearing the doorstep with some poisonous mixture. When such sorceries are discovered, the dread of the native has to be seen to be believed. A native woman at Fife fell into hysterics as soon as she saw such a horn placed by the doorpost of her hut, and was brought up for treatment by the villagers, who were afraid that she might die in the fit.

That deadly poisons are from time to time given in porridge or in beer by the sorcerers is undoubted, though rare nowadays. In a notorious case some years ago, held in the Magistrate's Court at Fife, an old and valued messenger called Sokosi was undoubtedly poisoned by these means, as was shown by the post-mortem, but owing to lack of satisfactory evidence it was extremely difficult to bring the crime home to the actual poisoner.

Such a sorcerer may so far forget himself as to openly curse a victim who has so far resisted his enchantments with the words, *uli nkulungwe (chisongo) wadya mwaka umo*—'You are devoted to death' (literally tabooed), 'you are to eat' (or live) 'only one year.' When the sorcerer so openly discloses his hatred, the man may call his relatives, denounce the sorcerer, and force him to take the *mwav* ordeal, whereupon, if found guilty, the sorcerer may be cut to pieces or burnt, as described in the chapter on 'Legal Notions.'

The belief that these sorcerers indulge in ghoulish banquets at the graveyards is deeply rooted, and is paralleled by a similar belief amongst the Mang'anja. When we remember the fact that the Awemba are an offshoot from the cannibal Waluba, it is not so incredible that certain depraved wretches may still gratify their primitive tastes in this fashion.

A few examples must suffice of the numerous amulets and charms which are used for protection from lions, to avert disease, scarcity of food, sterility, and enchantment. *Mpimpi* are small twin duiker horns worn sometimes to avert the evil consequence of adultery and so as to be popular in the village. *Mpinga* are two tiny cubes of wood strung on a string tied around the forehead to prevent head-

ache.   To prevent fever a small dried beetle is worn on the
forehead in the same manner.   Any localised pain is com-
bated by wearing a circlet of string upon the part, from which
are suspended certain charms.   Women who wish to keep
their husbands faithful wear two little horns of the klipspringer, and a similar charm is worn by men before starting
on a long journey.   Fetish horns are hung up inside the
huts to bring prosperity, whilst outside, often from the
jutting beam of a grain bin, dangles the horn of a roan
antelope, which prevent lions from visiting the village.
There is, however, no evidence of the worship of images or
idols among the Awemba.   It is true that small *tulubi* or
idols, made by the Wabisa and other tribes to the north and
west of our sphere, are sometimes to be found in Wemba
villages, but apparently no religious worship is paid to them.
Nor has the worship of fetishes assumed in their religion
such a prominent part as upon the West Coast of Africa.
The most noteworthy Wemba fetish is the *lilamfia*, which
was prepared by members of a kind of guild called *Bachamanga we 'lamfia*.   The nature of this fetish is shown in
the photo opposite.   It was peculiarly potent in war.
The first man taken alive, whether on the march or on
arrival at any of the enemy's villages, was seized and thrown
down.   A small hole was scooped out in the ground, over
which the victim's throat was cut by one of the captains.
The fetish horn was then steeped in the blood, and on
raising it, one of the Keepers of the Horn (*Bachamanga*)
blew down the small central horn, embedded at the medicine at the base, and danced.   Then driving a ramrod into
the ground, he balanced upon it the horn, which was held
in equipoise by the weight of the bell at the tip and the
medicine at the base.   Those who have been questioned
solemnly assert that the horn would by itself swing the
ramrod pivot, while the bell jangled.   When this uncanny
motion ceased, the *Bachamanga* noted where the base containing the medicine pointed, and prophesied that many
would be killed and a successful foray made in that direction.

As regards totemism and taboo upon the Plateau—it is
manifestly impossible, in the restricted limits of the present

'LILAMFIA' FETISH.

FETISH TO CHARM AWAY WILD BEASTS
FROM A VILLAGE.

FETISH AT KAMUTONIKI.

FOUNDATION STONE OF A WINAMWANGA
VILLAGE.

chapter, to attempt to fix the place of Plateau totemism amidst that galaxy of theories so ably championed by Dr. Frazer, Mr. Andrew Lang, and others. For many years the writer has questioned the older men as to their ideas of the origin of their totemism, but no satisfactory answers have as yet been given. Some say that Leza at the beginning, before the dispersal (*chipanduko*), (see *infra*) created the totems, but the usual reply is—' We have the same name as the animals, and that is all.' The institution and ordinances of the totem clans are accepted as something consecrated by immemorial usage, as to which it is vain and foolish, perhaps even impious, to inquire.

Wemba totems fall under the broad headings of animate, such as animals, reptiles, fish, birds, and insects, and inanimate, such as minerals and artificial objects. Plants and vegetable products, and nature phenomena, also supply totem names. The following list is given to show their variety :—

Animals.—Crocodile (*bena-ng'andu*, modern form *ng'wena*), elephant (*benansofu*), lions (*bena-nkalamo*), leopard (*bena-ng'o*, modern form *mbwiri*), dog (*bena-mbwa*), goat (*bena-mbushi*), pig (*bena-nguruwe*), fish (*bena-isabi*, and of certain species as *bena-mpende*), bees (*bena-nshimu*), birds (*bena-nguni*), mouse (*bena-mpuku*), tortoise (*bena-nkamba*), frog (*bena-fyula*), otter (*bena-mbowo*), duiker (*bena-nsengo*), ant (*bena-milongo*).

Minerals.—Slag iron (*bena-mbulo*).

Artificial Objects.—Cooking-pot (*bena-'nongo*), drinking-bowl (*bena-nsupa*), but totems of such artificial objects are rare.

Nature Phenomena.—Rain (*bena-mfula*).

Plants, etc.—Porridge (*bena-bwali*), millet (*bena-male*), to this phratry belong men who are chosen to be priests at Mwaruli ; castor oil (*bena-mono*), mushroom (*bena-boa*), plum (*bena-masuku*), banana (*bena-nkonde*), tree (*bena-miti-nsengo*), grass (*bena-chani*).

Some of these names are old and ancient ones given to

the animal which are nowadays not employed (compare the Wiwa totem name for lion and Muwaya for guinea fowl as different from the usual words used to denote them). Some of these totem roots can be traced back to the West Coast. In the case of the Leopard *ng'o* (modern form *mbwiri*), we find that Dennett in his book, *At the Back of the Black Man's Mind*, refers to Ngoyi as the Leopard totem, vide *s.v.* Wiwa totems do not cover so many classes of objects as those of the Awemba, as they are usually confined to the names of animals.

It is interesting to note that many of these clan names are common to many of the Plateau tribes, such as the Awemba and the Amambwe, who until quite recently were at war with each other, and it seems as if these phratries were constituted before the separation of the various tribes. In the olden times, possession of the same totem as some phratries of alien tribes, carried with it valuable privileges. If a stranger captured in war could prove that he was of the same totem as any of his captors, he would not be put to death. Even nowadays a travelling native will prefer to stay at the house of a man of the same totem, as he has the right to be suitably entertained by him. In some cases certain clans have become very numerous and powerful; so on Lake Bangweolo we find the totem names of Bena-ng'ona and Bena-ng'oma used in a general fashion to designate the two main branches of the tribe, and almost what we might term tribal totems. The same word *bena-*, ' the masters, or owners of,' is used not only to prefix totems, but also to prefix the name of the locality, so the Bena-Luwumbu or Bena-Ng'umbo are territorial terms adopted by the Bisa dwellers in that region, and not totemistic. Among the Awiwa there is no special reluctance to give their totem names except that of the chief, which is often noticed when questioning Awemba and Walungu. Among the Awiwa the totem descended on the father's side, but among the Awemba the maternal totem was the greater of the two.

Following the law of exogamy, no sexual intercourse is allowed among members of the same totem, for which crime the olden time punishment was death by burning. But whether this practice originated from natural horror of incest or from definite rules of exogamy or of totemism is hard to say. We have already seen that only members of certain totems were among the Winamwanga eligible for the priesthood, and again members of the Siwale and Simwanza totems were considered to be peculiarly acceptable as human sacrifices to the *manes* of the departed Mukoma.

When a member of the family dies, when burying him they turn his *face* to the quarter from which the original founder of the clan is supposed to have come ; this place is called Chipanduko (the place of the dispersal of the clans). The *head* itself, however, will be always turned facing the east. Among the Awemba, certain totems are considered higher than others ; for instance, a man who is a Mwenamfula (rain totem) is considered to be of good lineage and respected accordingly.

Unfortunately, every year these survivals of totemism are becoming fainter, especially amongst the Awemba. There is a tradition among the Awiwa that their ancestors would not eat or kill these animals, and that men of the Simwanza and Siwale (bird totems) would formerly release these birds if found in snares, and would not eat them. But nowadays the totem animal is in no way respected, and is killed and eaten like any other animal, without any feeling of remorse or any special ceremonies of the nature of a sacrament. Among the older men there is still a lingering feeling that there is some mystic and indefinable affinity between them and the totem. When a lion is heard at night roaring outside a village they exclaim *Lavwe mukanda*, at its fierceness, and use the same expression when they see a member of the lion totem in a passion.

The origin of Bantu totemism indeed appears to be as yet unsolved. Dr. M'Call Theal's theory of metempsychosis, however, seems hardly to be applicable to the Central African tribes in our sphere. The theory of transmigration of souls into those of animals exists, but it falls more under the head of what Dr. Tylor calls the doctrine of Were

Wolves (see Chapter XIV.), and is the privilege only of those of royal blood and those who have practised the arts of lycanthropy in their lifetime. There is no positive evidence to show that the transmigration is into the body of the respective totem animals of the 'shape-changers,' who usually become man-lions, man-leopards, or man-hyenas, and, moreover, such natives as have been questioned consider this doctrine quite apart from totemism.[1]

Unfortunately, too, the Wemba taboos throw very little light upon totemism, as they are not by nature totemic. An inquiry into any of the totem clans given previously shows that each phratry is not marked off from another by any particular observance of taboo law peculiar to its totem, in fact, as we have seen, the totem may be eaten by members of the phratry.

Broadly speaking, among the Plateau tribes this branch of what has been aptly called 'negative magic' may be divided under two heads—Tribal, and Particular or Class taboos. To the whole Wemba tribe, for instance, the flesh of wild pig and of bush-buck is interdicted, and similar tribal taboos are found among the Wabisa and the Wamambwe. Particular taboos are found assigned to various classes of men; thus no member of the Wiwa royal family may eat pork, which is, however, partaken of by the common people. Mambwe women, again, as a class may not eat eggs, and various grades of priests and medicine-men are bound by food taboos. The Awemba have a system of what has been called 'individual taboos,' and accordingly we find that certain individuals do not eat certain animals, which are nevertheless greatly relished by members of the same totem. For instance, if his father, an elephant hunter, has been killed by an elephant, the son will never again eat elephant meat. The medicine-men frequently impose food taboos, and when a man has become sick because of any particular kind of meat, the

---

[1] Since the above was written, the writer has consulted Dr. Frazer's great work on Totemism, where the East and Central African evidence has been collected in vol. ii. ch. xiii.; but no satisfactory explanation of the origin of Bantu totemism seems as yet to have been arrived at.

doctor will tell him that he must in future abstain from the flesh of the animal.[1] In the old time a warrior who killed say a Mushiri-mbushi (a man who may not eat goat) had in future himself to observe the taboo of his victim. A few other instances of taboos may be briefly referred to under the heads suggested by Mr. Andrew Lang in his article upon taboo (11th ed. *Ency. Brit.*), as they are dealt with in subsequent chapters.

Taboos of Women, Sexual Taboos and Avoidance.—Young girls on attaining puberty may not eat any food until they have been given a certain medicine called *imfu* by the Directress of the Rites (see Chapter XI.). Women again during menstruation must not touch the food or the fire-place, and must abstain from kindling a fire or from cooking, or else they will cause the inmates of the house to waste away with a disease called *ipembelela* (like consumption). The taboo imposed upon the parents of twins is dealt with in Chapter XVII., and the custom of avoidance of the mother-in-law is referred to in Chapter XVI.

Taboos of the Sick.—A man who is seriously ill is supposed to leave the village and to settle in grass huts (*mitanda*) in the bush until cured ; he must not contaminate the village with his disease, and, even if at the point of death, was in the old time carried outside to die (see Chapter XII.).

Funerary and Allied Taboos.—Funerary taboos and the lustral rites to remove them are described fully in Chapter XII., so it suffices to mention here that they affect all who have touched the dead body, and even the grave-diggers. In the important enterprises of life such as hunting and fishing, natives will submit to certain taboos. While a weir is being built and fish baskets are set, the Bisa fisherman who cuts the weir stakes, must live apart from his wife, and the majority of the Hunters, members of the society of *Uwanga wa nzovu* (see Chapter XIV.), are bound to abstain from certain foods, and live in the bachelors'

---

[1] In Chiwemba the word *chisongo* means not only taboo, but also a peculiar form of disease caused by violation of the laws of taboo.

quarters some days before starting in pursuit of a dangerous animal.

Taboos imposed by the Chief.—By breaking off a branch of a tree and laying it across the entrance of a garden ripe for harvest, a chief could stop all reaping. If a villager left his chief without permission, his gardens were thus marked (*ku-saka*) ; the crops then reverted to the chief who would make them over to any new comer or would reap them himself.[1]

[1] Considerations of space have caused the writer of this chapter to omit his notes upon the ancient cult of snakes, the doctrines of future life and of metempsychosis, and the annual feast to the spirits of the departed amongst the Amambwe, which is similar to the widespread custom of All Souls' Day.   He has, however, dealt with other aspects of Wemba religion in the *Journal of the Anthropological Society*, vol. xxxvi. p. 150 *et seq.*, from which certain extracts have been included in the present chapter.

CHAPTER VII

THE OFFICIAL CHEZ LUI

INASMUCH as official routine is the same all the world over, and in North-Eastern Rhodesia just as elsewhere the life of an official when actually upon his station is compact of routine, it is difficult to draw a picture of the daily round without laying oneself open to the accusation of inflicting tedium. Besides, the author of that delightful book, *Station Studies*, has already covered the ground in a fashion that forbids imitation. No matter that he deals with East Africa rather than with the Tanganyika Plateau —apart from the element which is there imported from India, and the fact that he is dealing with a station which lies in reach of the railway, life is very similar in the two dependencies.

There are, upon the Plateau, two distinct types of station ; one, usually the residence of a Magistrate or Assistant Magistrate, where there are at least two officials, a government doctor, and a trader—the other the ' one-man ' station, where there is only the official and, if he is lucky, his wife.

Upon the larger stations there is, naturally, rather more ' life ' in the shape of tennis parties, little dinners, rifle-range competitions and the like. But it must be borne in mind that at no station on the Plateau does the total resident white population exceed ten persons, of whom less than half are ladies. Social festivities are, therefore, somewhat liable to pall. Now and again, on red-letter days, an influx of ' outside ' officials, settlers and missionaries may occur ; but, for the most part, the same people meet each other several times every day, and may be forgiven if, in the course of months, they discover each other's weak points. Nevertheless, for the most part, the more populous stations of the Plateau are presided over by the Angel of Peace ; though, conceivably, he may be overworked at times. Moreover, it must be remembered that the relaxations of most up-country Indian stations, which no doubt represent in the mind of the man in the street the typical station throughout the uncivilised world, are here conspicuous by the impossibility of attainment. Minus a club, horses, a billiard-table, and the presence of troops, the average Indian civilian would probably send in his papers with ominous alacrity.

But the ' one-man ' station is, perhaps, the more interesting of the two classes ; though, to tell the truth, with the gradual spread of the Administration there are only a very few of the kind left at the moment of writing.

To those who have had experience of tropical admini-stration, what follows will be but the veriest dotting of i's and crossing of t's—a laboured exposition of matters which, by practice and usage, have come to be the merest common-places of life. But to others—to those who have lived their lives in the security of large cities, or in the no more eventful seclusion of sleepy English villages—it may, perhaps, be of interest to quote some details of the typical day of the typical official upon the Tanganyika Plateau.

Contrary to all accepted canons the life is neither very dangerous, very hard, nor very lonely. Most of the stations are built of brick, and neatly laid out ; fresh vegetables, fresh milk, and fresh meat—though this latter be only the swing of the pendulum between fowl and goat—are always available. The elements of tropical hygiene are, generally speaking, strictly observed, and in consequence the usual lurid picture of the miseries of the official stationed upon the Outer Edge would be a somewhat violent distortion of facts.

The danger, if danger there be, lies in quite other directions. To commence with, the work which the official is paid to do is of the most interesting possible kind ; that of dealing at first hand with a fascinating native race, whose view-points repay, and more than repay the closest attention and study. It may sound perilously like conceit for those who are themselves officials to draw a picture of the overworked Native Commissioner; but it must be remembered that it is the official himself who is usually to blame. For routine work there are the routine hours; and the man of average capacity can fit into those hours all that is demanded of him by headquarters. Thereafter he is at liberty to employ himself as he sees fit—either with a gun and a dog, since partridges, guinea-fowl and so forth abound, in the supervision of improvements which are always in progress, in gardening, tree-planting, or the performance of any odd jobs which may appeal to him.

The fact remains that the average official does not take as much exercise as he might. Casual matters involving the reference to books or the hearing of statements need attending to at all hours; perhaps an interesting case based upon some nice question of custom or tradition may be waiting to be heard—or there may be a few figures to finish up for some return or other. The offices are, as a rule, cool and comfortable; it is just as pleasant to sit there with a pipe as to be outside in the glaring sunshine—and so, for the most part, the office remains open from early dawn until sunset, and the official becomes soaked to the core with the routine of his profession. But he is pleasing himself—and does not, perhaps, deserve much praise for doing so.

That is the main danger of station life, and it is not of sufficient importance to need accentuating. In the early days, no doubt, things were different. Then, indeed, the terrors that lurk in solitude were real enough. It was no uncommon thing for a man to be six or nine months absolutely alone upon his station, so far as other white men were concerned; visitors were few and far between, supplies uncertain, mails irregular, and reading matter almost impossible to obtain. Those were the days when neurasthenia lay in wait for a man, when drugs and drink pleaded their charms and, in some cases, would not be denied. Those were the days when men dreaded sundown and the dark; when nerves were a-jangle, and the very rats in the roof were welcomed as living things; when a man longed for the society even of his station *capitao* or his personal boys. Incidentally, too, those were the days which taught the older hands most of what they know to-day—since it is the solitary white man, be he official or trader, who is cut adrift from his fellows, who penetrates into the inner sanctum of native life.

Nowadays, too, it must be remembered that station life, such as it is, is rarely lived for more than two months on end. There are always the needs of the district to be attended to; there is ever present the lure of *ulendo*, and so, when the official is surfeited with the work of his office, he adopts the simple expedient of locking it up, putting the key in his pocket, and calling up carriers from the nearest villages.

It is the merest truism to remark that no two men follow exactly the same daily routine. In Central Africa a man must spin his own mesh of interest in life, as the spider spins its web, out of his own particular Ego, and is apt, on occasion, to thank God for his hobby. With one, it is photography, with another botany, with yet another natural history; some may find intense pleasure in ethnology, others in native history and the compilation of genealogical trees with their roots in the Ark. But the following may, perhaps, be taken to represent a very average day as it is lived at any of the Plateau stations in the present year of grace.

One rises early; not from virtue, but because the morning hours before the sun is well up, while yet the dew is on the grass and the shadows of banana, pawpaw and lemon-trees are still long aslant the paths and garden beds, are, indubitably, the best of the twenty-four. Besides, in such matters, and when dealing with the unconscientious native, example is better than precept. Should the cattle-herd or the sergeant of police or the house-boys know that it is your practice to lie late abed, it is more than probable that the cattle will lose an hour or two of grazing, the *askari* will scamp their morning drill, and the porridge and eggs at breakfast be badly cooked.

Having, therefore, risen early, the half-hour or so before breakfast will probably be spent in going the round of the station, supervising the workers, watching the issue of prisoners' rations, instructing *askari* in musketry practice or investigating matters of routine. And, thereafter, breakfast and a pipe will fill the gap until nine o'clock, when office hours begin in earnest.

Yet, possibly, you will not visit your office until midday, or, conceivably not at all. The day must be spent in whatever manner may suit the needs of the district best. Perhaps there is a large village near the Boma which needs supervision—the natives, profiting by the words and example of the white man, have grown tired of their pell-mell jumble of huts, and are rebuilding in orderly lines. This means a day in the open with measure and tape, and later, a chat with the elders on matters of village policy. Or you may, for the day, be master foreman, since all kinds of jobs fall to the lot of the Native Commissioner. Thus the day may pass in the supervision of the stacking of bricks for a new kiln ; or in laying out station roads with a prismatic compass ; in the building of a new gaol or *askari* lines, or in a hundred and one tasks of the kind.

Let us suppose, however, that the day in question is one of hard, solid office work ; as, of course, the majority are. Probably, unless you have already attended to them before breakfast, the first item on the programme will be the treatment of the sick.

The ordinary householder in England would be staggered if he were suddenly asked to deal with a case of epilepsy, complicated pneumonia, malignant ulcer or, possibly, a broken leg. But the Native Commissioner has, long ago, given up being staggered at anything. He stands, to the native, in the position of Jove—ready to rain down lightning in the shape of exceptionally drastic pills, or to invoke the storm which follows upon certain drugs. Himself, he knows that with twelve, or it may be twenty, little bottles of tabloid products, no technical knowledge and a modicum of common-sense, he is expected to deal with any case which may arise. For the nearest doctor is, perhaps, five days away, and would not be best pleased at being called in to attend a sick native.

Certain broad and time-honoured rules are observed. Snake bite or lion wounds call for cautery and permanganate of potash ; if a native falls off a roof, keep his friends away from him and trust to luck. Non-surgical cases usually begin with a strong purgative and end with quinine ; if the patient does not choose to observe the usual rules of the game, so much the worse for him. With faith and Livingstone rousers, added to the firm, if misguided belief in the native mind that his official really knows what he is about, it is astonishing what cures may be effected.

It is, indeed, astounding to what lengths the native lust for drugs will go. A certain gallant officer, who shall be nameless, used, it is said, to issue to his recruits water tinged with permanganate or similar harmless dyes when the official drug supply was at low ebb. And yet, seeing that the same thing is very possibly often done in England in the case of nervous valetudinarians, perhaps the native is no exceptional fool after all.

The sick disposed of, any one of a hundred items may claim attention. In the next office the native clerk is dispensing hut-taxes at three shillings a time. Or, maybe, he is issuing calico, or weighing salt, or typing a report which is needed at headquarters. From without come the shrill voices of women who have brought grain or meal for sale, and are beguiling the passing hour in badinage with the *capitao*. Not that the consequent pandemonium disturbs the clerk one whit ; for, in this country, thirty shillings a month buys, body and soul, a native with a mission education, who is intelligent and conscientious, writes well, has a good head for figures, and may safely be entrusted with minor matters of routine.

Out in the sunshine the scene is peaceful enough. In the centre of the cleared space before the office the flag droops lazily from its tall staff. The sun is beginning to make itself felt, for it is nearly ten o'clock, and the white gravel of trim-kept paths shows up, glaringly enough, in contrast with cool stretches of dhoub grass and patches

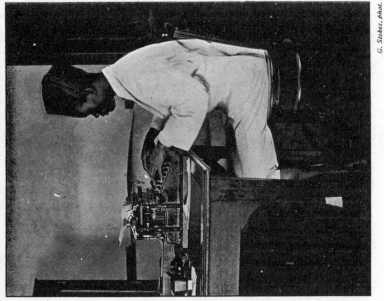

G. Stokes, phot.

NATIVE CLERK.

E. A. Avery-Jones, phot.

SERGEANT, N.E. RHODESIAN CONSTABULARY.

of shadow beneath *mitawa* or acacia trees. Mellowed by
distance come hoarse words of command—which may
once have been English, but which, transmuted by the
native tongue, are like nothing that has ever been spoken
since the days of Babel—for the army is on parade. Then,
of a sudden, the harsh blare of a bugle breaks in upon the
peace of the scene ; and, if there is a dog within hearing
distance, there will arise such a clamour of yelps and yowls
as to make one almost wish for the peace of deafness. For
the time has come for guard-mounting, and the native,
loving as he does ceremonial of any kind, may be trusted
to make the most of his opportunity.

But, in five or ten minutes, the hubbub is over ; the old
guard, which has been on duty since the morning before,
has been dismissed ; and the new guard has taken over
the details of rifles, ammunition, prisoners, flags—down,
even to the minute cake of soap which reposes in the
office washstand. Thenceforward, until the next *lipenga*
or bugle-call, which will occur at noon, one may look
forward to being able to hear oneself speak.

One glances for a moment at the row of figures squatting
on the cleared space outside the office. Here is a group of
youngsters, lying at full length, and passing the time in
rough chaff—these, obviously, want passes to look for
work, and may be allowed to wait for a while. The next
group—sad-eyed greybeards, with a woman or two among
them, and a skinny goat tethered by the leg to a convenient
tree—represent, no doubt, a case, which once embarked
upon may consume the rest of the working-day. Sitting
upon a corner of the verandah is one of the Sleeping Sickness Road Patrols, charged with the duty of seeing that
regulations as to ingress into and egress from the Area are
strictly observed. He, at least, having been taught the
value of official time, may be trusted to be brief—so in he
comes, accompanied by an exceedingly pretty little damsel
of perhaps twenty years of age. It appears that the girl
has been detected red-handed in the act of evading the
regulations, having been found without a pass at a village
well within the forbidden boundary. Having no reason-

able excuse to offer, beyond the claims of a *grande passion*, for Lothario, unfortunately, lives the wrong side of the boundary—she is sentenced to a fine, or, in default, imprisonment, and, the cash not being forthcoming, goes up the road at the back which leads to the gaol, with a smiling countenance. Her labour will not be hard ; perhaps the grinding of a few pounds of grain each day, or the cooking of the prison rations. Besides—who knows ?— Lothario, when he hears of her plight, will probably send in three shillings, carefully tied up in a dirty piece of bark-cloth, and the lady be free to wander where she listeth.

In comes another lady—this time of uncertain age and sadly devoid of charm. There is a baby on her back, and her left arm is swathed in a bandage. Behind her shuffles her husband—an unprepossessing person, with a vacuous, drooping mouth. This case has already been disposed of, and only needs a few well-chosen words to point the necessary moral. For the husband is half-mad, a beer-sodden, bhang-steeped individual, who, in some sudden access of brutish fury, has bitten deep into his wife's arm, leaving a huge, festering sore. There were, perhaps, faults on both sides, for the woman is known to possess a shrewish tongue ; but, for all that, *monsieur le mari* will not get off scot-free.

Thereafter follows a complicated case dealing with certain mythical goats which, some years before the Flood, apparently, were left in trust with a village headman. The genealogy of the goats is traced through, apparently, scores of centuries, each of the kids in successive generations having been, it would seem, personally known and cherished—the sole remaining survivor, which is none other than that same venerable ram whom we saw, half an hour ago, browsing off parched dhoub in the shadow of a stunted bush, is produced and duly admired by the court. And in the end a decision of a kind is arrived at ; a decision which, more by good luck than good management, appears to satisfy all concerned. Plaintiffs and defendants, witnesses and spectators, inextricably mingled, prostrate themselves before the office door, and there follow shrill ululations and deafening clapping of hands. Thereafter the parties vanish down the road which leads to the station village, with the ram in tow. There can be but little doubt that, within the next few hours, he will go into the pot to furnish a meal for the litigants, in despite of his venerable ancestry.

There is, it seems, yet another case down for hearing, and time is getting on. Précised by the station *capitao*—who, through long years of experience of the white men, has learned the value of conciseness and the omission of genealogical trees where not absolutely germane to the matter in hand—it appears that the question is one of the rights of a chief over his inherited harem, or *isano*.

The point is one which needs careful judgment. In a nutshell it stands thus. A paramount of importance has recently died, and, the due period of mourning having elapsed, his successor has been selected and, with the consent of the Administration, duly installed. Theoretically the new chief takes over the inmates of the *isano*—that is, the old chief's wives—lock, stock and barrel. But, in this particular case, the new chief is an old man, and many of the wives are young girls, scarcely out of their teens. They are tired, as well they may be, of the seclusion and tedium of life in the royal compound ; many of them, no doubt, have already bestowed their favours elsewhere. A break in the continuity of the old régime has determined them to make one bold bid for freedom ; and, in the particular case before the court, there can be no doubt that one girl, at least, has been found in most compromising circumstances in the hut of a youth who has no pretensions whatever to royal descent.

The marriage laws as at present enforced have, unfortunately, not yet been codified. Although native law is followed, in so far as it is not repugnant to ideas of English justice, yet it would be manifestly unjust to condemn a young girl to pass the rest of her days with a man old enough to be her grandfather. On the other hand, the prestige of the chief must be upheld. In the old days, misbehaviour on the part of the wife of a chief would have meant a speedy and unpleasant death for both the guilty parties ; and no one is quicker than a native to note the slackening of old bonds.

Fortunately the chief in question is a man of shrewd common-sense, and the matter can be put to him in a reasonable light. He realises that the white men will not enforce upon women marriages which are repugnant to them, and agrees to the decision of the court, namely : that the girl shall be free to leave the *isano*, providing that damages, much heavier than would be enforced in an ordinary case of adultery, are paid by the lover. So, once again, matters are settled amicably, and the court rises and retires to lunch.

These are some of the minor matters which, day in, day out, come up before the Native Commissioner for settlement. It would be impossible in one short chapter to give any adequate idea of their number or variety. Suffice to say that they range from a claim to a wife to a claim for a bracelet ; from murder to slander ; from ground tusks worth twenty or thirty pounds to a slab of soap. Boundaries and garden sites, the conduct of a Salt Market, the issue of Government Sniders for protection of lives and property in lion-infested districts, birth and death, marriage and divorce, witchcraft and sheer heathen superstition—these and such like are matters upon which the district official must decide. Usually it is plain sailing, since there are regulations and headquarter circulars which indicate broad lines of policy ; but many matters call for the exercise of judgment, and, it is to be feared, many cases must necessarily be decided in unwitting infringement of abstruse points of custom and belief. Still, in a complex case, native assessors can always be called in, and it is often a positive relief to the puzzled official to be able, for the moment, to shift the weight of responsibility on to the shoulders of those who are, undoubtedly, well able to bear it. Not a point is overlooked, nor, generally speaking, can the European mind detect the slightest injustice in such decisions. Why, indeed, should there be injustice ? since these same village elders have, in all probability, heard or assisted in the hearing of thousands of similar cases long before the white man came amongst them and set himself to learn their ways. Their justice may be rough and ready, it is true; but, for the most part, it is based upon common-sense, and will stand the application of the usual tests of right and wrong.

Probably the afternoon passes in much the same fashion as the morning. That is to say, at 1.45 the bugle will blare forth once more, and soon, from various bush paths and roads will come the workers, more slowly, one may be sure, than when they dropped their tools and fled at the midday signal. But by a few minutes past two work will be well under weigh once more, and will continue until the bugle sounds again at 5.45.

Perhaps the day in question may be a mail-day—that day of paramount importance in the whole week, when news comes in from the outside world. There is a scheduled time for the mail-man to arrive, and, as has been said in a former chapter, that time is observed with marvellous punctuality. As the time draws near one finds oneself scanning the road; when at last the familiar red-clad figure appears swinging along with his bag over one shoulder and an ancient gun over the other, one heaves an involuntary sigh of relief. This week, again, the mail has not been delayed by rivers or man-eating lions; both of which, it may be said, are, upon certain routes, factors to be reckoned with.

Occasionally, however, the incoming mail is not an unmixed blessing. Some one at headquarters is taking an irritating interest in the fate of two drums of cement which were despatched some months ago and have not yet been acknowledged, or a native has died upon the southern mines, and one is requested to trace his heirs who are entitled to the balance of wages due to him. But, for the most part, headquarters do not worry the outstation official overmuch, provided the requisite returns go down at proper intervals. Once a month comes the day of reckoning; the balancing of cash, the computation of revenue stamps and postal stamps and embossed stamps, the calculation of soap, and salt and calico and beads and flour and grain, and the heterogeneous mixture of game licences, gun permits, traders' licences, and the like. But it is only a matter of a day or two before the returns are safely packed and in the mail-bag; then one may return to one's muttons for another three weeks at least.

Every now and again, too, some one turns up—say, on an average, once a month. Maybe it is a Government Surgeon touring on Sleeping-Sickness duty—perhaps a trader, or a White Father, in the broad-brimmed hat and the picturesque gown of his Order. Or it may be some unfortunate who, minus carriers, a tent, perhaps, even a blanket, is trudging through the country in the vain hope of obtaining work ; stumbling from station to station, feeding at native villages by the courtesy of the headman, thankful enough to receive at each Boma some scrap of rations or clothing to help him on his way. Happily, such visitors are scarce ; the country as yet is not sufficiently civilised to hold out any chance whatever of employment, and such destitutes as do arrive are usually birds of passage, with the Congo, Nyasaland, or German East Africa as their ultimate objective. And they undoubtedly meet with far better treatment here on the Plateau at the hands of the natives than do their luckless brothers of the road in the south ; since the worst type of European has not penetrated thus far, and the natives have no cause to despise or to hate the white man who is down on his luck.

Once a year, as a cheerful break in the monotony of life, should it exist, there is a general upheaval of the accepted order of things. For the *Bwana Mkubwa*—the Administrator, in other words, is about to pay his annual visit. Some weeks beforehand the itinerary of his honour's journey reaches each out-station ; there is a general furbishing up of equipment, flying gangs scurry over the roads, that they may be spick and span ; messengers are sent to the various chiefs, and, in every way, the official house is set in order. On the day itself, or perhaps a day or two before, chiefs with their retinues pour into the Boma, and the station is black with natives, with, here and

C. Gouldsbury, phot.

RE-THATCHING AN OFFICIAL'S HOUSE.

F. A. Usher, phot.

SELLING GRAIN AT THE STATION.

there, a figure, borne shoulder-high under the shade of a gaudy umbrella. Tufted headresses, ceremonial pipes, spears and bows and knobbed sticks flash and whirl among the throng. Before the open court-house where, in peaceful, workaday times, cases are heard, the crowds are black upon the grass like flies. Usually the European population within reach of the station assembles, and the *Baraza* is duly held with all requisite pomp and ceremony. Grievances are aired and adjusted ; the chiefs, thoroughly in their element, speak their minds with the open yet courteous forbearance of one gentleman to another, and, later, take their presents, either of cash or calico in dignified content. Truly the annual *Baraza* is a valuable function, tending to weld close bonds of sympathy between the rulers and the ruled. And then, to the queer, half-toned melodies of their respective bands, and the high-pitched voices of their singers, the chiefs move out of the picture, down to the station village where, doubtless, the true festivities begin.

There are, indeed, many sides to the official's life, and space forbids us to touch upon more than a few, and those but briefly. Light and shade go to make up the picture ; in the morning one may be intent upon plotting out the district map, or entering up the district note-book ; in the afternoon engaged in the sad task of extemporising a coffin for a white man. And, too, there is the woman's viewpoint ; the ever constant problem of varying the menu, of preserving a garden threatened with total extinction under a scorching sun, of embellishing the house with some new fantasy. Usually the mail brings piles of literature, either from home or from the Tanganyika Book Club, which has its headquarters in Abercorn ; and it is an astonishing fact that, here on the Plateau, far from Mudie's or W. H. Smith and Son, most people, more especially those of the fair sex, get through far more reading than they would do in England. One has, at least, neither calls to make nor cards to leave.

Somewhere between four and five, unless there is a considerable pressure of work, office is over for the day.

The *askari* have finished their afternoon parade ; the clerk and the *capitao*, locking up the office, retire to the bosom of their families.   And, after tea, the official saunters round with a gun, or tinkers in the back-yard with a hammer, or trims his rosebushes, or prunes his lemon-trees, or sees to his beans and peas.   And then when the sun goes down comes the evening ceremony of saluting the flag.   The guard, presenting arms, lines up—the bugle sounds—and, very slowly and sedately, the flag flutters down, proclaiming to all and sundry that it is still well in the land under the rule of the white man.   When from one's verandah one looks out across the miles of hill and plain purpling in the twilight ; when one reflects that, between this present peace and the turbid barbarity of none so long ago, there stand, through countless miles, but a solitary white man and a handful of police, the truth seems almost too good to be true.

CHAPTER VIII

THE PLATEAU NATIVE (I)

In his *Last Journals* Livingstone, even after his perhaps unique acquaintance with the African physique, is never tired of referring to the physical beauty, not only of the Plateau people proper but of the surrounding tribes as well. The ' handsome and well-chiselled features ' of the men, the ' small hands and feet ' of both sexes, and most especially the neat features and graceful figures of the women, still drew forth his unstinted admiration.

The paramount Wemba tribe takes great pride in personal cleanliness, and much care in the cult of the body. A Wemba youth who is unkempt and does not avail himself of the innumerable *petits soins* in matters of teeth-filing, tattooing, and hairdressing, is jeered at by all his friends, who will, finally, assure him sarcastically that he is turning into the *Mulungulwa* or Missing Link. In parenthesis it may be mentioned that this fabled being is supposed to live always in the dense forest, in the shape of a man clothed only with a shaggy coat of hair which completely covers his body, and rejoicing in long, matted locks and bushy beard. He entices wayfarers, with plaintive cries, from off the beaten track, binds them to trees, and forces them to lead the simple life. Nor will he release them until his unfortunate pupils have themselves grown shaggy locks and flowing beards.

It is only logical to deal first with the physical aspect of our Plateau native, and to attempt to describe his gestures and his bodily aptitudes in health, his more common ailments and their treatment, with especial reference to surgery in disease. For the natives themselves, though, possibly, they make no such conscious distinctions, approach both mental and moral sides through the basic qualities of the body. Thus, many a native whose brain is tormented by some fixed idea, for instance, of possession by an evil spirit, will go straightway to the village doctor, and receive a purgative to dispel this mental obsession.

Some tribes pursue this idea even beyond the grave, since, if the ghost of a deceased relative proves obnoxious, they dig up and burn the body to cancel the power of the spirit.

A few of the more prominent gestures may be selected for description. Astonishment is usually expressed by rapidly lifting the hand to conceal the mouth, which gapes forth the ejaculation ' Yê, Yê ! ' To express impossibility and also to avert displeasure natives will hold out their hands with the palms upwards in a deprecating gesture. The act of giving is usually emphasised by the Wemba man with an expressive ' uumph ! ' grunted out with closed lips. If one hands one's tobacco-pouch, for example, to a raw native to hold, he will, in order to return it, first stand as far off as possible, and then, though holding the pouch in one hand only, stiffly stretch out both in delivering it. Contempt is displayed by slightly protruding the lips and sucking in the breath sharply, with a chirruping noise. When under the influence of any strong emotion, especially of fear, the *bouquet d'Afrique* becomes peculiarly pungent. Men laugh in a very hearty, but ordinary fashion ; but the women will punctuate a peal of laughter with the long-drawn, outlandish ' oh—oh—oh, we—eh—eh ! ' [1]

Livingstone comments upon the fact that, when King Chitapankwa was informed that the explorer's travels were made for the public benefit, he pulled down the underlid of his right eye. Such a gesture is common to this day, and is ridiculously in keeping with the schoolboy's question ' Do you see any green in my eye ? ' There are, in addition, many special gestures which are, to the expert, the hall-

---

[1] In the act of beckoning, very logically, the back of the hand, instead of the palm, is turned uppermost, indicating the ground to be covered by the person summoned. When pointing out long distances, the index finger is raised to the sky.

marks of various tribes, but which it would be tedious to describe in detail. There is, even, a fairly elaborate code of signs known to many natives for conversing with deaf mutes, and, indeed, many of the symbols employed bear a striking resemblance to those used in conversation with the similarly afflicted of our own race.

The upright and well-balanced movements of the men when walking, and the free and graceful carriage of the women have been commented upon, and are commonplaces in all books of Central African travel. Yet, on the other hand, it is only fair to remark that lake tribes, such as the Wabisa and the Waunga have often rounded shoulders and a distinct curve in the back induced by canoeing. The abnormal development of their triceps, moreover, in comparison with their ill-formed and puny legs only exaggerates their ungainliness. Waunga have been tested to see if they could carry loads, but, after the first day's march, their feet became very much swollen, and even bled ; no doubt from their being unaccustomed to walking save in swampy ground, which, coupled with their constant use of canoes, has rendered their feet excessively soft and tender.

The Awemba are excellent climbers, and the system of making gardens by tree-lopping keeps them supple until middle age. The toes find crannies in the trunks of trees where the most expert boy bird-nester at home would have to use climbing-irons. The big toe is slightly prehensile, and it is a common sight to see a carrier, in order to avoid stooping, once his load is firmly fixed on his head, pick up his spear and other odds and ends of his *ulendo* outfit with his big toe.

Such tests of their strength, endurance, and speed, as have been made at occasional station sports are hardly widespread enough to admit of very definite statements as regards the average native. No native has yet been found to run the hundred yards in under eleven seconds. But, in long-distance running and steady maintenance of pace from day to day the ordinary native shows considerable stamina. Mail-men, for instance, recruited from among all the tribes serve the mail routes all the year round, wet or fine, with unfailing regularity, averaging from twenty to twenty-five miles per day. Transport agents agree that the Awemba makes the best carrier, while the Amambwe and Winamwanga are the steadiest workers upon stations. A weight of fifty-six to sixty pounds is carried with ease by the average native, when accompanied by a white man, for about eighteen miles a day. A gang of porters, when left to themselves, however, will drop to an average of fourteen or fifteen miles, simply because time is, to them, no object, and further, because, as they can complete such a distance well before midday, they are able to save their *poso* (or food cloth) by doing odd jobs for the villagers at each hamlet where they halt for the night.

Owing, possibly, to the disuse of war and the chase, the skill shown by the average native in spear-throwing or with the bow is very disappointing. The Waunga, however, from their constant practice in shooting lechwe, are very expert bowmen. In Luena courtyard several Waunga, though not so expert at striking the centre of a target, transfixed running fowls and brought down pigeons perching on the hut-tops at a distance of sixty yards with the greatest ease. The Amambwe, Wabisa and Washinga do not show any remarkable aptitude in acquiring new sports and games, though they are keenly interested in football. The Awemba, however, learn physical and military drill in a very short time, and an officer of the King's African Rifles informed one of the writers that their quickness in this respect equalled that of the Nyasaland tribes, including Yaos, with whom they were trained at Zomba, and of whose cleverness in this respect Sir Harry Johnston speaks so highly.

One might, perhaps, conclude that their eyesight is far superior to that of the average European, but many white hunters contradict this apparent superiority, asserting that they themselves can, with a little practice, pick out game at a distance quicker than any native. The question is, however, open to doubt. The hearing of natives, so far as can be determined by the watch test, is distinctly more

acute than that of the European. It is true that natives
have the art of raising their voices to a peculiar pitch which
carries farther than the shouting of a white man, but the
distances at which instructions can be shouted and understood from black to black are none the less striking.

The question of transference of long-distance messages,
far beyond the range of either sight or hearing, has often
been discussed and commented on in books dealing with
native races. It is too abstruse a subject to enter upon
here, but it may be remarked that rumour has it that, at
the time of the Somali Campaign, when many Awemba
served in the King's African Rifles, wailing for the dead
took place in the Kasama Boma village many weeks before
written, or even telegraphic news, could have reached
that place of the death of members of the force.

No special tests of taste or touch have been made. As,
however, natives confidently assert that they can distinguish members of their own tribe by smell alone, even
on the darkest night, several experiments were made in
this direction, and, undoubtedly, some natives would seem
to possess this special faculty. One man, completely blind-
folded, did not make a single mistake in smelling out men
of his own tribe, and, though other natives of different
tribes were placed before him, he detected them at
once.

The hereditary transmission of natural or acquired
qualities from father to son is a moot point. In the Awemba,
for instance, all closely related to the royal blood bear a
distinctive cast of countenance, and are easily distinguished
from a crowd of ordinary natives. One might descant
upon the bravery and adroitness which seem to descend
from father to son amongst the nomad clan of Hippopotamus
Hunters, who used to be found upon the banks of the Luena
and Luapula, of whose daring hunting Livingstone gives
so graphic a description in his *Last Journals*; or upon the
inherited craft of the sons of the *fundi* blacksmith or ivory-
worker. But these are, alas, dying industries, and the
special types which they tend to develop are not permanent,
or ever likely to have any effect upon the race at large.

As in Europe, certain physical abnormalities repeat themselves in a curious fashion, and in several native families six-fingered children are born in successive generations.

In the light of actual experience the alleged marvellous powers of tropical natives in path-finding appear to be somewhat exaggerated. One of the writers was tracking a solitary eland through thick bush on a cloudy day, with a *capitao* and several boys from outlying parts of the district. As a test a prismatic compass was set down, and the boys were told to point to the east and also in the direction of the station which they had left in the early morning. They all pointed in the wrong direction, after ineffectual attempts to guess at the position of the sun, and were extremely astonished when by compass and *capitao* they were set right. It is difficult to get lost in the average Plateau bush, owing to the innumerable paths and even disused tracks, which lead to gardens and, finally, to a village. Where there are no such paths there are game tracks which lead to water, from which village finding is comparatively easy. Natives say that, if bushed at night, they first climb the tallest tree and sniff about for the smell of fire from the nearest village which, especially in the wet season, they maintain they can locate within a two-mile radius. Failing this guiding smell, and when no tinder can be found for the firestick, they make a rude perch in the boughs, and philosophically await the dawn.

We can discuss only in a general fashion the various questions of native health, diseases and their treatment, without any pretence at medical or scientific arrangement and method.

The often reiterated deadliness of the tropical climate is, of course, a myth where the natives themselves are concerned, and year by year its influence upon Europeans is mitigated, owing to the researches of the various schools of tropical medicine. Indeed, the *British Medical Journal* (p. 1291, October 1909) states : ' Having given statistics as to the decrease of mortality from different diseases, Professor Osler said a remarkable result had been that in

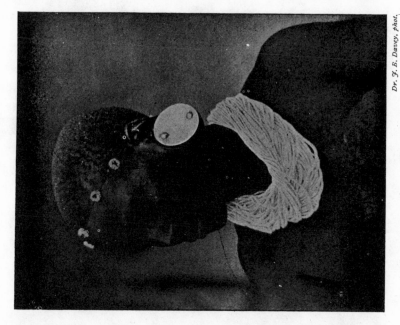

Dr. J. B. Davey, phot.

MAMBWE WOMAN SHOWING EARRINGS.

G. Stokes, phot.

WIWA GIRL.

1908 the combined tropical diseases, malaria, dysentery, and beriberi, killed fewer than the two great killing diseases of the temperate zone, pneumonia and tuberculosis.'

With the exception of minor ailments caused more by dirt and neglect of sanitary conditions than by the climate, the general health of the natives is excellent. Smallpox excluded, the country is very free from zymotic diseases, and at the present time there is no epidemic of even small-pox in our sphere. One of the writers was present on Lake Bangweolo at the time of the great epidemic of small-pox in 1903. The Wabisa understood thoroughly the value of isolation, and, in the first stages, instantly removed all suspects to grass huts in the bush, where they were attended by previous sufferers. When the disease reached its climax they pierced the pustules by rubbing the patient's body with sand, and finally removed the matter and sand with a banana leaf. The French Fathers considered that the Bisa practice of casting the bodies of those who had died of smallpox into the lake channels, often on a small raft of reeds was one of the most fruitful sources of contagion. At the south end of Chirui Island a medicine-man, who called himself Mulenga, was doing a roaring trade with little hookah-shaped gourds containing medicine which, he asserted, had been given to him by God, and which he had brought from the Luapula to avert the disease. For-tunately, all submitted to vaccination with good grace, probably because inoculation and rubbing medicine into an incision in the skin is a common device of native doctors —and, by burning the infected villages the disease was prevented from spreading to the mainland.

The native theory of the causation of disease being essentially a 'spiritual' one, diseases are invariably attributed to external, and usually supernatural influences —never to want of care by the patient in such matters as gluttony, excessive drinking, or dirty habits. Hence divina-tion is the final diagnosis. The medicine man, by various methods (discussed in Chapter VI.) will find out which of the ancestral spirits is displeased, or what living person has compassed the illness by his magic arts or witchcraft.

Treatment is, too, often pursued upon the lines of ' faith healing,' which would have delighted the heart of Mrs. Eddy! The village doctor, for instance, will give the sufferer a special horn containing remedies to be worn on the painful side, and special amulets to repel the disease. Drugs and actual medicines are used mainly as ancillary to the action of such charms. Though the medicine man will go into the bush to collect simples, and will powder various roots, yet these natural remedies are considered inefficient until rendered active by the addition of some charm from the medicine-man's magic box (*intangala*). Aperients and astringents are well known, but the nostrum given is such a mixture of various ingredients, such as roots and magic charms, that it is difficult to determine the action of any special root.

The larger organs of the body are regarded rather as the seat of the various emotions than assigned any definite functions in maintaining the harmony of the body. The natives have a very definite idea that at all costs the blood must be kept running through the veins, and they are exceedingly afraid that any sudden shock may cause it to desert the arteries and settle in the stomach, thus causing death. When a friend falls from a tree which he has been lopping to make his garden, whether his limbs are broken or not, the bystanders will first make sure that his blood be kept circulating all over his body, since they think that it may have been shaken out of its place by the shock. Accordingly they kindle fires round the patient, and massage his limbs. In one case of a cut finger, treatment consisted in pulling out one by one, first all his finger joints, then all the joints of his several toes, and was rounded off by spitting on top of his head—probably as a spiritual blessing additional to the physical first-aid.

A short description of the main diseases and illnesses seems necessary here.

Fever is the most common ailment. Towards the south-west of the sphere treated in these pages, in the swampy districts sloping from Luena (old) station to Lake Bangweolo this fever is usually a symptom of malaria.

Among the hill tribes, however, especially towards the north between Fife and Abercorn such fever may safely be attributed to other causes, as the malaria parasites are rarely found upon microscopial examination of the blood. The recurrent attacks of tick fever which, in the old days, was called intermittent malaria seems one of the main sources of this prevalent native disease. Mr. Winston Churchill, when travelling in Uganda, gave an excellent account of this hateful disease. Its worst features—at any rate in the case of Europeans—are the frequent recurrence of the attacks, as many as nine or ten separate bouts extending over a period of a month or six weeks, being by no means uncommon; high fever, and intense depression, while iritis is always to be feared as a sequela. Usually, however, it is not dangerous, and though quinine in the usual form appears to intensify the attacks, the disease will sometimes respond to Warburg's Tincture, warmth and rest.

The *ornithodorus moubata*, in other words the tick that carries spirillum fever, is to be found in the majority of the Plateau villages, but, happily, it is not always a carrier of infection. On the main trade routes, however, and at many Bomas where strangers are continually passing these ticks generally become infected with the *spirochaeta duttoni*, and thus produce tick fever. Old rest-houses are a favourite haunt of ticks, and the Government has just issued a circular warning travellers against camping in such buildings for the night. It must be said for the natives that they themselves quite realise the danger of such old buildings, and villages are usually moved to new sites after six or seven years—whereas round about an European settlement it is not always convenient to effect such drastic measures. At present the tick, called by the natives *Nkufu*, is under suspicion as being a possible carrier of Sleeping-Sickness.

An interesting point—though, unfortunately one which cannot be vouched for—is that some of the Angoni have, by repeated attacks in generation after generation, become immune. To preserve this immunity when travelling, and with the idea of importing immunity to their friends, they are said to carry these home-bred ticks with them from place to place.

Many varieties of skin disease abound on the shores of Lakes Tanganyika and Bangweolo. Leprosy is also found in various forms, but in spite of want of segregation it does not seem to make much headway, nor has it as yet spread to any great extent to the mainland or the High Plateau. The Wabisa subsist mainly on fish, which is often very putrid —and, since among the non-fish-eating Plateau tribes the disease is extremely rare, this fact would seem, to the layman at least, a good confirmation of Hutchinson's fish-theory in regard to the causes of leprosy. On the other hand, the P.M.O. of Nyasaland mentions that the eating of hippo-meat is viewed with suspicion as being a possible cause of the disease.

A form of Leucoderma is also a common affection among lake natives, and is by them attributed to eating certain kinds of fish. The breast and especially the hands present, in this disease, a curious mottled appearance, being covered with large white patches.

The ordinary skin diseases, such as itch, boils, carbuncles, and urticaria are common enough upon the Plateau. Native children are much afflicted with parasites, especially the painful body-maggot, *mutiti*, which occasionally appear even in Europeans. Fortunately, however, the guinea-worm—which an Irishman from Uganda described as entering the skin as small as a pin, and ' trekking-out ' as large as a python—has not yet made its appearance ; though ' jiggers ' are common enough.

Indeed Africa is most truly the paradise of the parasite. In a land of such vast distances it may seem paradoxical, but it is none the less true that the tiniest things are those that count the most, and are the most important in ultimate analysis. It is undeniable that more Europeans have died, or been invalided, through the bite of the insignificant mosquito and the fevers, including blackwater, which it engenders, than have met their fate in petty wars or from the attacks of wild beasts. The *glossina palpalis*, which would go in the smallest pill-box, is responsible for the spread of the dreaded Sleeping-Sickness, as is its brother, the *glossina morsitans*, for the cattle disease. These are but a few instances—but they may suffice.

In one of his reports, Mr. Young, Native Commissioner at Chinsali, remarks upon an eye disease common among the natives between the months of August and October. This disease is accompanied by acute inflammation and discharge, and to cure it the natives prepare a decoction into which they put alive a common or house-fly. They say that the fly is very cunning, and that, as it spreads infection from sore eyes to clean, so it may as well help to carry the appropriate medicine with it.

Abdominal diseases are many and varied, and are stated by some authorities—among whom is Dr. Kerr Cross—to be due to the fact that natives bolt their food without chewing it. But, as the staple food, porridge, does not require much chewing, it is perhaps more often due to habitual constipation and neglect.

Chronic diarrhœa and several forms of dysentery are very common in swampy localities. Dysentery of a virulent type occasionally becomes endemic just before or during the rains, and last year (1909) caused many deaths in the Fife division before it was suppressed. The natives often complain of *chulu* which they say is an internal sore or abscess, but since they point to it over the left side it may be merely spleen enlargement. Excessive constipation is called *lusuku*, and when the stomach is swollen up the medicine man is called in to give drastic emetics and purgatives.

The various groin-glands, septic or possibly of filarial origin they call *mupindo*, and assert that native doctors can soon reduce such swellings.

Natives can bear actual cold well enough, as is found in the case of workers transferred from the hot Luangwa Valley to a cold station like Fife ; but cold and wet weather combined are too much for them. Hence coughs and colds are very prevalent in the first months of the year, and often end in the dreaded *kabale* or pneumonia. If the ordinary colds and fevers which abound at this time of the year are not easily shaken off, they are attributed at once to the infidelity of a wife : indeed, a special word has been coined to denote this species. Consumption, though according to Dr. Kerr Cross, extremely rare in the adjacent North Nyasa district, is by no means unknown on the Plateau, and a certain percentage of deaths occur from it every year. Cancer, however, is said to be unknown.

The Awemba do not distinguish between attacks of epilepsy and insanity, but classify them together under the general word *kupena*. They distinguish between three forms : *Akakoshi musa* say they, is when a man has a mad fit which throws him into convulsions on the ground, but from which he quickly recovers and returns to his right mind ; *lupuma* is an acute attack of madness which sends a man suddenly raving mad until death ends his suffering ; but this form is said to be rare ; *chipupu* seizes its victim suddenly and causes collapse in a very short time, when the man lies absolutely rigid as if dead, and, if alone in his hut, is almost sure to be severely burned. This collapse often lasts a whole day, when the patient will finally awake and drop into a natural sleep. One of the writers was called in the middle of the night to assist in the case of a woman, and found the relatives, despairing of reviving her, in the act of prizing open the clenched jaws with an axe.

Another form is *chinsa*, where the insane man will eat leaves and grass, and live in the woods. Such men are, literally, ' wild men of the woods ' and are, perhaps, not so much insane as a throw-back to a very primitive type. One such man was brought before an official after being trapped by the villagers who were enraged at his continual monkey-like thefts of crops and pilferings from the village at night. The features of this man, especially the low, receding forehead, and the gait and movements were extremely simian.

Most tribes have the firm belief that for all these forms of insanity or epilepsy there is a special and very efficacious medicine, which produces violent vomiting, but, if persisted in, leaves the patient in his right mind, though very weak.

The following description of native surgery is taken from notes kindly given by Dr. Chisholm of the Livingstonia Mission.

The skill of native doctors is considerable. They treat fractures by setting and splints, but as they cause shortenings, callosities, and ankylosed joints, the treatment cannot be described as very satisfactory. Rest and position are not much considered in their surgery, but more in medicine. Hæmorrhage is stopped by boiling water or hot mud, but the principle of cauterisation does not appear to be known. Venesection, however, is practised, and the cut vein may be tied. Gaping wounds are stitched with fibre thread, and successfully closed. Ordinary wounds are washed with very hot water and medicines, composed of pounded bits of special wood, and are then covered with the leaves of a special bushy tree. Bad wounds are dressed daily, while over small wounds a fibre called *lukusa* is stretched, which acts as sticking-plaster. Blue-stone is in much request for snake-bites. When a man is bitten a ligature is at once fastened between the puncture and the heart, and the village doctor cuts the wound to allow the blood to flow freely ; then, after chewing certain leaves, sucks out the venom, afterwards cleansing his mouth with the same antidote as before. Charms against serpents, especially amulets made of the wood of rare trees, are much in vogue as preventives of snake-bites. Some Wabisa wear amulets of snake-skin to avoid being bitten by a certain kind of water-snake which is considered dangerous.

Abscesses, when nearly pointing, are opened with a knife. Cupping is frequently used, especially for headache and fever, sharp incisions being made with a native razor close to each ear, and the cupping-horn affixed, when a friend starts the flow into this horn by suction through a tiny hole at the tip, which is afterwards stoppered by wax.

The recuperative power of many natives after severe accidents is marvellous. A villager at Fife, whose head had been, literally, in the leopard's mouth, had, when carried to Mwenzo Hospital, part of his brain exposed, and yet recovered and leads an active life to-day. Natives recover well and rapidly after the most serious operations. Hundreds of people are living in the Awemba country to-day who have suffered the most terrible and unnameable mutilations at the hands of their chiefs, under which most Europeans would have died of shock alone.

Particulars of the various forms of mutilations inflicted for certain offences have been given in the chapter on Legal Notions. The following typical description is given by an eyewitness. The victim was thrown down on the ground, and his hands—sometimes placed on a block of wood—were amputated with an axe. The unfortunate, who was often unable to rise immediately, being stunned by a cruel blow on the spine, would rush away from the village to the nearest water, pursued by a volley of logs of wood and other missiles. The relatives, who were only allowed to approach him in the village in a case of mutilation by blinding, brought boiling water to the stream and dashed it on the bleeding stumps, holding the victim's arms above his head, and throwing on flour until, finally, the flow of blood was staunched. When the eyes were gouged out (with the thumb) the optic vessels were cut, and the relatives—out of kindness and, as they said, to prevent further inflammation —poured hot castor-oil into the sockets ! Such mutilations were not, however, confined to the savagery of the chiefs ; murderers often inflicting shocking mutilations on the bodies of their victims. This was done, it is said, to prevent the spirit of the murdered person from exacting vengeance, and even if only the joint of the first or the little finger were cut off, such mutilation would suffice for this purpose.

Abnormalities are very rare, owing, doubtless to the fact, strenuously denied by natives but nevertheless undoubtedly true, that abnormal children such as the *chinkula* are destroyed after birth. Albino children are occasionally found. Natives account for their partially white markings by saying that they are the children of the *Mulenga*, who, according to tradition, was a white man. The original *Mulenga*, the Azrael of the Awemba, is said to have come from Lubaland, and to have caused the great rinderpest (in 1894) to revenge himself upon Chitimukulu, who would not acknowledge his claim to be the real king of the Awemba. The natives say that Mulenga still moves as a wandering spirit from village to village in the Wemba country, and that Albino children are thus begotten by him from time to time. Though of this sinister parentage, Albino children are not the subject of any further superstition, or taboo, but marry in due course.

Erythrism is extremely rare, the writers having, so far, seen only one red-headed child ; they could not ascertain that any especial superstition was prevalent regarding it.

Dwarfs are, again, uncommon, and the writers have seen only two, and those in the Shinga country. Owing, perhaps, to their Congolese origin, the Awemba have many tales about dwarfs. For instance, on seeing a dwarf approach, one must salute him afar off to propitiate him ; he will then be much pleased, saying to himself : ' I cannot be so small, after all, if these Awemba can see me at such a distance ! '

Though children are occasionally born with webbed fingers, which are carefully separated later by their mothers, the rooted superstition of the Awemba that the Waunga, those quaint and primitive denizens of the Bangweolo swamps, have in many cases webbed feet, is a mere myth.

Umbilical hernia is extremely common among the younger children ; due, probably, to unsuitable feeding immediately after birth. Men with protruberant navels were frequently selected by the chief's messengers—who were known as the ' Neck-Twisters '—as fit victims for the human sacrifices decreed by the chiefs in case of shortage of rain. A fuller account, however, of this procedure is to be found in the chapter upon Native Husbandry.

CHAPTER IX

THE PLATEAU NATIVE (II)

IN the darkest shadows of the African forest there thrives a dwarfish shrub humbled, to outward insignificance, by the luxuriant overgrowth of rank grasses which surround it. The traveller passes it by as mean and ignoble. It is the expert alone who knows that, beneath the surface, its stems extend on every side in unseen ramifications, and that its underground limbs teem with a precious flow of the richest rubber.

So to the casual observer the treasures of the native mind and character are hidden from sight—obscured by the overgrowth of prevalent or fashionable theories which surround them. Hence, in approaching the mental and moral aspects of our Plateau native, we must resolutely clear such obstructions from the field of our mental vision, and brush aside that ungodly array of pernicious half-truths ; as, for instance, that the native is 'half-child, half-devil,' that he is a 'political idiot,' or that he is 'more non-moral than immoral.'

It cannot be too highly emphasised that, if we wish to study the native, we must begin from the *native* standpoint, patiently gleaning its expression from native languages and institutions. One must 'think black' to bridge the vast gulf between African and European conceptions. Better pasturage is to be found by an advance into the sympathetic and unprejudiced study of native life and character than by merely browsing upon the edge of the white men's theories.

Ten years of experience among natives—especially if many of those years have been lived alone in their midst—give far more insight than mountains of monographs or all the wealth of African literature.   The arm-chair scientist will, no doubt, look pityingly down upon so exiled an investigator, will contend that his mind has been warped by the influence of native life, will advise him, in half-veiled contempt, to cultivate more detachment from his subject, and to reconstruct his ideas on the basis of cold study of the problem and in the dry light of fact.   Yet how futile such advice must sound to those who have caught, even for an instant, a glimpse of the elusive in-wardness of the African soul !   Our exile knows his African, body, soul, and spirit, far better than does the scientist. That he cannot transmute such insight into terms of European thought, cannot reduce his knowledge so that it may be accurately measured by the ' ridiculous callipers of witless anthropology ' is unfortunate—and cannot be helped.   It is better to be inarticulate than inaccurate in such matters.   The study of African races on the spot is still in its infancy ;   perhaps some heaven-born genius may eventually arise and fuse into a brilliant monograph the inscrutable intellect of Tropical Africa.   But, in the meantime, it is better to flee from the devil of dogmatism and to cast oneself into the deep sea of native thought, even though it submerge us and render us dumb where we should be definite.

Bearing such limitations in mind, the impressions here-after recorded are advanced in no dogmatic spirit, but as subjective, tentative, and confined mainly to the dominant race in our especial sphere.

The genius of that dominant people is most clearly seen in its language and system of government, both of which evidence no small power of logical reasoning.   This is our first heresy against the generally accepted view that the Bantu is hopelessly deficient in logical faculties and reason-ing powers, so some attempt must be made to defend it. As the late Dr. Cust wrote in the Introduction to his erudite volume on the *Modern Languages of Africa*, ' some of these wild languages evidence a most intricate and elaborate organism, which, if they prove nothing else, at least point to the existence in the brains of the speaker of a logical power of reasoning.' If this argument may be followed—and it has been acutely said that to the modern philologist psychology is even more important than physiology—then, in Chiwemba we have, assuredly, such a language. The marvellous symmetry of its concords and its intricate tense system are, in the opinion of perhaps the greatest authority on Bantu philology, among the most elaborate yet discovered. The copious vocabulary and the almost unlimited capacity of forming derivatives according to fixed laws make us wonder at the genius of the race which evolved it. Again, the refinements and nuances of oratorical and idiomatic Chiwemba would appeal at once to any classical scholar, as would the simple yet sustained vigour of its folklore tales.

Nor is this language decaying or in any immediate danger of becoming debased ; on the contrary, it is gaining ground. And its very use at the present time postulates, from those who speak it well, logical and reasoning powers of no mean order.

Of the 'solemn foolery' of formal logic, or of logic as a theory of knowledge and scientific method, our Plateau native is, doubtless, ignorant ; nor does he grace his mental processes with labels of deduction or induction. Yet no one who has used native assessors will deny that their questions — especially in cross-examination—are directed, whether consciously or not, to the eliciting of proof by one of these methods. We may clinch the argument by pointing to the inherent logic in the development of such institutions as the Wemba form of government, which has been discussed in a former chapter.

The sententious wisdom of the old men is another factor to be reckoned with. Innumerable talks upon *ulendo* with chiefs and village elders can only confirm one in a high opinion of their shrewdness and mental capacity. Such chiefs as old Chitoshi, head of the Walungu and Zapaira—now, alas ! dead—were, in their way, true black philosophers, and their remarks anent the character of their peoples, doubtless derived from much experience in

governing them, would have dumbfounded any one apt
to be cynical in regard to native ability for reflection.

The denial of the logical faculty and of reasoning powers
is generally followed by the statement that the African
races are usually destitute of the capacity for abstract
thought. But this contention is disproved—at least to any
student of the language—by the existence of a special
Abstract Prefix, which is found more or less in most
Bantu languages, but abundantly in Chiwemba and the
kindred Chiluba. By the use of this prefix practically
any noun can be changed from the concrete sense
to the abstract. Abstract terms can, therefore, be expressed with greater ease and simplicity in Chiwemba
than in English. It is not necessary to go to the other
extreme and pretend that the natives are true meta-
physicians, or that they approach any conscious analysis
of the abstract. But the faculty and habit of abstract
thought are there and in constant use, as may be seen
from the numberless proverbs and pithy maxims of the
people.

This grasp of the abstract is accompanied by the sister
faculty of capacity for spiritual thought. Hence missionaries say that they do not find the often-quoted difficulty
of expressing the high moral and spiritual truths of Christianity in native terms. As Dr. Elmslie says : ' The native
lives constantly in an atmosphere of spiritual things. He
is consciously or unconsciously always under the power
and influence of the spirit world. Almost all his customs
are connected with a spiritual origin. It is in this power
of comprehending the abstract and spiritual in which the
so-called savage is at his best.'

Many officials fondly think that it is owing to their own
influence and that of a handful of native police that the
country is administered in peace and quiet. But is it not,
rather, that invisible backing force, the mysterious Europe
—the *Ulaya* of the natives—the maker of the ' Steamer
of the Mountains,' as the Awemba call the locomotive, and
the fashioner of long-range rifles that is the ultimate
restraining factor ?

The degree of brain-power and cleverness among the raw natives is a very moot point. It can only be said that up to the age of puberty black children educated with white show much the same share of intelligence. The native mind is in a constant state of receptivity, and its powers of assimilation are enormous. There is a constant yearning to learn to read and write, and to thus assimilate the knowledge of the white man. Boys reading by the camp-fire and by moonlight are a common sight. Such is the intense zeal for knowledge that many of the advanced boys who are sent to training-centres such as Kondowe, the head-quarters of the Livingstonia Mission, will injure themselves with overstudy and exhibit all the symptoms of neurasthenia and brain-fag. However doubtful we may be of the capacity of the average native, there is no doubt that some have considerable talent, and, in the opinion of missionaries who have trained them, could succeed in passing even such difficult tests as the medical degree at home with ordinary coaching.

The raw native is gradually being educated. In the Fife division, for instance, about ten years ago barely a score could read, out of a population of over 20,000 ; now about 7000 can read and write a little.

Memory, though undoubtedly not one of the highest qualities of the mind, is, nevertheless, not to be despised if found in a backward race ; and it may be safely said that the memory of our Plateau native is excellent. Finding on an old file the copy of a report on district travelling written nine years ago, one of the authors called up the messengers who were with him at the time and questioned them as a test. Though they had travelled many times over the same ground with other officials, three out of the four not only gave the exact route taken—a very devious one—but also recalled many forgotten incidents of the journey. Winamwanga boys at Mwenzo Mission can re-produce, faultlessly, pages of the text-book set for examina-tion, and at the French mission schools long catechisms are learnt by heart and repeated word for word with consummate ease. For this reason many missionaries denounce examination from text-books as a defective test, since it merely serves to train a faculty already highly developed, and advise that every effort should be made to stimulate thought instead of insisting upon a mere parrot-pattering of the text.

To turn to the obverse of the medal; we find that athwart the path of mental progress cleared by these qualities of mind are the two stubborn barriers of superstition and sensuality. The undoubted fact that mental development is arrested and sometimes crushed by these two obsessions must be fairly faced. Scientists have stated that this check is to be explained by the premature closing of the cranial sutures, by which the normal development of the brain is checked (Keane's *Ethnology*, p. 44). But this theory is now somewhat in disfavour. In the opinion of the present writers the intense sex instincts are the strongest bar, and it is in this direction, by gradually teaching resistance and restraint, that the best efforts of missionaries should be directed. The weight of witchcraft and the fear of magic has crushed any nascent critical faculty to death. Even the best-educated natives have a sneaking belief in lycanthropy—in other words, the power of a wizard to change himself into a lion or a leopard—and it is simply waste of time to point out to them that an open demonstration by the suspect should precede belief. Such beliefs cry for the strong corrective of a technical and scientific education, in which the phenomena of Nature which frequently underlie superstitious fear may be rationally explained. The lack of critical capacity perhaps accounts also for the want of a sense of proportion and the slow adjustment of relative values. The old, time-honoured standards of values in cattle, women, beer, and grain are well marked, but any new object fits slowly enough into its proper niche. Natives part with cattle, which represent so many wives, for the Brummagem toys, cheap striking clocks, and the like brought up by repatriated mine-boys from the south.

Mental instability and lack of power to fix the attention have been commented upon by some writers as a defect of tropical races. But in fairness it must be remarked that, when a native grasps the importance of a subject, he is all attention, and will follow the tedious windings of an intricate cattle case when even the interest of the white official has begun to flag. Again, missionaries who have had experience of teaching at home inform us that, in subjects which call for sustained attention, their black pupils' powers of concentration compare very favourably with those of a white class of the same average age in Europe.

The above are but a few aspects of the strength and weakness of the native brain. In fine, the mental gifts of the Plateau native, rooted deeply in the recesses of abstract and spiritual thought, are of the contemplative and unpractical type, wholly in harmony with the life of ease which he leads at present. The nimble adroitness, versatile energy, aggressive and inventive power of the white races, which make, no doubt, for practical success in life, are foreign to his nature. Yet it is the practical, workaday life of a Helot, the life of a ' hewer and drawer ' for a superior race, to which, by the irony of fate, he is, apparently, destined.

To turn to the general aspects of the moral and emotional sides of native character.

Let us examine the view taken by the native himself as to the source and effect of his emotion. He will attribute the baser emotions of which he is ashamed to an external source. ' Fear,' he says, ' seized me, and made my heart say *Pwa-a* ! ' (imitating a fluttering sound). ' Anger gripped me by the neck, and shame disturbed my breath.' The more noble moral qualities are, apparently, conceived as residing in the larger organs of the body, but are capable of being dislodged by lower impulses. Thus the seat of bravery is in the heart, yet the heart itself, by some crazy notion, is literally said to be driven down on occasion into the stomach. Intelligence is at once pointed out as residing in the right side of the forehead, and the expression ' He has a bee in his bonnet ' is paralleled by the coarser phrase ' He has maggots in his brain.' Vigour and energy proceed from the abdomen. Love and affection are spoken of as residing in the bosom, and the natives point to the

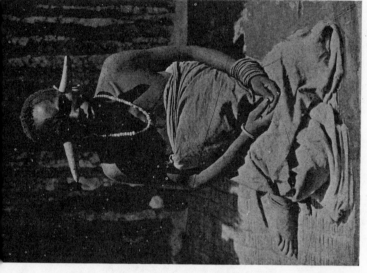

Bernard Turner, phot.

CUPPING.

G. Stokes, phot.

WIWA BOY'S ULENDO KIT.

centre of the chest to denote such feelings. Remorse is referred to usually as attacking a man over the region of the spleen.

The native conscience is very complex and varied. As an old trader put it grotesquely, but forcibly, 'an elephant could dance with hobnail boots on the consciences of most of the older men without any effect.' Yet the majority of the younger men are very sensitive to the various qualms of conscience, and are greatly disturbed by remorse and the fear of discovery. They will endeavour to lift this load from off their guilty minds by attributing their lapse to the fault of an evil spirit, and by the help of the medicine man, who often acts as father confessor in such matters, the spirit incubus with its load of guilty feeling is finally exorcised. Illness of any duration causes the patient to rack his conscience to discover what villager he may have injured, out of fear that the wronged individual may be inducing a chronic malady by his revengeful witchcraft.

The Awemba are, perhaps, the most emotional of the Plateau races. Yet, although some tribes seem capable of deep emotion—such as sorrow and real grief—no extravagant gusts of passion or outbursts of emotion sway them to the hysterical lengths which are credited to the Kafir. Natives think far more of a quiet, easy-going man, unemotional and slow to anger, than they would of a strenuous official stepping from the pages of Kipling, however admirable the latter might be with his driving energy and nervous Telegraphese. Hence the proverb runs, 'He is a fool who runs counter to a quiet man.' The most disturbing report is received with stoic composure. Glad news often causes the older people to break into an uncouth dance, but this seems more a matter of form than an expression of genuine emotion. How a native would act under the stimulus of a Salvation Army meeting it is difficult to guess, as this country has not yet been favoured with any outbreak of revivalism.

Before discussing the nobler qualities—such as honesty, generosity, confidence, fidelity to the given word of honour, and frank belief—it must be emphasised that these affections are mainly the outcome of the original sacrifice of the individual to the obligations of the clan system. The thraldom of the individual who, with all his rights, is bound in the altruistic trammels of primitive socialism is well worked out in a recent book by Mr. Dudley Kidd, so that no specific proof of this assertion is needed. Suffice it to say that on the Plateau the links of the chain are obvious. The individual is merged in his family, who are bound by various ties to similar groups, united in one village under the headman. The village headman, again, is subject to the influence of the various local overlords, who are in turn responsible to the paramount chief—the apex of the tribe. These bonds grip the Plateau native just as they do the Kafir in religious and legal affairs, in war, in hunting, in the everyday needs of life.

The unswerving honesty of the bush native is most remarkable. A wandering European hunter — an easy mark for plunder—may pitch his tent in any village, go out all day with his boys on elephant spoor, and return to find cash and goods untouched; they are under the protection of the headman, and no villager would dream of purloining anything. Native *capitaos* frequently send, by raw natives from the out-stores, bags of cash roughly sewn up in flimsy trade calico, which are faithfully delivered intact to the trader at his central station. At the principal *bomas*, owing to the constant influx of natives of different race, it would be unsafe to go out *on ulendo* without first locking up the house. But at an out-station such a precaution is unnecessary, and house and furniture may be left unguarded in perfect safety. Unfortunately, however, this high standard of honesty is beginning to deteriorate —possibly owing to the fact that the thousands of natives who have been south have returned with a lower code learned from less honest tribes. Thieves are, as a rule, natives who have seen the world, and very rarely are such acts brought home to the raw bush native.

The strong confidence which the natives place in each other is the best proof of this honesty. A Wemba boy, for instance, working at the mines will frequently hand over to a passer-by of his own tribe, who he may have only seen for a day, part of his wages for delivery to his friends, and such trust is very rarely betrayed. Contempt-of-court prisoners for default of hut-tax payments are free to do ordinary work unguarded on giving their word of honour not to escape, and this pledge is very rarely broken. The very frequency of the native phrase, ' to put one's neck upon a thing,' denotes that the utmost confidence is constantly given and received. Unprincipled white men sometimes take advantage of this simple trust ; in a recent case a gang of carriers worked cheerfully for six months in a neighbouring foreign territory for a party of hunters without pay, relying on the false statement that their wages had been deposited with the official of their own *boma*.

To complete this sketch of the nobler outstanding qualities of the natives, their conservatism, their sense of justice, and remarkable law-abiding qualities are merely mentioned here, as they have been already referred to in the chapter upon Legal Notions.

However, the reverse of the picture must not be ignored. Foremost among the defects stands the want of an aim in life. To this is due the sameness and persistency of the native type, which can be easily identified in Egyptian sculptures of four thousand years ago. The same shaped huts, the same primitive clothes, the same destructive methods of cultivation . . . but why run the gamut of a conservatism more than Chinese in its conformity to type ?

The absence of will-power among some natives is doubt-less due, to a certain extent, to the fact that the individual, as we have seen, has merged his volition in that of the clan.

The reserve forces of character—such as perseverance and reliability—are sadly wanting, and it is extremely difficult to engage boys in any pursuit for any length of time. The nomad instinct reasserts itself, and they are off in search of new masters hundreds of miles away, though, finally, they often return and admit their foolishness. Nor is it surprising that the factor of reliability should be a very minor quantity, and this applies to not only the ordinary run of natives, but to police, to messengers, and even to the ordinary run of educated native clerks placed in responsible positions. It is astonishing how often the most suave and soft-spoken *capitao* placed in temporary charge of an out-station will turn, as the natives say, into a lion. *Bukali bufumu*—' Cruelty is the mark of the chief '—so runs the typical native proverb, and so it is, perhaps, not surprising that a clerk, being for the time in the position of a ' little tin god,' is apt to abuse his prerogative.

This leads naturally to another phase of the native character. It is of no use mincing matters or denying —what is clear to any one of experience—that natives feel keen pleasure in witnessing the sufferings of others. When listening to the tales of mutilations carried out by one who had acted as chief mutilator for the late Mwamba, one could not help noticing how all the carriers gathered round and followed, gloatingly, the vivid description of detestable details. At the hanging of one of their own tribe, police were absolutely unmoved, climbing down into the pit with the utmost sang-froid to see if the execution had been successfully carried out. Of their callous cruelty to animals, the less said the better. Plucking a fowl alive and other horrors are committed by them without, apparently, the slightest shame. Whatever allowance may be made for their apparent insensibility to pain does but little to palliate their heedlessness to the manifest sufferings of even their own relatives.

A missionary report states that one youth objected to the eyes of an old and suffering woman—his relative —being operated upon because, he said, ' If she sees, I shall have to pay a three-shilling tax for her ; now she does not pay, being blind ! '   And when serious accidents happen—when, for instance, a man is severely scalded and lies in agony at an adjacent village—it is extremely difficult to muster carriers there to bring him to the

station ; usually men must be written on by the official
to bring the sufferer in.

Yet, in spite of this callousness, there can be no doubt
of the existence of family affection, deep-rooted, though
not often outwardly demonstrated. Among the Plateau
tribes the love of a native woman for her children is undoubtedly very strong. Frequently, a native woman will
assert in court that she would rather put up with the
ill-treatment of her husband than lose the custody of
her child. The practice of infanticide—of which McLellan
gives such terrible instances throughout the world — is
singularly less prominent in Africa. ' How poignant is
the cry of a child to a barren woman,' says the pathetic
native proverb, which shows the deep yearning of the
women for children. When a young child dies, the grief
of both the parents is intense. All officials who have
attended many inquests can testify that there is no
Oriental insincerity in the mourning ; and, again, those
who have witnessed the return of a son of the family
from the mines will never forget the outburst of joy and
affection with which he is welcomed.

Though faithfulness is prominent, the sense of truth
seems very vague. ' For we people are all alike in deceit
and cunning ! ' is the naïve ending to many a tale, wherein
deceitful ' slimness ' and low cunning are just as prominent as one might expect among what the Germans call
Nature Folk.

There is no exaggeration in the statement that a witness
in court cases will scarcely ever give a truthful reply
until he has perceived what he thinks to be the motive
of the question — hence the string of evasive answers
and, apparently, crass stupidity of many under cross-
examination.

The shortcomings of the native from the commercial
and business point of view are many and varied. For,
as Sir Henry Maine has pointed out, tribes still in the
status stage cannot understand the modern contractual
theory. Men who have engaged to work for a year on
the southern mines will suddenly feel the homing instinct,

and, despite the distance and the want of food for the return journey, will escape and arrive safely at their homes. A gang of natives engaged to work at Fort Jameson has been known to desert on the way down through encountering a bad omen. Fortunately, however, through precedents created by punishments in the Native Courts for this offence, the worker is being gradually educated as to the binding nature of agreements.

With the exception of the more conservative tribes, such as the Wiwa, it may safely be said that the Plateau native is thriftless and improvident. The custom in vogue among other Central African tribes of banking money by secreting it in a deep hole underneath the floor of the hut is very rarely met with here. Again, in spite of continuous warnings by officials to save grain against a bad harvest through dearth of rain, beer-drinking goes on unchecked until absolute want sets in, and the people are forced to live upon wild fruits and other indigenous roots and leaves. Boys who are paid, on return from Southern Rhodesia, sums varying from five pounds onwards will squander this money immediately upon creature comforts, and, in a few months, be compelled to turn out again to earn money for a three-shilling tax! In the same way, instead of purchasing cattle, pounds will be spent in collecting a wardrobe of flimsy and flashy clothes.

The native is absolutely without sense of the value of time. Thus the 'ticket system' of wage-paying and all manner of piecework devised to get a certain task finished in a certain time is regarded with the utmost disfavour. But there is no need to flog a dead horse in multiplying instances of so obvious a failing.

We come now to the final stumbling-block—the intensity of the sexual nature. It is not proposed here to enter at length into the vexed question of native morality, nor does it matter whether or not we agree with Sir Harry Johnston's statement that 'misuse or irregularity of sexual intercourse is not vice, and natives are rarely—knowingly—indecent.' Any mission doctor will confirm the enormous loss of nerve force and consequent mental degeneration at puberty of their pupils from this failing. It is all very well for anthropologists to sneer at ' books scrupulously dressed for the drawing-room table, in which accounts of native practices and beliefs are omitted as disgusting.' There must be a limit somewhere, and to describe the vagaries of native sex-impulses, whether vicious or not, would require the strong realism of Suetonius and a considerable facility for obscure and obscene Latin. One may, however, without wishing to dot the i's and cross the t's in this matter, note a few facts. First, that chastity is an unknown quantity in young girls over fifteen years of age ; secondly, that the immoral posturings and dances, kept up till late at night, cannot fail to inflame the passions of both the boys and girls who are invariably present ; thirdly, that early marriage merely gratifies these passions to the full. The older men, so soon as they feel at home with a mission doctor, will pester him for aphrodisiacs. One has but to listen to the filthy ingenuity of obscene abuse poured forth by two quarrelling women to realise that the fair sex do not lag behind in such matters. A few tribes are, by comparison, moral after marriage, but to speak of morality in the European sense with regard to such tribes as the Awemba is mere foolishness.

Nor may the fashionable defence that the native is more ' non-moral than immoral ' be here set up. The Awemba have a very definite code of sex-morality, as enforced by superstitious belief and definite sanctions, which included mutilation. All know that immorality is wrong, and that it runs counter to the laws of superstitious observance. Did space permit, it would be interesting to trace out the manner in which, according to the theory of native custom, sexual continence and faithfulness are essential in the daily conduct of life, and how immoral acts will—theoretically at least—vitiate and render unsuccessful the most ordinary pursuits, such as hunting and fishing. If, for instance, a woman who has committed adultery cooks her husband's food, he will be seriously ill. The moral code exists, without a doubt. It is not carried out in practice—that is all. Nor will any student of history be at a loss to quote parallels of the difference between the theory and the practice of national morality.

We have attempted to discuss both good and bad aspects of the native character from the mental and moral standpoints. To summarise the conclusions in a sentence—though possibly illuminating—would be manifestly very difficult. The grave defects of sexuality and superstition may be eradicated by the growing power of missionary influence and example, and by finding outlets for that readiness to work which distinguishes the natives of North-Eastern Rhodesia so favourably from the Kafir.

But all this is a matter of time—of centuries, even. When one reflects that Eugenics have not yet been adopted among civilised nations, it seems not only premature, but futile, to advocate, with some writers, their introduction among native races peculiarly impatient in matters of sexual restraint. It is, after all, the titanic task of our Plateau native himself to follow the advice of Browning—

> ' My business is not to remake myself,
> But make the absolute best of what God made.'

CHAPTER X

THE VAGRANT OFFICIAL

TIMES are, perhaps, changed since the early days when the natives of a certain division asked their official why all Native Commissioners seemed to be in such a perpetual bustle and hurry, scurrying round their districts as if their very lives depended on it. Nowadays we take things, it is true, in more leisurely fashion; but, for all that, the life of a district official on the Tanganyika Plateau is hardly one which would appeal to the confirmed lover of peace, whose habits have crystallised, whose daily round is set in a bed-rock foundation of immutable routine. For it is, during the better half of the year, a nomadic existence in the barest meaning of the term. No dweller in the ' tents of hide,' no wandering Mongol or Kurd can boast of more numerous camping-grounds than those which, in the dry season of the year, fall to the lot of the Native Commissioner who takes an interest in his district. Even the native proverb says, ' The scarecrow may rest o' nights, but never the watcher of men.'

A digression as to the term *ulendo*. It is what Alice would, probably, have called a ' portmanteau-word '; certainly its six letters comprise an extraordinary variety of meanings. First and foremost it means a journey; but it also represents, collectively, the various human units who go upon that journey. It is used as an adjective, qualifying the buckets, folding-tables, camp furniture, and provisions which stand to the Native Commissioners in the place of household gods. The way-bill which a native carrier presents with his load is called an ' ulendo-note,' and a somewhat strenuous brand of tinned meats is known under the name of ' Ulendo Beef.' *On ulendo* is the stereotyped phrase representing the normal condition of the average official during six months out of the twelve ; and, in preference to wasting further time in differentiating between what *ulendo* does and does not convey, it may be simpler to state that it corresponds exactly to *safari*, which, through the efforts of Mr. Winston Churchill, may be taken to be as much a household word in the England of to-day as ' veld,' ' kopje,' or ' khaki.'

Preparations for *ulendo* usually follow a definite routine. They consist in packing away anything of interest or value in the shape of books, pictures, photographs, or silver— since there will be no room for such frillings either upon the carriers' heads or upon the ground-sheet which is to be one's carpet for some weeks to come. The strictly utilitarian residue of frying-pans, enamel-ware, folding-tables, and the like may then be deposited upon the back veranda.

At this stage it is advisable to take a piece of paper and a pencil, and proceed upon the lines laid down in *Three Men in a Boat*, which will, at least, obviate the necessity of spending the first night in camp minus bed, bath, tooth-brush, or some similar indispensable. Mustard and pepper are peculiarly elusive articles, and appear, upon the average, in one *ulendo* out of four.

The next step is to pack—and it is a task which requires a clear brain and a level temper, plus an elementary know-ledge of mathematics and a specialist's eye for weights. There are two methods of packing for *ulendo*. One is to do it yourself, in which case your temper will suffer, and you will probably lose money over underweight loads. The other is to take a pipe and a book on to the front veranda, and leave your boys to distribute loads as they think fit at the back. The result of this method will probably be that, at the moment of starting, you will find a brawny Hercules stepping off gaily with an empty bucket, while a tearful child of ten will be pinned to earth beneath three portmanteaux and an iron bake-pot—upon the principle, no doubt, that to him that hath shall be given.

Having collected your porters and written them down,

having inspected your loads and entered them carefully—
special penalties being declared for the breakage of a whisky-
bottle—having finally selected your machila-team, allotted
carriers to your personal boys, and chosen muscular persons
to carry your tent, you will, most probably, retire to rest,
after warning the men that an early start is necessary.
And, next morning, three men will be sick, half a dozen
will evolve invalid grandmothers, and one or two will have
disappeared. This will necessitate an entire redistribution
of loads, and you will probably move off at midday,
ruffled and heated, with the pleasing knowledge that, at
the outset, you have wasted half a day.

But, after the first camp, all such difficulties will vanish.
The men will have conceived each an undying attachment
for his own load, no matter what its substance, size, or
weight. Your machila-men will skip like rams, and your
capitaos like young sheep. For, to the average African, an
ulendo serves the same end as does a trip to the seaside
to the jaded suburbanite. He will see many villages and
consume much meat, shot for his special delectation by a
benevolent *bwana* ; his work will be light, and at midday,
probably, will be over for the day ; there will be the many
and varied delights of the camp-fire, with its stories and
jests, its piquant little scandals and its somewhat salacious
merriment. In short, he is on a pleasure-trip, for which he
is to be paid at the rate of one shilling a week, and his
tax will be secured for that year at least.

Let us picture a typical camp—such a camp as falls
to the lot of every official night after night and for many
nights together ; such a camp as would be welcomed in de-
lirious frenzy by the dyspeptic money-grubber, jaded and
surfeited by an overdose of civilisation ; a camp, in short,
the memories of which will call to one in the years to come,
when the staff of the wanderer has been laid aside, and the
inexorable walls of the city have taken one into their grip
for ever.

In the shadow of a tall, gnarled old tree the tent has
been pitched—no skimpy bell-tent this, but a spacious
Edgington, with long, low fly. Round about it the ground

has been hoed clean—or the grass merely beaten down, according to individual taste—and the clearing is encircled by a hastily thrown-up fence of leafy boughs, which are still fresh and green and fragrant. In one corner of this enclosure a temporary office has been constructed of freshly lopped stakes roofed with grass and leaves—even now the poles are dripping with brilliant red sap, which one might take to be their life-blood. And, in the cool, dim depths, one can just discern a table, a chair, and a tin box —which, for the time being, represents to the native mind a concrete exposition of Government.

Over there, under another tree, is a heap of firewood and three or four piled rifles ; that is the guard, where malefactors will be looked after should any be found, where the bugler will sound his Lights Out and Réveillé, where the sentries will lie at night.   Over in the other corner is another grass-shelter—the dining-room this—equipped with tables and chairs, venesta-wood boxes, a bottle or two.   Behind this, again, is a kitchen, open to the winds of heaven, and, in close proximity, a serviceable tree, where meat can be hung, shielded from the sun by day, out of reach of four-footed marauders by night.   Round about the kitchen, too, you will see rows and rows of utensils filled to the brim with water —blackened, polished pots, or glistening gourds, which have been brought by the women of the village, and will be re-claimed by them after the exodus of the white man and his following.

In the centre of all is the main fire—the *bwana's* fire— the drawing-room and perhaps, too, the evening council-chamber of the place.   Here, when the spoils of the chase come in, will the meat be distributed ; hither, too, will come the old men and the headmen should the *bwana* feel moved to discuss the customs—manners there were none—of the olden days or the history of departed dynasties.

And, round the outer hedge, partitioned off by leafy screens into little booths, well to leeward of the tent, and at a decent distance, will be the quarters of the *ulendo*. Spears and bundles of mealie-cobs, little parcels of bark-

cloth or calico, battered cooking-pots wound about with
cord—or, perhaps, now and again a tin box that was made
in Birmingham and has come to see the world—charred ends
of stumps, and broken potsherds—these are the outward
and visible signs of native occupation. Three hours ago
the place was a forest sanctuary; near to the village though
it was, there was nothing to mark it off from other miles
and miles of illimitable bush. But, within the last three
hours, the servants of the white man have seized upon it
and marked it for their own; from a mere patch of forest,
uncharted and unknown, it has suddenly, with mushroom growth, blossomed forth into the abiding-place, for
one night at least, of sixty or seventy human entities.
And, so far as it is involved, the whole face of the universe
has changed. Beetles and crickets, crawling and jumping
things have either given up the unequal struggle and retired
to less tumultuous spots, or, disconsolate, wander to and
fro in the unaccustomed hubbub. While, in the middle
distance, a pall of bluish grey smoke, low-hanging, marks
a village—if, indeed, any mark were needed to point out
that which is self-evident from the hum of voices that rises
from it.

Such is the white man's camp—such the surroundings
where half his life is passed, amid the freshness of primitive
dawnings, the clean, clear-cut coldness of sub-tropical
nights. Cheerful enough, no doubt, when the great fire
casts flickering shadows upon the silver-barked trees
around, and is reflected in the pin-point glimmer of the
tiny fires of the carriers; eerie enough, too, in the dead
hours, when all save the sentry are asleep, and Heaven
alone knows what is lurking in the shadows outside the
encircling screen of boughs. For, perhaps, in those same
dead hours will come some sudden tumult and uproar and
the curious cry of natives who know that wild beasts are
abroad. Maybe some carrier, lying awake, has caught a
glimpse of a long, low form gliding round outside the
circle of fires—perhaps a hyena only, perhaps a leopard
or a lion. But, somehow, though lions are sometimes
heard, though their spoor is found often enough in the

vicinity of such a camp, it is but rarely—and that in well-known vicinities—that night attacks occur.

So much for the dream and the romance. Let us turn to more solid matters.

The average *ulendo* may be taken to consist of ten machila-men, thirty carriers, three or four native messengers, the same number of *askari*, four personal boys, and a hanger-on or two, with, very possibly, several women and babies, who will wake up when the rest of the camp has gone to sleep. In all, perhaps, some sixty souls. Needless to say, sixty stomachs require a considerable amount of food, and, since no rations are issued in bulk, each individual must shift for himself. In the majority of cases messes of two or three men, linked by relationship or village friendship, will constitute themselves automatically, and draw the sum of their calico uncut—since a *doti*, which is four yards, is the exact quantity required to clothe a man, and thus more valuable than four cut yards, which have eventually to be sewn together.

Upon arrival at a village the headman will invariably appear with a present of sorts, varying in size and value with his social standing — a basket or two of meal, perhaps a few wretched fowls, tied in an unhappy bunch and squawking lustily, heads downwards—maybe, even, a goat or a sheep. And, having thus rendered unto Cæsar, the village autocrat will squat himself down and wait for the return gift — since your African believes firmly in the principle of nothing for nothing, and precious little for a shilling. But a yard or two of calico will content him, and he will retire—only to make way for the female population who, bringing you gourds of water, will thereafter make the world hideous for a space with their shrill ululations.

Social matters having been thus disposed of in accordance with strict etiquette, the time has come to proceed to business ; and it may not be out of place here to sketch briefly the aim of the official *ulendo*.

The main object is, of course, to get into closer touch with the people in their own surroundings ; subsidiary

Dr. J. B. Davey, phot.

TRAVELLING IN MACHILLA.

Bernard Turner, phot.

MEN'S EARLY MORNING BREAKFAST.

matters are the checking of the census, the enumeration
of stock, inquiry into the condition of crops, the consideration of applications to move from village to village, and,
in general, the promulgation of any administrative decrees
which may have become operative since the last visit.

In the system of Administration at present in force
throughout North - Eastern Rhodesia the unit of all
calculations is the village—composed of several families,
mostly inter-related by marriage. These villages, each
represented by a headman, are sub-divided into groups
under the district headmen, selected by the Native
Commissioner upon the advice of the chief, and these
are again responsible to the chief who, in his turn, refers
directly to the official as regards matters of wider import
than mere census details. For instance, while such
matters as removals, deaths, births, and the like must
be notified direct to the *boma* by the village headmen
concerned, weightier matters of policy such as the cutting
of *vitemene*, the suppression of game-pits, and the like
fall within the sphere of the personal influence of the
chief, who will, as a last resource, be held responsible for
any widespread infraction of regulations. As a counter-
poise to this responsibility, however, he will derive a
certain influence from the authority which enables him
to adjudicate upon minor cases ; and, indeed, the keynote
of Administration is this relegation to the chief of all
matters which he is capable of adjusting.

Among the officials themselves the same principle of
centralisation holds good. Of recent years the system
has undergone certain changes. Formally the Magistrate
of a district was responsible to headquarters for the affairs
of his native divisions, and all reports were made to him by
his divisional officials. Under this provincial system the
Magistrate was responsible for the whole native policy
throughout his district, the advantage of the system
being that queries from Native Commissioners were dealt
with on the spot by a man acquainted with local conditions. Now, however, as far as native affairs are
concerned, the division and not the district is the

practical working unit, and Native Commissioners correspond direct with the Secretary for Native Affairs at
headquarters.

We will take it that the division under consideration
is one of average size and shape; that is to say, that its
farthest boundaries lie some three days' journey from the
boma, that it contains two or three distinct tribes, each
with half a dozen chiefs or, at least, superior headmen,
and, probably, about one hundred and fifty villages of
from twenty to two hundred huts apiece.

Probably there will be definite geographical features
which may be utilised as subdivisional boundaries, and
which will be likely to correspond more or less roughly
with inter-tribal delimitations. Each of these subdivisions will be the subject of a separate *ulendo*, and
they will be taken in rotation during the year until every
village has been visited throughout the whole division.
Some may be low-lying, swampy country, which it is
advisable to visit before the heavy rains ; others, perhaps,
are rich in game-bearing *nyikas* which it would be sin
and folly to visit before the grass has been burned—in
short, each subdivision will have its special characteristics,
and, after consideration of these characteristics, will take
its place in the touring programme for the year. And, in
addition to the foregoing considerations, such questions
as taxation and the labour supply, which go hand in hand,
must have close attention.   In some divisions labour is
called out in rotation from a definite subdivision each
month, in accordance with a prearranged scheme, formu-
lated in council with the chiefs themselves ; but, of late
years, labour itself has been so little in demand that such
a scheme is not so valuable as it was, say, five years ago.
Nowadays labour is drawn as much as possible from those
subdivisions where taxes are most in arrear, while it is
found unnecessary to press for taxes in the villages lying
closer to the *boma* until the end of the financial year—
31st March—is in sight. In short, a detailed programme,
based upon common sense, is a most important factor
in successful district travelling.

The distance between villages may, in the fairly well-populated portions, be averaged at between seven and ten miles. Assuming that every village in a division is to be visited at least once during the year, and allowing a full day now and again for the larger villages, usually those of chiefs and headmen, or mission stations, where there may be as many as three hundred or four hundred huts, it is frequently necessary to visit as many as three villages a day. And this is no light task. Usually the tent and sleeping gear are sent ahead to the last village on the list for the day, so that the camp may be ready against arrival, and then, in the glare and the heat—or it may be in drenching tropical rain—the intermediate villages are visited.

If the tents have been sent on, shelter of some kind must be found—perhaps in an *nsaka* or native council hut, a flimsy erection of grass and poles, some six feet high, with a floor of beaten earth, smoke-stained rafters, the remnants of wood-ash and charred stumps scattered amid shrivelled, half-gnawed mealie cobs, and, probably, a tangle of blood-stained game-nets hung from the roof. There, at the mercy of the winds of heaven, after the floor has been swept and garnished, the office table is set up ; pen, ink, paper, and the case books are produced from the depths of the office-box — and the villagers, marshalled by messengers, troop to the *nsaka* and squat around it. Here and there an individual grasps a skinny goat by the leg, trusting to the clemency of the *bwana* or the necessities of his larder to accept the animal as the equivalent of a florin or a half-crown towards the three-shilling tax. Others, with luckless fowls gripped by the neck, sit in stolid silence until their names are called. Now and again a ripple of laughter runs through the group ; some one has relieved the tedium with a jest. Or some old bag-of-bones who has passed beyond the limit of taxation receives his exemption paper, and, tottering out into the sunlight, lies down and gives the salutation of the women, amid the congratulatory jibes of his fellows. Or So-and-so has a grievance—wishes to build *mitanda*—is refused for the fiftieth time, and retires with a dubious shake of the head. So-and-so again, perhaps, has lost his wife, who has succumbed to the superior attractions of Someone Else ; he receives advice, and is told to produce his witnesses and his erring spouse, when the case will be heard. Various matters of policy are dealt with—various instructions issued, with hints of awe-inspiring punishments if they are not complied with—and at last, the work in that village being completed, the signal is given to move on. Like hawks upon their prey the carriers, who have been lurking in the shadows, pounce upon tables and chairs ; in the twinkling of an eye the *nsaka* is deserted. The women, having brought forth their little single ladders of notched palm-stems and, clambering up their grain-bins, deposited therein the precious tax-papers which have just been issued, descend again with the agility of monkeys and run, laughing and shrieking, through the village   The machila-men with much vociferation and expostulation clear a way through the crowds, and set off at a brisk pace ; it would seem that a miracle must be needed to avert catastrophe, as the long, unwieldy hammock swings through the lines of scattered huts, past projections, over stumps, through gaps in rickety fences. Then come the gardens, where the unfortunate passenger may think himself lucky if he is not bumped like a shuttle-cock upon the raised beds which line the winding path—and so out into the open country once more, the shrill cries of the women growing fainter in the distance, the song of the machila-men waking the echoes in the quiet land.

Now and again, in some unusually populous neighbour-hood, a two-day halt may be made. Then life is luxury. Proper shelters can be built ; flannels can take the place of ' ulendo kit '—usually khaki ' shorts ' and shirt, socks, boots, and a helmet—and in the evening or the early morning there is time and to spare for shooting. Then, too, there is always the joy of the evening hours—when a hush comes over the world, and the voices of the tax-payers are stilled, or so mellowed by distance as to become a

PITCHING CAMP.

F. A. Usher, phot.

CROSSING THE LUANSENSHI RIVER.

E. A. Avery-Jones, phot.

lullaby. Over by the fire, upon a carpet of boughs, lie vast joints of meat awaiting distribution, here and there a horned head, with great, mournful eyes, cocked at quaintest angle. The chink of bucket against bath falls soothingly upon the ear ; the rattle of tumblers presages a drink, which will rank not least among the pleasures of the day— for it has been more than earned. And then a few shrouded figures slip from the gloom and squat on the far side of the fire, to be joined a moment later by others. The headman has come to pay his respects, and to discuss affairs of State. So, while the clamour of voices rises in the village, and the carriers, over their tiny fires, sit and gossip of the day's march or the chances of meat upon the morrow, night creeps gradually upon the forests and the bushland spaces, and another day has died.

On *ulendo* the native character is, undoubtedly, seen at its best. Upon the station—overshadowed by the influence of the *boma*, by its awe-inspiring neatness, by the oppression of brick buildings, trim paths, and all the un-accustomed burden of the white man's routine — it is hardly to be wondered at that the native does not show in his true light. Instinctively, almost, he seeks to adjust his mental focus to that of the white man—and does not succeed.

But, when the official goes upon his journeys, conditions are reversed. It is then necessary for the *bwana* himself to adjust his outlook to the necessities of the primitive existence. He finds the native in the very midst of his household gods ; questions of village policy, of boundaries and of garden sites, of marriage and giving in marriage, come to him fresh and piping hot, and are discussed amid the very surroundings which have given rise to them. The native, too, is, undoubtedly, pleased to see his Native Commissioner—he delights in the opportunity of showing hospitality, and, incidentally, the presence of a large crowd of visitors, each of whom is anxious to do business upon the basis of calico for food, must necessarily tend to a short-lived but none the less pleasing prosperity. And, besides, the *ulendo* affords a connecting - link with the outside world ; it serves, indeed, the same purpose as does the arrival of the English mail upon a lonely station. There is all the news of the district to be discussed : what has happened to Simulenga's wife, who, when last heard of, had thrown a cooking-pot at her husband, and had taken up with Wadya ; whether little Mwali will be ready for the marriage rites this year ; whether it is true that Balazi died on the Southern Mines. Perhaps some one wishes to sell a cow — a matter of paramount importance in the native mind. Rest assured that the question in all its bearings will be discussed around the camp-fire. Or the headman may wish to move his village to a site where there are better hoeing-grounds — then, indeed, there will be discussion and argument prolonged far into the night.

On the other hand, no doubt, the advent of the official causes a fluttering in the dovecot, in so far as those unfortunates are concerned who have not discharged their obligations for the year. But it has always been the policy of the Administration to impress upon the native that the proper place in which to pay taxes is the *boma*. The *ulendo*, as we have seen, is intended primarily to allow the Native Commissioner opportunity to get into closer touch with his people, to study their economic and social conditions at first hand, and to lend tangible expression to the interest which is taken in their welfare by visiting them in their homes, and discussing with them all matters of importance in open council.

The charm of the touring season is intangible—but very real. One feels, perhaps, somewhat as a young adventurer of the Middle Ages may have felt when setting forth from the comparative security of mediæval England into the untried perils of fifteenth-century France or Italy. For the standard of comparison has changed since first one came to live in this wonderful country. The station—though it be but a pin-point in the wilderness, a mere congeries of bricks and mortar, thatched roofs, and outlined paths—has come to stand for home and civilisation. Outside it—among the tawny grasses, over the low lines of sprawling purple hills, on the other side of those patches of

dark bush and forest which stretch north, south, east, and
west—lies the district itself—the real abiding-place of the
curious peoples among whom one's lot is cast. Here, on
the station, is settled routine and a peaceful round of days.
Out there—down the long white road and over the rickety
corduroy bridge—adventures may lie in wait ; at the least,
it is there that the real zest and savour of life is to be found.

Let us thank Heaven for *ulendo* and all it means ; let us
pray that it may never be with us as with less fortunate
Administrations, where the soul of the official is cramped
and fettered about with bonds of red tape and the exigencies
of office routine.

So long as the year's work may hold days of open travel
—days compact of honest, steady tramping through tangled
forest-land, of gliding, boatlike, in *machila* through seas of
nodding grass—nights that throb and hum with the song
of insect life, or, maybe, with the raucous voices of evil
beasts—just so long will the life of a district official upon
the Plateau of the Great Lakes be one of the lives that is
best worth the living.

CHAPTER XI

INITIATION, MARRIAGE, AND DIVORCE

FOUR formal festivals—birth, initiation, marriage, and burial—stand clearly out from that 'codeless myriad of precedent' in custom and ceremonial which surrounds— one had almost said submerges — our Central African from the cradle to the grave. As Professor Tylor says, marriage should be described first, 'because upon it depends the family, on which the whole framework of society is founded.'

The ceremonies of initiation of the young girls at puberty —called *chisungu*—and the marriage rites are so intimately connected that we will discuss these and the various questions arising out of native wedlock forthwith. The ceremonies of birth, and death, and burial can be dealt with in the next chapter.

Among the Awemba and the majority of the Plateau tribes there is now no such initiation ceremony for boys as is described among the Yao tribe by Sir H. Johnston. The *butwa* rite, described in Chapter XVI., is, undoubtedly, a foreign and imported custom. In fact, all moral surveillance of young children is conspicuous by its absence. Little boys, when detected in the reprehensible practices mentioned in *British Central Africa*, are scarcely, if at all, blamed by their parents. Young children will rudely interrupt their elders when discussing important village business, and are merely gently reproved for such breaches of decorum, for which a white child would be soundly thrashed. The little girls, it is true, are bespoken at a very early age, and betrothed to the young men after the preliminary matchmaking. But this is purely a commercial transaction, in no way making for morality. The boy gives the girl a ring or some other token of his preference. The parents, after being informed by the young girl herself or the young boy's messenger, consider the offer carefully. The boy, if not straightway rebuffed, after a short time sends his messenger at sunset with a hoe or other offering as the *mpango* or marriage dowry. The family elders of both parties are called together, and deliberate as to the marriage. The hoes, etc., are instantly returned to the rejected suitor, whilst the dowry of the accepted youth is retained. The little girl, according to Wemba custom, is then taken to the young man's hut, and lives with him without further ceremony until she attains puberty. This pernicious practice is winked at by Wemba mothers, whose only care is to ensure that their daughter do not become *enceinte* before the *chisungu* (puberty) ceremonies of initiation. The unfortunate girl who found herself in such a condition became a byword in the village, and had to walk round the huts carrying a water-pot on her head, running the gauntlet of the older women, who filled her cruse with all kinds of filth.

The first real moral instruction for both sexes as to the duties and privileges of life was given at the *chisungu*. The boys, it is true, were merely admonished by the older men, and warned that they must observe the proprieties of married life, but the girls were very carefully instructed.

For the suitorless girl—a great rarity—the *chisungu* merely spelt initiation at puberty pure and simple ; but for a betrothed Wemba damsel the suitor joined in the rite, and the ceremony, when consummated, constituted marriage. We shall meet with other forms of wedlock later on in this chapter, but we must, at the outset, clearly emphasise the cardinal distinction between the *chisungu* and the *bwinga* forms of marriage.

The *chisungu* is, for the Awemba, the ordinary marriage ceremony, though the *bwinga* is not unknown. For the Amambwe, Winamwanga, Alungu, and other Plateau tribes, however, the *chisungu* is merely the young girl's initiation at puberty, since they have a separate and distinct ceremony called the *bwinga*, synonymous with our wedding. The *bwinga* is the most binding form. It is held to be a concession on the part of the parents, who thus, more completely, surrender their daughter to a favoured suitor known to them intimately, who has, more-over, probably worked years in their gardens for the privilege. ' My husband and I are twins ; we grew up together ! ' is the proud song of the Nabwinga bride, boasting before the lesser wives of her more intimate relations with her polygamistic spouse.

The *chisungu* form, on the other hand, is less binding, and hence arise the more frequent divorces among the Awemba as compared with other tribes. One can say with justice that the *chisungu* marriage is only tantamount to the ' temporary loan of a woman, revocable at will by the clan,' though this would hardly be true of the more binding *bwinga*. To take a classical parallel, the *bwinga* is as superior to the *chisungu* in point of solemnity and stringency as was the *confarreatio* to the *connubium* in the days of the early Romans.

Having thus cleared the ground, let us turn to the actual *chisungu* ceremony.

When a young girl knows that she has attained puberty, she forthwith leaves her mother's hut, and hides herself in the long grass near the village, covering her face with a cloth and weeping bitterly. Towards sunset one of the older women—who, as directress of the ceremonies, is called *nachimbusa*—follows her, places a cooking-pot by the cross-roads, and boils therein a concoction of various herbs, with which she anoints the neophyte. At nightfall the girl is carried on the old woman's back to her mother's hut. When the customary period of a few days has elapsed, she is allowed to cook again, after first whitewashing the floor of the hut. But, by the following month, the preparations for her initiation are complete. The novice must remain in her hut throughout the whole period of initiation, and is carefully guarded by the old women, who accompany her whenever she leaves her quarters, veiling her head with a native cloth. The ceremonies last for at least one month, and often even longer for a girl of well-to-do family, since beer and porridge are supplied to the guests without stint, and they are, needless to say, loth to abandon such free rations. During this period of seclusion, drumming and songs are kept up within the mother's hut by the village women—no male, except, it is said, the father of twins, being allowed to enter.

The directress of the rites and the older women instruct the young girl as to the elementary facts of life, the duties of marriage, and the minute rules of conduct, decorum, and hospitality to be observed by a married woman. It is, naturally, extremely difficult to find out what actually takes place, but there is reason to believe that, though many of the songs are obscene, yet, on the whole, the instruction given is wise and sound, and the 'filthy and putrid' customs remarked by Kidd as prevalent in South Africa, and noticeable even among certain Nyasaland tribes, are, happily, not practised. It must be noted that these old women are the only medical advisers available for the girl, and that, therefore, certain unmentionable practices should be regarded from a purely medical standpoint, and not as having any vicious origin.

The most peculiar feature of this instruction is the series of tests which the young girl is forced to undergo. These appear to us bizarre and eccentric, and the only explanation given is that they are intended to prepare the young girl and accustom her to all things she may have to encounter in her grown-up state. The following examples may be given of such tests devised by 'mothers of the rites.' They make fences of stout withies concealed in leaves, over which the girl-novice is forced to leap ; if she trips up, the older women jeer at her. Sometimes she is forced to thrust her head into a collar made of thorns. Again, in the middle of the night, one old woman will imitate the roaring of a lion outside the hut. Figures of animals are fashioned from a mixture of mud, lime and charcoal, and *nkula* (camwood dye) in the forms of lions and other animals ; the commonest objects of daily domestic life are also represented. After much reluctance one of the directresses of the rites allowed one of

the writers to inspect these figures inside the hut.   One
was an uncouth model of a lion, angular and grotesque, the
framework being of sticks driven into the floor of the
hut and plastered over with the above-mentioned mixture.
The eyes and mouth were clearly shown by means of beads
inserted, and the shaggy mane of coarse grass bristled all
over the image like the quills of an angry porcupine.
Another fearsome image represented a snake, but was,
in reality, more like an octopus, since its plaster tentacles
spread all over the floor of the hut, the spotted effect of
the skin being given by white beans cunningly inserted in the
camwood moulding.   (*See* the photo, opposite.)

The old women point to these in turn, and give a kind
of kindergarten lesson, emphasising the dangers from
wild beasts and the proper uses of the utensils ; the young
pupil must, meantime, listen with respect, regarding with
astonishment each of the quaint and crude objects presented to her.

Among some tribes she is carried to the stream on the
shoulders of one of the old women, and there immersed ;
grass bracelets and anklets are bound around her, and she
is finally escorted back to her mother's hut, enveloped
almost to suffocation in sleeping mats.   Upon arrival the
grass anklets and bracelets are wrenched off and thrown
on the roof of the hut.   The inside of the walls of the
initiation hut are painted by the *nachimbusa* with rude
pictures, each with its special signification and song,
which must be understood and learnt by the young girl.

Occasionally the novice is led into the bush close by,
loaded with a bundle of firewood which she carries, pretending to be heavily burdened.   Her woman attendant,
after lighting a fire, cooks a hotch-potch of all the grains
in the country, mixed with castor-oil, which unsavoury
mess the girl has to swallow.

Curious as the above customs may seem, many parallels
can be found in Dr. Frazer's *Golden Bough*, and Dr.
Haddon, in his book, *Head Hunters: Black, White, and
Brown*, describes similar customs as obtaining among the
Torres Straits islanders.

PAINTINGS AND FIGURES INSIDE THE INITIATION HUT OF THE GIRLS.

THE CHISUNGU CEREMONY, WEMBA.

THE 'MBUSA' IMAGES.

For the suitorless girl the foregoing rites conclude the initiation ceremonies, and she bides her time until a husband is found for her.

But when a suitor is already available, he is called the *sichisungu*, and the function is prolonged. The young man will suddenly appear towards the end of these observances, and, standing in front of his future mother-in-law's hut, brandish his bow and arrows, uttering the prescribed formula, ' Where is my game ? ' He peers around the open door and fires at a small target—often made of one of the clay images shown to the young girl—placed by the lintel, and having a black bull's-eye mark in the centre. He aims carefully, and, if his arrow strikes the centre mark, he shouts aloud ' *Eya !* ' dancing for joy. If he misses he is subjected to the jeers of the old women, who pinch and deride him unmercifully. On this occasion the hut is adorned with beads and calico, and the suitor must appear to be impressed with this show of wealth. After complimenting the parents, he returns to his own quarters.

On the following day the pair are shaved and anointed with oil, the youth—and, sometimes, also, the young girl— being bathed at the stream. Usually, however, the girl is merely anointed inside the hut, being then carried out on the back of her attendant and set on a mat in front of the house. Bows and arrows are placed across her knees, in token, they say, of submission ; possibly, however, this may be a relic of primitive bride-capture. She is attended by her sister and her mother and father, while the relatives of the suitor muster in front. The father of the girl then hands an arrow to his future son-in-law, with the words, ' With this you shall pierce the seducer of your wife.' Both parents address the young couple, the mother exhorting her son-in-law to be energetic in tree-cutting and garden-making, that he may keep want from the hut ; the father saying to his daughter, ' Now that you have grown up, little mother, be sensible, and keep desire from your eyes ! ' The bystanders gather round and offer presents of grain and flour to the girl, who receives all such gifts in silence. The village women have the right on this occasion to speak plainly to her, and are not slow to admonish her for her pride or haughtiness, telling her she must henceforth be obedient to her husband, a good housewife, and generous in entertaining her fellow-villagers. The girl, however resentful of any accusations she may think unjust, must bear them all in silence, until, finally, her husband leads her into the hut, and their joint life begins.

In dealing with the whole question of primitive marriage it is customary to draw parallels from authors, ranging from Aristotle to Andrew Lang, and to weigh in the balance the theories advanced by Morgan, Köhler, McLellan, and Westermarck. But the writers frankly shrink from such a task, and prefer simply to describe the ceremonies at the marriage of a well-to-do Lungu man, leaving deductions and parallels to be made by more competent experts.

Not the least interesting feature of note among the elaborate ritual observed is the long antiphonal Marriage Song translated at the end of this chapter, which is full of quaint conceits and inspired with a rude, but none the less genuine, poetic instinct.

In the case of a well-to-do and important man the ceremonies usually last three or four days, and the following description is typical of the full rite, there being, naturally, local variants and omissions, especially in the case of less well-to-do people. The mother of the bride sends her son-in-law two pots of beer to show that the preparations are complete, but the carriers take good care to finish the beer themselves *en route*, arriving before the bridegroom with the calabashes filled with water. Though he, as in duty bound, supplies them with food, they return again to the mother-in-law complaining of their hunger and the short commons received. However, as soon as fresh *provant* is set before them, the bride is shut up in her hut and must not appear again until the next day.

Meanwhile, the bridegroom goes a-begging in the neighbouring villages for the beads and other presents which he must disburse in order to conciliate the bride's family. They, however, have set a strict watch over all entrances that lead to that quarter of the village where the young girl is lodged, since, if the bridegroom can elude their vigilance and enter the bride's hut unseen, he is not required to pay any further dowry. Towards evening the bridegroom appears at the outside of the girl's quarter, followed in silence by a crowd of his own people. All are challenged by the bride's relatives to pay their footing ; after much haggling, on payment of a few beads they are permitted to occupy the central open hut of the quarter. Later on, fire, pipes, mats, and finally huts for the night are doled out and assigned to them, but for each of these luxuries some trifling payment must be made.

The bridegroom, meantime, has to wait outside in the cold ; he asks for a fire, which is given to him on payment of ten arrows. The bride's relatives, however, soon extinguish his fire with pots of water, so that he has humbly to ask for more embers, which are granted after further payment. A messenger from the parents then formally demands from the bridegroom the price of entry to their quarter, and returns with some arrows and beads which are rejected as insufficient ; but, having finally exacted enough from the eager suitor, he conducts him to a hut apart from his followers, where he passes the night.

The second day the suitor may not break his fast, but both he and the bride are anointed with oil mingled with the customary red camwood dye. Two little boys are likewise dressed up and anointed with the same red dye to act as pages (*bashindisi*) for the pair. The bridegroom comes forth adorned with a head-dress of plumes, carrying in his hand the ceremonial flyswitch of a zebra's tail. The whole party then perform the wedding-dance (*ntawila*) together. The bridegroom's friends dance up to the bride's hut singing, ' Come out, little mother, cook us porridge ; don't be niggardly ! ' while the womenfolk taunt the bridegroom, affirming that it will be a poor look out for their ' Bwadya ' with such an idle husband. The Sibwinga bridegroom, accompanied by his page, holds his spear of office, and whirls round in an extravagant dance, flicking the crowd with the zebra's tail. The women of his clan form up, carrying calabashes full of the various indigenous grains, and, shaking them in harmony with their own sinuous movements, finally empty the calabashes over the bridegroom's head.

Although these dances are kept up all the morning of the second day, the bride must still remain invisible in her hut. At length, however, she appears, standing between the doorposts of the hut, hiding her face, and holding a spear with the point reversed. The bridegroom shouts a greeting, and, levelling his spear (the point of which is carefully protected by a maize-cob), rushes at the girl, who escapes into the hut, hastily barricading the door. He storms at it ineffectively, but is not allowed entrance, and finally gives it up and rejoins his comrades.

The third day the band of followers is drawn up as before, but this time some friends carry the bridegroom on their shoulders, others bringing his mat and a stool.

On this occasion the wife sits on the stool, the husband being supported on her knees. The attendants shave his head with his spear, carefully brushing off the curls with a zebra's tail into a little heap, which is then collected and hidden away. This operation is repeated four times, while the bystanders resume their dances and singing. Four times, likewise, the bridegroom stands up and, turning towards the bride, who has also arisen, presses firmly with his foot upon her extended toes. He then takes a small stick from the hands of his mother-in-law and gently touches the girl with it, which custom, say the natives, is tantamount to proclaiming to all and sundry that she is henceforth his wife, and that he has full authority over her.

The people then proceed to the mother-in-law's hut. As the husband comes up, his mother-in-law takes off his head-dress and stretches out a mat for him, where the pair take up the same position as before.

The father-in-law then makes a solemn speech to the young couple, and, at the end, repeats the ceremony of giving an arrow to the husband with the same formula of vengeance to be exacted for misconduct. This arrow is carefully kept and returned by the bridegroom in case of divorce. The mother-in-law cooks porridge for the pair, throwing out a little with her stirring-spoon to the bystanders.

This concludes the ceremony, and both families, now united by marriage, forthwith set to work to demolish the numerous pots of beer collected for the marriage feast. And the proceedings terminate in a general carouse.

On the fourth day, albeit the marriage has been consummated, the young wife may not speak to her husband until he has tendered the customary offering of beads to induce her to break her silence (*kushikula*). Nor does the girl relent—especially if very young or of good family—until a heavy toll of beads has been paid.

We can but briefly touch upon the puzzling problems of polygamy and the complex quarrels, the jarring jealousies which are its inevitable outcome. Though there was, and still is, a superfluity of women among the Awemba, owing to the practice of sparing them in warfare, while destroying the males, yet it cannot be said that our Central African woman favours polygamy, as is asserted of her South African sister. For the Wemba woman polygamy may be truly described as serving as the battlefield of her status.

We must first get a clear idea of the feminine factors involved in such conflicts, and briefly describe the classes of wives commonly found in a polygamist household. This will, incidentally, illustrate other hitherto neglected forms of wedlock.

First in pride of place comes the ceremonial wife, or *nabwinga*, for whom the *bwinga* rites were solemnised. The *nabwinga* was the head wife and lorded it over the others, and, even though the inferior wives possessed separate huts, often, in outlying villages, she would maintain her mastery over all. The *chisungu*-made wife had, among the Awemba, the same prestige in relation to the inferior wives as the *nabwinga*, so we may class them together.

Next in rank came the dowry-acquired woman, who,

for want of a better term, we may call the ' commercial '
as opposed to the ' ceremonial ' wife, since she was
acquired with the minimum of ceremonial, passing into
the possession of her husband upon his paying the *mpango*,
or dowry. A polygamist who was already mated to a
nabwinga would approach one of his poorer neighbours
blessed with marriageable daughters with a suitable
dowry. If the woman had been already initiated, he had
to contribute some extra present to pay for these rites,
in which he had not taken part. The old women would
then carry the girl to his hut, and the marriage be
summated without further ceremony. Occasionally, however, the following short ritual was observed : A cock
and a hen were killed early the next morning, cooked
with a mess of porridge and beans, and partaken of by
the pair, who sat outside the house on a mat. A portion
of this food was then taken to be eaten by the parents.

The position of the commercially acquired wife was,
theoretically, somewhat equivocal. She was below the
nabwinga, yet, being a free woman, far above the
slave-wife. Her marriage was easily broken as compared
with that of the *nabwinga*, which had been riveted by
the sanction of ritual.

In the everlasting divorce cases arising out of this
' dowry marriage,' the parents always attempt to vindicate
their right to take away their daughter on restoration of
the original dowry, even after several years have elapsed.
They stoutly uphold the theory that their daughter is a
temporary loan, recoverable at will. Nor will they ever
admit that the acceptance of the dowry was, in any sense,
an act of barter, or that their power over their daughter
was thus transferred to the husband. The actual bride-
price they prefer to regard as a survival of traditional
gifts by way of a *douceur*, and not in the light of a business transaction.[1] Parents, however, who accept a large

---

[1] Indeed, among some tribes the *mpango* or dowry was more of the nature
of a marriage settlement placed with the parents of the girl as trustees
for the pair ; for instance, among the Winamwanga, when the dowry cow
calves, the son-in-law, if he behaves himself, recovers the young stock.

dowry are considered to have sold their daughters, and to have reduced them almost to the status of a slave. Hence we frequently find fathers refusing a substantial *mpango* and surrendering their daughters to poorer, but more complaisant, suitors, as against whom they reserve the right of recalling their daughters and revoking the contract. This non-committal caution of the parents, and the resultant elasticity of these contracts, renders this ' dowry-marriage,' from the legal standpoint, equivalent to ' mere concubinage, terminable at will.'

However equivocal her position might be, the Wemba commercial wife—especially if young and mated to an uxorious husband—would make stout resistance to the tyranny or ill-treatment of the head wife. The usual menial domestic duties imposed by the *nabwinga*, her superior, she would take as a matter of course, but if the husband, presuming upon the heavy dowry paid for her, began to treat her as a slave, she would at once escape, with the connivance of her parents. Or, to vindicate her independence, and to gain a temporary triumph, a Wemba woman would straightway leave her husband's house, and marry a lesser man in pique. Many a Wemba woman would thus sacrifice all to her pride, emerging from a course of successive husbands to find herself older, stripped of her reputation, and ultimately relegated to that slave-class which she had, all along, so strenuously striven to avoid.

Last in rank came the slave-wife. She was, usually, bought from the chief, and was considered as a mere chattel, to be sold with her children, if necessary, at the option of her master. A chief would often reward his warriors by allotting them slave-wives from the numerous captured women of the subject tribes. The Arab influence, which was strong at Chitimukulu's capital, undoubtedly fostered this slave-wife traffic, and hundreds of women were bartered and exchanged amongst the Awemba, the remainder being taken in gangs to the coast, where a great number are to this day.

Since the advent of the Administration the position of

the slave-wife has, naturally, improved. She knows that domestic slavery is not recognised, and that she can appeal to the *boma* against ill-treatment from the other wives. By thus boldly asserting her freedom she again enters into competition and strife with her fellow-wives, and this adds to the problems of the unfortunate husband.

To any one who has listened to countless cases arising out of the quarrels and jealousies of the polygamistic state, the foregoing description will appear by no means over-drawn. But, among the Wiwa and Winamwanga, polygamy, though not so prevalent, is acquiesced in by the women in comparative peace, when judged by the standard of the Awemba and the Wabisa. Yet the general attitude of the Plateau woman is adverse to polygamy.

Though, owing to the preponderance of women, polygamy was common among the tribes lying west of the Chambeshi, monogamy was the usual lot of those to the eastern half of the sphere indicated upon the map. The ordinary Wiwa or Winamwanga youth had to be content with one wife, and, after paying a small dowry, but doing many years of garden work, he would make her his *nabwinga*. For the native woman, the monogamous state is eminently satis-factory. It is a commonplace of missionary literature, and of the earlier books dealing with Central Africa, to comment upon the downtrodden state of the 'poor native woman.' This may have been true in the old time, when slaves abounded, but nowadays it is a mere myth, and deserves to be exploded, as giving a false impression. One may safely assert that the native woman is subjected to less ill-treatment and hardship than many a working-man's wife in England. The terrible economic pressure which forces so many married white women into occupations and constant toil too great for them to bear is absent among the natives. The physique of the average native woman is amply strong to cope with her usual domestic duties, which are easily performed, and give plenty of leisure. Again, the native woman has many safeguards against possible ill-treatment by her husband. Divorce is an easy matter, and her parents are only too ready to take her

back with open arms. While, if their son-in-law is not
attentive to them, and does not work in their gardens,
they will take the initiative themselves and remove their
daughter. Among the majority of tribes, indeed, it was
imperative for him to move into the parents' village, where
his mother-in-law would be at hand to keep him up to the
mark. The Wemba mother-in-law is always ready to take
up the cudgels on behalf of her daughter—and, indeed, she
possesses, in a sense, the virtue and advantage of im-
mortality, since on the decease of the true mother her sister
succeeds to the title and exacts the same respect from her
son-in-law. The fierceness of the Wemba woman is proverbial. On several occasions one of the writers has been
awakened in the middle of the night by a much-bitten
husband, who has plaintively asked that he may be placed
in gaol until morning, as the only safe place from his wife,
who was pursuing him like an avenging fury.

Among some tribes a woman can even choose her own
husband. Though this is rarely done in practice, yet
undoubtedly the Mambwe and Winamwanga girl can avail
herself of this right of choice, which is called the *mwata
wa kwingilila*, 'the custom of entering the hut.' When a
young girl is greatly enamoured of a youth, she will enter
his hut at dusk, and take from it his bow and arrows.
She breaks one arrow across, and then sits down in front
of the hut, placing the bow and arrows across her knees.
The youth tells the older men of this, and they usually
advise him to marry her. They admonish the girl that
she must be a model wife, as she has chosen her husband,
and never let her desires stray away from him. Her goods
and chattels are removed from her mother's hut, and she
lives with the man of her choice without further ceremony.
Very rarely will the young man refuse the honour done to
him ; but, if he does so, the girl is held as disgraced among
the village women, who taunt her with having offered
herself where she was not wanted, and her father has to
pay a goat to the young man to atone for his daughter's
forwardness.

We may now consider some of the innumerable reasons

which would serve, on occasion, as valid causes for separation and subsequent divorce.

Among the Awemba, when a woman has presented her husband with two or three children, she considers that she has fulfilled her marriage obligations towards him. With his consent, which, as a rule, is not difficult to obtain, she hands over her niece as a substitute (*mpokeleshi*). The niece inherits her aunt's position, and cares for her children, while the aunt retires to the peace of a single life or, very often, finds a new partner.

Again, the redoubtable mother-in-law often removes her daughter unless the husband comes into residence in her village, and, if he relaxes his garden-work for his parents-in-law, she will take away her child on pretence of a short visit, and marry her out of hand to a more energetic suitor.

Incompatibility of temper of either party soon leads to separation and practical divorce by mutual consent before the village elders. Among some tribes the husband cuts off the string of his wife's sandals as a token that she is henceforth free. Even on the wedding night trouble may arise. One of the girl's relatives, usually her aunt, keeps watch outside the hut until the husband throws out the customary firebrand to show that the marriage has been consummated, but, if he makes no sign, the woman, after a long vigil, enters the hut, upbraids him, and removes the girl for good.

Divorce, again, often arises from the barrenness of the wife. If, after the customary period, no child is born, the husband consults with the village medicine-man, who gives him the usual remedies and has recourse to divination to ascertain who has bewitched the wife to render her unfruitful. Cases are frequently brought before the Native Commissioner where an old lover of the woman is accused of retaining part of her clothing and, by bewitching it, causing her to be barren. Women, too, often ask to be set free on the ground that their husbands are sterile or impotent. This claim was, however, often avoided in the olden days, since by custom the husband might ask his brother to

Bernard Turner, phot.

BRIDE AND BRIDESMAID AT A NATIVE WEDDING.

Bernard Turner, phot.

NATIVE WEDDING.

The bride is veiled and the household gods are carried by friends.

visit his wife's hut secretly, so that she might have a child which should bear his name.   But, if this method proved unsuccessful, the woman herself was held to be barren and the husband obtained a divorce.

The jealousy of Wemba women is proverbial, and frequently severs even a long-standing union.   The head wife often, out of pure jealousy, threatens her husband with instant desertion unless he discards an inferior wife ; so that, no matter which alternative he chooses, his decision is followed by separation which, after a few years, operates as divorce.   Repeated adultery also causes divorce, as has been described in Chapter IV.

Among the eastern group of tribes—the Wafungwe, Wiwa, and Walambia—the introduction of cattle into the dowry makes divorce in many ways more difficult to obtain ; and, indeed, among the Wiwa very few cases are brought to court, as the cattle and wives are scarce and must be retained at all costs.

The native system of wife-inheritance often caused many forced divorces.   When a native loses his wife he dispatches a messenger with a present to his father-in-law, who must, later, send back another daughter to fill the dead wife's place.   If the nearest sister is already married, the next unmarried daughter is called out, but if she is too young the father must then provide a slave woman to replace her until she grows up and can inherit her sister.   If no unmarried female relatives of the dead woman are available, a married sister of the deceased must spend one or two nights with the widower ' to take the death from off his body.'   This leads to many divorces, since often a poor relation's wife is forced, not only to perform this ceremony, but also to fill permanently the place of wife to the richer widower.

Although the divorced state is very common, young women rarely remain for long unappropriated.   And widows, unless old women, very seldom remain bereft of a husband for more than a year, when they are inherited by the nearest male relative.   The widower soon consoles himself with the new wife, who must inevitably fall to his lot owing to the foregoing system of inheritance.

The ritual of inheritance is well worthy of note.

The widower carries a pot of beer to the tomb of his wife, placing it at the head of the grave. When the beer is sour, he opens negotiations with his father-in-law for her successor. As soon as his request has been granted he repairs to his wife's grave with a pot of beer, makes a little hole in the soil with his finger, and pours therein a small libation. The bulk of the beer is then disposed of by the villagers, who escort him back to his home. At sunset the new wife is brought, and, at nightfall, they enter the hut and light a fire. Near it a mat is laid down, and a stool placed upon it, on which the woman sits, supporting her husband on her knees as in the *bwinga* ceremony. Dancing begins around them until a relative enters the hut, gathers the embers of the old fire, and scatters them to the winds. A new fire is ceremonially kindled with the firestick, and, amid shouting, dancing, and beer-drinking, the husband and wife re-enter the hut.

It cannot be said that any such strict system of exogamy or endogamy, as exists among some of the native races of Australia, is exemplified in the marriage relationships of the Plateau tribes.

Among the Awemba we find two main principles regulating the laws of marriage affinities. The first is that a man may not marry a woman of his mother's totem ; for instance, an ' Elephant ' man may not marry an ' Elephant ' girl. The Awemba, it is true, are known by both the totems of their father and mother ; but, in marriage, the totem of the father is not considered, that of the mother being the determining factor. Thus, female cousins, who bear the totem of his mother, are taboo to the young suitor. Though the marriage of cousins is of common occurrence, yet we cannot assert that marriages are made within the totem. A man may, for instance, marry the daughter of his maternal uncle, or the children of his paternal aunt, because the totems of their respective mothers are alien to his own, which he derived from the distaff side. The Wemba elders say that even marriages of cousins were prohibited in the olden days, and deprecate the present universal system of cousin marriage. It is, undoubtedly, one of the main reasons which render the Wemba women less prolific than the wives of the Wiwa and other tribes where such close unions are prohibited.

The second principle is that a man may not marry the daughter of his 'potential' mother or father. On his father's decease the uncle inherits, and, owing to the generic system of nomenclature, takes the title of 'father.' The daughters of this paternal uncle are, therefore, always taboo to the prospective suitor, who is called their 'brother.' In the same way, since his aunt on the mother's side, in the event of the latter's death, assumes the title of 'mother,' he cannot marry any of the children of his maternal aunt, who are called his 'sisters.'

We may here contrast the marriage laws of the neighbouring Winamwanga, where descent is reckoned on the father's side, and where the son can inherit in default of a brother. They absolutely prohibit marriage with first cousins on either the father's or the mother's side. Yet the son takes over his father's wives as a matter of course, so in this we may see a form of endogamy. To give a concrete instance : a man, Kafyume, a polygamist, has a male child Kachinga. On his father's death, Kachinga will inherit and live with his father's wives, with the natural exception of his own mother, who is pensioned off. The Awemba express their disgust at a man marrying his father's wives, while the Winamwanga retaliate by asserting that the Awemba are so shameless in wedding their cousins that they would, no doubt, like to espouse their own sisters !

Though other tribes have their own peculiar rules of marriage affinity, yet the above main principles may be taken as fairly typical, and, moreover, it is scarcely within the scope of the present volume to delve into the difficulties or to explore the intricacies of polygamistic inter-marriage.[1]

ADDENDUM

TRANSLATION OF SOME STANZAS OF A TYPICAL WEDDING SONG

(*Note.*—This song was written down in the original and sent with a translation by one of the missionaries of the White Fathers.)

1 O thou Nightjar (Kambasa), preen thy plumes ; the winter is ended and spring begins.

2 The little Mulea has found her husband ; shake thy plumes for joy !

3 Let us, too, dance, though we be strangers, since they have wakened us for the wedding.

4 The huge roan antelope in the thicket hard by hears our song and awakes.

5 The Sibwinga, my bridegroom, is waiting at tne cross-roads to bring me a bracelet.

6 I see his beard : let us escape ! He is like a lion, and will devour me !

7 The form of my betrothed is as supple as the taut bow ; take him not from me, ye passers-by.

8 He is as swift as the *mpombo* and as agile as the gazelle, or like a little zebra gambolling before its mother.

9 The bride is no longer a child ; respect her, therefore.

10 She is like the stem of the nut tree, bending almost to the ground.

11 No longer does the bride weep, for she is stout-hearted.

12 Come, little mother—let us go bathe, and turn ourselves into crocodiles !

13 I do not want to marry another : I love my husband.

14 My betrothed, who could find only an old crone to marry him, is not like his friend.

15 Let not the Sibwinga stumble when carrying his bow, lest ill-luck come upon him.

16 The fish-eagle gnaws his bones in solitude, pining for want of a mate.

17 In our village there are no barren women—saving only my gluttonous aunt, who eats the beans and the stalks as well !

---

[1] Those who desire to gain some acquaintance of the Bantu laws of exogamy are referred to Dr. Frazer's great work on *Totemism and Exogamy*, published by Macmillan in four volumes.

18 In vain does the village sorceress point at me the finger of ill-omen, so that I may bear no children.

19 If the bride has jealous rivals, let us seize them and break their heads against the grindstones, so that they may die of shame and sink beneath the earth.

20 Every day the bride will sweep out the house, and, setting all in order, take victuals from the grain-bins that are full to over-flowing.

21 Young man, prepare thyself—to-morrow thou goest to the fire ! (Referring to the arduous *bwinga* ceremonies.)

This chant is recited alternately by men and women at the wedding of any important man. The men chant it antiphonally with the women.

CHAPTER XII

BIRTH AND DEATH

THE ceremonies at birth and death are so closely associated in the native mind that they can fittingly be dealt with in the same chapter. It is a common theory that the spirit of a dead ancestor will arise from the grave to act as guardian to the babe from the moment of birth. This is strikingly exemplified in the pathetic custom of cutting a hole in the blanket over the dead man's ear in the grave, so that the spirit may respond promptly if called out during the casting of lots at the name-giving, and rise from the tomb to act as the familiar of the living babe.

The Plateau tribes observe an essentially similar ritual at birth, so that the following description, though of the Wemba form, may be taken as fairly typical :—

The fortunate woman who becomes pregnant assumes an air of importance, strutting about with bark-cloths swathed so as to exaggerate her condition. The old women who superintended her initiation ceremonies now assume charge of her, and give her medicines and charms to avert accidents at birth—but on the sole condition that she shall make a full confession of all indiscretions she may have committed. She is subjected to a rigorous cross-examination after her first admissions, since the slightest concealment may impair the efficacy of the remedies given. As a rule the midwives will respect such secrets, and, being, as it were, the repositories of the moral conscience of the village, are held in great awe and esteem by all. If the midwife, however, is not sufficiently paid in food or beer for her services, she will sometimes, at a dance, publicly chant the various indiscretions of an ungrateful patient. Nevertheless, in

spite of this occasional betrayal, the practice of the confessional is in great vogue.

These midwives assist the woman in deliverance, and,
after this has been successfully accomplished, the child is
washed and a little salt is placed in its mouth to make it
take to the breast. The father is then invited to enter ; he
takes the child, and, holding it in his arms, looks searchingly
into the baby features to detect some resemblance to himself. If he is satisfied, he grunts out '*Chisuma!*' ('Tis
good!) and returns the baby to its mother's arms. But if he
has any reason to suspect her fidelity, and sees no point of
likeness, he roughly hands it back to her without a word,
and before nightfall—for a native has no sympathy with
a woman's suffering or weakness after birth—there is
trouble in that household.

If the child is born in the daytime, the proud
father rushes out and tells the neighbours, ' He is
for the axe!' if a man-child, or, 'She is for the mill!'
if a girl.

The women friends of the mother then enter the hut,
and, after the first '*Samalale mukwai!*' of congratulation
upon her safe deliverance, the conversation takes a distinctly
medical turn. The after-birth, if not already disposed of,
is buried deep beneath the hut.

In cases where the child is still-born, the midwives bury
it underneath the hut. Sir Harry Johnston, in his *British
Central Africa*, quotes an old resident here, Mr. J. B. Yule,
to the effect that among the Amambwe, when a child is
prematurely born, it is cut into five pieces (two legs, two
arms, and the trunk), and is then interred under the floor
of the mother's hut. Mambwe old men, however, when
questioned by one of the writers, have indignantly denied
this, and it seems unlikely that it was ever a widespread
custom.

In the event of abortion, the Wemba mother must bury
it herself, since the midwives would absolutely refuse to
handle any such untimely birth which they themselves
had not delivered. The mother, then, removes all traces
outside the village, and buries it deep beneath a *muvanga*

tree. At the foot of the tree she sets a black pot, inverted, and retraces her footsteps towards the village. Where two paths cross she lights a fire, setting thereon a broken potsherd, in which she places a small ball of unleavened dough, called the *mufuba*, which especial medicine she buys from one of her fellow-villagers. This is cooked with water and other *miti*, or remedies, are cast in ; she then dips her hand and rubs the decoction all over her body—the natives say, for purification. This done, she returns to her hut to resume her daily tasks, since no mourning or grief may be shown by her.

When both mother and child die in the birth-pangs, great horror is expressed by all, who assert that she must assuredly have committed adultery with many men to suffer such a fate. She is exhorted, even when *in extremis*, to name the adulterer. Whoever is mentioned by her is called *musoka*, the ' murderer,' and has, later, to pay a heavy fine to the injured husband. The bodies of both mother and child are, in this case, buried at the cross-roads outside the village. When any married woman passes by such a grave in the path, she will say—averting her eyes—' Is it well with you ? ' to conciliate the spirit of the dead woman, which, if not saluted with respect, might cause pain in childbirth.

The name-giving of a child is attended with much cere-mony. The village elders, with the medicine-man, meet together before the hut shortly after the birth of the child, who is then placed outside with its face turned towards the right lintel of the door. The *musunga*—a kind of gruel-pap—is cooked, while the mother sits with her hands resting upon an axe, to proclaim that she has borne a man-child, or, even more proudly, stands upright, leaning upon a hoe, to show that a lucky, dowry-bringing girl baby has appeared. The doctor places by the right foot of the mother the special ointment prepared for the purpose, with which she duly anoints her child, beginning at the right thigh and rubbing the unguent in as far as the neck, then turning the child over and repeating the process on the left side. The baby's first gruel-pap is then given by a

young unmarried girl, who just touches the child's lips
with it.

Young children, it may here be noted, are often employed to
administer drugs, remedies, even the Ordeal Poison, and to
sow the first seeds. Such acts, the natives say, must be performed by chaste and innocent hands, lest a contaminated
touch should destroy the potency of the medicine or of the
seedlings planted. It used to be a very common sight upon
the islands of Lake Bangweolo to watch how a Bisa
woman would solve the problem of her own moral unfit-
ness by carrying her baby-girl to the banana-plot, and
inserting seedlings in the tiny hands for dropping into the
holes already prepared. This practice—at least as regards
seed-planting—would appear to extend far into the Congo,
and is commented upon by the Rev. J. Weeks in his papers
upon the 'Customs of the Lower Congo People' (see *Folklore*, vol. xx. p. 311).

After the baby has been fed with this gruel, the young
girl then gives it back to the father, who hands it to the
mother. The medicine-man, who has been engaged meanwhile in consulting the lots or *ula*, proclaims the name
of the child, and is henceforth himself called the *mboswa*
or, as we should say, the godfather. Unless one of the
spirits of relatives recently dead signifies its approval by
the falling of the lots when called upon by the medicine-
man, the name is taken from the limited list of great
chiefs or chieftainesses, so we find even in the many
villages many little 'Mulengas,' 'Chandas,' 'Mutales,'
and 'Bwadyas,' and the parents are henceforth known
by the name of their child, *e.g.* Sichanda, the father,
Nachanda, the mother, of the baby Chanda.

The child is suckled until he can walk, often, indeed,
up to three years. During all this time the mother is
not supposed to co-habit with her husband, and, in any
case, pregnancy is avoided. The natives say that, if the
husband resumes intercourse with his wife, the child will
die. The old men quote this law of enforced abstention
in justification of polygamy, pointing out that the monogamist, when thus debarred from his wife, would naturally

solicit the wives of his fellow-villagers, and cause great trouble, whereas the polygamist had another wife to fall back upon.   As soon as the children are weaned and are considered old enough to be dressed—approximately, when they are between five and six years old—the little boys are made to sleep in separate huts, and in a different quarter from the little girls, who are, as a rule, placed under the supervision of an old aunt or grandmother.

If the first-born die shortly after birth, the fault is considered to lie with one of the parents, and the following test is imposed: Hunting nets are set, into which small game, such as duiker, are driven. If a male is caught, the father is blamed ; but, if a female, the wife is accused of having caused the child's death.[1]

We may briefly note the superstition found among many tribes throughout Rhodesia, connected with the cutting of teeth.   At the appearance of the first tooth the gums of the infant are bared, and the parents satisfy themselves that the upper teeth have not appeared first. The relatives are also called to the inspection, and, having ascertained that the lower teeth have been cut first, congratulate the mother, saying : ' *Waluka mwav* '— ' You are vindicated ! ' and anoint the mother with the red camwood powder. The unfortunate children who cut their upper teeth first are called *Chinkula*,[2] and are usually handed over to some old crone, in order that she may make away with them by drowning or exposure in the woods.   In the latter case the mother will often rescue her child, and have him conveyed secretly to one of her relatives, who is ignorant of the affair, in an out-lying village. Should the villagers, however, have reason to suspect that the mother had concealed such an ill-omened defect, they would instantly seize the child and drown it. The natives firmly believe that all relatives who allowed such a ' portent ' to survive would themselves perish shortly, root and branch.

---

[1] See page 183.

[2] *Chinkula* ; perhaps the derivation is 'that which may not grow up'— *Chi-i-kula*, from *Kukula*.

Bernard Turner, phot.

BANANA BAND TO SHEW MOURNING.

G. Stokes, phot.

TWINS IN A BASKET. THE TWIN CEREMONY.

Death is not such a 'King of Terrors' to our Central African as Dudley Kidd states he is to the Kafir.

The Plateau native is a thoroughgoing fatalist. Life, moreover, is held very cheap by men who have seen, little more than a decade ago, the frequent Angoni and Wemba raids and their attendant massacres, and the devilish disregard of life in the Arab slave-dealing caravans, of which the late Major Wissmann has given such a graphic picture.

The not infrequent Congolese custom of suicide, again, hardly points to any excessive dread of death. Nor can it be said that there is any marked disinclination to talk about death, and, in fact, many of the Bisa folklore tales are based on the cleverness of a man cheating his creditors or gaining some end by feigning to be dead, and inducing his followers to perform a mock burial. A well-known missionary, in writing of his talks with the Luban people (who were akin to the Awemba), mentions that the old men were much interested in the subject, and finally asked him if he knew the Death Secret! Again, one may often hear Wemba or Bisa relatives of the recently bereaved speculating, without the reticence noted in southern tribes, as to what had 'devoured their friend.' The elaborate ritual of purification after burial is no sign of actual awe, but merely shows that the well-known stage has been attained where 'the manner in which a thing is done has become more important than the thing itself.'

We shall describe the death of a commoner first, as being much simpler than that observed on the death of a chief. Since the ritual at burial of one of the common people is much the same all over the Plateau, we may first describe a Mambwe burial as typical, noting, afterwards, minor divergencies obtaining among other tribes.

When the sick man is at the point of death, his wives and nearest relatives gather about him, the brother often winding his arms around him over the region of the heart, as if to hold the fleeting spirit within the body. But, when the signs of death have fully developed, the eyes and the mouth are closed, and the dead man's knees are

bent up to his chin.   Wailing is immediately raised, and
taken up all over the village by the women.   All the
members of the clan and their friends then gather together,
some to dig the grave, and others to act as escort to the
corpse.   The body is buried usually the same day if there
is light enough, there being no process of embalming for
the common people.   Since the large thickets and groves
are reserved for the chiefs and their relatives, any spot
near the village is chosen for the resting-place of the body
of a commoner, so long as it be not too near to frequented
paths.   The side of an ant-hill is a favourite spot, but
there is no definite cemetery ground.   The body, swathed
in a blanket or common calico for the winding-sheet,
is wrapped in a mat, which is slung, as a rule, from the
' bitter pole ' and carried to the grave.   The pole used
for this purpose is henceforth accursed, and one of the
most solemn oaths is : ' By the cruel pole which took
my father to the grave ! '   When the body is light and
frail, it is, however, simply carried by one or two bearers.
The body is carefully deposited in the grave, which has
a niche hollowed out from one side of the vertical cutting
to receive it.   The head is placed facing the east, and so
inclined that the eyes may look towards the rising sun,
so that, the natives say, ' He may still bask in the rays
of the sun.'   The brother, or nearest male relative, finally
descends into the grave and cuts a hole in the blanket
over the ear of the deceased.   Curious reasons are given
for this custom, which is prevalent among almost all
Plateau tribes.   The Amambwe say that this is done in
order that the spirit may listen readily to appeals addressed
to him by the living, for instance, at the name-giving of a
baby relative, as we have noticed at the beginning of this
chapter, or in invocations for a safe journey, or for the
fertility of the crops.   The Awemba, however, simply say
that the hole is cut ' so that he (the dead man) may hear
when God calls him.'

One of the village elders will then take a handful of flour
and cast it over the corpse, while making a funeral oration,
the gist of which is more or less as follows : ' Thou didst

hold together the rafters of our house—now thou art dead our bonds are loosened. If the death thou hast died came from God, then art thou a spirit even now, and mayest rest in peace. But if witchcraft destroyed thee, return thou and take the sorcerer thyself. If this witchcraft has come from the womenkind, then suffer the female of (bush-buck, wild-pig, or gazelles) to fall into our nets ; but, if from the male side, then vouchsafe to us males. And ye departed spirits of our ancestors be nigh to guide us in our essay. Mayest thou ' (indicating the deceased) ' return as a good spirit, and prove propitious to our cattle and to our crops.'

This speech being over, the friends of the deceased, who have already placed beside the corpse little tokens of their respect, such as bracelets and rings, come forward and throw a handful of earth into the grave. When the earth is finally filled in, two relatives stand on either side of the grave, link their hoes together, and let them fall to the ground with a crash.

The grave-diggers, and those who have actually touched the dead body, then go to the nearest stream to wash. The others slowly return to the village, and are met, usually, where two paths intersect, by the medicine-man, who has prepared the infusion of ground-nuts and water for their cleansing. Each man, as he passes by, dips his hand into the simmering lustral bowl and rubs ground-nut oil all over his body. On returning to the village the mourners reassemble before the dead man's hut.

One of the relatives, after due preparation, enters the hut alone and carefully sweeps the floor, taking especial care to cleanse the spot where the corpse lay. The sweepings are carefully deposited in an earthenware pot, which is carried outside the village, inverted, and then smashed to atoms. The sweeper himself will forthwith bathe alone in the stream, and must, even then, be very careful not to strike or jostle by mischance any of his fellow-villagers, since it is firmly believed that whoever comes into violent contact with him will soon swell up and break out into evil sores.

The mourners, meantime, have dispersed to gather each his faggot of firewood, which is heaped into a little pyre by the medicine-man, outside the dead man's hut, and lighted by him ceremonially with the fire-stick. A fowl is then seized and decapitated by the door-posts, while the formula is repeated : ' If the death of our friend came from inside the house (*e.g.* from the wives) O fowl, enter within ; if not, remain without ! ' If the muscular twitchings and flutterings cause the fowl to enter the hut, it is considered a manifest sign of witchcraft. The fowl is then roasted, and both men and women smear the burnt feathers over their bodies.

Certain tribes, such as the Wawiwa, after the hearth has been whitewashed anew, cast on the first-kindled fire a piece of the root of the *muteta* tree—a knotty wood indigenous in the Lungu country, which fumigates the hut with a faint, incense-like odour.

The next day the mourners hoe a tiny garden near the grave, and sow in it a few grains of the common indigenous seeds. The natives say that they must use their hoes to perform some task for the deceased to show their respect for his memory, before soiling them in the common daily gardening.

The Wemba ceremonies differ little from the above, save that they do not observe such an elaborate system of purification. They content themselves with putting out all the fires in the village immediately after a death is notified. In the villages of the great Wemba chiefs, before the advent of the Administration, when a sick man was *in articulo mortis,* he was carried outside the village. The natives say this had to be done, as, otherwise, the chief would be angry if his village were defiled by death, and to this day, when a death is reported to the Native Commissioner, a fowl or a goat is brought to appease him as the chieftain.

After some days the hunting test is made, and the *Lupupo* ceremony—a kind of wake—is observed.

To go into mourning a man binds round his temples a circlet of bark—for four days if it is an infant, two months

for a grown-up boy, and at least three months or longer
if for his own father. The time of mourning also depends
upon the medicine-man's verdict after the hunting test.
The Winamwanga doctors hold an elaborate post-mortem,
especially over children, dissecting the organs with care,
to find out the cause of death. When the husband loses
his wife he takes no prominent part in the actual funeral
ceremonies, only later, when the question of inheriting
of her sister is brought forward. But, when the husband
dies, it is the wife's duty to mourn him with a wailing dirge :
' Thou hast cast me away, my husband ! I shall never see
thy like again ! '

As has been noted in Chapter II., until the old king
' slept ' and was buried at Mwaruli with the proper
ceremonies, a kind of interregnum was maintained. The
following description is taken from eye-witnesses, one an old
resident at Chitimukulu's village, the other being a villager
of Mwaruli, who lived close to the Sacred Burial Grove :—

At the king's village certain old men were always
selected who were called the *Ifingo*, or Buriers of the Chiefs,
and who must keep aloof from the reigning king during
his lifetime. When these *Ifingo*, whom we call the Masters
of the Ceremonies, heard the wailing, and knew that the
king was dead, they crossed the inner stockade which was
previously forbidden to them. After examining the dead
king's body they seized all his personal attendants and
servants that could be found. Three were straightway
killed, the first slave's lifeless body being put under the
king's head as his pillow, the second slave under his feet
as his footstool, while the third was slain at the gate of the
harem stockade, so that his spirit should act as guardian
and ward off evil spirits and thieves whilst the king slept.
Not unfrequently one of the favourite wives was killed
on the spot, and the court singers and jesters, if not killed
out of hand, were bound up to be reserved for future
sacrifice. The body was then laid out in state in one of
the principal huts, the walls of which were lavishly decorated
with calico, beads, and tusks of ivory. The *Ifingo* rubbed
preservatives into the body, so that it should not fall to

pieces during the customary lengthy waiting for the burial; among the ointments a decoction of *landa* beans was considered very efficacious for drying the corpse. When the nails dropped off, as the body became mummified, it was the duty of the *Ifingo* to collect them, and, finally, to hand over the full tale to the heir. Only the *Ifingo* had access to the hut where the remains were laid out in state. It was a crime, punishable by death, for any one to cross this tabooed ground, and one of the writers had, many years ago, to try a case in which seven men were seriously wounded for crossing the sacred ground in ignorance.

After a considerable time—frequently almost a year—had elapsed, and the millet had begun to ripen, the old men would say that the chief's spirit was preparing to arise and follow his body to Mwaruli, the royal cemetery. The Masters of the Ceremonies thereupon ground fresh millet, made an ointment therefrom, and dusted millet flour over the dried-up corpse; they then wrapped it up in an ox-hide, and slung it on a pole cut from the *muengere* tree. The captives collected by the young warriors in their raids to provide victims for the solemn journey, and such slaves as had been previously reserved by the *Ifingo*, were marshalled together and victims selected the same night.

Before the dawn a procession of the *Ifingo* and the old councillors gathered together in front of the principal gate of the village. Here one of the king's servants, bound as a *lipaki* (human sacrifice), was smitten between the eyes with a sacrificial club and the grim *machila* of the king passed over the quivering body. The cortège passed on, seizing any one found travelling on the path as a sacrifice. At each camping-place the body was carefully guarded all night in a hut. Next day, and again before the dawn, another victim was struck down at the gate of the village where the night had been spent, and Chitimukulu 'leaped over him.'

The next night, at the crossing of the Chambeshi, another attendant was immolated, and the grim burden crossed over him. In striking down the sacrifice the *Ifingo* smote only once with the club between the eyes, no second blow being permitted as a *coup de grâce*. If the victim still breathed, ' Chitimukulu despises him, and does not want him as a slave,' said the *Ifingo*, and passed on, leaving the unfortunate to crawl away to his home, as no one would succour him, or to fall a prey to wild beasts. If, however, the victim managed to sneeze before he was smitten, he escaped.[1]

From the Chambeshi the procession reached Mungu and tarried there, and, on resuming the march, another slave or servant of the old king was killed. The village of Chembe Kambasa was then reached, whence could be faintly seen the plains of Kukula and the distant fringe of Mwaruli Forest. Another unfortunate was sacrificed *en route*, usually on the Kukula Plain. When hard by Mwaruli, the procession was met by the headman, Mwini Mwaruli himself, and his people, who received the body of the dead king from the bearers. The Wakabiro and all the mourners from the capital, save the head wife, and the remaining victims thereupon retraced their footsteps, and Mwini Mwaruli himself assumed control.

On arrival at the Sacred Grove, Mwaruli sacrificed two more slaves and superintended the digging of the grave. The assistants then carefully lowered the body and filled in the grave. A hut was rapidly built over the spot, and some of the dead king's bows and arrows and spears were placed inside, a bed constructed, and the hut fitted up with the usual native furniture. Tusks of ivory were placed leaning against the walls. The attendants had, meantime, killed an ox, and, cutting the hide into strips, bound the rafters with them, sprinkling the blood on the floor.

The head wife was finally dragged into this hut and, the the natives say, dispatched (by strangling) by Mwaruli himself and buried, in cases where she was not instantly killed on the king's death.

This terminated these gruesome rites, and the hut was

---

[1] This curious respect paid to sneezing is a widespread custom; *vide* Prof. Tylor's *Primitive Culture*, vol. i. p. 101, as to Thugs letting captured travellers escape upon hearing a sneeze.

finally closed up and mudded over.   Mwaruli then told the people that ' Chitimukulu had accepted the sacrifices, and would now sleep in peace.'

Two of the king's elder wives, who were called Ba Muka Benye, were left at Mwaruli to attend to the occasional offerings of food and beer made to the spirits of the dead kings.   Whenever Mwaruli dreamed that one of the old kings had appeared to him, he repaired to the neglected one's burial-hut.   He carefully opened the door and pushed inside a lighted pipe of *bhang* at the head of the wooden bed, and, after he had prostrated himself and clapped his hands as if to a living king, he closed up the hut again.   At other times, offerings of beer prepared by the women caretakers and pipes of tobacco were taken to the grave by Mwaruli alone in the same fashion.   Mwaruli was much feared, and his prayers to Leza through the mediation of the ' Great Spirits ' were held to be singularly efficacious ;   his offices, in consequence, were greatly in request in times of drought or hunger.   But he could only bury one king, and no second.   To avoid any such ill omen, and to correct any tendency to longevity on his part, his own villagers, on a hint from the reigning king, would kill him forthwith and designate another village elder, who, subsequent to the approval of the reigning Chitimukulu or Mwamba, would exercise the priestly functions in his stead.

We may conclude with a description of the curious customs at the burial of the pa mount Mambwe chief, who is called the Sokolo.

A deep pit was dug for the grave, in which the body of the chief was placed in a sitting position, his wrists being crossed over his knees.   His wrists and ankles, moreover, were tied tightly together.   The mourners then lowered into the tomb the bodies of a youth and of one of the chief's wives, sacrificed to act as his attendants in the spirit Underworld.   The body of the wife was laid on the rigid breast of the sitting corpse, while that of the youth served to prop up the back of the dead chief.   A hollow bamboo was inserted in the chief's right ear, lengthy enough to project above the surface of the grave.   The mouth of the grave was thereupon roofed with stout poles and mudded over, and a hut was built above. The people believed that, after two days, came a spider through the orifice of the projecting bamboo, a little later a python, and later again a young lion.[1] The older men went to inspect the grave at intervals. When the python appeared it was fed and solemnly warned, before it glided away into the bush, that it must seize game only, and never molest a man. When the lion cub came forth they placed on one side a mixture of flour and water, and on the other a kind of pottage tinged with *nkula*—the red camwood. The young lion was exhorted to lick the flour, to show that it was a good spirit. If, however, it licked the mess of *nkula* instead, it was, manifestly, an evil were-lion, and the old men withdrew in haste and dread, admonishing the evil spirit at a safe distance to beware of molesting them. If, however, the cub licked the flour, it was a good spirit, and was fed regularly. When strong enough to fend for itself, the young lion was taken into the bush and shown the fresh spoor of game, with the strict injunction that, though it was free henceforth to hunt the beasts of the forest, it must abstain from hunting men or women of the tribe.

[1] For the myth of the young lion emerging, cf. Speke's *Journal*, p. 221 (Edinburgh, 1863), relating the death of Rohinda VI., as told by his grandson.

CHAPTER XIII

GAME AND THE CHASE (I)

BY slow degrees, yet none the less surely, North-Eastern Rhodesia is winning the suffrages of big-game hunters, and year by year the number of visitors in search of horns, tusks, and skins increases.   But trophies have to be earned ; the country is, indeed, no lotus land in this respect. Captain Stigand, in *The Game of British East Africa,* states : ' In the countries in which I had shot before (*i.e.* North-Eastern Rhodesia and Nyasaland) practically every animal has to be hunted and tracked with the utmost care before being brought to bag.   In East Africa, on the contrary, the majority of the game wander about in a semi-tame state, and live on the open plains, where all the world can look at them.'

It is, of course, true that even the confirmed ' machila-hunter ' can—and does—obtain a good many head ; but, speaking generally, the country is none too easy-going.

Nevertheless the presence of a native population greatly simplifies matters for the sportsman.   Most natives of Central Africa have been hunters from childhood ; the pursuit of meat is, indeed, one of the essentials of their existence.   Nowadays, with the introduction of (from their point of view) vexatious game laws, devised to prevent the wholesale slaughter of elephant, rhinoceros, eland, hippopotamus, and the larger animals, their ancient privileges have been curtailed.   Their game-pits are forbidden by a humanitarian Administration ; their nets, it is true, remain, but the use of them is confined to the capture of small game.   No wonder, therefore, that they leap gaily enough at any opportunity of accompanying the white man who goes a-hunting, seeing that, in many cases, it is the quarry itself—as representing so many pounds of raw meat—rather than the actual pursuit which appeals to them.

Thus the European finds no difficulty in obtaining men to perform the laborious part ; rather will his energies be directed to preventing half the male population of the village where he is encamped—greybeards and toddlers included—from following on his trail and waking the echoes in hideous glee when the game is viewed. And it would seem to be an unwritten law of the country that, when game is killed, a certain portion of it shall be the perquisite of the gun-bearers and spoorers, but that, when a blank is drawn, the liability of the white man shall be nil.

The game found upon the Tanganyika Plateau is too well known to need detailed description, and, in any case, this is not a treatise upon Natural History. Most of the specimens to be bagged in North-Eastern Rhodesia are to be met with, though more sparsely, in South Africa. Black lechwe alone, perhaps, are not found below the Zambesi. For the rest, eland, roan and sable antelope— —the latter less widely distributed, though plentiful enough in its local habitat—hartebeeste (Lichtenstein's), koodoo, waterbuck of the smaller variety, reedbuck, red lechwe, puku, klipspringer, pombo (the South African duiker), tsessebe, oribi, bushbuck, and katiri (the South African steinbok) comprise practically all the specimens of buck and antelope to be found. A curious furred hartebeeste has also been shot in the vicinity of Katwe. Sitatunga, too, are common enough in certain northern localities, though the nature of the ground—heavy swamps—renders their shooting difficult.

Of the larger game, buffalo are common enough in parts, as are also zebra and rhinoceros. Hippopotamus are to be found in most of the larger rivers, and elephants are fairly widely distributed. Giraffe, unfortunately, miss the Plateau proper—they live across the German border on the north, and again south on the Loangwa river, where they are strictly preserved. On the other hand, vermin, *i.e.*

lions, leopards, cheetahs, hyenas, wild dogs, and crocodiles are far too common to be agreeable.

Among the smaller mammals the following are the principal : Red lynx, civet cat, serval, booted lynx, wild cat, genet (two species, *tigrina* and *rubiginosa*), lemur, bush-baby, tree cony, three or more kinds of mongoose, squirrel, giant swamp rat, several field rats, mice, and voles, six or seven species of rodent moles, otter, ant-bear, porcupine, and two kinds of jackal.

The principal game birds are geese (five or more kinds, including spurwing and knob-nosed), eight or nine kinds of duck, two kinds of guinea-fowl, three or more kinds of francolin, teal, snipe, korhaan, pauww, marabout stork, crested crane, egret, and wood pigeon.

The reptiles of the country do not merit a lengthy description, though there are numerous varieties of snakes, most of which have been captured by the White Fathers at the instance of Bishop Dupont, and their venoms sent to Paris, in order that anti-toxins might be found. The more usual kinds are the python, the black mamba, the puff-adder, and many kinds of grass-snakes, which are, presumably, non-poisonous. There is also a snake called by the natives *ngoshye*, which is usually found in holes in the vicinity of water. This snake is dreaded by the natives more than any other kind ; it is said to be the fiercest of all known reptiles, and is credited with the capacity not only to attack its prey but to stalk it as well. There is also the cockatrice, *inondo* or *itea*, which is said to climb trees, and, hanging by its tail, to strike downwards at men or animals passing beneath it. It is supposed to crow like a cock—and, whether this be true or false, white hunters of repute asseverate that they have heard the crowing of cocks in the bush far from any known village. Probably, however, it is like the *Ndhondhlo* of Zululand —a purely mythical creature.

There are also found the iguana, the chameleon, a large, brightly-coloured tree-lizard, and many varieties of frogs and toads.

Speaking generally, the best season for ordinary buck-shooting is, in North-Eastern Rhodesia, from August to December, although the tendency of the native seems to be to burn the grass later every year. In the old days it was a heinous offence—some say punishable by death—for any person to set fire to grass until the signal had been given by drum in the chief's village. And nowadays, with *mitanda* and *vitemene* scattered throughout the country, and grain-bins in almost every patch of bush, the hunter, European or Native, who sets the grass alight, incurs a considerable risk of being held liable for compensation.

By the beginning of October, however, at latest—and in some districts much earlier—the old grass on the plains has been thoroughly burnt off, and the new shoots are sprouting ; while, in addition, all but the main waterways have run dry. Then it is that the buck, which throughout the rest of the year are dispersed through the bush or in the vicinity of old native gardens, collect in large herds and frequent the grassy plains or *nyika* with clockwork regularity. From dawn until the sun is well above the skyline, and again from four o'clock until dusk, hardly a *nyika* can be visited—with due regard, that is, to the direction of the wind—without several head of roan or reedbuck, hartebeeste, eland, or zebra being found upon it. It is, however, a fact worth noting that, when the moon is growing on to full, the buck do not come out to feed in the plains until much later than usual ; at full moon, indeed, one is lucky to meet them early enough to have light to shoot.

Only average caution and an adherence to the laws of common sense are needed to bring the hunter within reach of his game, even though in this ' *nyika*-shooting ' shots are rarely taken at more than 150 yards distance—usually, indeed, much nearer. And, supposing that meat in large quantities is needed—as it usually is when a *ulendo* of forty or fifty natives, each blessed with an infinite capacity for raw meat, is in question—it is by no means difficult, with careful shooting, to bag say, nine or ten animals with a dozen shots.

For, curiously enough, the mere report of a rifle, or even the sound of the impact of the bullet, does not at first seem to scare the average herd. This is, probably, because they cannot for the moment locate the danger. Most buck—more especially, perhaps, roan, hartebeeste, and puku, will merely stand with heads uplifted in bewilderment, provided they have not caught sight of the hunter, or got his wind, until several of the herd are lying dead. And not until then will they move off—as often as not to stand again a hundred yards farther on. On the other hand, when a herd is in full flight, a bullet pitched discreetly in front of them on their line of progress is often sufficient to bring them to a standstill.

Naturally, however, wholesale slaughter of this description is to be avoided, unless the condition of the larder imperatively demands it. The one unpardonable crime is to leave meat lying ; not, indeed, that such a condition of affairs often occurs, since natives are like vultures, and will collect from miles around upon the slightest rumour of meat going a-begging. Generally the objective of the hunter is a good head, and, although ' records ' are as difficult to obtain in North-Eastern Rhodesia as elsewhere, the very quantity of the ordinary species increases the chance of bagging a good specimen. Bushbuck, koodoo, and good roan are, perhaps, the most difficult specimens to obtain—though, curiously enough, roan is by far the commonest buck of the Plateau, except in the North-West.

Once the game is down, nothing remains but to instruct the *fundi* to cut its throat, to send a runner back to camp for carriers, and to adjourn to the next *nyika*, where the process may be repeated. Except in the case of the very small animals, all meat is, of course, cut up on the ground —for an eland scales close upon 1200 lb., a roan from 500 to 600, a waterbuck 450, a hartebeeste 300, and it is impossible to transport them wholesale to camp except under very exceptional conditions. An excellent method of scaring vultures from the carcase is to lift the head slightly by tying the neck to the hind leg, for instance—and attach a piece of white calico to the horns ; while, if the animal has been shot during the evening, it is always advisable to leave at least one native in charge of each kill, equipped with a fire, to provide against the visitation of lions, leopards, or hyenas.

Now and again, of course, the above simple programme undergoes necessary alterations. It may well chance that an animal has not been struck in exactly the right place —just behind the shoulder or in the neck being the spot generally recognised as the most deadly—in which case, more especially if it be hartebeeste, puku, or eland, a stern chase, which is often a long one, begins. The tenacity of life among buck and antelope is proverbial—perhaps the hardiest of all is the little puku. Puku, with two legs broken and no interior left worth mentioning, have been known to travel over two miles through dense matted growth —a pitiful sight, indeed, and one tending to disgust the hunter to the extent of inducing him to swear off shooting altogether. But, after all, meat is a necessity of life, and even the best of shots cannot be always certain of hitting his quarry in exactly the proper place.

It is in such stern chases that the shooting-boy begins to earn his wages. Anxious and alert, with eyes that must scan both the ground and the surrounding bush simultane- ously, a grass-stalk in hand to point out the spoor—he will follow—perhaps for miles—over country which would be unintelligible to the average European. From the imprint of the hoof he divines the speed of the beast ; from the quantity and position of the blood, the nature of the wound. Rock or swamp, leaf-mould or grass, it is all one to him ; sooner or later the wounded animal will be sighted, probably in dense, close bush, and the end will come at last, though the white man aches in every sinew, and would sell his soul for a long, strong drink.

Many writers, it is true—Lugard and Grogan, for instance —scoff at the shooting-boy ; it is, indeed, fashionable to assert that the wild man of the woods is much over-rated as a huntsman and tracker. And, no doubt, there are to be found so-called *fundis* who know not the tail of an animal from the head, a roan antelope from a hippopotamus, or the muzzle of a rifle from the butt. But, on the other hand, there are men who hunted—perhaps for the chief—long years before white men came to the country—who speared their elephants in dense, matted forests—who have eyes like hawks, and an instinctive knowledge of the workings of the animal brain. Such are the men of whom we write.

For the shooting-boy, be it remembered, has his reputation to maintain. It is his province—and his alone—to clean the guns of the *bwana*, in full view of an admiring village populace. It is he who is responsible—so far, at least, as other natives are concerned—if his master's bag does not equal that of other sportsmen ; he who will, undoubtedly, be blamed if a wounded animal escapes, if the *bwana* loses his way, if any untoward accident befall. Moreover, in the evening, when others are chattering round the fires, it becomes his duty to look to skins and trophies, to prepare the *masks*, to clean heads, to make fly-switches out of freshly lopped tails, and the like. And, for the most part, he is worth his salt.

So much, then, for the programme of an average day's ' *nyika*-shooting.' Now and again wart-hog may come into the bag—curious beasts, that seem almost like a link with the prehistoric ages. Unsuited by nature to the burrowing of holes of their own, they usually appropriate the vacant dwellings of ant-bears, and—no doubt because of the utter disproportion in size of the head to the rest of the body—invariably enter those holes tail-first, with the result that no spoor is ever found leading to a hole, but always away from it. The native method of killing wart-hog has the crowning merit of simplicity. They take station above the hole armed with spears, and stamp violently. It is not long before, annoyed by a shower of falling earth, or, perhaps, frightened by the noise, the lodger rushes forth, to be promptly speared by the expectant hunter.

It is, perhaps, worth noting that big tushes are not often to be found among wart-hog dwelling in rocky ground, whereas in sandy places, where there is little or no friction to contend with, the tushes often attain to considerable size.

The wart-hog undoubtedly suffers considerably from

WART HOG.

J. Stuart Wells, phot.

LION.

Dr. J. B. Davey, phot.

LIONESS.

J. Stuart Wells, phot.

rinderpest. Possibly from this reason he is not so easily
found as buck, antelope, or the common bush-pig. Very
early in the morning one may meet him upon the *nyika* ;
at any time during the day there is a chance of a *rencontre*,
but it is a remote one enough. And yet, very short-
sighted and intensely curious as he is, it is usually easy
enough to get a close shot once he has been viewed,
though it is commonly believed that, owing, perhaps,
to his lack of height and deceptive colouring, the novice
is more likely to miss his first wart-hog than any other
game.

It is sometimes said that the wart-hog, when wounded,
is an ugly customer to tackle. Some sportsmen even
asseverate that he has been known, unwounded, to charge
natives gratuitously, when escape would have been the
simpler policy. But it is more than probable that his
pugnacious attitude has been exaggerated. Like any wild
animal, his first thought is to escape ; when driven into a
corner he will, naturally, show fight, and can certainly
inflict a very nasty wound with an upward rip of his
tushes. But, for that matter, even bush-pig are held
in great respect by natives, who will refuse point-blank
to enter a *musito* where wounded pig have taken refuge.
And the roan, when badly wounded, often proves himself
a most formidable opponent. There exists, to testify,
the well-known case of a hunter of considerable reputation
who, having incautiously approached a wounded roan,
found himself in the unpleasant predicament of having
to dodge round a tree for a quarter of an hour to evade
the attack of the infuriated animal. Indeed, of all the
buck and antelope tribe, perhaps the eland alone is never
known to show fight—which is a merciful dispensation
of Providence when it is remembered that he is, in size
and weight, not much inferior to the average cart-horse,
and that his horns, heavy but sharply pointed, would
inflict a fatal wound with very little power behind them.
Even the little bushbuck—undoubtedly the prettiest of
his family, with his daintily spotted chocolate skin and
his delicate curving horns—is an animal to steer clear

of when wounded, and there are men who go so far as to
state that a wounded bushbuck is quite as dangerous as
a wounded lion.[1]   This is, no doubt, an exaggeration,
although, quite recently, a settler saved himself by
gripping the horns of a bushbuck which was making for
him ; nevertheless, they are savage little brutes, and, were
it not that their skins are very soft and pliable, it is
probable that the natives would leave them severely
alone, since the meat of the bushbuck is, in many tribes,
tabooed for superstitious reasons.   Women will not wrap
their children in the skins, lest they should become
spotted, and many natives will not seat themselves upon
the skin for a similar reason.

Of the really dangerous animals buffalo, when wounded,
are, perhaps, as deadly as any.   Sullen, sulky beasts,
feeding, as they do, at night or in the early morning,
wandering during the heat of the day in almost impenetrable *musitos*, they resent the presence of a human being
immediately, though—unless wounded—they will usually
do their best to escape.   But, once wounded, the buffalo
is a foe to reckon with.   His vindictiveness is very nearly
human ; for no object that can be surmised—except that
of revenge—he will almost invariably turn at a sharp
angle to his track and wait for his pursuer, charging at
short range with incredible energy.   No rifle that was ever
made will suffice to stop or turn him, unless a vital spot
is struck ; and herds that have been frequently disturbed
will often charge *en masse* upon one of their members
being wounded.

For the successful pursuit of buffalo a knowledge of
their habits is indispensable.   Generally speaking, they
leave the *nyika* at sunrise, feeding slowly through the
bush until about ten o'clock—though for perhaps an hour
after the sun is up they may be found standing just
inside the edge of the bush.   About ten they lie down
and sleep until about two, when they once more move
on towards the *nyika*, feeding as they go.   All through

[1] Recently, indeed, in the Fife division, a native was ripped up and killed
by a bushbuck which he had caught in a net.

the night, from sunset, they continue to feed, leaving the open ground once more as the sun begins to rise. It is probable that they water morning and evening, though this, of course, depends upon the time of year ; in the rainy season they will frequently make wallows in the swamps, and lie there deep in the mud all day long. They are very fond of thick *musitos,* and feed upon young bracken to a large extent.

Until about four or five months old the calves are not allowed to travel with the herd, although, a week after birth, they may join them with their mothers for an hour or so during the day. It has been said that the old cows hide them in thickets and feed them at stated times, but this is not fully substantiated. A herd with young calves will usually travel very much more slowly than one consisting entirely of adults. Lions are believed to be particularly fond of the young calves, and it is said that they will follow a herd for days together, subsisting in the interval solely upon the droppings of the herd.

A somewhat noticeable instance of the presence of mind of a native face to face with danger of a very real description occurred recently. A white man, having wounded a buffalo, was charged by it in country which admitted of no escape. At the crucial moment his *fundi* sprang to his side and, reversing the spear which he carried, struck the animal with it violently upon the nose. It may be remarked in parenthesis that, had the native inflicted a flesh wound, neither he nor his master would have lived to tell the tale.

With regard to the rhinoceros, but little of interest is known at present. The only species hitherto found in North-Eastern Rhodesia is the black rhinoceros, Burchell's white rhinoceros being unknown. At certain times these beasts herd like elephants ; one official has stated that he has seen as many as fifty in a single herd, and that the tracks of twenty together are seen with comparative frequency.[1]

It is the habit of the rhinoceros to scatter his dung with

[1] In 1909 a three-horned rhinoceros was shot by Captain Pisiscelli, A.D.C. to H.R.H. the Duchess d'Aosta.

his horn ; the natives say that he is mad, and that he does this in the idiotic belief that the procedure will effectually prevent the hunter from following him.

Ant-bears, though common enough throughout the Plateau, are but rarely met with. The natives call them *nengo*, and are especially fond of their flesh, which is very fat. The animals themselves subsist mainly upon ants, and their method of capturing these is to dig into an ant-heap until the inhabitants, alarmed, commence to scurry to and fro. The ant-bear then inserts its long, thin tongue, and holds it motionless until it is thickly coated with ants, when it is withdrawn and the ants devoured.

As is but natural in a country where lions abound, these animals form the basis of many native superstitions, which it would be wearisome to detail at length. But the super-stition anent the *chisanguka*, or were-lion, is interesting, as having its parallel in most of the primitive systems of folklore. It is implicitly believed that certain lions are not merely animals, but human beings, malevolent and endowed with magical powers, who, for their own evil ends, have assumed the dreaded form of the king of beasts. A native will tell you, confidently, that such-and-such a lion is well known to be So-and-so *sanguka'd*—that is to say, transmogrified. And there is a story, widely believed, of a certain so-called were-lion which, being slain by a boar, was thereupon at once declared to be no *chisanguka*. Again, the lion plays an important part in the fortunes of the Mambwe dynasty, it being a universally accepted fact (as previously stated) that the Sokolo, or Mwenemambwe— the reigning chief of the Amambwe—is, at death, trans-formed into a lion.

Two distinct species of lions are known to the Plateau— the ' white ' lion and the ' black-maned ' lion. As a pendant to this, one may consider the swamp leopard—if, indeed, this is a distinct species. An official who has had experience of these animals gives it as his opinion that the swamp leopard is not a different species, but that leopards who, on account of the flat, swampy country around some parts of Lake Bangweolo, have taken to frequenting the edges of the swamps for the purpose of catching fish become longer and darker in the coat, and, apparently, longer also in the leg. The swamp leopard is said to hunt only in couples. Definite information concerning this animal would probably be of great interest to naturalists.

Considering that the crocodile is the totem of the reigning Wemba dynasty, there is a regrettable paucity of interesting superstition or tradition connected with these reptiles. They are very common in most of the larger rivers of the Plateau. It is said that there are always two crocodiles in every egg that is laid. When the young ones are hatched —that is, if they are lucky enough to escape the fate of providing a meal for their parents—they do not take to the water at once, but live among the reeds until they are old enough to look after themselves. It is a well-enough-known fact that crocodiles usually kill their prey by pulling it under water and floating above it until it is drowned ; they then hide it in a cranny under water until it has putrified, but take it on to dry land to devour it.

It is believed in some parts that there are special crocodiles which are possessed by the spirits of departed chiefs, and will do no injury to human beings. It is also a common superstition that, every year, a crocodile eats a white stone ; when the beast dies the stones can be counted, and the age thus computed. The stones are said to be carefully preserved and taken to the Chitimukulu of the crocodile totem.[1] The gall-stone and the bile-duct (*ndusya*) are kept by witch-doctors as medicinal ingredients. Under certain exceptional circumstances men are, in some parts, believed to turn into crocodiles.

The following notes taken from the *Luena District Note-book*, compiled by G. M. E. Leyer, Native Commissioner, will afford a clear insight into the various methods of trapping game and procuring fish :—

' TRAPS.—Hunting-net (*sumbu*). These are made of bark-rope, with large meshes, and are about six feet high. They are put up

[1] It is a fact that stones are found in the bellies of crocodiles, and also of elephants.

in lengths so as to extend about a mile, and, for choice, arranged so as to be supplemented or flanked by some obstacle like a fence or river. The beaters form a large circle, of which the net is a segment, extending over the ground to be hunted. The game is then beaten up and driven to the net, where it becomes entangled and is quickly dispatched by men concealed in shelters of twigs, etc. Game thus caught includes all the smaller buck, and often the young of the larger antelope.

'GAME-PITS (*buchinga*).—These pits may be open or covered, with or without sharpened stakes at the bottom. They are dug in game-paths, or in gaps in fences. In them are caught all kinds of large and small game, except the full-grown elephant, which is, perhaps, too sagacious. Similar pits for hippopotami, dug along the banks of rivers, are usually fitted with spears instead of stakes.

'SNARE-TRAP (*mupeto*).—The principle of this trap is a rope, or string, forming a running noose. The spring-force is supplied by a young tree or sapling, bent to sufficient tension with a second rope. Any animal stepping into the noose, which is hidden from view, releases the string, and is caught by the leg. These snares, which are often very strongly made, are placed in tracks where the game is likely to pass. Even the largest antelopes are sometimes caught in them. Tiny variations of the same idea are also often made, and baited for small animals, mice, and birds.

'SUSPENDED LOG or WEIGHTED SPEAR (*ikunku*).—A sharpened log, pointed downwards and often provided with a large spear-head, is suspended in the branches of a tree above a path frequented by elephant. In connection with this weight a string is stretched across the path in such a way that the former drops instantly the spring is touched.

'BOX-TRAP (*chimpangu*). — This is used chiefly for leopards, and is built after the mouse-trap pattern. It is made of stout timber in the shape of an oblong box. At one end a goat is placed as bait. When the leopard enters to seize the goat the other end closes automatically by means of a falling log. If well made it is most successful.

'HARPOON (*chiwingu*).—This is, in principle, an ordinary harpoon with a log attached, and is used to kill hippopotami from canoes.'

The use of poison to destroy beasts of prey is unknown. When they did not possess firearms, natives killed elephants simply with their spears. Dogs were sometimes sent forward to annoy the elephant, and while they were thus occupied spears were thrown by men at close quarters.

LEOPARD.

Bernard Turner, phot.

SABLE ANTELOPE.

(Published by kind permission of the B.S.A. Co.)

There is a good deal of superstitious belief in regard to hunting and woodcraft. Some of these have already been referred to. When setting out, the sight of certain animals is a good omen, that of others spells bad luck. But such superstitions are of little practical importance.

' FISHING.—Along the large rivers, and in the vicinity of the great lakes, Tanganyika and Bangweolo, fishing affords perhaps the most important means of subsistence for a considerable number of natives. Native methods of catching fish do not appear to vary from those in use elsewhere. Nets are, of course, the chief implements, both fixed and for dragging. Another favourite method is to build fences (*bwamba*) across running water, leaving gaps in which are placed cone-shaped traps (*miono*) made of reeds, of which the bases are turned up-stream.

' Fish-hooks are used, and also a kind of iron gaff. A very reprehensible, but common, practice, is that of killing off all the fish in a certain stretch of river with fish-poison. This is called *wuwa*, and is of five distinct kinds, all vegetable. Also, though fish may have been killed by this poison, it does not thereby become dangerous or unfit for human consumption.

' The method of using the *wuwa* is as follows : A quantity, say ten to twenty baskets-full, is poured out on to the ground—preferably on ant-heap clay. It is then pounded to flour. Then the ground is raked up with a hoe and mixed with the poison. This is put into the baskets, which are immersed in the river, being stirred and spun round until the contents have dissolved and the baskets are empty. The dead fish shortly begin to rise to the surface and to float down-stream, where they are caught by a fence and gathered in. This poisoning can, fortunately, only be practised in small rivers, and then only when the water is at its lowest, *i.e.* October and November. . . . '

Many of the species of fish collected from Lake Bangweolo by Mr. F. H. Melland, F.Z.S., were entirely new, and have now been classified by Mr. G. A. Boulenger, F.R.S.

On the whole, the attitude of the native to the members of the animal world that teems about him is a quaint one enough : a curious mixture of shrewd hunting-lore and childish superstition. In one breath he will tell you that lions hunt men more frequently in the rainy season because, their skins being wet, the scent is stronger and the difficulty of approaching game consequently greater. This theory, whether true or not, argues keen reasoning powers. But the next instant, you will find him babbling of some weird were-lion which is impervious to spear-thrust or bullet-wound. Equally illogical is he in his respect or contempt for dangerous animals. One day he will refuse to walk along a hoed road in broad daylight without a gun (whether loaded or not is immaterial) ; the next, armed only with a spear, he will drive a lion off a kill with the utmost sang-froid.

Indeed, when far from a white man and compelled to act upon his own initiative, the native is often astonishingly plucky. In almost every case of natives being attacked by lions—say in a village at night—the whole male community will turn out and do their best—often successfully—to rescue the unfortunates, while cases are on record of old women, children, and even badly mutilated men killing savage beasts in defence either of themselves or of members of their family.

In the accepted sense of the word, however, the native is not a " sportsman." His nets and his fences, his poison and his traps, are repugnant to our ideas of fair dealing—though, perhaps, one may except the Waunga, who kill otters by spearing them from canoes. But, after all, he has to live. Meat is not, it is true, essential to his existence, but it is, perhaps, the greatest luxury which life has to offer ; and one cannot blame him if, being out of reach of butchers' shops, he procures that luxury in the simplest and most effective manner that is known to him.

Nothwithstanding that every hunter has his own ideas upon the matter, no review of hunting conditions would be complete without reference to the all-important question of the ' battery ' most suited to local conditions.

For use in ordinary *nyika*-shooting—that is to say, excluding elephant, rhinoceros, buffalo, lion, and leopard—popularity wavers between the ·303 magazine sporting rifle and the 8 mm. Mauser. The former is cheap, serviceable, and has the crowning merit of taking standard ammunition which can always be obtained in the country ; the latter has the advantage of superior penetration, and, a clip being fitted to the cartridges, all five rounds can be loaded into the magazine in one motion.

Elephant hunters again are divided into two schools—those who believe in the head-shot with a small-bore rifle of great penetration such as the ·303, and those who, pinning their faith to the body-shot, prefer heavier bores such as ·600 or ·450. It may be submitted for the decision of experts whether there is not safety in compromise—for the 9 mm. Mauser has been found by many hunters to carry a sufficiently heavy charge for body-shots, while retaining enough penetration for head-shots as well. It is, however, necessary to calculate upon the possibility of an elephant charging, in which case a heavy rifle is, undoubtedly, a comforting weapon. A double ·400 hammerless ejector is favoured by many.[1]

The ·350 cordite rifle may, perhaps, be considered ideal for all African game except rhinoceros and buffalo. The two latter beasts are so often met with in thick bush that a heavy rifle—not less than ·450—is essential in dealing with them. In the case of a sudden charge at close quarters a bullet from a ·450 or ·600 should turn any beast, whereas with a small rifle the bullet must reach the brain or prove useless. In elephant-shooting the conditions are somewhat different, inasmuch as a shot should, under ordinary conditions, be taken at from ten to thirty yards, and it is generally possible to use the greatest deliberation. Under such circumstances the brain will usually be aimed for, and, of course, much more accurate shooting can be made with a small than with a large-bore rifle. With the ideal battery it is probably best to take the first shot with a small-bore rifle at the brain (since the body is often covered with thick bush or grass), and have a trustworthy native at hand with the heavy-bore, to provide for a sudden charge.

Lions, met in the open, can usually be settled with a

[1] In writing the above the authors are greatly indebted to Major V. G. Whitla, who has shot in most parts of the world, including North-Eastern Rhodesia.

·350 or 9 mm.; but for wounded lions, followed into
' thick stuff,' a big-bore should be carried, double-barrelled
if possible. For hippopotami there is no doubt as to the
superior merits of the small-bore, since the shot—unless
the animal is met on land, which is exceedingly rare—is
always at the head, and the greatest accuracy is needed.

In selecting large-bore rifles, it is advisable to choose
one with hammers and rebounding locks, the reason
being that this rifle, being usually in reserve, will probably
be carried up to the last moment by a native. Under
such circumstances hammer rifles are infinitely safer than
hammerless, as the mere rubbing on the bearer's shoulder
or against bush and branches may easily put the safety-
catch to danger, whereas with the hammer rifle it is
necessary to actually cock the hammers. And here it
may be mentioned that one of the everlasting difficulties
of the Plateau hunter is to induce his gun-boy to carry
his rifle in any other position than directly pointing at
the eye of the person immediately behind him. In narrow
bush paths this will be found a drawback. Another
favourite method is to grasp the rifle firmly by the barrel
—with the result that it becomes badly strained and
the sights corroded with perspiration. Those who bring
out rifles—such as the ·303 magazine—with screwed-on
stocks should make sure of having also a long butt-trap
screwdriver, since the dry weather—the proper hunting-
season—causes the wood to warp and the stock to become
loose, with disastrous effects to accurate shooting. In
an emergency the faulty screw can generally be reached
with a spear heated and beaten down.

A double-barrelled 12-bore shot-gun is an indispensable article, as are also, of course, good field-glasses
and a serviceable cartridge-bag. Except when using a
rifle adapted to clips, which can be easily carried in the
breast-pocket of the hunting-shirt, it will be found advisable to have a small leather flap on the belt, carrying
five or ten cartridges fitted in holes and ready for immediate use. Nothing is more annoying—and, on occasions, dangerous—than to find at some critical moment

that the heathen in charge of the spare rounds is some fifty or a hundred yards in rear.

For those hunters whose eyesight is defective, light spectacles will be found more useful than pince-nez, which are perpetually being caught in branches, etc. A hunting eyeglass, attached to the brim of the hat or helmet, might be useful.

The telescopic sight is most useful in shooting black lechwe, ostrich, and sassaby, as it is usually most difficult to approach nearer than 250 or 300 yards. Also, when an animal is standing in the shade, the advantages of such a sight are keenly realised, as it tends to make him stand out distinctly.

With regard to bullets for the ·350, ·303 or 9 mm.— that is to say, the rifles used in ordinary shooting—the best are those with a very little lead and a small cavity in the head, not more than a quarter of an inch in depth. For elephant, hippopotamus, or lion, solids, of course, are used. The correct bullet for buffalo would seem to be a moot point.

On the whole, the following may perhaps be taken as an ideal battery for all kinds of shooting in North-Eastern Rhodesia : (1) Double ·600 cordite hammer ejector, with rebounding locks ; (2) double ·400 cordite hammerless ejector (as a reserve rifle) ; (3) magazine ·303 or ·350, with a telescopic sight ; (4) magazine ·256 Mannlicher ; (5) D.B. 12-bore shot-gun.

For protection after dark a shot - gun loaded with S.S.G. is far more useful than a whole battery of heavy rifles.

The following may be quoted from notes by Mr. C. P. Chesnaye upon the fauna of North - Eastern Rhodesia, embodied in the Reports of the British South Africa Company, 1898–1900 :—

' Lake Tanganyika, the fauna of which is of a distinctly marine type (see *To the Mountains of the Moon*—Moore), is full of fish of great variety. The electric fish, called by the natives kunta, is of the cat-fish variety, pale yellow, with dark blotches ; the electric tissue covers the whole body, and the fish gives a powerful shock when handled.   For the table the fish called by the natives masupa, pamba, mkupa, numoi, can be recommended.   There is an endless variety of others, from the nsembe, resembling whitebait, to the pamba, weighing 80 to 90 lb., and measuring 4 ft. in length. All the lake fish are eaten by the natives, and are greatly prized. The nkupe is as good as a haddock, and the masupa quite equals mackerel.   Sponges are also found. . . . The Medusa fresh-water jelly-fish is, with one exception, supposed to be the only one of this class found in fresh water.   Turtles are also found. . . . The eels of the lake are curious, the nose being split into three pieces.   Another fish, the ndomo, has the nose elongated till it is like an elephant's trunk, with only a small mouth at the tip.

'BIRDS.—In addition to those previously mentioned, the following are found : Heron, flamingo, pelican, eagles, vultures, sparrow-hawks, falcon, owls, parrots, paroquet, three kinds of hornbill, finch, cardinal, weaver, tick-birds, mocking-birds, goat-suckers, night-jars, cormorant, gull (Tanganyika), pigeons, turtle-dove, Turaco quail.

'INSECT PESTS.—Tsetse-fly (*Glossina morsitans* and *palpalis*), mosquitoes, locusts (rare upon the Plateau), the *Pulex penetrans* or jigger, and the Kufu bug are among the most common.'

ORIBI.

WATERBUCK.

(Published by kind permission of the B.S.A. Co.)

CHAPTER XIV

GAME AND THE CHASE (II)

ELEPHANT-HUNTING is, undoubtedly, one of the finest sports in the world; it is also, unfortunately, one of the most expensive, unless good ivory can be obtained to cover the outgoings. And upon the Plateau we are still in the stage when it is regarded more or less as a commercial speculation. Certainly the palmy days of old, when the hunter could bag as many elephants as he pleased, irrespective of sex, have gone, never to return. It is just as well for the present generation, for instances have been known of one European having killed as many as a hundred elephants in a single year.

Elephants are as plentiful as ever they were—indeed, their numbers are, no doubt, increasing; but the big tusker is a thing of the past—or fast becoming so. The recent Government Notice increasing the number to be shot upon a £25 licence from two bulls to four of either sex has, undoubtedly, given a temporary fillip to the sport so far as amateurs are concerned, since the risk of incurring a heavy fine by accidentally shooting a cow—quite an easy mistake for the tyro to make—has now been obviated. But, concurrently, the export duty on ivory has been raised from 9d. to 2s. 6d. per lb., and it is the general opinion of those skilled at the game that conditions are, on the whole, no better than they have been for the past two years.

Tusks, as a rule, run much smaller in North-Eastern Rhodesia than in Uganda or British East Africa, the average for bulls being about 30 lb. per tusk, and for cows about 11 or 12 lb. With ivory at, nominally, 10s. per lb., but actually nearer 6s., local price, the total value of a full-grown bull elephant is something between £20 and

£30. From this must be deducted the cost of travelling and — if not sold locally — the cost of export duty. Travelling is quite a serious item when it is remembered that the hunter may often travel a week or more before striking spoor that is fresh enough to follow, and much longer before he sights an animal really worth shooting. A very big bull may, upon the Plateau, be reckoned at anything over 60 lb. per tusk.

It is difficult to lay down definite rules regarding the habitat of elephant. But certain facts are known. In August, September, and October, when the smaller water-courses are dry and there is no food elsewhere, they are to be found in the vicinity of large rivers, and at these times they drink at all hours of the twenty-four—presumably because this is also the season of wild fruits, especially *masuku* and *mpundu*, of which they are inordinately fond, and which have the effect of engendering great thirst.

Native opinion is to the effect that the large bulls are never—or but rarely—found with the rest of the herd, being generally two or three miles away, though within call, and that such bulls as are found running with the cows are either *tondos* (tuskless animals) or small bulls with insignificant tusks. Some white hunters, however, asseverate that this segregation of the sexes depends upon the time of the year, and that, while in August, September, and October the bulls do not accompany the cows, they usually do so from February to May.

The natives believe that elephant, like cattle, calve once a year, and, in proof of this, allege that cows are not infrequently seen with three or more calves of varying sizes, all small. This argument may, however, with equal logic be taken to prove that the calves mature but slowly, from which it would be reasonable to assume that the period of gestation is also prolonged. It is probable that this period is, in fact, from twenty to twenty-two months, and that cows calve every two and a half years. There would seem to be no definite breeding season.

Another curious fact in connection with the young

calves is—according to native evidence—that they do not suck. The mothers are said to strip bark from trees, masticate carefully until soft and pulpy, then, exuding their milk over it, give the milky mass to the calf. Possibly some white hunters may have witnessed the process!

In the old days, before the white men came to the country, the hunting of elephants was, in practice, restricted to a certain class of *fundis* or skilled hunters. These men —the aristocrats of sport—were held in great esteem by their fellows ; they were banded together into societies— *uwanga wa nzofu*—which had their own language, initiation ceremonies, body-marks, and the like. The tail and one or both tusks of all animals killed belonged to the chief, and it may here be mentioned that the generally accepted theory of 'ground tusks' is hardly in accordance with native custom. The *chimbo* — or left-hand tusk—was held to represent the lordship of the country, and was invariably given to the chief, who would have suffered severely in prestige had he allowed the *fundi* to retain it. In cases where this *chimbo* was exceptionally small, the chief usually kept both tusks, and compensated the *fundi* by presents of calico, wives, etc. It is worthy of remark that, at the burial-ground of Wemba chieftains at Mwaruli, it is always the *chimbo* that is used in the ceremonies for obtaining rain.

Part of the tail—a most valuable article, seeing that high prices were, and still are, paid for a single hair—was usually given to the *fundi*, and if he killed two elephants he usually received one in its entirety as a perquisite—though still ceding the *chimbo* to the chief—while the particularly expert *fundi* with an established reputation would receive various presents, such as salt, calico, blankets, and barkcloth, and was usually, in the course of time, given a village of his own to govern.

The following account of the ceremonies attending the initiation of a postulant for the privileges of the *uwanga* were supplied to one of the writers by two *fundis* of repute, who had, probably, between them, been in at the death of over a hundred elephants :—

The would-be initiate applied to one of the *bachibinda* or elders of the *uwanga* for permission to enter the association of elephant-hunters. He was then sent out into the forest with an ' old hand ' and told to fire at some small buck or other animal which was pointed out to him. It must be remembered that, in those times, guns were supplied in plenty by Arab traders, and most of the elephant-hunters possessed one at least.

If successful, the novice was informed that his application was granted. Next morning, at dawn, he appeared before the initiates, bringing with him four *dotis* (16 yards) of calico and a hoe—or a goat—which was handed to the principal *chibinda*.

The actual ceremony of initiation—which consisted of tattooing—took place on the outskirts of the village. Only initiated men were present. One *fundi* was detailed to make the necessary incisions, which was done with a native razor. The ' medicine ' used was concocted of the following ingredients : the *nkolomino* (Adam's apple ?) of a lion ; small bones of the *inondo* and *ngoshye* snakes ; certain portions of the *ingufwilila*, a kind of snake, ' larger than the python,' which was said to be found in German territory, which were mixed—bones, blood, and all—into a paste worked up with honey (and of which mixture a piece the size of a matchbox was said to be worth one large bull tusk !) ; a small piece of the *munganunshi* and *mulama* trees ; the *nsomo* or nerve of the tusk ; skin from the ribs, the forehead, and the tail of the elephant ; and scrapings of the elephant's toe-nails. These ingredients were pounded up, dried in the sun, burned or charred, and then cut into little pieces, which were then powdered and rubbed into the incisions, with the effect of raising small oval cicatrices.

On the day of initiation the novice received five marks below the second joint of the right thumb, one on the right shoulder, and one just above the right eye—that is to say, upon the hand, shoulder, and eye which he would there-after use in shooting. Subsequently, for the first elephant he killed he would receive seven more such marks higher up the right forearm. When the right forearm was completely covered, the marks would be continued on the left forearm.   Evidently, however, the exact number of marks varied, since as many as fifteen were sometimes given for a single kill, and it would seem that, after a certain number of elephants had been killed, the expert became entitled to finish tattooing his arm with as many marks as he might think fit.

When a man had killed two or three buffalo, he was admitted to the *uwanga*.   A rhinoceros equalled an elephant, but a hippopotamus was evidently regarded as very tame game, and a good many had to be killed to qualify for admission.

The effect of the *uwanga* medicine seems to have been considered as rendering the hunter invisible to his quarry. Lions, probably for superstitious reasons, were not included in the *uwanga*, but a special medicine could be obtained which would ' hold up ' an attacking lion until the hunter had time to shoot.

The *mulamba*, or special doctor, whose province it was to make the incision, was paid large prices for his good offices.

After the initiation the *fundis* returned to the village, where beer was drunk, a white cock killed and partaken of by the *bachibinda*, and the women and children joined in dancing and singing until a late hour.

Well-defined ceremonies undoubtedly attended the cutting-up of an elephant—but they are not practised nowadays in their entirety, and seem to have varied in different districts, so that it is difficult to vouch for the accuracy of the following :—

In some districts a torch of grass was passed around the body of the dead animal, under the legs which were upper-most when the beast was down, and finally the elephant was slapped with it upon the forehead.   At this stage the song ' *Chonde chalima* ' was sung, and continued for some time after the ceremony, while one of the hunters stood upon the carcase and the people danced round about it.   The skin was then cut, a beginning being usually made at the neck.

The next undertaking was the cutting-up of the tusks.

First the head was severed and stood on end, with the tusks pointing upwards, supports of branches being made in the case of very large animals. The skin and meat between the tusks was then cut away, and afterwards the osseous matter was removed with an axe. The tusk was then drawn by its point—or sometimes carried—to a fire which had previously been lighted, and was allowed to remain upon it for a few moments until it could be scraped clean and the *nsomo* or nerve easily drawn out with the point of a knife. Leaves were chewed and spat out upon the tusks as they were being chopped, and also upon the *nsomo* the moment that it was withdrawn from the tusk. This withdrawal of the nerve was, indeed, the crux of the ceremony, and was always performed out of sight of whosoever might be present at the cutting-up. The general belief was that if an uninitiated man caught sight of it he would become impotent—while, if even a properly initiated *fundi* attempted to cook and eat it, the same fate would befall him, and, in addition, he would be cast out with ignominy from the fellowship of the *uwanga*.

When the meat had been cut into long strips it was placed on stakes (*malambo*) and dried by lighting fires under it. In the evening a dance called the *chiriri* took place, which was attended by the hunters, who carried the tusks under their arms. A modern variant is for the *fundis* to refuse to put down the tusks until the white man, whose first elephant it is, has paid his footing in calico or otherwise. The meat was finally packed in grass or reeds and carried to camp, the appropriate song being ' *Yombwe nama waingila mu chipiya, ingolowola.*' ('The elephant—the one with the thick tusks—has gone into the bush !')

In the old days there were three or four well-known methods of hunting elephant. In one the *simunini* was used, one of the hunters climbing a tree towards which the elephant was driven by the others, when the *simunini* or heavy spear was thrown downwards into the skull as he passed beneath.

Another spear, used in a different fashion, was the *kalongwe*—a weapon about eight feet in length, heavily

weighted near the blade, which was twelve inches in length
and about three inches at its broadest part. The younger
men, armed with spears, first harried the elephant until
he retreated to some little distance for his last stand;
whereupon the more experienced hunters, armed each with
his *kalongwe*, lined up silently at right angles to the expected
path of attack. The infuriated animal was then, by a
flank movement, driven out past the line of *fundis* and
speared by them as he went.

Elephants were, in some districts, killed when crossing
streams, when the natives would surround them in the
water, and stab and hack until the waters ran with blood,
and the poor beasts emerged to die upon the farther bank.
It may be noted that it is the opinion of experts that
elephants can swim, though natives deny this, stating
that their feet are always on the bottom, even though
the very tip of the trunk only may be above water. Many
hunters, however, affirm that they have seen elephant in
waters which, when sounded, proved to be far too deep
to allow of them wading on the bottom; and there is no
doubt that the broadest and deepest rivers offer no bar
to the advance of a herd.

The two native hunters above referred to tell the story
of an elephant which, being caught by the leg by a crocodile
in crossing a river, dragged the brute across and, carefully
selecting a patch of firm ground on the opposite bank,
stamped on its head, crushing it to death. They also state
that they have known elephant to be attacked and killed
by lions on at least two occasions—in one case by four
lions, in the other by two. The elephants in each case
were full-grown bulls, and the trampled condition of the
grass and bush bore witness to their mad rushes to and fro
in their endeavours to escape.

Many superstitions exist as to the possibility of governing
an elephant's movements (though it is noticeable that
genuine *fundis*—who are, nowadays, few and far between—
scoff at such superstitions, and refuse to admit that they
were ever generally accepted). For instance, grass was
knotted at intervals along the edge of a *nyika* to prevent

a herd entering gardens, and if, when following fresh spoor, the herd appeared to be travelling too rapidly, a large white bead was frequently placed near the droppings to hold them up for a while.   There is a story of a particular *fundi* who chanced to annoy his chief, and, as a penalty, was ordered to kill six elephants within two days or suffer death.   His wife, hearing of the sentence, whittled some pegs of wood and, going out into the bush, drove them in at intervals round an area some ten miles in circumference. The next day the *fundi* found his six elephants and slew them without the slightest difficulty.

It is related by a European hunter who has shot many elephant that, on one occasion, the spoor seemed hopelessly and irretrievably lost.   The grass was dense and matted, the *fundis* had lost heart, and the hunter sat himself down to smoke before returning to camp.   Whereupon up came an ancient load-carrier, saying that with a basin and three beads he would undertake to find the lost spoor.   There being no basin available, he was accommodated with a saucer and three white beads.   After shuffling the beads in the saucer for a while, mumbling and mouthing, he shook them out upon the ground, and confidently pointed in a certain direction.   Within an hour the herd was viewed and an elephant killed.

Left alone, the elephant is an amiable animal enough ; one feels, indeed, rather sorry for him, seeing that his only protection lies in his sense of scent and hearing, since he is so short-sighted that he can hardly distinguish a motionless man from a tree at thirty yards.   But once wound him and one must take the consequences, which are apt to be serious, since he weighs anything from three to four tons, and can travel at the rate of a cantering horse.   Nor can any shelter avail the hunter against him ; high, dense bush will be lashed through, tall trees uprooted, and his trunk will search out any nooks and crannies in the ground. Casualties are, comparatively, few and far between, but they occur ; and the man who adopts elephant-hunting as a permanent pastime is practically certain to come to grief sooner or later.   Quite recently a well-known hunter,

who had bagged his 112 elephants, was killed by the
113th; still more recently, in German East Africa, a man
who had wounded an elephant and was following its
spoor came upon what he thought was the same animal
lying dead. He advanced, looked at its tail, and began
to measure its tusks; when, suddenly, the elephant, which
was a different unwounded animal that had been sleeping,
rose to its feet and trampled him to death. In another
and happier case, a hunter crawled out alive from between
the hind legs of an infuriated bull which had pursued him,
and escaped with nothing worse than a severe shaking.
In one case, it is said, when a spear had been driven through
the trunk and the tail cut off, an elephant rose and went
off, and was never seen again. Vaughan Kirby tells a
similar story.

Some natives say that the *tondo*, or tuskless elephant,
can see better than the animal with large tusks, which
serve to distort its vision. Probably the explanation of
this theory is that the *tondo*, having no tusks, can cover
the ground quicker when charging or escaping in thick
bush, and is thus credited with better sight than the
ordinary animal. It may be remarked that, though
Captain (now Sir Frederick) Lugard queries the existence
of *tondos* in Africa, there can be no doubt that they exist;
and, though opposed to the belief of many European
hunters, most natives claim to have seen, and even killed,
tuskless cows in different localities. The *tondo* would
appear to represent a distinct species, seeing that the skull
is formed after a different fashion, the space between
where the roots of the tusks should be being hollow in
tuskers, whereas in *tondos* it is filled with solid, bony
matter. *Tondos* usually keep with a herd — probably
because they cannot strip bark for themselves—and they
undoubtedly rely upon the labour of others for their sustenance. On being asked why, if this were so, the remainder
of the herd did not drive them out, an old native hunter
gravely replied with a cross-query—' Do we drive out
our children who have the misfortune to be born cripples,
and cannot fend for themselves ? '

In the dry season elephants often powder themselves with dust, scraping with their feet until they obtain a very fine powder and then shampooing themselves, so to speak, with their trunks. This is probably to keep off insects ; and, for the same reason, they indulge in mud baths during the rains, which account, no doubt, for the various shades of colour which they present at different times, varying from almost jet black to pinky brown.

The accepted theory that elephants pull down trees with their trunks is probably inaccurate. In the case of small trees it is, no doubt, true ; but, confronted with a large tree, they usually rest their foreheads against it and sway gently backwards and forwards until it goes by the roots. Once down, the tree would appear to lose interest for them ; one would almost say that it had been up-rooted in sheer devilry, though, especially in the case of *tondos* who cannot strip bark, they are said to be fond of the roots of certain trees.

In following elephant—as, indeed, with all game—the distance between the droppings is a good indication of the speed at which the herd is moving. Elephant travelling fast may be said to average seven miles an hour. Before finally holding up they usually scrape the ground, either looking for a soft patch, or to make sure that there are no ants, and the presence of these scraped patches is sure indication that the herd is near. Another explanation of this, and one generally preferred by natives, is that the elephant kicks up the dust—just as the native himself does —to ascertain the direction of the wind ! An elephant invariably chooses sloping ground—preferably the side of an ant-heap—upon which to sleep. When an elephant has been wounded and is down it is a common practice of natives to drive a spear through the trunk close to the end, so that his attention may be distracted should he rise and attempt to charge. In some districts this practice is denied, but a hole was often made in the trunk and a string passed through it and secured to a stump, so that the trunk should not shrink before reaching the chief.

Among themselves elephant have the crowning virtue

BULL ELEPHANT.

CUTTING UP.

of loyalty to wounded comrades, and have often been known to assist a stricken beast by walking beside it and holding it up. In this they differ from most buck and antelopes, which seem to have an unconquerable aversion from a wounded fellow, and which will almost invariably drive it from the herd. One member of a herd of elephants will also draw the attention of others to danger by touching them with its trunk and emitting a kind of blowing noise, while a hunter states that he has seen an elephant take up some grass, upon which he had been sitting a moment or two before, and pass it to his companions, whereupon the whole herd turned off into the bush.

Mr. Young, in one of his reports, has an interesting note about the Mushiri Forest, which may perhaps tally with the widely spread belief that elephants have a special burial-place. It is to the effect that this forest was one of the late Nkula's game reserves, and a favourite retreat for elephants. There is some superstition about the place, and the natives will not go there themselves or take any one through, although they will go all round the actual spot, and afterwards say that they have been through. After the undergrowth has been burned, at the time of the grass fires, native hunters will venture in, but only after special doctoring and ceremonies.

The sport itself is, undoubtedly, one of the most fascinating in the world. There can be no telling whether any given beast will yield his life or claim that of the hunter—and therein, perhaps, lies one of its greatest fascinations. The merest trifles—the variation in a puff of wind, the crackling of a dry twig underfoot—may turn sport to tragedy. It differs, too, from other kinds of dangerous shooting in that the strain is more prolonged. With lion or buffalo the chances are that the actual encounter will occur quickly, and last but a few moments; with elephants, on the other hand, if good tusks are sought, there must often be an hour or more of cautious manœuvring, often within twenty yards of four or five unconscious animals, which may, at any moment, realise their danger and either flee headlong—or charge. This, too, usually as the culmination of a long and tiring day, in the wet season as likely as not, when one has left camp at the merest peep of dawn and followed the tangled spoor through matted, sodden grass, through thicket and thorn, until at last one stumbles forward almost in a dream, without hope of ultimate outcome. The mere spooring is a strain upon both eyes and brain, for the tracks will cross and interweave—now crowded together into a narrow space, when no separate mark will stand out distinct, now branching away in a huge loop that may or may not join the main track farther on. Even the native tracker cannot follow spoor at any pace for more than an hour or so at a time ; and, indeed, when it is all plain sailing, the work will usually be left to comparative amateurs. Then, when there is a block—when four or five ineffectual casts have been made to right and left—the skilled *fundi* will elbow his way through the admiring throng and, with a grunt of contempt, cut out the spoor of the bull and swing away upon it—to fall back again once more when there is no longer danger of its being lost again for the moment.

Very typical, too, is most of the country in which the work must be done. Now and again elephant may be found and killed in the open ; but such chances are rare. For the most part it is forest land, very silent and dark — a primeval setting for the primeval beast — matted bush, dank, grassy undergrowth, or, for a change, a patch of the curious 'white country,' as the natives call it, where silver-barked trees extend for miles, set thick and low, though there is no undergrowth beneath. Then, as the spoor grows fresher, one comes upon the signs— trailing strips of bark, where the sap is not yet dry, fronds of bracken trampled by giant feet and even now curling upwards in the last instinct of life before they become parched and dry for ever.

Here the *fundi* will stop for a moment and examine more attentively than before some twig or crushed leaf —and then point ahead with a smile. It is the time for rope-soled shoes, for the halting of such carriers as are near at hand, for looking to rifle and cartridge-belt, for the last few words of command. Somewhere in the gloom —just ahead, or, it may be, two miles or more distant —great beasts are moving slowly to and fro or standing motionless, save for the rhythmic flapping of their huge ears, the switching of their mighty tails.

On again—carefully but swiftly—for even this is not quite the last stage. That will come when a low, dull rumbling rolls through the forest, varied by the swift, sudden snap of a branch broken and dragged to earth. When that sound comes it is safe to wager that the novice will, for a moment at least, repent bitterly of his temerity.

And then, suddenly, the *fundi* stands on tiptoe and points. Just ahead—so close that it seems one could almost touch it—is a great, grey, motionless shape wedged in beneath the overhanging branches—a very part of the forest. As one's eye becomes accustomed to the sight, another and yet another mass looms up into view—ahead, to right, to left. The hunter is well within the herd, and—especially if it be the wet season—it behoves him to make the best possible use of his time, lest a sudden puff of wind from an unexpected quarter should result in a dangerous scramble for life or, at best, the loss of a day's hard work.

Yet this is, essentially, a case where ' hastening slowly ' is the best policy. Nothing can be seen but the great, grey shapes—' furniture vans,' in the apt words of a well-known hunter who recently met a terrible fate among these very woods. It is impossible to say if they be cows or bulls, and—if the latter—whether the tusks are worth bagging.

There is a small tree close at hand, and the hunter climbs it cautiously to spy out the land. Just so !—the four or five animals within the immediate range of vision prove to be cows, one or two with calves at foot, which were, before, hidden in the thick grass. Rejoicing at a *mulandu* averted, the hunter slides to earth again, and, moving with the utmost caution, a handful of dust kicked off an ant-heap or, better still, a pepper-pot in his hand to test the wind at every second yard, he steals cautiously round the bunch of cows to a solitary animal standing asleep a little farther on.

This, surely, must be a bull! The great arch of his back curves up well above the lower branches of the tall tree near which he is standing—from behind he looks like an enormously stout old gentleman in very baggy trousers. His ears flap and his tail swings lazily — for the rest he might be carved out of stone. Slowly and cautiously the hunter steals round, and, peering through an opening in the bushes, sees what he was looking for— a pair of huge white tusks curving gloriously out on either side of the great trunk.

It is the moment of a lifetime. Round about in the vast forest are Heaven knows how many more similar monsters ; it is difficult to gauge with any accuracy the precise direction in which they will charge when once the shot has awakened them to headlong panic. And yet— that shot must be fired, or the bull will go free.

Quite unconcernedly, in almost his ordinary voice, the *fundi* discusses the merits of the beast in question. Yes, he is a big bull—not but what the *fundi* himself has seen others twice as big. But the *bwana* may as well shoot him. There is a village quite close, whence men will bring flour for meat, and, with that little stream down there, the place will make a good camp. There may, of course, be a bigger animal farther on; but the wind is choppy, and the cows are getting restless. Yes—on the whole it will be as well to shoot.

This affectation of superiority is but a blind—a mere concession to the claims of his dignity. In his heart of hearts the *fundi* longs for that mass of meat to be lying motionless, and cares not a jot for the tusks, every bit as much and as little as do the lesser lights, who are shivering with excitement and imploring the white man to shoot the largest bull that has ever been seen in the forest, while a glance to the rear will detect heads bobbing up at intervals among the bushes—the heads, these, of machila-men who were warned only five minutes before to remain well in rear.

Shoot—yes! that is the obvious duty of the wretched hunter. But at this particular moment it seems more easily said than done. What utter presumption to attempt to stretch so colossal an animal on the ground with a tiny rifle and a bullet no bigger than one's little finger. And what about the mothers, and the calves, and the possibly bigger bulls hidden away in the gloom?

Still, the situation is one which has been voluntarily sought, and must be faced. Suddenly the tremor of nervousness passes : here one is face to face with a big bull elephant, and every precious moment may make the capture of those tusks more difficult. The rifle is ready cocked—that was done some time back. It only remains to slide back the safety and press the trigger.

Then, at the last moment, comes the question—head-shot or body-shot? followed by an agony of indecision worse than all that has gone before. Just for a second both are possible. Odd remarks of casual friends, ' tips ' from sporting manuals, diagrams of the vulnerable points come to sway the mind now hither, now thither—and the valuable moments spin by.

Suddenly the elephant himself solves the problem. With a lazy movement he turns half round, until his head comes well into view. Very slowly the great ears sway; then—is it imagination?—they seem to move more rapidly. That is the spot—just there where the outer edge of the ear falls upon the massive shoulder, or a trifle below. But surely there is something wrong, for the ears are working now, and the great trunk is thrust aloft. Suddenly there comes a puff of wind on the back of the hunter's neck, and in the twinkling of an eye the huge beast has swung round with a wicked bellow and a dangerous light in his tiny eyes and plunged into the forest. Pandemonium reigns where a moment before all was peace—a rush like the wind, the trampling of gigantic feet, which shakes the very trees—and silence. So much for wasted opportunities!

Such misadventures, however, only serve to whet the

appetite. With the next beast the hunter will take no chances and waste no time in idle speculation. A good, steady head-shot at twenty or thirty yards, and there will be a fine bull on the ground, as dead as mutton. And thereafter there will be orgies in that silent forest. Camp must, for obvious reasons, be pitched wherever the elephant falls. From near and far villagers will come like vultures to assist in hacking up the mighty carcase. Scenes of blood and offal, which must be witnessed to be realised, will make the very night hideous : natives, more like madmen than human beings, stripped mother - naked, wading in pools of blood, hacking indiscriminately at their own limbs and those of their fellows in the effort to obtain an ounce more of the precious meat, small boys staggering to and fro with huge baskets of intestines, women trailing strips of meat and sinew, gory ruffians peering out of the very carcase itself or standing tiptoe under the arching ribs to reach some tempting morsel—all these are sights familiar enough to the hardened hunter, but hardly meet to be set down in print. And then, when night comes, the dancing and the singing, the rows and rows of stakes— each marked by a twinkling fire, each holding strips of drying meat—perhaps, in the small hours, the visit of a hyena, or even a lion, to see what man has left him—all these are part and parcel of the biggest and the best sport that the world has still to offer.

APPENDIX TO CHAPTER XIV

Some Notes on the Game Regulations

The following notes are extracted from the Summary of the *Game Laws of North-Eastern Rhodesia*, published by the Administration Press, Fort Jameson :—

'*Import of firearms and ammunition.*—No permit for the introduction of arms or ammunition is now required. Sportsmen proceeding from England *via* Broken Hill should consign their firearms to Broken Hill in North-Western Rhodesia as "in transit to North-Eastern Rhodesia," and may then obtain their release from the Customs officials by signing a Customs Bond. On arrival at the first administrative station in North-Eastern Rhodesia— Serenje or Petauke if the country be entered *via* Broken Hill, Fort Jameson if *via* Blantyre or Tete, Fort Hill if *via* Nyasa and Karonga—Customs dues at the rate of 10 per cent. *ad valorem* must be paid on all arms or ammunition introduced, and any Broken Hill Customs Entry Forms will then be signed by the administrative officials (the Magistrate or Native Commissioner, as the case may be), and should be returned to Broken Hill. The administrative officials will then register each gun, and will grant to the owner a " permit to use " at a cost of ten shillings, no matter what number be introduced.

 ' *Birds or animals strictly protected.*—On account of their utility : Vultures, secretary birds, owls, rhinoceros birds, or beef-eaters. On account of their rarity and threatened extinction : The giraffe ; also the mountain zebra, wild ass, and white-tailed gnu, none of which latter, however, have so far been found in North-Eastern Rhodesia.

 ' *Game reserves.*—An area to the east of Lake Mweru, and an area on the left bank of the Luangwa river, near the Sasare Mine.

 ' The protected animals may not be hunted within any part of North-Eastern Rhodesia under pain of a heavy penalty, nor may any game be hunted within the reserve. Hippopotami are protected on one reach of the Luangwa river.

 ' In special circumstances—of the nature of the collection of specimens for public museums or for scientific purposes—the Administrator will grant a permit to kill a limited number of the protected birds or animals, or to hunt within a reserve. Such licence costs £5.

 ' *Game licences.*—Game which may ordinarily be hunted under licence is divided into two schedules in *The Game Regulations of* 1902, and subsequent amendments have modified the schedules until to-day they are as follows :—

 ' Schedule II.—Game which may be killed under a special licence issued by any official in charge of a district and costing £25 : Elephant (four only), rhinoceros (five only), gnu (blue wildebeeste) (unrestricted), zebra (Burchell's) (six only), eland, and all game which is classed under Schedule III.

 ' Schedule III.—Game which may be killed under an ordinary licence issued by any official in charge of a station and costing £2 : Buffalo, sable and roan antelope, koodoo, hippopotamus (four only), wart-hog, bush-pig, puku,

  lechwe, inyala, the chevrotains, and all other gazelles and
  antelopes except eland and gnu.

'Guinea-fowl and the various kinds of bustard and francolin are
not included under the head of " Game."

'Fish, which are plentiful in some rivers, are protected in so far
that dynamite may not be employed in effecting their capture
except by special leave of the Administrator.

'If a sportsman on entering the territory takes out a £25 licence, it
will not then be necessary for him to take out a licence to carry a
gun as well; but if he has first taken out the gun licence, no refund
will be made.

'*General.*—It is permitted to any licence holder to employ natives
as gun-bearers and to assist in spooring and following game ; but no
employee may himself hunt game unless he is himself also provided
with the necessary licence.

'The Administrator has power to alter the schedules either generally
or in respect to any particular districts. It is therefore advisable,
before taking out a licence, to state where it is intended to hunt,
and to inquire as to any alterations in the schedules.

'The hunting is forbidden of (1) young and immature elephant
(immature meaning one whose tusks do not weigh 11 lb. each);
(2) the female of any animal when accompanying its young.

'Hunting game by means of snares, traps, or pitfalls is generally
forbidden.

'A licence to hunt does not in any way grant the right to hunt on
private property without permission. Only a very small portion
of North-Eastern Rhodesia has, however, been taken up by settlers,
so this restriction does not mean much interference with the sportsman.

'A licence to hunt game is current for twelve months—1st January
to 31st December ; it is not transferable, and it must be produced
to an official of the Administration on demand. Gun permits expire
on the 31st March in each year.

'While the officials of the Administration will grant every facility
to sportsmen in the way of supplying information at their disposal
as to the best shooting-grounds in their districts and other matters,
they cannot undertake to provide carriers or, as a matter of duty,
guides.

'Sportsmen must remember that the presence of tsetse fly
(*Glossina morsitans*) in numerous belts renders the employment of
horses or oxen impossible, and that, as the only alternative to
walking, *machilas* or bicycles are used.

'Taken all round it is probable that North-Eastern Rhodesia offers the cheapest shooting-ground now available to the big-game hunter ; £50 *per mensem* from the date of leaving Blantyre or Broken Hill until his return would probably cover all the expenses (exclusive of the licences) of a comfortable trip.

' A fishing-rod should be included among the impedimenta. In some of the streams tiger-fish offer excellent sport, and spoons, mounted on piano-wire traces, should be at hand for their capture. Other kinds of fish—many excellent for the table—may be lured with meat and various natural baits, using large perch hooks and strong tackle. Fly-fishing has not generally been found successful.

' On completion of a shooting trip, and before a sportsman leaves the territory, he should make, concerning the trophies he desires to take out of the country, a " Declaration of Origin " before a government official in charge of a district. He will then, on application, be granted an " Export Certificate," which will enable him to take his trophies through North-Western Rhodesia, Nyasaland, Portuguese East Africa without obstruction or the payment of further dues. A small stamp duty is charged on the export certificate, but no export duties are levied on game trophies going out of North-Eastern Rhodesia except in the case of ivory, on which a duty is leviable—2s. 6d. per lb. on elephant ivory, 2d. per lb. on rhinoceros horn or hippopotamus teeth. (The duty on otters is 1s. 6d. per skin.)

' At the present time, owing to the precautions taken against the spread of sleeping sickness, all game licences will be endorsed with a condition to the effect that they do not cover those parts of the country known as the " Sleeping Sickness " and " Guard Areas." The portion thus shut off may be roughly described as the country north-west of a line drawn from Abercorn to Mporokoso, thus shutting off the southern shore of Lake Tanganyika, and west of a line drawn from Mporokoso to Mwana Mwapi on the south-eastern corner of the Bangweolo Swamps, thus shutting off Lakes Mweru and Bangweolo.[1] There is not the slightest danger of contracting sleeping sickness in other portions of North-Eastern Rhodesia, which is—especially in the dry season—a very healthy country.

' A recent map of the territory to a scale of 15·78 miles to the inch may be obtained from the London Office of the British South Africa Company, or from the Secretary to the Administration of North-Eastern Rhodesia, on payment of 10s.'

[1] An additional "Sleeping Sickness" area now exists upon the Luangwa river to the south-west.

Wemba Names of Game and of Some Other Animals

Elephant	Nsofu.
„ (single tusk) . . .	Chipembe.
„ (tuskless). . . .	Tondo.
„ (male tusker) . . .	Nkungulu.
„ (female)	Ninansofu.
Rhinoceros	Chipembere.
Hippopotamus	Mfubu.
Buffalo	Mboo.
Sable	Nkanshilie.
Roan	Mperembe.
Waterbuck	Chuswe.
Puku	Nseula, mpolokoso.
Mpala	Mpala.
Reedbuck	Imfwi.
Zebra	Nkoloto, cholwa, chingalika.
Hartebeeste	Nkonshi.
Wildebeeste	Nyumbu.
Koodoo	Ntandala.
Oribi	Nsele or kasele.
Duiker	Mpombo.
Klipspringer	Chibushimabwe.
Sitatunga	Nzobe.
Tsessebe	Ntengu.
Crocodile	Ng'andu.
Lion	Nkalamo.
Leopard	Mbwili.
Hyena	Chimbwi.
„ (spotted)	Chinseketa.
Jackal	Mumbwe.
Hunting dog	Mbulu.
Eland	Nsefu.
Wart-hog	Njiri.
Bush-pig	Kapole.
Porcupine	Innungi.
Serval cat	Mbale.
Felis ocreata Mellandi . .	Pati.
Lemur (galago garnetti) . .	Changa.
„ (small) . . .	Kawundi.
Felis caracal	Lubwabwa.
Civet	Mfungo.
Bushbuck	Chisongo.

Mongoose	.	.	.	.	Lipule.
Honey-badger	.	.	.	.	Chiuli.
Ant-bear	.	.	.	.	Innengo.
Hare	.	.	.	.	Kalulu.
Lechwe	.	.	.	.	Inja.
Sharpe's steinbok	.	.	.	.	Katiri.
Monkey (small)	.	.	.	.	Kolwe-ka-mpenga.
,, (black)	.	.	.	.	Sange.
Baboon	.	.	.	.	Kolwe-wa-mpiri.

CHAPTER XV

THE MISSIONARY AND HIS WORK

RELIGION and politics are, admittedly, dangerous subjects with which to meddle ; and, were it not that some consideration of the missionary question is absolutely essential to the proper understanding of the conditions which govern life upon the Tanganyika Plateau, one would be sorely tempted to avoid the subject altogether. But to do that would be, indeed, to play *Hamlet* without the Prince of Denmark. All that we can do is to state at the outset that we wish to approach the matter in no carping spirit. Our task is in no way to criticise the truth of the beliefs which are disseminated by the various missionary bodies with whom we deal, but to discuss as fairly and impartially as possible, the effect which must of necessity accompany the introduction of any alien religion into a pagan country, and the more obvious results of the various systems upon which those beliefs are disseminated.

In his *Kafir Socialism* Mr. Dudley Kidd writes as follows : ' If the missionary were to raise the question of method, and if he were to admit that there is room for improvement in this direction, he would take a step which would prove the most progressive he has ever taken. At present he is apt to put down (colonial) hostility to mere prejudice, and thereby loses all the stimulus he might receive from level-headed criticism. By admitting some failure the missionary would short-circuit much current opposition. . . . '

The above is perhaps true of the south.

In this country, however, compared with other African states or dependencies, relations between the missions and the Government are so surprisingly cordial that criticism on either side is daily accepted in good part. Just as there are many points upon which the knowledge and experience of the missionary is of inestimable value to the *boma*, so are there many points upon which the *boma* might conceivably offer suggestions to the mission. The two should work hand in hand, and, upon the Tanganyika Plateau, they undoubtedly do.

For many reasons North-Eastern Rhodesia offers exceptional facilities for a fair and unbiased study of the missionary question. Here the missionary is given every chance of carrying out his work to the best advantage. The European population is small and, as a general rule, the laymen are not of pronounced religious views. If he does not receive active sympathy and encouragement from private individuals, the missionary is not, at least, handicapped by bigotry and prejudice as is often the case where the white population is larger and of more varied opinions. Again, the missions in this country have the advantage of the Administration in point of length of residence. And, moreover, the natives themselves have been subject to European influence for so short a time that it is still possible to compare the present state of affairs with that of the earlier days.

The stock complaints against missionary work in Central Africa are so hackneyed as hardly to bear repetition. Briefly, they may be summarised as follows :—

1. That the missionary, anxious for tangible results, devotes too much time to the intellectual training of his people, and pays but scant regard to the moulding of their character.

2. That insufficient time is devoted to instruction in manual labour.

3. That the net result would seem to be a personage who considers himself the equal of the white man, but who is, in truth, little better than a precocious child.

4. That mission teaching tends to create dissension and rupture of family ties among the natives themselves, the average mission-boy being an outcast among his fellows.

5. That the native, always thirsting for instruction, is

apt to regard the mission as a place where secular learning is imparted either free or for a merely nominal sum, and, in consequence, professes a faith which he does not really hold, with the result that the majority of professed conversions are of no real stability.

6. Finally that the native, in assimilating the learning of the white man, develops concurrently failings which were not so apparent in his natural condition, in consequence of which the average European employer has, as he expresses it, ' no use for the mission-boy.'

Let us see whither a fair consideration of this objection will lead us.

1. *Intellectual training.*—Whatever one's own religious views may be it must be conceded that the mere presence of the missionary in a pagan country teaches the native the critical attitude. And, furthermore, since no country can become civilised without the aid of education, the choice must for a time lie between an utterly barbarous people retaining their pristine virtues and vices, and a semi-civilised community which has lost its own faith and has not, as yet, acquired the faith of its conquerors. This, says the missionary, with truth, is merely a transition stage.

Were it possible to eliminate the intellectual progress induced by mission teaching during the last twenty years, the country would be denuded of the educated native, and the general standard of intelligence would be considerably lower than it is.

2. *Industrial training.*—Most missions nowadays realise that faith must go hand in hand with works. In North-Eastern Rhodesia special attention is paid to industrial training, and the work now turned out, be it in the direction of brick-laying, carpentering, joinery, blacksmithy, or the like, would probably surprise many who believe that the mission-bred native can do no more than croon the alphabet and put on a collar inside out. Moreover it must be remembered that, owing to the extremely small European population, the market for skilled work is very limited, and industrial work is an expensive luxury where its proceeds cannot be turned into cash.

3. *The curse of the swollen head.* — Here, in common fairness, it must be said that no one realises the danger more acutely than does the missionary himself, and the fault lies rather in the natural vanity of the native than in the teachings of his preceptor. Precisely the same symptoms become apparent in the young *boma* messenger who is suddenly promoted to the task of 'writing on' men, or checking census papers. There are but few Uriah Heeps among the African races, nor is the sign altogether an unhealthy one, though vastly irritating at times. The following quotation from the advice of the Moravian Mission Council goes to show that the missionaries themselves are alive to the weakness in question : ' When converts from among the heathen are established in grace, we would advise not immediately to use them as assistants in teaching, but to act herein with caution and reference to the general weakness of their minds, and consequent aptness to grow conceited.'

It must be remembered, too—and this is a point which missionaries would do well to emphasise unceasingly, since it is not fully grasped by the ' man in the street '—that many young natives, moved by a zeal for learning, attend school and assume the outward appearance of mission-boys, though they are not regarded as such by the missionaries themselves. Far from being ' converts ' they are often not even ' hearers,' but 'scholars ' pure and simple. Secular instruction can, in most missions, be obtained without any profession of faith whatever. It is often these ' scholars ' who give a mission a name for producing bumptious youngsters.

4. *Family dissensions.* — If this objection can be substantiated it should be considered more as a serious difficulty against which the missionaries themselves have to fight than as a weapon to be used against them. But conditions here are not the same as in India or China, where the danger is recognised as a very real one. In Central Africa the pagan father is rather pleased than otherwise that his son should come into close contact with the white man ; it means, in all probability, that he will eventually

attain to a responsible position carrying high wages in which the family will participate. But with daughters the case is very different, since education ultimately leads to emancipation, and the advocate of Women's Rights is not a *persona grata* in a native village. The following opinion upon this point is valuable as having been furnished by a missionary, Dr. J. Chisholm, of Mwenzo Station, Livingstonia Mission :—

' The " man in the street " among the villagers is ready, usually, to declare that the schools are a good thing, in so far as they enable the boys to get good pay as *capitaos*, store-boys, clerks, etc., but at heart he does not love the change. He sees his sons learning what he does not know, getting proud and " swelled head " and giving up the sacred customs of their fathers. What affects him more, he sees his daughters freely mingling with others in school in a way that arouses his suspicions, he finds them expressing notions and opinions as to their rights to choose their own husbands, and to refuse the polygamous connections which he has long ago arranged for them, and he can see that very soon he will be landed in no end of trouble in pacifying the men to whom he has promised his daughters, and already " eaten " the price paid for them. It is never difficult to find such individuals who can see no good in the work of the missions in their midst.'

5. *Interested conversions.*—It is a sad, but unimpeachable, fact that the average mission-boy looks upon the mission as a place where secular learning can be had for the asking, and upon residence there as a stepping-stone to higher things—not to the higher things of the spiritual, but of the temporal, world—not as leading to spiritual advancement, but to worldly profit. How many mission-teachers of even long standing would be proof against an offer of a Government billet at similar or even less wages ? As C. J. Bennett in the *Southern Workman* says : ' With the negroes, as with the whites, I conceived that too much attention has been paid to the sharpening of the intellect and the fitting for money-making.' There is, indeed, no real ' culture ' in the true sense of harmonious development—and, since in Central Africa there is no economic pressure, the rigid educational standards of the English Board School seem somewhat out of place.

6. *The development of new failings.*—It may be doubted whether this argument against mission-work is of any real value. The teachings of the missionaries make, at least, for common decency, which, in the end, must improve both the physical and the mental standard of the native.

Indeed, upon reflection, it will be seen that the quarrel of the European settler or official is not with the missionary himself nor with the majority of the Christian community, so much as with the bumptious, self-assertive, native teacher. With the best will in the world it is difficult to believe that these are, as a rule, sincere. They know that their ability surpasses that of their fellows ; they regard their work as that of a *capitao*, carrying better wages than fall to the rank and file ; as a class they require distinctive handling from the administrative point of view ; they frequently become embroiled with the wives of other men ; their religion is, at the best, but skin-deep. They get a veneer of moral training, but the substratum is mainly educational. In some cases out-stations in charge of native teachers are situated two or three days from the mission. The inspector criticises the efficiency of their schools, it is true, but they have more serious temptations to combat with than have their fellows, and but little help in doing so, while their very position and the influence which it carries with it is a menace in itself. In all the main essentials there is no real difference between the mission-teacher, the *boma* capitao, and the store-boy. Together these three represent the native aristocracy, holding aloof from the *wa-shenzi*, they are merely interchangeable units of the same class. But whereas the *boma* capitao and the store-boy are usually under strict supervision, the mission teacher, from the very nature of his work, is left for a great proportion of the year to his own devices.

The gospel of such a teacher is to get on in the world— and he will make but few sacrifices for his faith. It is when considering this class of teachers that one is most inclined to agree with Ruskin when he says that, 'Modern education, for the most part, signifies giving people the faculty of thinking wrong on every conceivable subject of importance to them.'

On the other hand, it must be remembered that there are good, earnest teachers as well as bad, and that the white man, in employing natives without strict inquiry into their antecedents, as often as not has only himself to blame should the speculation turn out badly. Many natives— not necessarily teachers, though a good proportion of them are such—are dismissed from missions for misconduct and refusal to submit to discipline. No guarantee is given as to their characters, which are, in such cases, imperfectly formed. They wander about the country seeking situations, and often obtaining them through superficial smartness and ability to read and write. In almost every case they eagerly quote their mission training as a recommendation. Sooner or later they inevitably succumb to temptation, and the white employer promptly blames the mission which produced them.

What the native himself thinks of the missionary is a most difficult matter to decide. Probably he does not give him credit for purely disinterested action ; but he is an adept at the concealment of his thoughts, and when questioned will suit his answers to his company. He realises that there is some subtle difference between the mission and the *boma*, though he may not be prepared to define it. None the less he is shrewd enough to observe that the latter usually has the last word, which naturally tends to handicap the missionary. On the other hand, he knows that the missionary is better able to penetrate into his home life, and that he deals with individuals where the *boma* deals with masses, advises and assists where the *boma*, with the best will in the world, is compelled to administer.

Again, the missionary has the *boma* at hand to protect his interest, and all questions of punishment can be relegated to it, so that he is left at liberty to become popular with his people.

Most probably, however, the native does not worry his head about the why and the wherefore of it all. He sees

F. A. Usher, phot.

TYPE OF MISSION BOY.

Bernard Turner, phot.

WHAT THE NATIVE CAN PRODUCE WITH WHITE SUPERVISION.

that the missionary—with the exception, perhaps, of the White Father—lives quite as comfortably as the official, and with certainly more style than the average trader ; it is only reasonable to suppose that he should assume that it is the missionary's particular way of obtaining a livelihood.

Again, the very nature of the missionary's calling prohibits him from resorting to rough-and-ready methods of redress on offending natives, and it is possible that he loses some measure of prestige in consequence. Muscular Christianity is quite as necessary here as in England ; and though, as a matter of fact, the mission doctor who will travel one hundred miles to visit a serious case is just as much of a sportsman as the heavy-handed settler who bags his lions and his elephants, it is the latter rather than the former who appeals to the native mind.

Self-sacrifice, again, though excellent in its way, is not a virtue which appeals strongly to savage peoples ; and thus the missionary, while foregoing his pleasures, is denied the just reward of approbation by his flock.   In fact, from this point of view the missionary is strangely unfortunate, since those Christian virtues which he possesses are mere drugs in the market of native public opinion.

Again, it is the especial prerogative of the chief—and so of the *boma*—to decide *mulandu*.   The missionary — to his credit be it said—is most scrupulous to avoid embroiling himself in any case whatever, referring all such matters to the proper quarter.   This conceivably tends to diminish his authority in the eyes of the native.

Indeed, taken on the whole, the missionary has a hard task. Public opinion at home is apt, no doubt, to exaggerate the dangers, difficulties, and discomforts which he is called upon to undergo in the exercise of his calling. Many people would, no doubt, be surprised at the degree of comfort which he manages to extract from his surroundings ; but, even when this fact is discounted, there remains the knowledge that he is compelled, from force of circumstances, and with no blame to any one, to carry on disheartening work in a difficult position.

Having thus briefly discussed the missionary question in the abstract, it may be of interest to examine the history of the three societies with whom we have to deal.

I. THE LONDON MISSIONARY SOCIETY.— The first in the field were the London Missionary Society, and for the following notes upon the history and scope of this mission in this sphere the authors are indebted to the kindness of the Rev. Dr. Wareham of Kawimbe Station.

The Society began work in this country in the year 1887, by the opening of a station at Fwambo's village, near the site of the present Kawimbe. This became a centre for the Amambwe people, and here evangelistic, educational, medical, and industrial work have since been carried on.

In 1889 Niamkolo was established as a centre for work among the people on the shore of Lake Tanganyika, and, by means of canoes, boats, and the steamer, *The Good News*, these people were regularly visited.

In 1904 Kambole Station was opened, and from it were worked the populous districts of the Isapa and the Iendwe Valley. These three stations practically reach all the Amambwe and Alungu in British territory.

From time to time the question of commencing work among the Awemba was considered. Mporokoso's village was visited more than once, and finally — in 1900 — a station was opened at Mbereshi, on Lake Morfwe, of which Mporokoso's was constituted a substation under a native teacher. After ten years' existence as an out-station, Mporokoso was occupied in 1908 as a European station, and thus the chain from Tanganyika to Mweru was completed.

While the aim of this mission has been, and is, to preach the gospel, its work has been by no means limited to preaching. Various other branches have been undertaken, of which the most important has been educational. The method employed has been one of gradual expansion, new villages only being occupied when they could be efficiently supplied with teachers for a definite number of weeks in the year. Year by year teachers are being better trained, and the results therefore show steady improvement.

As regards the evangelistic side, it cannot be said that

the people are rushed into Church-membership. All inquirers are enrolled in the ' Hearers' ' class, which they must attend for one or two years. They then apply for admission into the Catechumens' class, in which they must receive at least two years' instruction before their application for Church-membership is considered.

Turning to the medical side we find excellent work being done. There is a dispensary at every station, and at Kawimbe, in addition, a brick hospital, well fitted and furnished, and in charge of a doctor, while there is also a doctor at Mporokoso, where a hospital has just been built. At the dispensaries thousands of attendances are made each year, and the number of patients who enter the hospitals for medical and surgical treatment is steadily increasing.

Industrial work is by no means neglected. While every station possesses a workshop where all that is necessary for housebuilding and plain furniture can be made, there is an industrial centre at Kambole, under skilled supervision. Here boys are apprenticed and trained as carpenters, builders, blacksmiths, plasterers, etc., and the furniture made compares favourably with that turned out from the larger workshops of Nyasaland and Southern Rhodesia. At present, however, the market for furniture is but small.

The outlook for the London Missionary Society's stations would appear to be hopeful enough. The years of foundation-building are over, and with them, it may be hoped, the retirements and deaths which have in the past so hindered the work of the mission. There exists, at least, a native church increasing steadily in numbers, a school system by which children are being taught the Bible and the three R's, and a body of trained workmen ready to meet the small needs of the present and the greater needs of the future. It is hoped, too, to establish shortly a central training-school for teachers, which will take the place of the several teachers' schools carried on at the various stations.[1]

[1] Now an accomplished fact (November 1910).

A weak point in the system, and one admitted by members of the Society, is the dearth of lady missionaries to especially look after the welfare of the women and girls.

II. THE WHITE FATHERS.—The following sketch of the history of this mission was most kindly furnished to the authors by the Very Reverend Monseigneur Dupont, Vicar Apostolic of the Vicariate of Nyasa (translation of Extracts) :—

The first White Fathers arrived at Mambwe in 1891 ; after some tentative missionary endeavours they found that this site was not favourable to their work, and began to dream of penetrating into the Luwemba country, then rigidly closed against Europeans. In June 1895 they reached Panda, and founded the mission of Kayambi, near Mipeni, the capital of King Makasa. Difficulties and even threats of death were not wanting. Chitimukulu himself rose and advanced with an army to attack the missionaries, but, restrained by some inexplicable reason, halted *en route* and put the inhabitants of Musamba's village to death.

In spite of these difficulties the mission of Kayambi prospered rapidly, and, a year after its foundation, possessed a school which already comprised five hundred boarders. In 1897, being desirous of penetrating into the very heart of the country, the missionaries made a bold journey to the village of the redoubtable Mwamba. Here they were, at first, well received ; but after a few days, probably owing to Arab influence, a rising took place, and they were obliged to withdraw. On returning to Kayambi, they found Mgr. Lechaptois with the necessary documents appointing Father Dupont Vicar Apostolic of Nyasa. Mgr. Lechaptois appointed his colleague at Kayambi on the 15th of August 1897.

The missionaries were in the act of projecting a new expedition when three of them died of blackwater in a few weeks, and the school at Kayambi had to be closed for want of a director.

During the early part of 1898 two missionaries travelled in the Mwalule, Muchinga, Wabisa, and Wawemba countries, and Chitimukulu insisted on their establishing themselves near him. They returned to Kayambi, having promised to revisit him.

In September of the same year they again revisited Chitimukulu, and found themselves once more confronted with difficulties. Just at this moment Mwamba's envoys arrived, and implored the missionaries to accompany them to that chief. On the very eve of their departure one missionary died of exhaustion on the Chambezi river, and only two started for Mwamba's capital.

They arrived at the chief's village on the 11th of October. Mwamba was at the time seriously ill, and greeted them with this remarkable proposition : ' You have excellent remedies and can, no doubt, cure me ; if you do, I will give you half my country. On the other hand, if I die, I will give you the whole—and you will look after all my wives, children, and people, so that they may not be killed ! '

The missionaries wishing to establish themselves about twenty miles from the capital, Mwamba objected, saying that it was too far, and that his people would be killed passing to and fro. He went so far as to supply men to build a house for the missionaries two or three miles from the capital.

Mwamba's condition gave no hope of a cure ; he died on the night of the 23rd–24th October. Then arose indescribable panic and disorder, and the whole population gathered round the house of the missionaries. When a chief dies all his people are held responsible for his death ; all the neighbouring chiefs, relatives, and friends must avenge him, by killing large numbers of his people, after which the remainder are distributed. On the day after the death of the chief, bands of pillagers were reported from all directions. The missionaries were lucky enough to stop them all, merely by threats, and not a drop of blood was spilled. The grateful population christened the site of the mission ' Chilubula,' that is, the place where they had escaped death.

The missionaries then hastened to write to the Administration at Zomba inviting them to occupy the country. Some days later Messrs. M'Kinnon and Young arrived. The missionaries were delighted to welcome them, and to see them occupy the country in the name of the British Government. Little by little things quietened down, and the peaceful occupation of the country was completed.

In April 1899 the mission at Chilubula was transferred to the Luombe, where it still stands. Brick houses were built in this year. The brick house at Kayambi had been built the previous year ; these were the two first European buildings in the Luwemba country.

In the same year three missionaries were sent to found the mission of Kilonga, near Mpika.

In 1900 three missionaries made an attempt to enter the Lunda country under Kazembe. Harassed by various difficulties they returned to the Kalungwisi river, and finally, in 1903, quitted this locality and installed themselves upon Chirui Island, where they have an important station for the islands, the Lunga country, and the east coast of Lake Bangweolo.

In 1905 they founded the mission of Ng'umbo on the west of Lake Bangweolo in the Fort Rosebery district. The same year they founded Kapatu in the Mporokoso division, and, at the present moment (July 1910) three missionaries are on their way to found a station at Mushyota's in the Kalungwisi district.

Looked at as a whole, it is impossible to have aught but the greatest respect for these White Fathers. Hardy, simple men, pursuing under the most trying tropical conditions their austere rule, bound by the vows of humility, chastity, and obedience — cheerfully acquiescing, nay, delighting in the prospect of an exile which is in most cases lifelong [1]—one must, indeed, be a carping critic to dissect, be it ever so kindly, the sum total of the good they do. And, indeed, this good is widespread, and of a very vital character. It is true that their scholars do not rise to the intellectual heights attained by those of other

[1] Since this was written arrangements have been made for furlough after ten years in necessary cases.

A DWELLING HOUSE, L.M.S.

Bernard Turner, phot.

F. H. Melland, phot.

KAYAMBI CHURCH (WHITE FATHERS MISSION).

missions; but it must be remembered that they profess to mould character rather than intellect, that they are teaching a foreign language (English), and that they are but poorly equipped with funds for the purchase of school requisites. Their pupils, indeed, are of a simpler type—even as are the missionaries themselves, when compared with the married missionaries of other societies.

There must, according to the rule, be at least three men on each of the mission stations. This is partly because itinerating plays a very important part in their educational system, sections of their spheres being visited month by month—and also, no doubt, because, notwithstanding their indomitable pluck, the severity of their lives often has regrettable effects upon their constitutions. At the Maison Carrée—the training-school in Algiers—they receive a special training for five years, during which time they are taught to deal with Arabs, and are tested as being men of perfect character.

Contrary to the general idea, they belong, not to a regular order, but to the class of secular parish priests. For this reason the vow of poverty is excluded, and each member has his own little income—small enough, but sufficient for his simple tastes. Many of them are keen hunters, and no doubt expend some portion of such private means upon the purchase of rifles and ammunition. The bishop himself, Monseigneur Dupont, is known as a genial and plucky sportsman, and many a story could be told of his adventures in the early days.

Each mission is run upon lines of the strictest economy, and, with the exception of some few staple articles, such as tea, coffee, and sugar, which they procure from Europe, each station produces all its own food-stuffs. On all the older established stations are glorious fruit and vegetable gardens, and there is always an Économe—a kind of overseer or agent—who sees to the domestic side.

As has been said above, there is neither luxury nor extravagance upon these mission stations; but, for all that, the missionaries do not by any means abase themselves to the level of the natives. Indeed, their sense of discipline is very keen, and their pupils and teachers are usually civil, respectful, and willing. The Fathers themselves, whether of high or low birth—and there are men of both classes, from the aristocrat of La Vendée to the simple Breton peasant—are intellectual and well-read, and seem to keep well in touch with European politics and events. At the same time they are simple, open-hearted, and intensely hospitable, and evince a boyish interest in their work which makes them very pleasant companions.

Though perhaps rather apt to neglect their own health, their medical skill is considerable. They have made a complete and thorough study of native ailments and diseases, are acquainted with the properties of most native drugs, and understand the ordinary appliances of the medical profession, having, in most cases, undergone a special course of medicine at the Maison Carrée.

At two of the stations—Kayambi and Chilubula—there are houses of White Sisters—and the influence of these is most important as replacing the wives of married missionaries. Nevertheless, it may be doubted whether the natives themselves quite understand the position—and, in any case, the celibacy of the White Fathers is—to quote the words of Bishop Dupont himself—the ' heel of Achilles ' of their system from the native standpoint.

Undoubtedly the influence of ritual upon the native mind is very great ; it supplies to the native just that element of the mysterious which he feels to be wanting in the more prosaic observances of other missions. And, too, the influence of the confessional is not the least among the weapons with which the White Fathers are armed.

At all the stations the Algerian style of building is adopted ; all the work is picturesque and massive, and the red tiles, made, like everything else, upon the station, lend an air of finished work which is extremely pleasing. The churches, too, are tended with the greatest care, and most carefully painted and decorated—so much so that the whole life of the station is made to revolve around the church, which, at least in the case of the two older established stations, Kayambi and Chilubula, is used solely for purposes of worship, and not also as a school.

III. THE LIVINGSTONIA MISSION.—The following sketch of the Livingstonia Mission—of which Mwenzo Station, near Fife, is the only example in this sphere—has been compiled from notes kindly furnished by Dr. J. A. Chisholm of that station :—

The Livingstonia Mission, commenced in 1875 as the memorial to David Livingstone, raised by the Scottish churches unitedly, confined its work both at the beginning and for many years afterwards to Nyasaland, labouring chiefly among the Angoni and Atonga tribes. Soon, however, it looked across the artificial boundary to Rhodesia, and in the gradual expansion of schools from the established stations, the mission year by year spread farther and farther into Rhodesia, the Central Livingstonia Institution recruiting its apprentices to carpentry, building, agriculture, printing, quarrying, etc., from Rhodesia in no small proportion.

At the end of 1895 it was decided to transfer the station which had been carried on at Mweni Wanda (Fort Hill) to Rhodesia, and a beginning of a new station was made at Mwenzo, near Fife. During the first four or five years little apparent progress was made, partly owing to several changes in the staff, due to resignations and furloughs, and also to the fact that at times no European could be placed at Mwenzo.

When the Administration of North-Eastern Rhodesia, in a praiseworthy desire to help the different missions, drew out suggestions for boundaries, the Livingstonia Mission found allotted to it the whole of the Fife, Chinsali, and Mirongo Divisions, and large parts of Mpika, Lundazi, and Serenje. The Livingstonia Mission has, ever since, attempted to work these districts in accordance with its own policy and methods of mission work.

The Nyasaland stations opened up schools, itinerated by European ministers and doctors, and sent selected pupils to the Central Institution for training as pastors, evangelists, and teachers, or in the different trades.

Mwenzo extended to the south and west in the same way.

The schools are very primitive, are staffed by badly trained teachers in many cases, are often too far away from European supervision, and are poorly furnished with educational necessities. But it is the aim of this mission to teach the people to read as quickly as possible, to be able to write, and do a little arithmetic—excepting for those who are to be teachers nothing more serious seems to be attempted in the way of Higher Education. The teachers, etc., are trained at the best stations and at the Central Institution in Nyasaland—and at the out-schools also one sees some attempts at singing, drill, etc.

The mission [1] has at present (1910) over 250 of such schools in North - Eastern Rhodesia, which means over 15,000 native children under some kind of education. The schoolhouse, road, playground, and cleanly dressed teachers, no doubt, act on the whole as an object-lesson to the natives on the advantages of cleanliness and order, and the intelligence of the rising generation cannot fail to be raised in some measure by what they see, hear, and attempt to learn at these numerous schools.

The personal knowledge of the writers is limited to the work done at the Mwenzo Station. Here a medical missionary is in charge. There are, at present, over 160 schools worked from this station. The whole district is divided into seven divisions, each of which is under a certificated schoolmaster, who is continually on the round of the schools in his division. At the end of each month he returns to the station, and goes through his diary with the missionary, who through him directs the work. The missionary himself also spends several months of the year itinerating in the villages. But even with this organisation of missionary, native schoolmaster, teachers-in-charge, and monitors it would seem that one trained European schoolmaster, at least, should be in charge of these 160 schools, and the training of the native teachers who are to staff them.

[1] These figures include the Serenje Station.

At Mwenzo there are some 300 baptized members and some 500 in the preparatory classes. No natives are baptized without at least two years' preparation, and teaching in special classes is compulsory after baptism also.

In medical work the Livingstonia Mission has a fully qualified doctor on each of its stations, and many of them have specially qualified themselves for tropical work by taking the 'Diploma of Tropical Medicine.' At Mwenzo there is a good hospital, and many serious cases are being treated, while several operations are performed each year. There is a trained nurse who also has charge of a small band of girl-boarders, and works among the women and girls of the villages.

A weak point on this station is that little is done in training the native in manual work—but the different buildings on the station have been put up by natives trained at the Institution, and, indeed, the large majority of natives in the whole district who are capable of building, making furniture, and the like, have been trained in the Livingstonia Mission.

With regard to the treatment of polygamy—perhaps the most important question with which the missionary has to deal—the following may be said to summarise the views of this mission :—

When a monogamist heathen is baptized his previous marriage is recognised. The mission objects to the marriage of a Christian with a heathen—but if, after warning, the Christian remains obdurate, he or she is married on the understanding that the heathen party binds him—or herself —to monogamy. At present polygamists are not admitted as Catechumens. No polygamous man is baptized until he has put away all wives save one, and the wife so retained must be the one first married by him.

This, then, is briefly the position as regards the mission question in North-Eastern Rhodesia at the present day. To the London Missionary Society belongs the honour of being first in the field—in this sphere at least. Ever since 1887, when the station at Fwambo's was opened, there have been missionaries upon the Plateau, and though results may, perhaps, appear disappointing, those who live on the spot and are in touch with the actual conditions of the country can have nothing but admiration for the steadfast manner in which these devoted workers have clung to the task before them—a task Herculean in its magnitude.   Friendly criticism of the ultimate ends need not necessarily spell belittlement of the energy and determination exhibited in their attainment.

None the less one may, perhaps, be forgiven for sur-mising that the most searching test of all is yet to come. Hitherto the converts of the missions have been put to no great strain ; since the religion which they have embraced is, theoretically, the religion of all the Europeans with whom they have hitherto come in contact. When the native finds himself face to face with the doctrines of Islam, when he learns—and the time is surely not far distant when learn it he must—that Christianity is not the only religion in the world outside of his own creed—then, indeed, it will be time enough to say whether this house of Christian belief which so many earnest men have given their lives to erect is builded upon firm rock or shifting sand.

Mohammedanism must come to us as it has already come to the Western states, to German East Africa, and the regions of the North. Once the German railway is an accomplished fact followers of Islam will pour into this country in their thousands ; slowly, no doubt, at first, but later as a great swollen stream gathering impetus as it moves.

That missionaries themselves are not blind to the danger is evidenced by the recent World's Missionary Conference at Edinburgh. On Wednesday, the 15th June, the subject of the Advance of Islam was the dominant topic of the afternoon session. *The Irish Times* of Thursday, 16th June, in reporting the Conference, states :—

'A still more pressing aspect of the situation was urged . . . the advance of Islam, and the urgency of making at once a vigorous effort to stem the advance where it was declaring itself, and to anticipate it where it is at present only threatening. It told of the

renewed activity of the Mohammedan propaganda over a large area.
. . . But the great field is Africa. Two forces are contending for
Africa—Christianity and Mohammedanism. If things continue as
they are now tending, Africa may become a Mohammedan continent. Mohammedanism comes to the African people as a higher
religion than their own, with the dignity of an apparently higher
civilisation and of world power. It is rapidly received by these
eager listeners. Once received it is Christianity's most formidable
enemy. The absorption of native races into Islam is proceeding
rapidly and continuously in practically all parts of the Continent.
Mohammedan traders are finding their way into the remotest parts
of the Continent, and it is well known that every Mohammedan
trader is more or less a Mohammedan missionary. The result of
this penetration of the field by these representatives of Islam will
be that the Christian missionary enterprise will, year by year,
become more difficult. Paganism is doomed. Either Christianity
or Islam will prevail throughout Africa.'

Expert views upon Mohammedanism as a religion for
Africa are of undoubted interest. Dr. Blyden, the great
authority upon West Africa, lauds it to the skies. As the
Koran itself says, religions must be suited to the peoples,
and to the African races Mohammedanism is as fitted as
is the camel to the desert. Hudson, the Attorney-General
of Sierra Leone, says, in the *Journal of the African
Society* :—

' Missionaries should copy the Mohammedan system of grafting
and pruning, and, taking the native worship as a fact, gradually
eliminate inhuman, immoral, and unchristianlike factors — not
knock away the props of the people.'

While, in the same periodical, Mr. Allen Upward, speaking of Northern Nigeria, says :—

' It is unanimously agreed by non-missionary observers that Islam
is the religion which yields the best practical results in this part
of the world.'

On the other hand, Stewart, in his *Dawn in the Dark
Continent*, p. 71, says :—

' The religion that is purest in itself, and most elevating in its
influence, and best fitted to the moral and spiritual necessities of
mankind, and which will most fully and readily adapt itself to the

advancing civilisation of to-day—which Mohammedanism does not —is the one that will outlive the other and finally hold the field. Of the two, Christianity is the one that most completely fulfils these conditions, and the prospect that Africa will one day become a Christian continent rests rather on a sober calculation of causes and effects than on pious desire or missionary prophecy.'

Whatever the eventual result may be, there can be no doubt that a struggle is inevitable. In such a struggle cohesion and combination must have their value, and it is therefore reassuring to learn that a Code has recently been agreed upon between the various Central African Missionary Societies—exclusive of the Church of England and Roman Catholic bodies — which will ensure that uniformity of work and policy of which the lack has, hitherto, been so acutely felt.

No chapter upon missionary endeavour in Central Africa would be complete without some reference to the African Lakes Corporation, and the authors feel that they cannot conclude better than by again quoting Dr. Stewart, who says (*Dawn in the Dark Continent*, p. 219) :—

' Its (the African Lakes Corporation) chief object was not primarily to provide openings for the investment of capital or to secure new markets, but to assist the missions, to act against the slave trade by supplying the natives with goods they needed, to keep communication with the sea open, and to do a great deal of work which a trading company might do, but which a mission could not and ought not to do. It was an association genuinely existing for the objects set forth in its articles or memorandum ; and it is to its credit morally if not financially that it held on for fifteen years, although during that time it paid a dividend only once. Since then, however, it has paid dividends ranging from $7\frac{1}{2}$ to 10 per cent., besides placing considerable amounts to reserve.'

CHAPTER XVI

VILLAGE SOCIAL LIFE

AMONG the Plateau natives the love of ceremonial is linked to an equally strong sense of courtesy and innate respect for the punctilious duties of social life. A Wemba young man is nothing if not a polished gentleman, and well versed in matters of tribal etiquette. He must maintain good form in dress and appearance, which includes not only clothes but personal ornaments, and the refinements of tattooing, teeth-filing, and hair-dressing. The duties of hospitality must be strictly observed, dances and beer parties being given in due rotation by each village. For in beer and dances lie the natives only idea of an evening's entertainment, since the Plateau tribes have no such theatrical performances with masked players as are in vogue among certain Congolese races.

To deal first with the important subject of dress. Before the introduction of calico the Wemba, both men and women, usually dressed in bark-cloth. The Senga and other tribes near the Luangwa river wore a coarse cloth woven by themselves, while others, such as the Bisa, used antelope skins for covering. Nowadays Wemba men wear a loin-cloth of calico, held in position by a rough, often native-made, leather belt. The Bisa men of the lake wear a loin wrapper made of the skin of some small antelope, and this fashion is followed by many tribes east of the Chambeshi. For instance, the Winamwanga and Wiwa tie a string round their waists and suspend from it two duiker skins so as to form an apron in front and behind called the *nsuli*. The Yombe and Wafungwe content themselves with one antelope skin, which is passed between the legs after the fashion of bathing drawers.

Some Yombe men have simply a short skirt composed of tousled fringes of bark-cloth.

One has only to listen to native songs warning women against extravagance in their dress to infer that the feminine passion for clothes sways Central Africa as much as Bond Street. Though the men may sing, 'One bracelet should be sufficient adornment for a contented woman,' or 'O woman, you are like a greedy wagtail, pecking up all you can get,' yet the fashions of the native women change capriciously, and are the despair of the struggling trader who, in his desire to meet them, is frequently left with a large stock of unsaleable goods. Around most Boma stations the women wear the trade *nkanga* (native woman's cloth) swathed round below the armpits. But the poorer rustic woman must make shift with bark-cloth, which, indeed, is warmer and—when quaintly worked with fibre thread and reddened with camwood — more artistic than flashy trade 'prints.' Underneath this wrapper of bark-cloth is worn a small apron, called the *buchushi*, which hangs from a thick belt embroidered with white or blue seed beads. The belt or *mushingo* is as important, ceremonially, as the Homeric zone, and the phrase 'she took up her sister's belt' signifies that a woman has married the widower of her deceased sister. The Winamwanga women affect an apron of dressed antelope leather, worn behind and called the *inguwo*, while they wear in front a smaller apron of dark cloth, which, in the case of the younger and more fashionable girls, is fringed with seed beads. The Bisa married women wear the beautiful skins of the black or red lechwe, as baby-slings, while the women of other tribes have to be satisfied with the common duiker or sheep-skin. A skin sling is rightly valued as a great protection for the children, especially when on the march. Owing to the prohibition in force for a short time against the killing of even small game, a great outcry was raised by the women, who asserted that their children, being reduced to calico slings, would certainly perish.

In war the young fighting men were adorned by their

chiefs with gaudy raiment, called *miala*, and wound coloured turbans round their heads, some even flaunting a spiked iron headpiece (*ngala shya Waluba*), or a turban sur-mounted by the gaunt beak of some large hornbill. The chiefs, however, were plainly dressed to avoid detection in battle.

Turbans, twisted Swahili fashion, are often worn, yet occasionally, on the lakes and in the hot valleys, natives will wear broad-brimmed hats rudely plaited from native straw.

Sandals are only worn on the march, and, as a rule, only just before the rains, when the soil becomes parched and burns the feet. Ideas of decency vary so much, not only among tribes but in individuals, that any sweeping state-ment would be unwise. With the Winamwanga women, as with the Wankonde, the removal of the back cloth by an enraged husband is considered a greater indignity than taking off the front apron. Again, some women, clad in a string and a most exiguous front apron, will parade without any sense of shame, while others of the same tribe caught bathing at a stream will run up to their necks in water—even though the river be infested with crocodiles—rather than be exposed.

Personal ornaments are very varied. Modes of hair-dressing are legion. The most common styles among the Wemba are, *misoso*, where two parallel strips of wool are shaved off from the nape of the neck round the crown to the forehead, and *chiteta*, where the hair is cut right back from the top of the forehead, leaving a semicircular fringe high up on the skull. Some Bisa and Wemba will shave the head all over save for a small circular tuft at the back. Winamwanga and Wemba women frequently use the seeds of an aromatic plant to scent their hair. Even wigs of coarse matted fibre are occasionally worn, especially by the older men on Lake Bangweolo. The Bisa are fond of teazing out the curls of the hair and training them into wisps, which are gradually stretched out and added to by weaving in dark fibre or bristles till they hang down in matted, string-like bunches. The Bisa women weave red and white beads

into their wool, so that the hair on the crown of the head
and down to the nape of the neck is quite concealed.
Some Shinga chiefs, like Chitunkubwe, wear their hair in
fillets and rolls not unlike the types of hair-dressing seen
in bas-reliefs in the Egyptian Gallery at the British Museum.

Both men and women wear rings, which are exchanged
as a sign of friendship. When leaving on a long journey
natives are given small bracelets or rings as keepsakes,
which they sling from their belts, and must retain to show
to the owners on return. Long ago only *fundis* and persons
of royal blood were allowed to wear necklets and bracelets
of elephant hair, but now they are frequently worn by commoners. Some women, especially among the Wabisa and
the Washinga, love to wear huge coils of thick brass wire
wound snake-wise round the wrist up to the elbows, and
weighty anklets of the same wire up to the calf of the leg.
But the smaller bracelets of thin, drawn-out copper or
brass wire are more in request, and richly dowered girls
wear hundreds of these as armlets and anklets. Their
poorer sisters try to keep up the same pretence of fortune
by weaving imitation bracelets from the finest straw-
coloured grass, which, at a distance, resembles the real wire.
The huge, circular, white shells introduced by the Arabs,
which in the old days were bought for a cow, are still
worn by the chiefs, though they are now valueless as currency. To a native woman her brass and copper bracelets
and ivory armlets and rings are what jewels are to a Gaiety
girl, and her desire for them is insatiable. The husband,
passing through his village with a gang of carriers, will
sing out dolefully to his wife, ' I am a bond-slave to the
bracelet maker ! You cry out to be adorned ! Look you,
here am I load-carrying, earning money for you ! '

Small knives, as a rule, form part of the camp outfit of
the native, and with his bows and arrows, spear, and goat-
skin bag, the ornamental snuff-box suspended from his
neck, and his axe from his shoulder, he is fully equipped
for the road. When merely walking from village to village
on pleasure bent, the young dandies carry small swagger
axes, and the women little swagger hoes.

Most natives oil their bodies with castor oil, and polish them with the inevitable camwood. To avert disease they smear their faces with lime and the *mufuba* dough, and rub camwood well into their bodies, as the latter is supposed to be especially efficacious in keeping off evil spirits, which are often laid for good by the medicine-man's cunning in enticing them into circles of powdered camwood outside the village.

Wemba women still whiten their faces with chalk when the moon appears. In the villages of big chiefs the keepers of the Lilamfia whiten one half of their faces with chalk, the other half being reddened with camwood. In the *butwa* ceremony the bodies of the neophytes are whitened all over with lime or chalk, and in the *chisungu* ceremony the bride has white rings painted round the eyes, while the bridegroom has a white ring smeared round one arm. Painting of the body, it will thus be seen, is mainly reserved for solemn rites and important functions.

Tattooing, in the strict sense, is unknown—the cicatrices raised being more of the nature of keloid scars, blackened and rendered prominent by the application of charcoal. Such tattooing is the province of the women, who sometimes employ small steel forceps to lift up the skin, which they cut with a lancet-shaped knife. Children are, as a rule, first tattooed at the age of about six years. It would be tedious to give details of the various tattoo marks employed by each tribe. The distinctive mark of the paramount race, the Wemba, is the vertical line in the middle of the forehead, ending between the eyebrows, and the crossed tattoo bars on either side of the face. The marks on the back vary amongst the Wemba, but the *mtoso* vertical marking, from the nape of the neck partly down the spine, is the commonest. The arms are usually reserved for marking to denote the number of big game killed by each man. The back of the legs are occasionally marked, but there seems to be no special significance in this, and natives say it is merely a matter of fashion. Though frequent questions have been asked, one cannot discover if any special and private body marks are tattooed as distinctive of the totem clans. The elaborate tattooing on the abdomen is, in the Wemba tribe, found only among the women.

There are many methods of teeth deformation. Many Bisa and Wemba file their teeth down to a sharp point, giving a cruel, shark-like appearance to the mouth, and this fashion is said by them to be derived from the cannibal tribes of the Congo. Other tribes file their teeth in serrate fashion, but no special deformation can be said to be the peculiar hall-mark of one tribe, as it seems to be more a matter for the taste of each individual. Mambwe and Winamwanga men usually knock out two, or even four, of their lower teeth. In each village there is a dentist who performs these operations, knocking off the teeth level with the gums with the sharp blow of an axe-head driven home with a wooden mallet.

The hideous *pelele* or round disk of wood, which, as Sir Harry Johnston states, causes the upper lip of the Munyanja woman to project like a duck's bill, is only found among the Senga tribes, and even then in a somewhat modified form.

Senga women likewise pierce the nostril on one side, and insert a tiny rounded disk of wood or tin (called the *chipini*) like the Swahili, who derived it from India.

Some Bisa women pierce the middle cartilage of the nose and hang therefrom a small string of minute beads.

Certain Yombe women wear as a lip ornament a plug of wood inserted in the lip like the *pelele*, but tapering to a sharp point. The only reason vouchsafed for this peculiar custom is that it is the fashion, and that Yombe women ' who love their husbands very much ' drop this plug into his beer ! But whether this ornament was supposed to sweeten the beer, or was placed in it as a proof of a woman's fidelity, cannot be discovered.

To the Wemba the scrupulous niceties of salutation and discharge of hospitality due are of the utmost importance. The prescribed Wemba greeting, ' *Mwapoleni ?* ' (' Are you well ?'—perhaps more strictly rendered,' Are your wounds healed ? ') is answered, ' *Endi mukwai,*' which may be rendered, 'Yes, my dear sir.' On returning from a journey the Wiwa wayfarer is greeted with the words, ' Have you journeyed in safety ? ' to which the regular answer is, ' Yes, God has spoken for us on the way.' For the husbandman returning from his garden there is the regular formula of greeting. The Wiwa hunter is greeted by the phrase, ' What luck, *fundi* ? ' to which he will reply, ' There is meat,' or, ' I saw grass only,' as the case may be. The Wemba ' *Samalale mukwai*,' to the mother after the birth of a child, has already been noticed, and there are other formulæ connected with these important customs too numerous to mention.

The following description is given of the reception of a relative from afar :—

' When his own people know the path by which he is coming, they send out their children to greet him, whereupon they embrace him and say, " *Kû Kû*, are you all flourishing at your home ? " And he will reply, " Yes, we are all well." The children then escort him back to the village, and the head of the family or clan conducts him to his hut. A beer-pot is brought forth, and a new gourd is handed to him to drink from. Only when he is satisfied may the clansmen pass round the beer and discuss with him the news he brings of other members of their totem in distant villages.

' On the eve of his departure his host's wife grinds flour and furnishes other provisions for the way. Before he sets out the children are gathered together again, and in case of an elderly relative, the host says, " Will you not bless our children before you go ? " The uncle will then gently spit upon the chest of each child in turn, and say, " May you keep well, my child."

' His host and his wife then conduct him outside the village—usually to the first stream—and then with the formula, " *Kafikeni-po* " (" May you arrive safely "), which is answered by the phrase, " *Syaleni-po* " (" May you remain here in safety "), the guest resumes his homeward journey.'

Native hospitality to strangers is a well-worn theme,

but it must be remembered that it is mainly confined to those of the same tribe. The Winamwanga, when carrying loads within their own tribal boundaries, usually leave their *poso* (calico allowance to buy food) with their wives, relying upon free rations *en route*, although when the road leads into the Wemba country they will load themselves up with flour.

Many travellers, impressed by the fact that a carrier will pass around any delicacy given to him, have used it as an example of the profuseness of native hospitality. But, as Mr. Duff justly says in his book, *Nyasaland under the Foreign Office*, the truth is that native hospitality 'is more or less a system of give-and-take. Food can usually be had in abundance, and, after all, if the titbit makes but a mouthful, it is preferable to divide it rather than break the custom which forbids eating by oneself.'

But when it comes to the distribution of meat which will make a meal worthy of serious attention, there is a stern tussle for the last scrap of gory skin.

The well-known African system of 'age-classes' is, upon the Plateau at the present day, in such decay that accurate information is very difficult to obtain. In the olden times the children class was kept very distinct, and they lived in huts together, called *itanda* or *ntuli*. It was only when they had 'danced the heads'[1] that official notice was taken of them. Those boys who had 'danced the heads' together, formed a kind of society, and fought in a band together, shared in the spoil, and were supposed to help each other. But nowadays, though Winamwanga and Wemba lads live in *ntuli* by themselves, there seems to be no survival of such a system. Among the hill tribes in the Fife division the relics of this system are clearer. The elders of the Wafungwe say that there are four definite ranks : First, the children who live in the *ntuli*. Next, the striplings 'who have been taught by the older men,' and the young married men. In the third rank are the young men who have had children, and who are qualified, therefore, to sit in the village council. The last class is that of

---

[1] See Paper quoted on p. 29.

NATIVE GAME " INSOLO."

"SPINNING SEEDS" GAME.

the old men—the wiseacres of the village—whose advice is listened to by the headman with great respect, and who have married sons or daughters. It is very difficult to elicit exact information as to the social privileges which mark off each rank. When a young man sees one of his elders of a higher class smoking, he must never go up to ask him for tobacco. He may approach and sit near him, but must give no hint until the older man deigns to notice him and give him a little tobacco or snuff, upon which he must *tota* to the giver. A young man who has not had a child is, among certain tribes, not supposed to be able to 'speak his case,' and hence in many of the cases which come to the *boma* the elder brother will always speak first, although it is not his own case.

Women, until they have borne children, are still considered in some tribes as children themselves. But their standing when they attain to the dignity of mother-in-law is high, and, as Professor Weule points out, the relation between the son and mother-in-law—the butt of jests in European comic papers—is, in African life, 'nothing short of ideal.' Thus, if a young man sees his mother-in-law coming along the path, he must retreat into the bush and make way for her, or if she suddenly comes upon him he must keep his eyes fixed on the ground, and only after a child is born may they converse together.

The larger clans, such as the Mwenimwansa or the Mwenamboa, whose ramifications extend from one tribe to another, formed a loose kind of society which, in the olden time, was bound to assist even members of a different tribe ; but the mutual duties of members of such a clan are gradually weakening, and, the Awemba say, are only properly respected nowadays by the Wabisa.

In the south and towards the west of our sphere there are very interesting secret societies, which form a kind of lodge in each village. The Rev. Dugald Campbell mentions, in the *Aurora*, the Society of the Butwa on Chirui Island, and states that there are five similar societies, mainly residing across the Luapula River.

The following description of the Butwa Secret Society

has been kindly furnished by Mr. H. T. Harrington, Assistant-Magistrate of the Luapula district :—

'The ceremony came here with the migratory tribes of Kazembe's, the Walunda and the Wausi, from the west about 1760. It is practised now by Kasembe's Walunda, the Wena Kisinga, the Watabwa of the Mweru district, also probably by the Wena-Ng'umbu of North Bangweolo. Possibly other tribes practise it, but I have no evidence. The Wemba deny doing it. The ceremony itself is called *butwa*; the master of the ceremonies is called *nangulu*; the large temporary grass house built outside the village for the ceremony is called the *mulumbi*; the drink brewed for the ceremony by the *nangulu* is called *malawa*. Each village arranges for its own *butwa*, which may take place yearly, or less frequently. When it is decided to hold a *butwa* (usually at the request of the women), the *nangulu*, with some assistants, goes about a mile from the village into the bush and builds a large grass shelter (*mulumbi*), usually large enough to hold the entire village population. This done, he brews the *malawa*, a strong beer which when drunk causes the drinker to become highly excited. The *nangulu* enters the *mulumbi* and starts the drums going as for a dance ; all the villagers flock there and start dancing, the *nangulu* giving them frequent drinks of the *malawa*, which works them up to frenzy. When night is well on, at a given signal the men and women, young and old, enter the *mulumbi*. They are paired off, male and female ; it seems usual for a young girl about to arrive at puberty to be paired with a full-grown man, also for a young lad to be paired with a full-grown woman. This is because the *nangulu* are members of a secret society for teaching and accustoming the young to their relations with the opposite sex, and to destroy all false modesty on the part of the young. This orgie of licentiousness is kept up sometimes for days ; when it is declared over, the people, after making a present to the *nangulu*, return to the village. The fact of the ceremony having taken place is never mentioned at all, and all the people behave as if none of them had been there.'

Mr. Harrington adds that the above details may be taken as fairly correct, as they transpired in a case which came before him as Acting Collector of the Mweru district in 1898. A young wife who was *enceinte* was so abused by the *nangulu* at a *butwa* ceremony that she died. The young husband was away at the time. On his return he was so exasperated that he ran in to the *boma*, and in spite of his dread of the *nangulu* and the witch-doctors divulged the details. In the case which followed some of the witnesses came forward and spoke freely.

With reference to the special features of the *butwa*, as practised by the Wabisa of Chirui Island, these further details are compiled from notes taken by one of the authors on the spot, and recently checked by an old Bisa initiate. The strong beer—which they here call *mwewe*—is drunk, but also a special medicine is pounded on the flat surface of a hoe which has been used at a *butwa* burial. Late at night, when all are excited with drink, this special potion is administered by the *nangulu* to the neophytes, who, after frenzied dancing, as the drug begins to work, speak strangely, and finally fall to the ground in a kind of trance. The *nangulu* then says that they have ' died *butwa*.' When they revive a little the *nangulu* gives to each his special name, by which he is to be known in future to all the members—Kalepa, Chifita, Mukobe, Chisanshi, etc. Assisted by those who have been previously initiate, the *nangulu* leads the new members into the *mulumbi* house. Among the Wabisa this house is divided into partitions ; on one side recline the initiate *butwa*, while on the other side the neophyte boys and girls are paired off together.

Among the Bisa the period of this ' instruction ' varies from several weeks to three months. The relatives of the neophytes bring flour for their sustenance and the other presents which are left outside the *mulumbi* house. If a woman becomes pregnant at these rites she cannot return to the village until the *nangulu*, by the use of certain medicines, has caused abortion. When the master of the ceremonies wishes to conclude the initiation, he marshals the band of the newly initiated and issues to them the fancy cloths, oil, and camwood sent by the relatives, to adorn themselves. Shortly afterwards a gaudily dressed procession of initiated boys and girls returns to the village, but they may not show the slightest sign that they recognise even their nearest relatives until the *nangulu* has introduced each of them to the members of his household.

In the olden times the members of the Butwa Society held very closely together. They had to tend each other when sick, raise a collection if one of their number had to pay damages in a *mulandu*, and in case of the death of a *mutwa*, it was their bounden duty to seek out the wizard. As a secret society they were greatly feared, and some of them formed a kind of guild of highwaymen, attacking carriers on the path and robbing them. There are probably special signs by which a member of the *butwa* may make himself known. At Matipa village any *mutwa* visitor who comes in will play upon a special instrument called the *chansa* (like a rude guitar) the peculiar *butwa* song, whereupon the other members of the village lodge must receive and entertain him. When a *mutwa* initiate dies they may not bury him at once, nor is any immediate wailing allowed. His relatives bring beads to adorn the corpse, dress it up in fine clothes, and anoint the body with oil. Around the eyes white circles of chalk are painted. After two weeks or so all the members of the *butwa* have gathered together from the surrounding villages, bringing offerings of camwood and beads in honour of the departed. They beat drums and sing the *butwa* chants for another week or so, after which the body may be taken out for burial. When carrying the corpse to the grave they intone the following chant : ' Our friend has bitten the white shell ' (referring to the *mpande* shell which is placed between the lips of the dead man). ' While you are holding him, bear him gently to his grave.' The body is not slung from a pole in the usual fashion, but borne to its resting-place upon the arms of brother initiates.

Such is the ritual of the Butwa Society among the Bangweolo people. There was a big lodge in 1903 in Matipa village, but as the Administration's influence has gradually increased, and the White Fathers have established mission schools on the islands, the power of this secret society has greatly declined, and their immoral practices have abated.

Of all village festivities, beer-drinking holds pride of place. It is the customary finale of the four great native rites of birth and burial, marriage and initiation. For completing the garden work, too, beer is an important factor, whenever a tree-cutting ' bee ' is organised. The acrid smell of the beer-pots pervades all village social life—is, indeed, the true essence of native joviality. Of its evil influence a missionary in the *Aurora* writes as follows :—

' We have pointed out that where beer is there is a dreadful waste of land and of food-stuffs, that it is the greatest enemy of industry, that men care for nothing else when beer is ready, and sit stupid all day or rove far and wide to seek villages where there may be a supply. And we assert that nine-tenths of the village quarrels, adulteries, broken heads, and murders arise out of beer-drinking.'

In the Wemba country these evils are, perhaps, not so manifest as in the part of Nyasaland referred to, but it is a good description of the state of many tribes in the Tanganyika district. One may admit that—since from its gruelly nature the beer is a kind of food as well—the actual *physical* evil of intoxication is slight, but its effect *morally* is decidedly pernicious, as it awakens the sensual side of the natives' nature to a deplorable extent.

Bhang-smoking is another resource for whiling away the evenings. In the delirium produced by this drug—much like that of the hashish infusion—the savage and cruel side of the native character is inflamed, and a goodly number of murders have been committed by men under the influence of *bhangi*.

Next to beer-drinking, dancing and singing, perhaps, take rank as stock amusements. It is at the midnight *chila* or dance that the impetuous soul of the Central African reveals itself, flaring forth in the fitful gleams of an outlandish art. One may have been charmed with the subtle spell of Cairene dances, have mingled with the crowd fascinated by the Swahili *ng'oma* at Dar-es-salam, or in the far interior have watched the Bisa women dance the *kanyungu* by the gloomy shores of Lake Bangweolo. Wherever one may be, the throbbing witchery of the tom-toms and the wild cadences of the singers assail the senses with the same elemental, irresistible appeal.

A few of the Winamwanga dances may be described as

fairly typical of those in vogue among the other Plateau tribes. In the *kanjenje*—which is a dance for women only—a ring is formed, and the dancers, singing in unison, clap their hands in strict time with the beats of the drum. A young girl, who has previously been given a special potion, is set in the middle. Her waist oscillates at first with slow and gentle tremors, soon giving place to rapid twitchings, which ripple all over the body, and are then succeeded by convulsive quiverings so powerful that the girl has to be steadied by the outstretched arms of the women encircling her. Faster and faster beat the drums, and more rapid and violent grow the muscular quiverings, until they appear to rend her frame, when of a sudden the girl will fall upon the ground in a senseless heap. In Musengakaya's village, where such a dance was witnessed, the natives said that medicine had been placed in the girl's feet.

The dance peculiar to the men is called the *chilongwe*. This is usually performed at a beer drink, when the topers in turn execute an eccentric crab-like dance, singing and praising their god, Kachinga, the giver of the good things of life.

The *chikweta* dance, in which men and women take part, is by far the most popular. A young man will dance out to the ranks of the women opposite until he faces the girl of his choice, upon which he retreats to the centre of the ring. The girl then dances up to him—with the sinuous abdominal movements which constitute for them the fine art of dancing—and, after footing it together with jigging steps, they both retreat to give place to another pair. When the *chikweta* is kept up until the small hours of the morning, dancing of an obscene character is often indulged in.

In the step called the *mung'wanye* the men and women stand in rows facing each other ; the women then 'go to be married,' as they phrase it, each approaching the man of her choice. As she slowly retreats he comes forward, and she plucks at his belt or pulls out his knife, returns it, and dances back again.

E. A. Avery-Jones, phot.

WEMBA DRUMMERS AND DANCERS.

E. A. Avery-Jones, phot.

WEMBA PROFESSIONAL DANCERS.

An ancient form of *chila* was called the *mukondo*, being a representation of war and of bride capture. The men went, with bows in their hands, dancing out to marry the women. Each young man, when dancing in turn with the girl he favoured, handed her his bow and arrows, while the other men circled round about the pair.

Among the Winamwanga, at the end of the dances, a collection was made for the drummers.

Among the Wemba there are skilled performers on the various kinds of drum, and these artistes are in great request, travelling from village to village on a professional tour. Those drummers who favour the 'mother drum,' the large *mpilingi*—having a drum-head at both ends—are accompanied by two assistants, one of whom beats the *mpikwe* drum as a second, while the other beats the 'stripling drum' or the *kalume*, singing at the same time to keep the chorus together. Some are skilled executants upon the *kamutibi*, which has only one drum-head. In the *kamutibi* a louder tone is obtained by inserting at the side a kind of circular stop, over which is stretched the stout papery-like film spun by a kind of spider called *lembwe-lembwe*; this stop also produces the peculiar rattle made by the gut strings or 'snares' affixed to military side-drums. Another expert is more of a dancing-master than a drummer, and is known as the 'dancing-man' all over Central Africa, being called *simuseba* by the Wemba. His special instrument is the *chilimba*, a kind of guitar with a gourd as a sounding-board. He sustains the solo parts, singing to his guitar, while his assistant beats a small kind of drum and joins in the chorus, which, with its appropriate dance, is soon learnt by the village folk. A *simuseba* must be an adept at the art of improvisation, and will soon weave character sketches of the village people into his recitative, not forgetting to praise 'the beautiful red bodies of the women' (to quote from a typical song) at the villages he visits, or the skill in hunting of the men.

In some districts there is a class of professional dancers, jesters, and contortionists, whose performances are always a popular feature.   A few years ago a pair of dancers—who were soon named the Luapula Twins—toured North-Eastern Rhodesia, and reaped a rich harvest at each station. Their dancing costume consisted of a kind of ballet skirt (made of fringes of threaded reeds like an arras curtain), which swished at each step; their arms and legs were covered with bracelets and anklets of tiny bells or of rattling seeds.   The 'twins' sang and danced at the same time, causing their anklets and bracelets to clash like castanets and jingle to the shake of rattles.

Another virtuoso was a native of Simumbi village, who called himself the *mung'omba*, a kind of giant hornbill. As a headpiece he wore the huge beak of the bird, while its pinions were spread over his arms.   In season and out of season he raised his discordant song, crouching and flapping his wings in clumsy imitation of the ungainly dance of this great bird, chanting as his refrain its strident cry of ' *gûh-gûh-gûh, êh-ĕlĕ-ĕlĕ*.'

The ministrels of the chief were called the *siwaomba* or *ng'omba*.   The chief would give a favoured singer three drummer assistants to support him, and assign to him a chorus of young men (*banku*) to be trained.   As we have noted in a previous chapter, these court bards were frequently blinded so that they should not run away. Many an *ng'omba* was the evil genius of the reigning king, inciting him in peace to oppress his own people, and in war urging him to slay and spare not.

To attempt any appreciation of native music would be impossible within the limits of the present chapter.   There is a tendency to regard barbaric music with contempt, mainly because the African modes are unfamiliar to us, but it is a subject which would well repay attention and careful study, as the material is very considerable on the Plateau alone.   The actual words of the songs are the least important point ; they are often clipped to suit the exigencies of the metre so as to be almost unrecognisable, *e.g.* the word *maka* is not ' strength,' as one would imagine in a certain song, but short for *makanga*, a guinea-fowl.   It is rather the plaintive lilt of the music, with its quaint halftones and the perfect rhythm kept by a native chorus, which is so fascinating. Wemba youths are, as a rule, very musical and have a good ear. They are too fond of singing falsetto; but many who have been tested possess good tenor voices, several being able to sing up to B♭ with ease. Bass voices are uncommon, although baritones and tenors abound. It is interesting to note that singing in harmony has advanced to the stage when three and sometimes four parts (as in the case of Muvanga's band) are sustained by skilled singers. When one recollects the late development of harmony in civilised Europe, this fact is somewhat remarkable in a Central African tribe.

The Plateau musical instruments are numerous, but in the main conform to well-known Central African types. For instance, we have first the primitive *Lumonge*, a strip of rafia palm bent as a bow upon which the playing string is stretched. Women play this much after the fashion of a jews' harp, holding one end of the bow in the mouth and twanging the other with their fingers.

The *Luntonga* is apparently a development of the *Lumonge*, having a bridge in the centre, and a gourd sounding-board below; it is played with a rough kind of bow.

Several other instruments known generically as *Malimba* are in vogue. The *kalimpango* and the *mpango* are species of these made much after the principle of the guitar, and are twanged with the fingers. The *kasese*, with its gourd resonator and its fiddle-like neck with three stops, is the nearest approach to a violin, but it is usually played with the fingers.

The *sansi*, or so-called native piano, with its iron keys fixed upon a wooden sounding-board, is too well known to merit detailed description.

As a trumpet the Wemba used the horns of a koodoo, but among the Walungu a tusk of ivory was sometimes used for this purpose (see Sir Harry Johnston's *British Central Africa*, p. 465). The small reed flute or *chimpeta* is similar to the *chitoliro* played in Nyasaland.

The above instruments are usually played alone; those

of the *malimba* class, however, being frequently used to accompany the voice.

Of choruses and chanties there is an unending variety, since when doing any concerted work, such as machila-carrying or hauling timber, each gang will sing to keep in time and to relieve the tedium of the work. Many are old traditional songs sung by slave gangs in the past, but new melodies are composed every year, spreading over the country like popular comic songs. Before entering each village it is only common politeness for the *machila* men to sing to warn the inhabitants of the approach of a caravan.

'You who are in the path move out of the way, the Dreadful thing (the white man) is coming, or else—The thing from the East is coming along, the skilled player upon instruments of music.'

for every white man who possesses a gramophone is a true virtuoso to the natives.

And as the Msungu emerges from his hammock, the finale '*koloke woo*' is smartly rapped out. Later on, the long line of carriers will file in, some perhaps singing dolefully :

'The *capitao* has cheated us of our poso.
Don't cry, mother ; we shall get back all right.'

Or on the march each carrier when mountain-climbing will sing his own peculiar chant, half patter, half song, to strengthen his heart in the rough places, while others may encourage their fellows with such songs as these—

'Friend Mulenga, don't be slack in singing;
Go to Blantyre and learn cleverness.
The *lamia* (telegraph wire) goes all the way to show you the road ;
If you find the work hard, you needn't go again.'

Or as the day wanes the woods will echo with the songs heralding the approach of the successful hunter to camp, as, for instance—

'The buck wounded by the *bwana* ;
They quench the flames, they quench the flames,
With their fatness, with their fatness.'

In case of an obviously new hand, whose knowledge of the language is somewhat sketchy, his *machila* men will soon improvise songs touching upon his little failings and peculiarities with rude satire.

For the native has a sharp eye for the character of what he calls in his slang the 'chalk-faced people,' and a niggardly man comes off badly in their *machila* songs.

'You in the village, what are you afraid of ?
  We are only carrying a large stone (and consequently you won't
    get much out of him).'

The songs of the Wemba women when pounding maize or grinding corn are usually of a plaintive type, ending in a kind of meaningless chantie.   For instance—

> 'Let us dance the *kapamba*,
> The dance the smart girls dance
> On the banks of the *Manyowe*,
> *Bwadya e wayaya yawe yo*.'

Even the dandy does not escape sarcasm, as witness the following—

> 'Oh, Queen of England, yours is a brave brood.
> Have you not brought forth the great ——
> Who is always shooting his shirt cuffs ? '

There is a vast wealth of folklore tales awaiting collection among the Plateau tribes.   Some Wemba folklore stories are translated in the *Journal of the African Society* by one of the White Fathers, in which are described the adventures of the hare, the counterpart of the fox in English folklore.[1]

The Lake Bisa folklore stories are interesting as not being of the usual animal type, and out of a collection, made by one of the authors, the following specimen is given below :—

THE TWO BROTHERS AND GOD

'Long ago these men they were two—the elder and his younger brother.   Now the younger was a man of much wealth, while his

[1] Many of the Winamwanga folklore songs have been written down as far as possible in the English notation by Mrs. Dewar of the Livingstonia Mission, and are published in a little book called *Chinamwanga Folklore Tales*.

elder brother was a beggar and of wealth he had none. On a tall ant-hill was the hut of the younger, though his brother was left alone and forsaken in Mitanda (a wretched hamlet). One day Great God brought out a piece of iron, and said : " Take it to that man whose hut is upon the ant-hill ; let him forge from it a supple sling for carrying my youngest born child, and see that he tattoes it with the proper pattern inside." So they took the iron to the younger brother and said : " Son of man, forge this into a baby sling, and do not forget the tattooing." But the man was dumb-founded, and said to his fellows : " How may I compass this, since no man may forge baby-slings from iron ? " His fellows replied : " No, indeed, but first ask the advice of your elder brother." The younger man went to his brother and said : " How can I forge a baby-sling ? " And the elder answered : " I know not ; have you not always despised me ? " But the younger entreated him, saying : "I beseech you, child of our blood," and he besought him and straight-way gave him a woman for his wife. Then said the elder : " Fetch three water-pots and take them before God, and say to him, ' Give these water-pots to your royal wives, and ask them to fill them to the brim with tears, for with tears alone may the iron be tempered.' " So God assembled his wives : to each jar he set ten women to weep. And they wept and wept ; three whole days they wept, yet the jars were not filled. Then said God : " Dry your tears, I shall take back my piece of iron." And forthwith the sky was darkened with clouds, and the thunder fell upon the hut wherein the younger man had hidden the iron, and it was borne away with a flash of lightning. When the rain abated, the younger man sought for the iron, but could not find it. Then God spoke and said : " Cease from your search ; I shall find you another piece."

' But in truth the man's troubles were over. For God said to himself : " He will get no more iron from me, because I can never find tears enough to fill his jars, or to forge my sling." So the story goes.'

Of proverbs and riddles there is an endless variety. The Wemba are very rich in proverbs, perhaps because of their Congolese origin, while the Winamwanga and Wiwa delight in riddles. A few examples of Wemba proverbs are given here :—

   ' " If you are killing a snake destroy its mouth also."

   ' " The owner of the porridge has not dirty hands."

   ' " Your fellow-wife will never wash your back " (referring to the constant jealousy of the wives of a polygamist).

WOMEN'S DANCE.

Hubert Sheane, phot.

MEN'S DANCE.

Hubert Sheane, phot.

' " The master of the dogs need not call them " (used sometimes when family property such as women or children are in question, who will follow the man who has been kind to them).

' " The hungry man burns his mouth " (more haste less speed).

' " I shall come to-morrow," says he, when 'tis his neighbour's wife that is dead.'

Asking riddles is a favourite method of passing the time. The Wemba start by saying : ' *Cho ?* What is it ? ' and he who accepts the challenge says : ' *Chilika*, Cut it short,' upon which the riddle is given as follows :—

' *Q*. What is long ?
' *A*. Your mother's snout as long as a field rat's.
' *Q*. A band of mutilated men across the stream ?
' *A*. The lopped trees of a native garden.
' *Q*. A basket woven by cunning craftsmen ?
' *A*. A honeycomb.
' *Q*. The fool we beat around the village ?
' *A*. A wooden grain mortar (which is common property and pounded by every woman in turn).'

Where games and amusements are concerned, the African boy is far more resourceful than European children of the same age. The multitude and variety of native games is astonishing, and there are few European games which have not their African equivalents. Diabolo, for instance, was known long ago among the Plateau tribes and was called *nsengwa-nsengwa*, and Winamwanga boys are very expert at throwing and catching their rude spools.

To indicate the general character of Plateau sports a few specimens of Winamwanga games may be given.

The game called *Chityatya* gives good practice in spear-throwing. A solid disc is cut out from the soft putty-like wood of the *chiombo* tree, and the players stand facing each other. One at the head of the rank throws the *chiombo* wheel so that it rolls swiftly down the ranks of the players, and as it passes each player, he swiftly casts his spear. When all players on one side have made hits, they dash for their opponents, and put them to flight.

In the game known as *Mulambilwa*, the boys again are divided into two sides, and kneel in two rows facing each other. Each player then places in front of him a tiny kind of ninepin, about the size of a sparklet bulb, usually employing the hard conical berries of some tree. At a signal all throw other berries at the ninepins of their opponents. As soon as all the men are down on one side, the vanquished players spring up and take to their heels to escape a drubbing from their conquerors.

A swinging rope is soon woven from the fibre of maize stalks and slung between two trees. As the boys swing they sing quaint songs, such as—

'We are wee bats flitting up and down in the twilight.
Mother Muleya is far away, in our hearts is gameful joy,
In our hearts is gameful joy.'

Another popular game is a kind of mimic warfare, in which captains are chosen for each side, and bullets of wood, toy spears, etc., are used as missiles.

The boys and girls play at setting up house together. Outside the village they build small grass huts, to which the girls bring grindstones for preparing the meal, which they cook and serve like grown-up women. At midday they pretend to retire for the night, barring the doors like their elders, and sleep until one of them imitates the morning cockcrow, when they wake again.

Little girls have their own special sports, which they play by themselves, usually a variety of round games. One popular form is called the Cattle Kraal. A circle of girls is formed, who lock their hands together. One, standing in the centre of the ring, makes a desperate rush, holding up her hands, trying to break through the fence with the weight of her body. Wherever the fence is broken the offender has to take her place in the middle.

In some tribes the little girls play with rude dolls carved with a truly Egyptian angularity of outline. Among the Wiwa, when a young girl dies prematurely her doll is buried with her. After the initiation ceremony all such dolls are abandoned, though very occasionally one will find a grown-up woman keeping her doll. For instance, the wife of a *capitao* at Fife—a Namwanga woman—carries, wherever she goes, a doll which she calls her daughter, though she has grown daughters of her own.

Hoop-trundling and top-spinning are common pastimes. There is a form of peg-top wound round with string, but thrown differently from a schoolboy's peg-top. Four or five peg-tops are kept going at once by the players, the object being to throw each top so that it upsets that of its opponent, the player who clears the ground first being called the conqueror. Another is a very light form of teetotum, and is twirled between the fingers and thumb. As in the Malay Islands, the top spinning the longest wins, and great skill is shown in spinning them.

Of string tricks and puzzles there is a great variety; but unfortunately they are quite indescribable, since some, which are supposed to be working models, as it were, of animals or of common objects, like our cat's-cradle, are extremely intricate. The ball games are those common to Nyasaland, played by boys and young men, and need no special description.

ADDITIONAL NOTE *re* BUTWA, ON PAGE 261.

The late Father Foulon (who worked on Chirui Island for many years) informed the writer that the instruction given was not wholly immoral, but designed to impart to the initiate extraordinary powers, such as that of invisibility at will.

CHAPTER XVII

VILLAGE CEREMONIES, ARTS, AND INDUSTRIES

BEFORE the advent of the Administration, villages were larger and the sense of village life and its obligations far stronger than at the present day. Even now the village is still, to the native mind, far more of a living entity, corporate and spiritual, than can be realised by any European. Its site was on sacred ground, hallowed by the foundation ceremonies, and placed under the protection of the ancestral and local spirits. Its sanctity must at all costs be preserved intact. Any extraordinary occurrence, such as death, the birth of twins, or of an ill-omened child, would defile not only the inhabitants, but also the place itself, and hence we find this purification extended to inanimate as well as to animate objects. These ceremonies peculiar to village life are of its essence, and have a prior claim to our attention before the more mundane description of village arts and industries.

To consider first the foundation rites for a new settlement. Some of these customs for founding a village are still observed among the hill tribes on the Nyasaland border, and Headman Namusamba gives the following description of the Fungwe rite :—

' The headman tells his head wife to grind flour, which is distributed to the village priests (the *Simapepo*). One of these priests proceeds to the selected site, and casting the flour on the ground, utters the following prayer: " You spirits of this country, this flour I set down here. If I myself, and the headman may settle and walk in safety upon this site, then let me find this flour undisturbed and unpolluted ; but if it be otherwise, then I shall know that I may not dwell here in health." Early the next day the priest will revisit the spot, and, on finding the flour undisturbed, will rejoice and gather the headman and the people to begin the fence. The *Simapepo* himself cuts the first stake, and all the others pile their fence poles upon the spot where the flour was laid. When the circular trench is completed, the *Shin'ganga* takes medicine from his magic horn and moistens the first stake of the fence with it. This stake is held by the headman and his wife until firmly rammed in, and all assist to drive in the other fence poles. When the fence is completed, the priest, the headman, and his wife, standing by the fence pole last staked, make intercession as follows : " O ye spirits, hold steadfast our fence and our village, and may ye abide propitious to us all ! " '

Throughout all the Plateau tribes it is necessary to have the ' foundation horn ' fixed before the village is inhabited. Among the Lake Wabisa the medicine-man procures a roan horn and inserts it tip foremost in the ground, and drives in stakes of the *mulunguti* and *mutaba* trees on either side. The headman thereupon calls the people together, and says : ' All ye people listen ! if any man is ill and about to die he must be taken outside ; he must not die in my village.' It these precautions were observed, the villagers firmly believed that their headman would not be killed by his enemies even if his fence was stormed.

The ceremonies already described, enacted at the birth of a *chinkula* child (one whose lower teeth were cut first), and the rites which take place upon the birth of twins, are said by the natives themselves to be absolutely necessary for purifying the village from defilement, and for averting the Nemesis which would inevitably follow if such portents were unexpiated.

The Awemba ceremony at the birth of twins has already been described in the *Journal of the African Society* (1906), p. 43, and therefore a description of the Fungwe ceremony is given as showing some divergence in matters of detail.

Among the Fungwe, as soon as the children are born, the midwife calls out ' *Wuwi, wuwi,*' to proclaim to all that twins have been delivered. The midwife anoints herself with oil and commences to dance and sing with the other village women. The father of the twins goes straightway to the village doctor and receives from him medicine which is steeped in water-pots in which all the village people wash themselves. The medicine-man also mixes other lustral medicine, called *mulombo*, in a bowl of porridge, and gives a portion to each of the villagers to drink. After a day or two, when the umbilical cords have dropped off, the rite (referred to in general terms in the above-quoted *Journal*), is performed by the husband and wife in the presence of the midwife and the elder village women. Later on in the same morning a procession, headed by the medicine-man carrying the twins in a basket, wends its way to the cross-roads outside the village. The basket containing the twins is placed resting upon a bed of small stakes, but although spectators may view afar off, only the fathers of twins and women who have borne children are allowed to dance around it. There is much rejoicing, and the women wave about bunches of green leaves, but insult the father of the twins by vile curses, and sing obscene songs about the parents. The twins are then removed from the basket, which is left in the cross-roads. On return to the village the father of the twins kills a goat, and mixes the blood with a decoction made by the village doctor ; with this he sprinkles the feet of the midwife. In the evening he makes a tour of the village, sprinkling the blood in front of each door, over the grain-bins, the pigeon-cots, and the goat-pen, and, lastly, over the cattle kraal. Unless these rites are performed the natives say that a blight would fall on the village. Those villagers whose huts were not sprinkled would fall seriously ill and swell up all over, the grain would rot, and the live stock would die. The father of twins himself, unless he received medicine from the doctor, would assuredly die, and, if he refused to complete the ceremonies, he and his wife would be driven from the village. In course of time, when the mother gives birth to a single child, the village doctor brings another medicine and tells the midwife and husband that they must wash in it, saying to the husband, ' Now your twinhood is finished, you are no longer a *shimpundu*.'

To turn to some description of an average Plateau village. In general appearance there is very little to distinguish one Plateau village from another. The same circular, grass-roofed huts, the cylindrical grain-stores, the neat pigeon-cots, the women pounding grain in mortars, or grinding flour upon the primitive mills underneath the eaves of the huts, the grimy little children playing by the unswept spaces between the huts—where slinking curs snarl among the refuse—are all familiar and somewhat monotonous components of a village scene.

But, taking these components in details, there is considerable divergence among the different tribes. Take the huts, for instance. The most common type of hut, that of the Wemba, is constructed with poles bound together with withes, the interstices being filled in with mud. The framework of the roof is woven upon the ground. In the Luangwa Valley the Walambia and the Watambo make wattled huts of split bamboos woven transversely around the framework of stout poles, so that the hut looks like some giant basket in the making. The interstices are filled with a thin layer of mud, but—probably on account of the heat—the outside wall is not mudded over, and the verandas are rarely built in. From fear of marauding tribes the timid Wapakwe on the Nyasaland border, until recently, used to build small, squat huts, snugly ensconced in almost inaccessible crannies and nooks of the hills. The floors are sunk in the ground, and the roofs turfed over to render them as inconspicuous as possible. The Waunga and Wabisa build their huts when possible upon mounds raised well off the ground, and strengthen the base to resist the encroaching waters, which, in the height of the wet season, often creep up almost to the door lintel. Many of the Waunga have, however, solved the problem of floods ingeniously by building each hut in their fishing villages upon a buoyant platform of reeds, which rises with the water and keeps each homestead high and dry. The floors of these floating houses are mudded firmly, so as to permit of cooking without burning the reeds underneath.

There is no need to descant upon the general methods of hut-building (wall-making, roofing, or mudding), as they are similar to those in vogue in Nyasaland (fully described in Miss Werner's book, p. 141–143). Square, rectangular huts or *tembe* are found near stations, and where East Coast influence has made itself felt.

In 1900 the majority of villages were fenced in, but nowadays it is very rare to see a stockaded village except where lions are abundant. The Lake Bisa still plant a cactus-like shrub around many of their villages, which makes a good fence, and, if broken at any point, will cover the body of the intruder with its milky sap, which produces agonising itching and painful swellings.

The following detailed inventory of the goods and chattels in a typical Winamwanga hut may be of interest, as showing how much may be placed and stored within a small circular space. As one entered, on the left of the door, the porridge pot was boiling upon the triangular hearth made by two cones of ant earth facing the clay hob which was let into the wall. The hob was littered with odds and ends, which included small iron tools for drawing out brass wire. Directly above the hearth was a wooden rack upon which, as it was the wet season, firewood was being slowly dried by the smoke, and suspended from the roof above were maize cobs, black and shiny with soot, preserved for the next sowing. From the centre pole which supported the roof a native guitar was suspended. To the right of the door were four short-forked stakes driven into the ground upon which, at night, the cross supports would be laid lengthwise and then covered with a mattress of split raphia palm unfolded as a bed. At the head of the bedstead were two pots filled, from time to time, with beer to propitiate the guardian spirits of the husband and wife. Near the foot of the bed, perched upon the three prongs of a stake driven firmly into the floor, was a nest of woven grass in which a hen was quietly sitting. Upon pegs projecting from the circular walls hung a graceful gourd bottle containing scented oil used by the wife for her toilet, and, close to it, dangled a reed-

Bernard Turner, phot.

BEGINNING A NATIVE ROOF.

This framework is inverted and placed on hut to the left.

Bernard Turner, phot.

HUT INTERIOR SHEWING THE HEARTH AND NATIVE POTS.

buck horn, full of mysterious medicine—the property of the husband. Around the segment of the floor, directly opposite and farthest from the door, were arranged several water-pots, above which, suspended from pegs, were various kinds of baskets nested within each other. Behind the reed door were the husband's bow and arrows hanging from a peg, while his spear was leaning against the veranda outside.

The picture drawn by many writers of the men-folk sitting idly in their villages whiling away the time in ' divine carelessness,' however true it may be of South Africa, is hardly applicable to the Plateau. A glance at the table of agricultural work performed month by month (see Chapter XVIII.) will show that there is work to be done throughout the greater part of the year. Moreover, many tribes have their special industries to pursue.

The Awiwa, for instance, are energetic iron workers, and, during the dry season, smelting is vigorously carried on. When looking out of the tent at night in a Wiwa village the tall, red-hot kilns make an impressive sight, standing sentinel, as it were, round about the outskirts of the village with their cylindrical pillars of flame. The Awiwa are not such skilled iron workers as the Washinga, but as their method of smelting is that usually adopted upon the Plateau it is described in preference. A kiln is first mudded by the side of an ant-hill. Occasionally the iron shale is dug out of the gneissic rock upon the hills, but, as a rule, the Awiwa dig into the swampy plain (such as those by the side of the Katonga river), where, at the depth of about 10 ft., large lumps of hæmatite quartz are found among the gravel. These are hammered into small pieces with a large iron hammer or *mpando*. Firewood is then collected near the kiln and charcoal is burnt. The kiln (which is a cylindrical structure from 10 to 12 ft. high, about 6 ft. diameter at the base, tapering to 3 ft. at the top), is packed from the base with a layer of firewood, then with charcoal, and then with the broken hæmatite lumps until it is full. Fire is then introduced from one side near the top, and, owing to the shape of the kiln

and the orifices at the base, a sufficient draught is obtained.
The slag and dross pour out of several earthenware pipes
leading obliquely from the ore itself to the outside of the
kiln, and, finally, the smelted metal drops to the bottom
of the furnace. As soon as the kiln has cooled off, this
cake of metal is loosened and hooked out with tongs and
then handed over to the blacksmith.   Among the Washinga
large goat-skin bellows are often used to create a forced
draught.

The Winamwanga blacksmith plies his trade in a small
open hut. Two boy assistants keep blowing two goat-
skin bellows, whose bamboo nozzles face each other, to
keep up the small charcoal fire to the requisite heat.   When
the mass of iron is red-hot it is placed upon a small stone
anvil, and an elder assistant beats it flat with a huge stone
hammer bound with handles of bark rope. The blacksmith then beats the flattened mass into the form of an
axe or hoe, putting on the finishing touches with a small
iron hammer. Such a blacksmith *fundi* can forge spears,
knives, hoes, hammers, sickles, arrow-heads, axe-heads,
and fish-hooks. The Shinga blacksmiths show considerable skill in the making of knives, and a specimen sent
home to be tested was declared to be of good steel and
well-tempered. Senga *fundis* are very skilful at mechanical
repairs, and clever at making small castings of broken
parts of machines. A blacksmith who is at Mwenzo can
make new nipples for guns and repair locks, and has even
repaired bicycle frames and forged new parts on being given
the pattern.

The *kafula wa nsambo*, or bracelet-maker, is in great
request, and he must be supplied with beer and fowls
when working. He will first estimate the number of
bracelets to be made from a coil of brass bought from the
local store, and is then held rigidly to his bargain. This
brass is heated over the forge until it becomes sufficiently
malleable, when it is beaten into strips. The strips are
dipped in oil, drawn to a point at one end, and then pulled
through an iron die with a large slot ; then through dies
with graduated slots, which reduce the wire to the required

fineness. The core of each bracelet is composed of *bukonge* (*sanseviera* fibre), or a wisp of hair around which the wire is wound. Copper bracelets are also fashionable, and some years ago Katanga natives used to bring ingots of copper, cast in the form of Saint Andrew's cross, for the Shinga blacksmiths to forge into bracelets. Thick brass wire is usually bought by the coil direct from the store, then heated and wound into the heavy snake-like armlets by the *nsambo*-maker; but in the outlying districts these artists can cast the same thick tubes of brass or copper by running off the molten bars into bamboo moulds.

For the Lake Bisa fishing is the paramount industry. In Chapter XIII. the various methods of fishing have been briefly dealt with; but a few further remarks as to the customs and superstitions connected with the industry of fishing may not be out of place. When fish are narcotised with the *wuwa* poison, the first fish caught is presented to a pregnant woman immediately, ' so that many fish may float on top of the water.' Nets are usually woven from the fibre called *luimbwe* ; when a quantity of this fibre is prepared, the fisherman gives a beer-party to induce his fellow-villagers to assist him in net-making. The method of fishing is as follows : Nets are let down in a wide circle from canoes around a likely spot. Each large net is given a name, such as ' the greedy mouth,' ' the tireless eater,' and the names of chiefs or of chieftainesses, such as Mwila, Chanda. If a shoal of fish is entangled in ' greedy mouth,' for instance, the name of this net is shouted out, and the canoes flock together to haul up the weighty net. The first basket of fish taken must not be eaten, since the fish are placed upon the grave of the village chief, or else before the ancestral spirit huts, so as to ensure a good catch. The Wabisa are also expert at fish-spearing, which is sometimes done at night by holding a torch over the water. When a good haul of fish is made, they are dried in the sun and packed in elliptical, shield-shaped crates, and sold at the nearest station. Askari and messengers are very fond of these dried fish, and one of the writers began to take in crates at a shilling a time in lieu of hut tax. Unfortunately, these crates became speedily too lively and demonstrative, and were on the point of overpowering the station itself, when the sergeant was drastically ordered to burn and bury what he sorrowfully called ' good stink-fish.'

For making large canoes the Wabisa search for large trees in the Luwumbu country, the wood of the *mupapa*, *mulombwa*, *saninga*, or *mupundu* trees being suitable. When one of the writers ordered a large canoe to be built, all the villagers engaged for the work camped near Movu, where a large trunk of *mupapa* had been located. Several days were spent in cutting down the tree, whereupon half of the workers returned to fetch food, leaving the skilled boat-makers to shape the bows and the stern. In a week the log was trimmed into a solid boat-shaped block, by which time all the workers had returned, and began to cut out the interior. The outlines were marked in charcoal, and the workers fixed their axe heads flatwise in new handles so that they could be used as adzes to hollow out the core. When the inside was sufficiently hollowed out the boat was turned over, but only skilled workmen were allowed to shape the outside lines. It took nearly six weeks to make this large canoe, which was dragged by ropes and wooden rollers to the nearest waterway. Smaller canoes are hewn out in much the same way, since natives believe that burning out the core would spoil the wood and weaken the shell. There was a large canoe on the lake, about 30 ft. long and 8 ft. broad, which was seaworthy and strong. It was called the *Kapopo*, after the mythical monster which was said to have once inhabited the lake. This monster, according to the story-teller, an old Bisa man named Chiwawa, used to come out of the lake and make periodic descents upon villages by night. Its body was as large as seven oxen, and its neck was long and sinuous like that of a python. From its head projected one horn, from underneath which glared a fierce, lidless eye. When it emerged on land the earth shook, and when it roared the sound was heard all over the lake. This blatant beast would make a sudden descent upon a village, and, inserting its long neck through the narrow doorways, would peer round and drag out and devour the unfortunate inmates one by one. It had a special *penchant* for chiefs and their offspring. When one remembers the veracious native tales about the famous *chibekwe*, or water rhinoceros, with three horns, which used to devour the hippopotamus on Lake Bangweolo, not to mention the Tanganyika sea-serpent, it is not difficult to account for the origin of such stories as have appeared recently in papers about the *dinosaur*, which (according to those who have relied upon such native myths) is said to live, move, and have its being in the vast swamps south of Lake Bangweolo on the river Lunga !

Last of the major industries which are mainly in the hands of the men, is that of salt-making. In 1902 the Assistant Native Commissioner of Mpika Station gave the following account of the salt-making in his division :—

' The grass is cut in such a manner as to leave a little earth on the root, and this is tied in small bundles to dry. When the grass is quite dry the natives burn the bundles, taking care only to char them ; for this purpose they take water into their mouths and blow it on to the hot ashes—in other words, making the grass into charcoal. The cinders are then carefully gathered up and taken into the grass shelters which have been built by the riverside. It is not unusual for several hundred natives to congregate at Kibwa during the salt-making season. The women in the meantime have made a large earthen pot in the shape of an inverted cone, with two orifices called *Nshiko*. This vessel is suspended from a post and filled with the cinders containing the salt. On these cinders is poured a large quantity of water, which percolates through them, and runs out at the small holes in the vessel, which are stopped with grass or straw ; the water thus filtered but charged with salt is caught in a wooden trough placed to receive it. This salt water is placed in new pots on the fire, and boiled until the water is evaporated, leaving the salt at the bottom. To evaporate enough water to make 12 lb. of salt, the natives are obliged to boil it for thirty-six hours, or, roughly, three hours for each pound of salt. They generally have from four to six pots on the fire at the same time. When all the water is eva-porated they break the pot and place the cake of salt on the fire to dry thoroughly. According to the trouble taken in filtering the salt is white or otherwise.

' Where there are no salt pans, a kind of potash salt is made from the ashes of certain kinds of reeds and grasses burnt over the fire.'

Having dealt with the main industries allotted to the men, we may turn to the industries which are the special province of the women. For the Plateau woman the principal industry is the preparation of food. The pounding of grain in the mortars, the winnowing and subsequent grinding at the primitive hand-mill, are the inevitable daily task. The woman must also collect the various spinach-like grasses used as a relish for the porridge, which often involves a lengthy search for suitable varieties. Beer-brewing is, again, in the woman's department. Beer is made from eleusine, from white millet, maize, and cassava in the following way : A basket of grain is left in the stream for two days until it begins to sprout, upon which it is placed out on mats to dry and is then ground. This malt is subsequently mixed with gruel made from unfermented flour, and this mixture is allowed to stand for a day or two until the fermentation sets in. The next morning water is added, and the mixture is boiled, after which fermentation is allowed to continue for a few days. The brew is then strained off into beer-pots through a native sieve, and is then ready for drinking.

From our point of view the staple diet of millet porridge seems very monotonous, though in the rainy season maize, pumpkins, beans, and potatoes vary the menu. No set time for meals is observed, as natives eat when opportunity offers and as any special relish in the way of meat or fish becomes available ; but before retiring the evening meal is a regular institution. The Awemba, Walungu, Amambwe, and Winamwanga prefer porridge of red millet, the Wabisa of cassava flour, while the Wasenga use white millet. As a relish, the Bisa mix the oily *mushikishi* bean with their porridge. The Waunga and Watwa gather the seeds of the lotus-lily, dry and pound them into a kind of meal, and subsist also to a great extent on a large potato-like tuber.

For an able-bodied man at work, two pounds of flour

a day is an ample ration, and this is the recognised allowance for station workers. This ration, however, must be varied judiciously with beans and other relishes, since unless natives are allowed their usual diet of green food as well as meal they are extremely liable to scurvy, and to this cause, doubtless, must be attributed the numerous cases of this malady which occurred among North-Eastern Rhodesia natives when working in the mines.

A few customs in eating may be noticed. Chiefs eat by themselves at a special fire. Wemba guests take lumps of porridge haphazard from the basket, while the host divides any relish available. Among the Winamwanga, however, it is customary for the host to taste the mess of pottage first, it is said, to show that no obnoxious thing or poison has been put with it. Each man after rolling his lump of porridge into a ball makes a dent in it with his thumb, and then uses it as a dipper to catch the gravy from the relish bowl. Before and after each meal it is customary to wash the hands. There seem to be but few instances of perverted tastes or of morbid longings for noxious food. The disease of *safura*, or dirt-eating, mentioned by Livingstone, is rare among the Plateau tribes. Wiwa women, when pregnant, eat a special red earth obtained from ant-hills, which is said to ensure a speedy delivery, and some of them continue this habit after childbirth.

To the Central African the hearth and its fire are sacred. For instance, if any serious disease breaks out, the headman will call upon the medicine-man to place medicine at the cross-roads, the village fires are then raked out, and the smouldering embers thrown upon the bowl of medicine at the cross-roads. All shout aloud and make as much din as possible, while the medicine-man departs alone to produce a new flame with his fire-stick, from which all fires are rekindled. Again, a woman after intercourse with her husband may not approach the fire or cook until she has washed after the prescribed fashion, nor may she draw near during menstruation (cp. Chapter VI.); only after this is finished may she draw near and whitewash the hearth, and kindle a new fire from embers taken from a neighbouring hut.   As has already been noted elsewhere, when a death occurs, all fires are extinguished, and a new fire for the village ceremoniously kindled. Whatever may be the real reason for these rites,[1] it would seem as if there was some idea of preserving the hearth and its fire as pure from contagion and taint as possible.   When a thunderbolt falls, for instance, the chief kindles a new fire from it, and dispenses the embers, ordering his people to quench their old fires and use this fresh flame sent from God.

The minor industries which have some claim to be termed Arts in vogue among the Plateau tribes comprise : pottery, bark-cloth making, basket-making, cloth-dyeing, wood-carving, and the preparation of skins and decorative leather work.

Pottery is the special province of women.   The Wemba woman shown in the photograph used as her only implements a lump of clay, a maize cob, a black powder formed from an old potsherd ground down, a piece of broken gourd, and a shell.   After moistening the clay and kneading it, gradually mixing in the powder to give strength to the clay, she first fashioned the circular sides of the pot, leaving the bottom open.   After carefully edging the upper rim with the shell, she turned over the pot, and with the maize cob the sides were skilfully worked inwards to the centre, until the rounded base was completed.   By way of ornament a girdle of herring-bone marks was quickly pricked round the middle of the pot with the sharp-pointed gourd shell.   The next day the pot, now quite dry, was burnt by heaping brushwood all round it, while the woman kept carefully turning it with two charred sticks used as tongs.

Bark-cloth is made by men only, and until recently it was the duty of every suitor to make such clothes for his betrothed as part of the dowry.

---

[1] Father Torrend, in the preface to his *Comparative Grammar*, thinks it possible that fire-worship may have penetrated from the Persian Colonies on the East Coast into the interior, instancing the Barotse as fire-worshippers.

The best trees for bark-cloth are the *mitawa, muombo,* and *ngalati,* since they are washable, whereas cloth made from the bark of the *ching'anse* or the *misoko* trees will fall to pieces if wetted in a heavy shower. A bark-cloth weaver goes into the forest and cuts samples from the bark of various trees until he finds a strong but pliant rind. He then fells the chosen tree, and by slitting it lengthwise, and, after knocking off the outer bark, skilfully peels off the inner rind intact. These strips of inner bark are placed in the sun to dry, or sometimes upon the rack above the hearth to be cured by the smoke. When he wants to make a cloth, he steeps the strips of bark in the river overnight, then scrapes the outside with a knife, after which he beats out the bark with a hard wood mallet scored with criss-cross lines. By this means the bark is teazed and hammered out to an even thickness all over. The cloth varies from a light tan colour to a pretty shade of grey, and is frequently oiled and coloured with camwood, and decorated with fibre thread from the *chieni* or the *usamba* tree.

Several dyes are known. Natives dye calico black by crushing the berries of the *musangati* tree, and steeping the cloth in the juice mixed with a coal-black swamp mud. If the *musangati* berry is used by itself, a dark blue colour is obtained. The roots of the *kaminda* or of the *makashi* shrub are also used as black dyes. A red dye is obtained from the leaves of the *usishi* tree, or else by boiling the cloth with camwood ; while to obtain a khaki dye the bark of the *muwawa* and *namuenshi* trees is employed.

The Wabisa are expert at tanning and decorating skins. Lechwe skins are moistened and then rubbed down with a kind of pumice-stone ; they are then dressed with oil, and a lozenge-shaped pattern is pricked with a needle upon the inside of the skin.

All leather-work, such as the making of belts, pouches, and of goat-skin bags, is the work of the men. Cord-making from the coarsest rope to thin twine for hunting or for fishing-nets, and even the sewing and patching of their wives' clothes, is the work of the men.

The weaving of baskets and mats from split bamboo, reeds, and osiers calls for no detailed account, as it is the same as that in vogue in Nyasaland, which has been described by many writers. The four kinds of basket in common use are : the *mtanga*, woven by the Wasenga, used as a reaping basket for maize, and for keeping calico and odds and ends inside the hut ; the *museke*, made with reeds, is used for carrying grain and provisions on *ulendo* ; the *lupi*, a broad, shallow basket woven from reeds or from osiers and used for winnowing grain; while last of all is the *chipe*, a small, flat basket used as a plate for porridge.

One has only to attempt to make a good collection of curios to realise how hopelessly inartistic are our Plateau natives. The only objects of any pretence to decorative art are the snuff-boxes, the ornamented bark-cloth boxes, and the pottery, and even these are insignificant and crude when compared with the Luban work across the Congo border. It is obvious that races who have at the most only three or four adjectives for designating colour are somewhat deficient in artistic sense. It is true that bushman paintings have been discovered on the southern fringe of our sphere near Serenje, but so far, except for the grotesque wall-paintings made by the midwives at the *chisungu* ceremony (as described in a previous chapter) no other specimens of native painting are extant. Occasionally a boy will show a distinct skill in clay-modelling of animals, but this gift seems to be rare. Indeed, the various crafts of the native artist are now moribund. Idol-making was once a fine art, and there was a famous one-legged artist on Chirui Island who could carve lay-figures most skilfully, but he is now dead, and with him has perished his art. About ten years ago there were a good many ivory workers who did a fair trade in turning ivory bracelets and rings with their bow-string lathes, but since, nowadays, the bulk of the ivory is exported, they have disappeared.

The cheapness of calico and of fancy clothes has almost killed the cloth-weaving industry still practised by the

Bernard Turner, phot.

NATIVE ARTIST DECORATING BARK BOXES.

Bernard Turner, phot.

MATMAKING. MULUNGWANA WOMAN WEAVING PRAYER MATS.

Walungu and other tribes on the Loangwa Valley. The loom is similar to that in use in Nyasaland. A spindle whorl is used for spinning the thread from the raw cotton.

In bartering the produce of these various industries a fair amount of inter-native trade is done. The Washinga carry on a good trade in ironwork, bartering spear-heads, fish-hooks, axes, and hoes with the Wabisa in return for dried fish nets, mats, and baskets. In a Native Commissioner's Report, dated 1902, it was shown how the Wanyamwezi trader would tour round the country, and, by continual exchanges, finally procure a good profit. He would buy three pounds of Senga tobacco for half a yard of calico, and then sell this tobacco in the Wemba country for two yards. With this two yards of calico fifteen pounds of salt would next be bought in the Mpika division, and the salt would buy at least three sheep in the vicinity of Ft. Hill. These sheep in their turn would eventually be sold for three shillings each to Europeans at Karonga or Fife. Assuming that a man started with a load of sixty pounds of tobacco, it is obvious that a handsome profit was made.

The Awemba seem to have no special inclination for trading, since they buy all they want at the local European store.

Owing to the Sleeping Sickness Regulations, the native trade which existed until recently between the Wanyika of Central East Africa and the Winamwanga and Awiwa— the former trading tobacco, salt, and other wares for the bark-cloth, hoes, and sheep of the latter—is closed down for the present.

About nine years ago a full-grown bull could be purchased for from 10 to 15 lb. of salt, a full-grown cow for from 20 to 25 lb., but nowadays, owing to competition of European buyers for the southern markets, prices have risen considerably, and the price of cows among natives ranges from £2 to £3 a head. The Awiwa are willing to exchange two young bulls with farmers going south in return for a heifer, but are very averse to parting with their female stock. The mine-boy repatriates are now most anxious to invest their deferred pay in cattle, and as they possess a considerable sum of money (from £1500 to £2000 being paid yearly in many divisions), inter-native trade, especially in cattle, has received a welcome impetus and is gradually improving all round.

CHAPTER XVIII

NATIVE HUSBANDRY

Our Plateau native is first and foremost an agriculturist. His pastoral instincts are dormant and undeveloped. The dominant Awemba possess merely a few hundred head of cattle which, owing to the presence of the tsetse fly over the greater portion of the Wemba country, increase but slowly. Even tribes, such as the Winamwanga and Mambwe, who can boast of a few thousand head of cattle, exhibit none of the pastoral skill and aptitude for cattle-raising which distinguish their Nyasaland neighbours.

The making of gardens and agricultural work is of paramount importance. When a native has any definite garden work to do, such as tree-cutting or fencing, it is extremely difficult to make him realise any other obligations, such as that of working for his tax or the necessities of transport. For the most important thing in life from the native standpoint, namely, the acquisition of wives, can be only achieved by the cutting and gardening efforts of the suitors. Time itself is reckoned by a kind of rough farmers' calendar, inasmuch as the very names of the months are given according to the state of the weather, of the food supply, and of the garden work done in each. Indeed, among some tribes agriculture is of such supreme importance that in order to remove any hindrance to its pursuit the natives have been known to resort to human sacrifices.

To avert a drought the following rites are described by Dr. Chisholm as having taken place among the Winamwanga :—

' The head chief sends special messengers (*mavyondongo*, from *kuvyondongola*—to twist the neck) to capture persons—men, women, or youths to be sacrificed to the spirits of the chief.   In the Winam-wanga tribe they may want three or four.   They prefer persons of the family of the priesthood, or those with a large umbilical hernia, or those who have had twins, also twins themselves, or those who have a squint, mothers (*nakatote*) who have borne only one child, or pregnant women.   These are taken to the shrines and are killed in a special manner by these special messengers. They are known to be killed by twisting of the neck, and are never seen again, but what is really done with the bodies is kept very secret.'

Nowadays the spirits of the Winamwanga chiefs have to be content with meaner offerings, such as sheep and pots of beer, which are taken to their shrines with much pomp and beating of drums.

Among the Senga a woman was sometimes sacrificed to cause rain.   Among the Wemba, in case of drought, the *Shing'anga* was summoned to divine the cause.   If the spirits of the chiefs buried at Mwaruli were responsible, a bull was sent to Simwaruli for sacrifice, and—by way of a douceur—a slave woman as well.   When the drought was acute, a human victim would be conveyed to Mwaruli, and the high priest would keep him caged in a stoutly woven fish-basket, until his preparations for the sacrifice were made.

Before going into details of sowing and reaping and their attendant rites, it is necessary to give in brief out-line a summary of the garden work throughout the year. The natives divide the year into two parts—the work of the dry season (June to October), tree-cutting and pre-paration of gardens, and the work of the wet season (November to May), sowing and harvesting.

Work of the Dry Season

June.—Men begin cutting trees for the new gardens. Grain stores are completed for the previous harvest, and the women are engaged in harvesting, threshing, and storing of grain.

July.—Cutting of gardens is continued.

August.—More cutting and heaping of branches in layers upon the garden patches.

September.—Scuffling over the *male* gardens reaped in June, for planting with a second crop. During August and September very little work used to be done, but there is a growing tendency to cut later every year.

October.—After the first shower has fallen the circular gardens of heaped-up branches are fired. If the rain sets in by the end of October, early crops of *male* and *masaka* (red and white millet) are sown.

THE WORK OF THE WET SEASON

November.—After the first rains vegetable marrows, pumpkins, and cucumbers are planted.

December.—Monkey nuts and many varieties of beans are sown, and more marrows, pumpkins, and maize— usually in the gardens which have borne the staple crop of *male* in the previous year.

January.—The first early crop of *male* is reaped. A dwarfish species of *male*, called *chifwifwi*, is sown in the old gardens. The larger kinds of *male* are then planted in virgin soil as the main crop. January is the month of hunger, when many have to subsist upon wild fruits and roots. Those who are hungry will carefully fence their pumpkins and marrows and the edible grass called *luwanga*, upon which they exist, reserving the hard labour of fencing the *male* crop until February, when food is more plentiful and, as they say, ' their bodies come back to them.'

February and *March.*—Maize is reaped. More beds are hoed for the planting of potatoes and other tuberous roots. Fencing of the *male* crop is begun.

April.—Early crops of *male* are reaped. The gardens are kept clear of weeds and guarded against the depredations of game.

May.—The reaping and storing of the *male* begins, and is continued until June.

This finishes the work of the wet season.

The ceremonies at sowing and reaping vary considerably among the different tribes, so only a few examples can be given. Among the Wiwa the chief, Kafwimbi, collects together men from the outlying villages to help him with his sowing. Early in the morning all go out to sow, beginning at the gardens of Kafwimbi's head wife. When the baskets of seed are distributed to all, mothers throw a handful of sand into the tiny sowing-baskets issued to the children, warning them that they must on no account eat any of the first seed dispensed from the granaries of the chief. It is firmly believed that greedy children will swell up and die if they eat instead of sowing the grain of the chief.

Wemba, when sowing millet, deposit in their large sowing-baskets little balls of medicine composed by kneading together the pulp of the roots of various trees, so that the seed may yield a plenteous return. Men, women, and children sow together, dipping their small baskets into the large panniers set in the middle of the garden. Forked sticks are used as rakes to furrow the ground for the scattered seed. When monkey nuts are planted, special charms are placed in the seed baskets. A tortoise shell, they say, gives the nuts a hard and stout rind which resists boring insects. A fat grasshopper, dried, pounded, and smeared over the seeds, causes the ground nuts to grow as fat and lusty as itself !

Harvesting and partaking of the first-fruits are accompanied by elaborate ceremonial among Central African tribes.

Among the Yombe no one is allowed to partake of the first-fruits until the ceremonies are completed. Escorted by a band of drummers, his medicine-men, and the village elders, Chief Njera ascends in state the Kalanga Mountain, until he reaches the hollow fastness held by his forefathers in bygone days against the marauding Angoni, and the spot where the body of his grandfather lay buried. Before the tomb of the departed chief a bull is slain, and pots of freshly made beer and porridge made from the first-fruits are deposited before the shrine. The ground is then carefully cleaned of weeds, and the blood sprinkled on the freshly turned-up soil and on the rafters of the little hut. After offering the customary prayers in thanksgiving for the harvest and beseeching the spirits to partake with them of the first-fruits, the procession withdraws. On return to the village the carcass is divided, all partake of the fresh porridge and beer awaiting them, and the day closes with beer-drinking and dancing.

Kafwimbi, the Wiwa chief, is tabooed from eating the first-fruits, and can only use porridge made from grain of the previous harvest. In his courtyard at the present day are huge grain-stores, in which the grain from each harvest is kept separate. Whenever a new granary is opened, a sheep is killed and the blood sprinkled round the grain-store, after which its contents can be cooked and eaten by the chief and his family in safety. The reason for this taboo is that the chief is the seed-giver to the tribe, and is debarred from partaking of the fruits of one harvest till the success of another is assured, ' so that the seed may never be lost in the land.' Indeed, the preservation of seed for the next sowing is no easy matter for natives, owing to the ravages of the rats, which swarm in every village, and of the borers, weevils, and other insects, which soon infest the grain-bins. Thus the finest maize cobs are selected, and either hung up to dry from the topmost boughs of the village trees or else placed within the hut on a shelf over the fire to be dried and preserved by the constant smoke.

Of the two main systems of preparing the soil the most prevalent upon the Plateau is that which is known as the *vitemene* system—of pollarding the trees, burning the branches, and manuring the soil with the resultant ash. The subsidiary system—simple hoeing of raised beds—calls for no particular comment, and is customary mainly among the Lake Bisa and other tribes living on the banks of the larger rivers, for whom cassava forms the staple food. The *vitemene* system, however, being a peculiarly native method of cultivation and mainly confined to Tropical Africa, deserves more explicit explanation.

To make each garden—which is a circular patch of about fifty yards in diameter—the following procedure is adopted : The trees within a radius of from one to two hundred yards from the selected spot are all pollarded, after which the branches are dragged to the chosen site and heaped up to the height of two and even three feet. When thoroughly dried in a month or two, this mass of heaped-up branches is fired, and the potash in the ashes makes a good fertiliser.   Certain tribes—such as the Bisa of the mainland—are even more destructive of forest areas ; not being contented with mere pollarding, they fell the trees over a large area, dragging the logs to build a pyre over each chosen garden site.   The Lake Bisa, however, owing to the dearth of trees on the islands, migrate about July to the southern swamps towards the Waunga country, and make their gardens by cutting down and heaping up reeds which are fired when dry.   Such *male* gardens are cultivated chiefly for brewing beer, as cassava flour is mainly used for porridge.

In a large village all the people of one *chitente* or quarter go out together to select sites for their yearly tree-cutting.   Choosing spots where the trees are thickest, and where, consequently, the work of dragging branches will be least arduous, each head of a family cuts down a few branches to bespeak the soil and to show the limits of his tree-cutting.   For the first day of actual work each man goes out alone to his own site, and after pollarding all day rests the next, saying, ' Let my spirits, if they like the site, have a day to cut there too.'   The following day, if no bad omens are encountered at the garden or on the way, he cuts without ceasing every day until the work is finished.   If on cutting down a tree he finds the nest of a large bee with a white mark round the neck (called *chipashi*), it is a very bad omen, and if he persists in tilling the spot he will surely die.   Great care is taken to avoid cutting close to the garden of any villager who is suspected of witchcraft.   Such a wizard is popularly supposed to dispatch every night during the harvesting season his servants, the owl and the crow, to

Bernard Turner, phot.

"CHITEMENE" CUTTING.

Hubert Sheane, phot.

A "CHITEMENE" GARDEN SHOWING DESTRUCTION OF TREES.

all gardens close to his own. They pluck the ripe bunches of millet, flying the whole night long to and fro, bearing grain to the wizard's store. While this aerial harvesting is in process, the wizard is described as sitting at ease by his grain-bin, rating each bird soundly if it delays or flies with too light a load. Nor can it complain of overtime, as the wizard has previously taken the precaution of cutting out its tongue !

Among some tribes a tree-cutting 'bee' is held. A villager whose garden is too large for him to go out unaided sets his wife to brew a large supply of beer. When the beer is nearly ready he calls upon all his neighbours to help him. All leave the village at dawn and keep cutting vigorously until late in the afternoon. By then, as a rule, the beer-pots are requisitioned for the thirsty workers, and the work begins anew. Many a worker, in drunken irritation at the mocking jeers of his comrades, will valiantly venture on the topmost boughs to show that he can still lop branches with the best of them—frequently, alas ! to fall with a crash upon some jagged tree-stump, whereupon the pitiful moaning of his relatives will succeed the joy of the revellers with tragic swiftness. Such accidents are by no means infrequent, and many of the crippled folk met with by Native Commissioners in their district rounds ascribe their deformity to this cause.

This custom of collective tree-cutting provokes many quarrels. Even a cautious host, who has kept the beer in his house until the work is done, will frequently run in hastily to the *boma* to complain that his intoxicated guests have broken each others' heads and even burnt down his hut in a drunken quarrel.

Tree-cutting is left to the men, the women's work being to collect and pack the branches in layers over the circular plot. If the soil is 'hard and strong' the branches may be piled up to the height of three feet; but care must be taken, as, if branches are heaped too high upon a lighter or more sandy soil, the natives say the strength of the soil will be burnt away, and the millet will dry up ere it is half-grown.

The burning of these heaped-up gardens begins about October. Each man must give due notice before firing his gardens, so that the neighbours may prevent the flames from spreading to their own unprepared plots. At sunset each man runs around his garden with a rude grass torch and sets it aflame. Using boughs as a flail, he beats out the flames in the surrounding grass, since to spread fire and to cause the destruction of a neighbour's garden was one of the most serious offences at native law. A short time ago in the Fife division an elderly man was so distressed at having destroyed another's garden by accident that, having no means to recompense the sufferer, it preyed upon his mind and he committed suicide. In such cases the grain-bins of the offender would be forfeited by the chief making them taboo. If the gardens of a chief were destroyed by fire spreading from a neighbouring village, it was in the old days a just and sufficient cause for an instant raid in reprisal.

The virgin soil thus prepared by burning is sown with *male* for the first year ; white millet succeeds it as the second crop, while ground nuts and beans are planted in the third year. With this rotation of crops the goodness of the soil is finally exhausted.

To give some idea of the diversity of food-stuffs cultivated, the following table is given of the main varieties and their names in Chiwemba :—

CEREAL GRAINS AND OTHER CROPS

Eleusine, called *male* (*Eleusine coracana*), a dwarf species of millet, is the staple crop. There are eight varieties of this millet known to the Winamwanga.

Dhura (*Sorghum vulgare*).—This is the *dhura* of Northern Africa, called (in the south) Kafir corn, which grows in bunches on a stalk ten to twelve feet high, much like maize. There are many varieties among the Plateau tribes.

Millet (*Pennisetum typhoideum*).—The white variety

(*masaka*) is mainly cultivated by the Wemba. The red variety (*kanchewere*) is popular among the Asenga.

Maize (*Nyanji*).—There are five or six varieties of maize seed, but they are all inferior to the best South African or American species.

Rice.—The natives say that they cultivated the red variety of rice long before the Arabs introduced the superior white seed.

Beans and peas.—The common French bean and seven other varieties of beans are cultivated. Of these the *nkamba* (a large bean growing on a tall shrub) and the *nkalanga* (a ground bean which buries its seed as ground nuts do) are excellent vegetables. The native peas are sturdier than the common English variety and more suited to the soil, growing without the support of sticks.

Marrows, pumpkins, melons, and gourds.—Red and white varieties of pumpkin are common all over the Plateau. There are various kinds of vegetable marrows, three species of cucumber—which are coarser and thicker than the English variety—and two kinds of water-melon.

Cassava.—There are two species—the poisonous (*manangwe*), which has to be steeped before use, and the non-poisonous (*nkaka*).

Potatoes.—Of sweet potatoes there are two varieties— the red and the white. Of another long tuberous root (called *mumbu*, and very like Livingstone's potato) there are four kinds. *Mumbu* are rather watery when boiled, but fried in chips make an excellent vegetable.

Monkey nuts.—The smaller variety (*Arachis hypogaia*), is mainly grown, but the larger species is occasionally found. The White Fathers make a splendid cooking oil from this nut. Natives boil or fry them as a vegetable and squeeze out the oil, which is used for various purposes. The castor-oil plant is common all over the Plateau, the oil being mainly used mixed with fragrant seeds for anointing the body and for dressing bark-cloth. Besides the above food-stuffs, special foods are grown in certain districts. For instance, the Wasenga grow arrowroot, sugar cane, and papaws, all of which were probably introduced by the Arabs.   The Lake Bisa grow quantities of bananas and *mushikishi* beans.

In reviewing the above list it must be borne in mind that for the generality of the Plateau tribes there is only one staple crop—namely, of red millet.   The other grains—maize, beans, tuberous roots, and the like—are considered as quite subsidiary, and are sparsely cultivated.   The Wabisa of the Lake have their fields of cassava to fall back upon in times of scarcity of food.   But on the Plateau proper any failure of the *male* crop is a serious affair, since the Awemba have but meagre subsidiary crops to fall back upon, and hence the hunger stage is soon reached, being most acute from the months of December to January. Most Native Commissioners recognise this fact, and make strenuous efforts to induce natives to plant cassava.   Fortunately at this season many wild fruits are ripe, and wild plums, figs, wild oranges, custard apples, and wild dates abound.   In the Fife division alone a collection of no less than twenty-two different species of edible wild fruits was made.   On asking the Winamwanga headmen on what they mainly subsisted when short of food at the beginning of the year, they brought in eleven varieties of roots of wild plants and nine specimens of leaves of various plants, which are boiled and eaten, mashed, like spinach.

In the hunger season, again, locusts, caterpillars, and many other insects form part of the menu ; traps are set for the smaller animals, duiker drives are organised, and pits, though prohibited, are doubtless still made for the larger buck and antelopes.   Towards the end of the year 1907 there was a great scarcity of food in the Wemba district.

Fortunately the Plateau has of late years been very free from swarms of locusts ; but in certain restricted localities where game is abundant the crops are exposed to their depredations at harvest-time, and official reports testify to the damage done by elephant, eland, and the larger buck and antelope.   In the West Awemba division, one of the authors saw a village wrecked by elephants, who had taken possession and had put the villagers to flight the previous night. The grain-stores had been pulled down, and grain had been scattered and trampled under foot in all directions. The irreparable damage which can be done to crops in a single night in spots frequented by elephant, eland, or roan is one of the strongest native arguments in favour of the *mitanda* system (of garden huts). For obviously, since the gardens must perforce be guarded at night, some shelter on the spot, as a protection from wild beasts, is necessary. Hence, though *mitanda* are strictly forbidden, most Native Commissioners wink at rough grass shelters (*tute*) being erected while the crops are ripening, on condition that they are destroyed after the harvest. Where elephants are plentiful, quaint watch-towers are built on stout poles, overhanging the gardens like the huge nest of some antediluvian bird. However, with stout fences flanked by game-pits (which we have already described in a previous chapter), the gardens are fairly secure against all game except elephants.

Among the beds of cassava, ground-nuts, and sweet potatoes, wild pigs do no small damage. As a protection the Amambwe dig shallow pits and throw up small mounds around such plots, which, however ridiculous they may appear as a barrier, seem to scare away the pigs, who, perhaps, suspect traps on such uneven ground.

Native garden tools are of the simplest description. The small axe with the narrow cutting head, and the common Central African hoe, are familiar enough and have been described and photographed in nearly every book of Central African travel. These two implements serve every ordinary garden purpose, though among some tribes a sickle-shaped knife inset into a long handle is used for clearing weeds and brushwood from the gardens.

Such is a short outline of native agricultural methods, of the principal food-stuffs, and of the problem of famine due to shortage of rainfall and the ravages of game.

The chief problem is that of the deforestation of the country owing to the present wasteful system of tree-cutting. As fresh forest land is cut down each year for the staple crop, the forest areas are being slowly converted into straggling scrub and stunted trees. This problem has so far been found extremely difficult of solution. In 1906 to 1907 attempts were made to induce the natives to abandon the tree-cutting system, but were met with such passive opposition and dissatisfaction that they were abandoned. Although one Native Commissioner showed by practical experiment how well *male* could be cultivated by merely hoeing the soil, the natives were unconvinced, attributing the success of the crop merely to the white man's magic. Even when one pointed to the splendid crops of wheat, vegetables, and other food-stuffs grown by the White Fathers at their stations throughout the year by a simple system of irrigation, they would only say, ' That is all very well for white men. But is not each male child born for the axe and each female child for the hoe ' (referring to the formula at the birth of each child). ' How can we hoe the ground like women ? ' ' How again can we find wives if we do not cut trees for our fathers-in-law as in the olden time ? ' Nor were the independent Wemba women slow to oppose most vigorously any system which would throw the bulk of the garden work—namely, hoeing, which the men refuse to do—upon their own shoulders.

Besides the tree-cutting, the present system of late burning of the bush is most destructive to the young trees. Mr. Neave, in a paper published in the *Journal of the Geographical Society* (February 1910), p. 137, states that among Wemba and other tribes this burning frequently does not take place until the trees have assumed the foliage of the following year. Hence, on the Plateau at least, it would seem most advisable if such burning as is necessary should be made earlier, and restricted to definite months as in many parts of South Africa.

Again, far more forest areas are denuded of trees by natives each year than are necessary for their actual food supply. A Magistrate of long experience has estimated that, at least, half of the produce of gardens thus wa te-fully cut is squandered in beer-drinking.

At present the path to improved methods is blocked

by the blind prejudice and crass conservatism with which the Plateau tribes — like most 'nature peoples' — cling to their crude and antique methods of soil culture. It must in fairness be admitted that many of the plains, especially in the Wemba country, are what is known as sour soil, and therefore out of the question for raising crops. But it is curious that the good soil on the banks of the streams is not more used for the sowing of the staple crop.

For instance, the European gardens, maintained with a little irrigation throughout the year by the side of streams at every white settlement, show what different kinds of food-stuffs can be grown successfully on river-bank soil. Considering that such fertile soil is available in abundance —for a population which in North-Eastern Rhodesia does not exceed two to the square mile—it is all the greater pity that deforestation still continues. Warnings as to final penalties of unchecked deforestation are writ large in the majority of agricultural reports upon Tropical Africa, and there can be no question but that the denudation of the forest areas leads to deterioration of the climate and ultimately to the impoverishment of the country. In the neighbouring territory of Nyasaland, the Director of Agriculture, in his Report for the year ending 31st March 1910, remarks that already—owing to the previous deforestation by natives—the supply of firewood and timber in the vicinity of the larger European settlements is becoming a serious question. On the Plateau, fortunately at present, owing to the scanty white population and the absence of mining or other timber-consuming industries, the problem does not call for immediate treatment. But in years to come, as the population increases (with that singular fecundity which distinguishes the Bantu races under British rule) and white settlers arrive, the problem will call for serious attention. It is to be hoped, however, that by gradually fostering the cultivation of rice and of cassava, the natives will, in time, become alive to the easiness with which these foods are grown, and slowly substitute them for their more uncertain crops of millet, just as certain tribes upon Lake Nyasa have abandoned to a great extent their primitive foods, and now rely upon their crops of rice, which was first introduced by the Arabs and encouraged by the Nyasaland Government.

Doubtless, too, when the necessity becomes more acute, a Forestry Department will be established, which, by afforestation and by encouragement of tilling as against tree-cutting, will gradually eliminate obsolete native systems, and—at least among the younger generation—finally reduce· their primitive prejudices to a vanishing point.

To turn to the pastoral side of native life, Sir Harry Johnston gives an admirable description of the origin of Central African cattle, so nothing need be said on this head. On the Plateau the humped and shorthorn breed of cattle are the most common, although occasionally one finds to the south of the North Loungwa district long-horned, straight-backed cattle of the Cape type, which probably have been traded from the Angoni. The native cattle on the Plateau are, as a rule, of small size. The important fact from the point of view of the European farmer is that, with the exception, of course, of sickness caused by the tsetse fly, the native cattle are remarkably free from the many cattle diseases prevalent in South Africa. Thus in the Fort Jameson district a few imported head of cattle died from red water—a disease from which the local cattle are apparently immune, as it did not spread. In some seasons there are local outbreaks of stiff-sickness or three-days' sickness—a disease which, as a rule, passes off without any subsequent ill-effects, and which is the cause of only a small mortality. Many of the broken remnants of tribes in the Fife division have con-siderable skill in tending cattle and knowledge of cattle medicines. Accordingly, when the Awemba raided as far as the Songwe river, they spared the lives of the Wenya and Wandia herdsmen to look after all captured stock. The Wawenya show considerable skill in delivering cows in calf. After the calf is born the roots of the *chiloke* plant are mixed with saltish earth, which is much sought after by game, and is obtained from certain ant-heaps. With

NATIVE GRAIN BIN.

Gibson Hall, phot.

Bernard Turner, phot.

HERDING GOATS IN VILLAGE BY DAY.

this mixture the cow is massaged from horns to tail, and finally the udders are bathed. This treatment, they say, soothes the cow and causes it to give milk immediately. The Wenya cattle kraals are long rectangular buildings of strong poles, the interstices being usually plastered with mud. The roof and rafters are stoutly woven and thickly grassed, thorn bushes being thrown on top, since lions attack these kraals from above. Wenya cattle are taken out very late to grass; the natives say that this is not mere indolence on the herd-boy's part, but because the heavy morning dew is most dangerous for all beasts. As a rule cattle are herded by young boys close to the village, and very rarely are they taken far afield or is pasture specially burnt for them. When the grass is dried up and the pasture near the village is exhausted, cattle are driven into the old cassava gardens and mealie patches, where they browse on the dried mealie stalks and on cassava leaves. The women of the Wenya tribe may on no account milk the cattle or touch the udder—a superstition found also among the Wankonde and the Zulu. The old men say that since the *sotola* rinderpest in 1894 they have had no outbreak of epidemic disease among their stock. Scab occasionally appears, but is soon cured. The leaves of the *sambwe* shrub are pounded in a mortar into a greenish pulp, which is rubbed into the sores, a portion being diluted with water and given to the affected cattle to drink. Small black frogs are occasionally swallowed by cattle, and to get rid of these the Wawenya drench the beast with copious draughts of charcoal and water. When a newly-born calf refuses to take the udder, biting ants or cockroaches are rubbed upon its gums, so as to irritate them and cause the calf to suck. If a cow has twin calves the owner must hand over both to the chief.

The Nyika tribe—of which a small number inhabit the Fife division—are renowned for their pastoral aptitude and skill in cattle-breeding. Should a cow be snake-bitten, the root of a shrub named *mukololo* is pounded and mixed with water. The Nyika cow-doctor takes a mouthful of this decoction and squirts it into the wound, then blows another mouthful up the beast's nostrils. A cow mauled by a leopard is treated by rubbing into the sores the boiled juice of the tree called the *chipeta*, by massaging the bruised parts with boiling water, and by rubbing in this liquid as a liniment. But for wounds made by the claws of a lion, the Wanyika admit that this remedy is useless. They firmly believe that after certain ceremonies have been performed inside the kraal by the village medicine-man it will be able to resist all attacks by lions. A part of such ritual consists in burning a spear over a strong fire until the head melts off; upon the smouldering flames are then thrown the shells of a species of tortoise, which give off a most powerful smoke, the stench of which clings around the walls and rafters for a long time, and is said to render them impervious to attack.

Many tribes upon the Plateau uses the fish poison *wuwa* as a remedy against scab. The leaves of this plant are pounded in a mortar, and the juice therefrom is rubbed into the scabs. As this lotion is very poisonous to all but infected beasts, those treated must be carefully tied up. Government herd-boys often use this remedy for outbreaks of scab, with excellent results.

About the Wemba or Mambwe methods of tending cattle there is little to say. They prefer, as a rule, open kraals, and these are usually in an indescribable condition of filth, the cattle often being seen standing up to their girths in mud and ordure. The time-honoured story of a lion having sprung into a Mambwe cattle kraal by night and being found there by the villagers the next day—having been unable to struggle out of the mire, much less to seize the cattle—though it seems somewhat fabulous, would be easily credited by any one who has seen the abysmal filth of Mambwe cattle stalls.

Among the Winamwanga, cattle are usually slaughtered by a sharp blow on the back of the neck with an axe while the animal is licking salt, the neck being immediately ripped open with a spear. The Walungu are accustomed to cutting out the in-growing horns of cattle, which they prefer to do with a hot knife instead of a saw. Cow dung is not put to such a multitude of uses as among the Wan-konde, who use it as a fuel and for washing out the interiors of huts to drive away insects ; but among the Wandia tribe it is used for plastering and mudding their huts.

Other Central African domestic animals have been so faithfully and fully described by Sir Harry Johnston in his book, *British Central Africa*, p. 432, that only a few remarks on the Plateau varieties need be appended.

Each village has its little flock of sheep and goats. The sheep are, as a general rule, skinny and small boned as compared with English breeds. They are a cross between the two breeds of maned and fat-tailed sheep, the colour varying from dark to reddish brown. On Lake Bangweolo a large variety of fat-tailed sheep is to be found, abounding on Mbawala Island. Unfortunately the Lake sheep do not stand the journey well to the high Plateau, and among flocks sent to Fife the mortality was high. To lessen this the natives usually bring some of the Lake soil and mix it with the drinking-water for some time after the arrival of a flock on higher ground. The Bisa and Wiwa slit the tails of their sheep and dissect out the tail bone. Into the cavity they rub salt, and say that by this method the tail becomes heavy with fat. No particular attention seems to be paid to goats. They wander round the village picking up what refuse of cereals they can find, and, as the ground is usually littered with winnowing chaff and other food refuse, they do better than might be expected.

The African *nkuku*, or fowl, is supposed to have reached Africa first through Egypt at the time of the Persian occupation, not before 400 B.C. No special food is given to fowls, which live on the refuse of the village grain-bins.

Sitting hens are placed in a grass net woven on top of a forked stake, which is driven into the floor of the native hut. In a very few villages guinea-fowl are reared by placing eggs, found in the bush, under a sitting hen. Pigeon cotes are erected in the majority of villages. The first stakes of such cotes are driven in by a woman who has borne twins, in order, they say, that the pigeons may multiply.   Dogs are usually of the pariah type, and live on the village refuse and offal.   Among the Waunga there is a larger breed of dogs used to hunt lechwe, and in other tribes such dogs as have shown skill in hunting are usually well fed.

To describe the innumerable kinds of insects used for food and other purposes is beyond the scope of this book. Professor Drummond has described the insect life on the Tanganyika Plateau, the native traps for flying ants and the habits of termites at considerable length.   In spots frequented by bees an artificial hive (*munshinga*) is built in the following manner : A log of wood is cut in half lengthwise, each half being hollowed out like a canoe. The two parts are then put together and slung from a tree, and a little slot is cut so that the bees may have ready access to the interior.

In conclusion, the Plateau as a whole is essentially suited for the raising of cattle.   Though there are extensive fly belts in part of the Awemba District, yet, fortunately, the northern parts of the Tanganyika and North Loungwa Districts have been for many years free from fly.   Native cattle, however, do not increase as rapidly as they might, owing to the native practice of permitting many bulls to run with the herd, and allowing too much inbreeding.   Castration is rarely practised by the Winamwanga or Amambwe, and it would be an excellent thing to send round Nyika herdsmen who are expert castrators.   It is to be hoped that, as the country becomes more occupied and cultivation is extended, the fly will disappear as it has done in South Africa ; at present, however, it shows no signs of decrease, but forms a decided check to the free circulation and consequent widespread increase of the native cattle in our sphere.

CHAPTER XIX

WAYS AND MEANS

IT is often difficult enough to commence a fresh chapter ; there are so many ways of doing it that one casts around in despair for some method of deciding upon the best. But in this particular case—perhaps because the chapter in question is to be a strictly utilitarian one—there seems but one opening possible. And that is—to impress upon the intending visitor the central fact that upon the Tanganyika Plateau every man is, to all intents and purposes, his own storekeeper, and that he should act accordingly when purchasing his equipment prior to leaving England.

It may perhaps be as well, at the outset, to consider the various methods of entering the country. They are three in number : from the south *via* Cape Town and Broken Hill, from the east *via* Chinde and Lake Nyasa, from the north *via* Mombasa and German East Africa. There are, of course, others as well ; for instance, a traveller in search of varied experiences might elect to land at Lobito Bay and proceed to Railhead, and work his way eastwards through the Congo, or, striking northwards from Beira or Salisbury, arrive *via* Tete, Feira, and Fort Jameson. Neither of these routes can be considered advisable.

The following hints upon the Cape and Chinde routes may be of value :—

Via Chinde it is well to remember that no river steamer ever repairs the rents in its mosquito-nets, and to have a needle and thread handy. Good cooks can be engaged at Blantyre or Zomba, but the wages, which are much lower upon the Plateau than in Nyasaland, should be arranged in advance. The same applies to Broken Hill. It is often very rough indeed upon Lake Nyasa, and sea-sick passengers may cheerfully anticipate a repetition of their ocean experiences. At Chinde itself everything must remain in the Customs House, which is in the British Concession ; a handbag should therefore be packed with requisites for the night, which is usually spent at the A.L.C. boarding-house.

There is not much to be said in connection with the Cape route, except that ladies need dust-cloaks and veils for the train. A filter should be kept out for the journey between Livingstone and Broken Hill, and a hamper, well stocked, should be packed for this portion of the journey, as the restaurant car does not go further than Livingstone. Heavy baggage not wanted on the voyage should be sent a month ahead *via* Beira to escape the heavy passenger luggage dues, and consigned to Broken Hill or Ndola.

Fares and freights require careful consideration, as they are perhaps the heaviest initial expense.

By the Chinde-Nyasaland route the cheapest method is to go by the Rennie Aberdeen Line from London to Chinde, then by river steamers to Port Herald, rail to Blantyre, *machila* to Fort Johnston, and steamer to Karonga on Lake Nyasa.   The fares are :—

First class (single)	£63	0	0
Second class	53	11	0
Intermediate steamships (one class only)	57	15	0

By the Deutsch Ost Afrika Line to Chinde, and thence by the British Central Africa Company's steamers, train, and *machilas* to Karonga, fares are quoted as follows :—

First class	£81	10	8
Second class	61	19	8

All the above rates include food during the actual journey.

By the Union Castle Mail Line from England, by the Western route to Chinde, and thence by the A.L.C. to Karonga, the fares are :—

	London to Chinde.	Chinde to Karonga (first class only).	Total.
First class (minimum) .	£47 5 0	£29 0 0	£76 5 0
Second class „ .	34 13 0	29 0 0	63 13 0

The average duration of the trip from London to Karonga is from six to seven weeks.[1]

By the Cape Town Southern Rhodesia route the fares are as under :—

	Union Castle Line, London to Cape Town (intermediate steamers).	Railway, Cape Town *via* Victoria Falls to Broken Hill.	Total.
First class .	. £28 7 0 (lowest)	£19 9 7	£47 16 7
Second class	. 23 2 0 ,,	13 7 5	36 9 5

The cheapest rates for freight to the Tanganyika Plateau are still *via* the Nyasaland route. All particulars can be obtained from the British Central Africa Company, 20 Abchurch Lane, London, E.C., who quote rates from Liverpool to Fort Johnston at the south end of Lake Nyasa, varying from £13, 18s. 5d. per ton to £12, 15s. 11d. per ton, according to the class of goods imported. These rates are per ton *weight* or per 40 cubic feet of *measurement*, at the Company's option. To this must be added £8 for transport to the north end of Lake Nyasa at Karonga. The African Lakes Corporation are at present the only Company who run a through freight service from Chinde to Karonga, and all particulars can be obtained from their Head Office, 14 St. Vincent Place, Glasgow.

The freights quoted by the Rennie Line from London to Chinde vary from £2, 10s. to £3, according to the class of goods ; the A.L.C. rates from Chinde to Karonga, namely, £18 per ton, must be added, making the whole freight about £21 per ton.

Heavy baggage *via* the London, Beira, and Rhodesia route to Broken Hill varies from 17s. 3d. to £1, 15s. 2d. per 100 lb., according to the class of goods imported. In the Appendix to Chapter XIV. the procedure with reference to dutiable goods, namely, arms, ammunition, and liquor, has already been dealt with.

---

[1] The Union Castle Line run intermediate steamships *via* the East Coast to Chinde. The fares are 42 guineas first class (minimum) and 30 guineas second class (minimum).

Having thus discussed in detail the various ways of entering the country, with approximate cost and duration of journey, let us consider what are the absolute necessaries which must be taken. At the outset it may be stated that all the following articles can be procured more cheaply and of more reliable quality in England than anywhere in South or Central Africa. It is sometimes said, ' Buy as little as you can at home ; wait till you get to Cape Town, or Bulawayo, or Broken Hill, as the case may be. There you will find everything you need, and you will have saved the cost of carriage from England.'

Not a bit of it. Goods of the kind required on the Plateau are not manufactured in either South or Central Africa ; at the best—for instance, in the case of tents, which can certainly be bought in Bulawayo—they are merely made up from materials imported from home. The Southern storekeeper is not going to be a loser over the deal ; his customer must pay the original cost of freight and something over to represent middleman's profit. Besides which, all articles bought in South Africa carry South African duty, whereas at the moment of writing there is no import duty in North-Eastern Rhodesia except upon arms, ammunition, and liquor.

For all practical purposes 6d. per lb. added to the retail price of an article in England will represent its price landed upon the Plateau. There are, naturally, variations according to the distance of the particular station from the port of entry, but 6d. may be taken as a fair average.

The following list, compiled by the late Mr. Robert Codrington when Administrator, was intended to serve as a guide to officials entering the country for the first time. It may be taken as representing the minimum required by a bachelor, and thus serves as a good basis for discussion :—

1. Sporting rifle and D.B. shot-gun.
2. Light vests or undershirts.
3. Light drawers.
4. Merino socks.
5. Cotton or flannel shirts without collars.

RHODESIAN MAHOGANY.

(Published by kind permission of the B.S.A. Co.)

6. Suits of light tweed.
7. Suits of khaki or similar material.
8. Strong, but not heavy boots and shoes.
9. General clothing as worn in England in summer for use at headquarters of districts.
10. Sweater.
11. Waterproof.
12. Overcoat.
13. Strong camp-bed (A. and N.).
14. Blankets and sheets.
15. Camp table and chair.
16. Travelling-bath.
17. Tin uniform-cases.

Let us consider the above in detail. Item No. 1 has been discussed in Chapter XIII. Items 2 to 4 are indispensable, and may be passed without comment.

No. 5. Silk and wool will probably be found preferable to either cotton or flannel, and will better stand the loving attentions of ultra-energetic washboys. A supply of good drill shooting-shirts, with turned-down collars and breast-pockets, should be taken; half a dozen will probably suffice. The most important point is that they should be of dark khaki, which will not fade in washing, preferably a kind of heather-mixture shade in which green predominates, if suitable material can be found. If thorn-resisting, so much the better; but it is useless to attempt to have them waterproof, and the merits of ventilation would be sacrificed to very little purpose.

No. 7. It is a good thing to have half a dozen pairs of white drill trousers for changing into for the afternoon game of tennis. But complete suits of white drill are a mistake; they attract the sun's rays, instead of making for coolness, and they need double the washing of khaki. Tussore and mercerised silk are excellent materials.

No. 8. Boots and shoes constitute perhaps the most important item. The former should be plentifully equipped with nails. If a choice must be made, weight is less objectionable than flimsiness. Riding boots and leggings are not, at present, of the slightest use. It is useless to attempt to obtain a waterproof boot; African rains will

penetrate any leather, and the more comparatively waterproof the boot is the longer will the water remain inside ;
it is almost better to have holes purposely bored in the
soles to let the water out as quickly as possible ! For
shooting and careful stalking some consider that stout
shoes with rope soles are preferable in many ways to boots.
Putties are most useful, and several pairs should be taken,
although many residents discard them and wear only
socks below their 'shorts.' And it may be noted here
that 'shorts' are also indispensable—half a dozen pairs
are none too many, and they should be cut a good inch
above the knee. The freedom given by 'shorts' on
ulendo must be experienced to be fully appreciated—
breeches and gaiters being far too hot, and trousers most
uncomfortable for a long march. Nevertheless, a pair of
khaki trousers and leather spats is by no means a bad
kit for pottering round the station after birds in the wet
weather, or the season of 'blackjacks' and grass seeds.

No. 9 needs but little comment. As hinted above,
shirts and underclothing suffer severely in the wash,
partly through the fact that the native washboy will just
as soon beat out clothes upon a board with a nail in it as
not, and partly because clothes are washed more frequently
than at home, and are apt to rot in the sun when drying.
A pith helmet is a necessity—the 'Tent Club' pattern is
perhaps the best. One for each year of intended residence
is a fair allowance, and three or four waterproof covers
should be taken. Needless to say the covers should be
khaki, though some people prefer the helmet itself to be
white for station wear. Double Terai or Stettson hats
are most suitable and necessary—and a tweed cap is
often useful in a *machila*.

No. 10. A sweater is a matter of individual taste. It
is useful after tennis, when one is apt to sit for half an
hour or so upon a veranda and contract a chill, but is
not much used upon *ulendo*.

No. 11. The waterproof should be fitted with a cape.
Nothing else will keep out the rain over the shoulders, at
any rate after the first year. The African climate is

notably hard upon rubber articles, and it would probably be true economy to purchase two moderate-priced waterproofs than one expensive one.

No. 12. Overcoat. Perhaps a superfluity, except upon the voyage and in the train. It may be used in camp, but as there is usually a large fire it is not essential. Nearly all its purposes can be better served by a good dressing-gown, which is indispensable.

No. 13. The camp-bed is an article upon which all sporting authorities love to expatiate. It must, of course, be light and portable, and should pack in a bag. For most purposes the X pattern is probably the best. A new X bed has recently been produced which is considerably broader than the old pattern, and has special improved sockets for mosquito-net poles.

No. 14. All blankets should be white. The reason will be better appreciated when a night or two has been passed in the near vicinity of a native village. Sheets are useful for *ulendo* during the dry weather, but dangerous during the rains. All linen brought to the country should be thoroughly good : it will prove far cheaper in the end. A Wolseley waterproof valise is one of the most valuable articles which the traveller can posesss.

No. 15. Camp table and chair. Here again the X pattern cannot be beaten, at least for tent use. Folding, dining, or office tables can, however, be made in the country at the various mission stations, and such are better suited to individual requirements. A strong, comfortable deck chair with arm-pieces is invaluable. When the canvas rots, as it invariably does sooner or later, *puku* or reed-buck skin makes an excellent substitute. The Indian Rhorkhi chair is useful.

No. 16. The travelling-bath should be of tin, fitted with cover and lock. It can then be packed for the board-ship voyage with linen, etc. The collapsible bath propped up with wooden slats is a delusion and a snare.

No. 17. Tin uniform-cases are essential. Leather is useless. One case should be fitted with a double cover, for important papers or books.

Jaeger cholera belts are most useful, though it is not every one who can wear them. Handkerchiefs should be taken in abundance, preferably of coloured silk. The native loves them, and pouches them without scruple, but a bandana is comparatively easy to trace. Evening dress must not be forgotten—a dinner-jacket is most necessary. A few stiff shirts should be taken, but for ordinary use soft or frilled shirts are preferable. Black boots and evening shoes are also liable to be overlooked. Each suit should have two pairs of trousers.

So much for the question of clothes and outfit in general. The following list of little things, so liable to be forgotten, and between the having and not having of which so great a gulf is fixed, may be of use to the new resident :—

Good travelling inkpot.
Ink pellets, or concentrated ink.
Plenty of foreign stationery.
Spring balance.
Candle lamps, collapsible, with Talc and spare globes.
Acetylene lamp, for use in lion districts for sportsmen.
Blue lights and magnesium flares for big game, for sportsmen.
Good camera, preferably with metal body.
Bootlaces.
Buttons.
Studs.
Needles, darning wool and thread.
Small box of haberdashery supplies.
Pocket compass.
Good knife.
Belt and swivels with chain.
Boot repair outfit and leather.
Spare shaving brushes.
Tool box.
Small despatch box.
Watch glasses. (A wristlet watch is the most serviceable. A really good watch is a mistake ; far better half a dozen at half a guinea than one at ten pounds.)
Hair scissors or clippers.
Grindstone.
Safety razor (as two months will elapse in sending an ordinary razor to be set).

Strong galvanised iron Army bucket canteen.

Luncheon basket (made to order—bought ones are never suitable, and usually far too heavy).

Thermos flask.

Light wooden (Venesta) bottle box, fitted to hold say ten bottles, Sparklet bottles, etc.

Seccotine.

Luminous matchbox for camp.

Hunting knife in sheath.

Hinges.

Bolts.

Plenty of Willesden canvas.

Twine.

Sail needles.

Good field-glasses.

Alpenstock as shooting stick.

Sparklet bottles.

Airtight (screw-top) bottles and jars.

Good assortment of vegetable and flower seeds.

Strong cartridge bag or belt, made to fancy.

Canvas water-cooler.

Garden tools.

Watering-can.

Syringe.

Spare pipes and tobacco pouches.

Tennis racquets and balls.

A map of the country.

A handy guide to sportsmen has been compiled by Dr. Dunbar Brunton.

Before leaving England a subscription for well-selected periodicals, newspapers, and cheap books should be arranged with a good newsagent. There is a great dearth of reading matter. All newspapers, especially those on glazed paper, should be packed in waterproof coverings, and the thin-paper editions sent where possible. A cheap parcels rate exists *via* Beira—7s. 6d. for 11 lb.—and quantities of stores such as tea, hams, biscuits, etc., can be sent this way at stated intervals.

A bicycle is indispensable, and can be used on most native paths. It should be fitted with tandem tyres, double cross-bar, raised pedals, and extra strong saddle-springs, but on no account with a back-pedalling brake. A good foot-pump should be brought. Punctures can be mended with raw rubber straight from the tree. Bush cars appear to be a failure, except on the main roads.

Health.—The following note is extracted from the *Official Handbook* published in 1903 :—

' The new arrival should take every precaution against exposure to sun, wind, or rain. Flannel clothes should be worn and changed immediately after exercise or exposure to wet ; he should eat, drink, and smoke moderately, and retire early to rest. Food should be of the best that is procurable, and always fresh in preference to tinned. English vegetables, milk, eggs, and fresh meat, or game, are procurable at all the large stations throughout the country. Mosquito nets should be invariably used, and three to five grains of quinine taken daily as a prophylactic during the unhealthy season.

' Apart from malaria and its sequelæ, the country is remarkably free from other tropical diseases, both among natives and Europeans. Dysentery, diarrhœa, typhoid, and insolation occasionally occur.

' The first two years of residence are the most trying to Europeans, who afterwards seem to acquire immunity to a certain extent, and enjoy long periods of uninterrupted good health.

' The unhealthy season of the year is during and just after the rains from December until June ; the most unhealthy months being April, May, and June.

' Hæmoglobinuric or blackwater fever occurs as a sequela to malarial fever. Those who neglect to take sufficient precautions against malarial attacks, and expose themselves to harmful influences while harbouring the malarial parasite, are those who generally fall victims to this pernicious type of fever. While the mortality stood at about 25 per cent. of those attacked, it is satisfactory to note that with improved medical treatment and nursing the mortality from this disease has considerably decreased during the last two years.'

During the seven years since this was written, as the country has become more settled, attacks of blackwater among residents have been very few and far between.

But little can be added to the above. Kufu fever has already been referred to in a previous chapter. A hot-water bottle for use during attacks of fever should always be carried when travelling. Permanganate of potash, a

caustic pencil, and a lancet should also be carried on
ulendo, preferably attached to the belt—more for the sake
of the carriers than of oneself. Sleeping in, or even near,
villages should be avoided whenever possible ; it is quite
unnecessary in the dry season. For similar reasons the
quarters of servants should be at a considerable distance
from the dwelling-house. Every one in sleeping-sickness
area should wear putties, as it is said that the fly
bites almost invariably on the ankles and legs. When
travelling, the journey should be made either early or
late, thus avoiding the heat of the midday sun as much
as possible. Regular daily exercise is of prime importance.
Before leaving England every one should be vaccinated,
unless the operation has been recently performed, and—
a most important point—should have his teeth thoroughly
overhauled. The evils arising from unsound teeth are
legion and often most serious.

Most filters are unsatisfactory, but water should always
be boiled if there is any suspicion of its being impure. At
most stations this is unnecessary.

Medicine chests, fitted with the drugs necessary in Central
Africa, can be obtained from Messrs. Burroughs & Wellcome.
The principal remedies needed are quinine (hydrochloride
is preferable to bisulphate), two or three kinds of suitable
purgatives, Warburg's tincture, chlorodyne, Dover powder,
phenacetin, ammonium or potassium bromide, hazeline,
iodoform, castor oil, blackwater palatinoids (Hearsey's
preparation), permanganate of potash, and corrosive
sublimate. Jeyes' fluid and ammonia are most useful.
Surgical bandages, lint, and goldbeater's skin should also
be taken, while jaconnette is a handy article. Two or
three spare clinical thermometers are invaluable. Persons
using glasses are advised to bring a good supply of spare
lenses. A stock of medical comforts, such as *good* brandy,
port, champagne, and Brand's essence should always be
maintained.

Tents.—Money put into tents is well invested. More
misery is caused by small, ill-ventilated, or unsound tents
than the unsophisticated newcomer dreams of ; and, con-

versely, the extra initial cost or payments to extra carriers for dining and kitchen tents is a pardonable extravagance —that is, of course, if any considerable period each year is to be spent in travelling.

The tent should have a double fly, and should be made of thin Willesden canvas, which does not absorb moisture and so render the load heavier. An excellent pattern, but one little known in this country, is the ' Indian Field Officer's '—which includes a curved porch in front and a bathroom behind. The fly comprises both veranda and bathroom, and makes one load ; the body of the tent is a second load, and the ground sheet and poles make the third. The body of the tent should not be less than 10 by 12 ft. The ' porch ' and bathroom should be identical in size and shape, and the ' petticoats ' made to lace on to the top, so that porch and bathroom can be interchanged. The sides of the fly should come almost down to the ground, so as to allow plenty of space for loads in wet weather. Inside walls should be at least 4 ft. high, as every inch of height means, in reality, more floor space. Ground sheets should be made of Willesden canvas also, as it does not rot, and is not damaged by ants. Pockets in the walls are most useful, as are also straps and hooks to buckle round the poles, for clothes or rifles. The walls of every tent should be made to roll up and tie, to allow plenty of ventilation when camped at midday.

Machilas.—*Machilas* are an invention of the devil ; but unless one possess a bicycle they are practically indispensable. The hammock should be slung well off the ground, to avoid stumps when travelling through bush. In wet weather, however, the cords contract, and it is necessary to loosen them, or it will be found impossible to wriggle into the *machila*. The flaps should come well down on each side ; there should be a wooden framework, fixed to the pole, to hold the cover out from one's head, and the cover itself should project beyond the hammock at each end, otherwise it will drip on to one's boots and down the nape of one's neck. Carriers should be, as much as possible, of the same height. Pockets in the flaps will be found a useful addition for storing a book, cap, etc. Pillows or a couple of blankets should be placed in the *machila*, especially when used by a lady, as serious damage may result from contact with a jagged stump.

Housekeeping.—It is practically impossible to give any estimate of the cost of living, since individual tastes vary so much, and the matter depends mostly upon the individual in charge of the commissariat. It is certainly a country in which it is cheaper to be married than single, so far as actual cost of stores goes. No matter how good a manager a bachelor may be, it is impossible for him to keep so sharp an eye upon domestic economies as a woman.

Living expenses for married settlers vary from £3 to £4 a month. As we have seen in Chapter I., meat, eggs, and vegetables are very cheap—for instance, about £5 a year plus the cost of cartridges spent on a native hunter (50s. for licence and say 50s. for his pay), should keep the household well supplied with meat.

It has already been said that all stores should be ordered from home. Dutiable articles (in England) can be brought out in bond. They should be packed in venesta-wood cases, each fitted with a padlock and hinges, and not weighing more than 60 lb. nor less than 50. Such boxes will be worth almost their weight in gold upon subsequent *ulendos*. All stores and heavy furniture should be sent forward as freight to Broken Hill or Chinde, at least two months in advance of the traveller. Whisky and paraffin cases should be enclosed in another case, as thefts in transit frequently occur ; on one occasion *empty* beer-bottles were substituted for full bottles of whisky. Liquor should be packed in fifteen-bottle cases, to save head transport.

Many household articles can be procured in the country, or can be replaced by substitutes. Sugar can be bought at Musidi Mission in Nyasaland ; paraffin at Kassanga in German East Africa (at a much cheaper rate than in the A.L.C. stores, though not, perhaps, of quite equal quality) ; good brown and white flour is produced by the White Fathers at Chilubula and Kapatu, and also excellent oil distilled from monkey-nuts, which can be used in cooking to save marrow-fat, a most expensive item. Salt-petre should be taken for salting meat; and for this, and other culinary purposes, good native salt is usually procurable. It is very dark in colour, but goes much further than ordinary table salt. Coffee can be got from Nyasaland; a good coffee-grinder must not be forgotten, and a small hand-mill for grinding other things—such as mealies, which make excellent bread—is most useful. Pigs do well, and during the cool season good bacon can be made. An excellent substitute for beer can be made from fermented honey, which is very plentiful at certain seasons. Jam may be made from Cape gooseberries, tomatoes, lemons, limes, carrots, and pine-apples, all of which thrive. Desiccated soups and Maggi's *consommés* should be brought. Local (Nyasaland) tobacco and cigarettes are cheap and good. Starch for most purposes, except collars and shirts, can be made from cassava, and baking-powder from ground-rice, and bicarbonate of soda with a little tartaric acid. Rice can be bought in Nyasaland, and also upon Lake Tanganyika,—it requires careful cleaning, but is good. Mealie-meal makes excellent porridge, though it is apt to pall unless mixed with oatmeal.

As regards kitchen utensils, it is equally difficult to lay down any hard-and-fast rules. Every lady should bring a stove, which should be carefully packed with instructions for refitting. A mincing machine, rolling-pin, and pasteboard are also essentials. A good meat-safe is obviously indispensable, but this can soon be made out of a small roll of mosquito wire-netting, since any native carpenter can soon make a frame. Some people are in favour of aluminium cooking-pots, as being light and strong, while others maintain that they impart an unpleasant taste to food. The only saucepans which will stand the rough treatment which they receive from boys are those of seamless steel, which can be bought with detachable handles, so that they can nest inside each other.

A CENTRAL AFRICAN INTERIOR.

C. Gouldsbury, phot.

BRIDGE-MAKING.

J. Stokes, phot.

With regard to furniture, the less brought the better. Good beds, lamps, one or two folding easy-chairs for drawing-room use, the usual bedroom fittings in coloured enamel, plenty of light fancy stuffs for curtains and draperies, door plates, handles, picture hooks and eyes, and the Army and Navy folding chests of drawers are among the most useful articles for married settlers, but the average bachelor acquires these slowly at the various sales. If the settler is a handy man, he can knock up out of the cases in which his outfit arrives very passable furniture, which can gradually be cheaply replaced by engaging a native carpenter to work for several months.

Carpets may be dispensed with and replaced by native mats, which are cooler, and do not harbour so many insects. Most ceilings in the country are made of mats or calico. For a man intending to build his own house, a case or two of alabastine or some similar wash should not be forgotten.

Glass can be got from Bulawayo. If building is intended, a spirit-level and mason's square should be included.

Boys.—This again is a matter of taste. The usual establishment consists of : Cook, 7s. 6d. to £1 *per mensem* ; table-boy, 7s. 6d. to 10s. ; house-boy, who can also wait at table, 5s. to 10s. ; wash-boy, 5s. ; *sukambali* or plate-washer, 3s. ; *sukampika* or dish-washer, 2s. ; garden-boy, 3s. All the above wages are exclusive of *posho*, which usually consists of four yards of calico, value roughly 1s. 6d. per month, which is given in lieu of food.

The *sukambali* and *sukampika* can usually be rolled into one. Both are little black devils in the superlative degree, and the patience of the average householder usually extends to one only. In some cases an *ulondo* or night-watchman is kept ; as, however, they mostly favour the historic individual who asked a mission doctor for medicine because he could not sleep soundly at night, their services can usually be dispensed with.

The Central African servant is vastly irritating at times ; but he is generally very efficient. He looks after his master's interests to the best of his ability ; and though he may now and again pilfer himself, he usually takes care

that no one else should do so. He has also the great merit
of becoming attached to his own particular master or job,
as the case may be, and rarely leaves except to take a
short holiday. During the master's absence on leave he
is usually either placed on board wages or given a holiday,
and almost invariably comes back upon his employer's
return to the country. And though he may ask for a rise
in wages, he rarely gets it more than once a year—usually
at Christmas-time, and at the rate of an additional shilling
a month.

In conclusion, it may be said that everybody's own boys
are the best in the country and possess all the cardinal
virtues ; while, conversely, the boys of other people are
usually unmitigated scoundrels—a happy state of affairs,
and one which speaks volumes for the capacity for adapta-
tion shown by the Plateau native.

With regard to the taking up of land, the following
notes may be of interest to intending settlers :—

So soon as the settler has definitely selected his piece
of land, he must forward a written application for a farm
through the local Native Commissioner or Magistrate,
describing the situation of the land and attaching a sketch-
map, while stating what native villages or gardens are
upon the site selected and the position of other grants of
land in the vicinity.

Except where natives are located in large numbers,
there is generally no difficulty in arranging with them
to move upon the payment of a small fee for each hut
so removed ; but the British South Africa Company will
not grant a title unless it is made quite clear that the
natives have agreed to move.

When the application has been approved, the settler
must beacon off the angles of his land. Upon payment
of quit rent—£1 per annum per 1000 acres—occupation
is granted for a period of one year in which to pay survey
fees. If the settler desires to purchase the land and not
remain merely a tenant, the price for farms not exceeding
6000 acres is 6d. per acre, and the payment of this price
may be extended over two years if desired.

The survey fees of a farm of 2000 acres may vary from £24 to £30.

A limited number of cattle can be hired from the herds of the British South Africa Company for 10s. per head per annum. The cattle will be left in the hands of the farmer for a period of three years, provided that proper care is taken of them. At the end of this period an equal number of cattle—as many as possible being of the same age and in the same condition as those originally received—must be returned by the farmer.

Young male calves can be bought cheaply from natives for final sale as slaughter or trek oxen in the Southern Rhodesia market. The rancher pure and simple who does not go in for catch crops of cotton frequently ekes out the unproductive years of waiting until his stock matures by starting small native stores, and by growing his own wheat, vegetables, rice, coffee, and fruit speedily reduces his living expenses almost to vanishing-point.

CHAPTER XX

LOOKING AHEAD

The fate of the prophet in his own country is so well known as to have become a truism, contumely and the derision of men being least among the terrors which await him. And to prophesy as to the ultimate fate of this Plateau of ours would be, indeed, to give hostages to Fortune, since there is, at present, but little to indicate the lines along which the country will ultimately progress.

By the thriving farmer, desirous of finding a market for his cattle, the enterprising rubber-planter, the trader with his eye upon the pockets—or substitutes therefor — of the native population, and by the general speculator, waiting, Micawber-wise, for something to turn up, progress must be spelled in block-capitals, since to these it is the consummation of all others most eagerly desired. But to the man who prefers the peace of Nature to aught besides, progress may not stand as so rosy a vision, for assuredly North-Eastern Rhodesia is the last country on the map to preserve its old simplicity, unharassed by the attentions of the financier or of the speculator.

Our awakening must, and can only, come with the advance of the railways. Mr. Rhodes once drew a pencil-line from north to south of the map of this territory, saying, 'That is where the Transcontinental—the Cape to Cairo—Railway will run!' And dare we limit the possibilities of any country which has not yet been placed, by railways, in communication with the outer world ?

Yet the consideration of such an advance involves us at once in a vicious circle of argument. For there is at present no one particular asset in the country which would justify the expenditure of the vast sums which would be needed, and yet it is vain for us to hope that such an industry could be developed without a railway.   Minerals are believed to exist, mountains of coal have been found to the west, but the Plateau has never yet been properly prospected.   Cattle are known to thrive, but the southern border—across which, for the moment, the only market lies—may be closed again as it was before.   The southern mines are crying out for northern labour, but so long as such service involves a long and tedious journey, its popularity must remain dimmed in native eyes.   Un-limited faith and almost unlimited capital are needed before the first sod of any Plateau railway can be turned. Rhodes would have done it had he lived ; now that he is dead, we may only hope that his mantle may fall upon some other equipped with his peculiar genius for opening up the silent places of the earth.

Yet, even now, such possibilities loom large in the minds of men.   Recently *African Engineering* prophesied that Katanga would shortly become the Clapham Junction of Central Africa.   And it went on to state : ' With Katanga as the centre of the Central African railway system, the value of North-Eastern Rhodesia as an agri-cultural centre will be greatly enhanced, on account of the great market which will be opened up by the radiating lines starting from an immensely wealthy centre almost on the border of British territory.'

At the present moment railways are beginning to con-verge upon us from the north, in German East Africa, from the south *via* Broken Hill, from the west *via* Katanga. The Germans seem likely to outdistance us in the matter. Probably in about five years from now the Daressalaam-Tanganyika line will be an accomplished fact, a branch-line arriving, ultimately, at Langenburg on the north-eastern border *via* its already projected route, Kilimatindi-Iringa-Ithaka.   When once completed, this line will divert considerable trade and traffic to the east coast ; and, in all probability, the country will be at once overrun with Swahili and Indian traders.

One must also bear in mind the probability of the Congo interior becoming, almost immediately, a 'free' country in fact as well as in name. There would then lie, within reach of the Plateau, an inexhaustible supply of rubber, and a huge market for European manufactures. In order that we may secure our share of the trade thus waiting to be developed, transport facilities should be brought right up to the eastern border of the Free State at the earliest possible moment. And, with this end in view, the Nyasaland route from the mouth of the Zambesi and across the Plateau will probably be found the most suitable. But existing conditions must first be altered. The Nyasa-land Railway must be continued to Lake Nyasa ; steamers must be added to the wholly inadequate fleet now plying on that lake, and a line must be laid, say from Karonga, on its northern shore, to some point upon Lake Tanganyika. That railway—a matter of 250 miles—could probably be built at a fairly reasonable cost, although there is a stiff gradient from Karonga to be climbed.

But the most probable route of the near future—and the one which, at present, bulks most largely in practical politics—is that *via* Ndola. Already a mail-route is projected which, entering the Plateau on the south-west, will bring us a full week nearer England. Already, too, Broken Hill has lost some of its former importance, since Ndola has absorbed the distribution of up-country traffic. And, in consequence, the heart of the country, so to speak, has been displaced. Fort Rosebery and Kawambwa, which, a year ago, were but mere outposts, have sprung with mushroom growth into centres of activity. No doubt the railway construction work in comparatively close proximity to these stations, with its consequent demand for labour, has had much to say to this result ; but the fact remains that it is on the west of the Plateau at present that the main influx of civilisation must be looked for. The original route from Broken Hill *via* Serenje, Mpika, and Kasama has vanished for a time into the limbo of forgotten things.

With a railway—even of narrow gauge—once within

the territory, the whole aspect of affairs would change. Not only would the white population increase with a bound —a change which would, necessarily, bring in its train the usual economic developments—but the outward, if not the 'essential,' character of the natives would undergo corresponding alteration. Along the line of rail on either hand farmers could grow rice, cereals, Indian corn, cassava, and the like, with the reasonable hope of eventually bringing these products to market in the south, and that at a fair profit after deducting freight. For hitherto, under native hands, the soil of the country has been merely scratched—and, in some parts, that soil is richer than the southern farmer has dreamed of. Presuming reasonable rates, it would be well worth while to breed cattle and even horses, since the railway would obviate the long, tedious, and dangerous journey to the south, with its ever-constant risk of fly belts. Where, nowadays, horses must be imported almost literally with prayer and fasting —with the concomitants of night-treks, clothing the animals from head to hoofs, dousing them with paraffin, paying rewards for the capture of fly upon them, and the like—once the railway arrived they could be off-loaded from fly-proof trucks within three days of their entrainment in Bulawayo—and their progeny returned thither at a profit in the years to come !

With the advent of the railway, too, the necessities of life would at once become cheaper and more certain of delivery. Head-transport would, of course, quickly die the death in the vicinity of the line. Roughly speaking, such transport costs at present 1d. per three miles per 50 lb. ; but it must be remembered that 100 miles takes five days to cover, and, when time is money—as one day it may come to be, even upon the Plateau—such a consideration must carry weight.

With the railway in existence, internal communication by telegraph and telephone could be at once commenced ; not only along the actual line of rail where it would appear in the natural course, but in cross-sections—since the cost of importing the material is the main factor which, at present, militates against the spread of the telegraph system.

Failing a railway, motor-cars or road-engines might be utilised, though it is doubtful whether they would be of much use except for the conveyance of mails. At present they would be out of the question for transport purposes, a fact which was amply proved by the Graetz Expedition in 1908, which, though simply and solely an advertisement, demonstrated conclusively what was already well known, namely, that the roads of the country were constructed for pedestrian traffic only, and are adapted merely to that purpose. The labour necessary to put these roads into the condition requisite for motor traffic— and to maintain them in such repair—would probably cost considerably more than does the head-transport over those roads at present. And, in any case, the question of bridges would constitute a very serious difficulty; although it might, perhaps, be avoided by a system of relay cars, each performing a stage between two large rivers, and trans-shipping cargo by canoes or boats.

In this connection one may well consider the feasibility of utilising the main waterways of the country for transport. The principal river of the Plateau is the Chambeshi, and this, according to Mr. Melland, Assistant Magistrate at Mpika, is navigable to Kavinga's. But, though deep at Kavinga's, at the Bangweolo estuary, where it diverges into many channels, it would necessitate boats of extremely narrow draught. During the dry season it is navigable, for light-draught steamers, to within 50 miles of its mouth, where the first rapids are met with. Thence, up-stream, the river is full of rapids and shallows. When in flood it is navigable to from 130 to 150 miles of its mouth, for light-draught steamers, and this condition of affairs lasts for about six months out of the twelve. All the year round flat-bottomed boats or barges could be used to about 130 miles from the mouth. On the lower reaches the average depth is from 19 to 20 feet. A great extent of deep water is covered with a species of long grass growing on the bottom, but the Wabisa find no difficulty in sailing their

canoes through this, and the Chambeshi itself, its tributaries, and the other rivers flowing into Lake Bangweolo
are used by them all the year round, since they never walk
where they can use a canoe. Native traders also use the
waterways, hiring canoes from the Wabisa, in which they
come from the west side of Bangweolo right up the Chambeshi to the mouth of the Rukuru river, and thence up the
Rukuru to within 25 miles of Kasama. Other tributaries,
such as the Luansenshi, the Munekashi, the Lulingila,
and the Luena are greatly used, being available for flat
barges, canoes, and light-draught steamers for a considerable distance.

The Luitikila may, perhaps, be navigable as far as
Nkandochiti, but there are rapids 4 miles higher up that
river. And boats burning fuel would be absolutely useless in that vicinity, as there is no fuel there. Something
in the nature of a sailing-punt—with centre not lee-
board—might be used for river navigation only. It is
also probable that the Lofu river, flowing into Lake Tanganyika, could be utilised, and in this case porterages
could be made from the Bangweolo river system.

While on the question of transport, it must not be
forgotten that elephant, zebra, and eland abound. The
last-named have already proved most successful in South
Africa, and a cow eland (with her horns off) should prove
an ideal saddle animal, her paces being, as far as can be
judged from observation, all that could be desired. Zebra
exist by the thousand—one night almost say the million—
and their capture should be no difficult matter. Indeed, a
certain gentleman, who is the fortunate possessor of a couple
of horses, recently drove an eland some five miles along
a road with a fly-switch to shorten the distance over which
the meat would have to be carried when it was eventually
shot ; and he is now endeavouring to capture and train
zebra upon which to ride.

The Indian Khudder system might, surely, be introduced
into this country with advantage.

‘ It has long been considered that the African elephant cannot
be trained like its Indian brother, but, though far less docile, it

evidently yields to training in time, as the fact has been proved beyond question by Commandant Laplume at Api in the Congo State. There the young elephants are caught during the dry season, the older animals being frightened off, and the hunters pursuing the calves on foot. Losses are considerable, and the greatest care must be taken of the calves, as they die from all manner of causes, such as hæmaturia, dysentery, pining, and insolation. The training is a very gradual process. For carts and waggons the elephants are usually harnessed in pairs, but for ploughing they are driven singly—and they get through a tremendous amount of work. They are used for riding, and carry the rider's baggage, travelling at the rate of five kilometres an hour for about five hours ; but they ought not to be worked in the heat of the day. The farm at Api now owns some fifty trained elephants ' (*African World*).

From the foregoing it may be seen that elephants should not be neglected when considering the questions of locomotion and transport.

Let us pass to the consideration of the agricultural future of the Plateau. It is very doubtful if this country can ever be colonised, like Canada or Australia, by numerous small peasant proprietors. Our Plateau sphere is essentially a plantation country, that is, a country for white planters working rubber, cotton, etc., with native labour, as is done in Ceylon and other parts of the world.

To select any particular industry as being likely to prove the ultimate mainstay of a country which, like the Tanganyika Plateau, is so rich in potentialities, would be somewhat premature. But in rubber we have at least a tangible asset ; at the worst, it will afford occupation to a limited number of settlers ; at the best it might open up possibilities of tremendous magnitude.

Five years ago Mr. Blyth furnished the Administration with an excellent report upon the agricultural possibilities of the Plateau, in which he stated that, in the Saisi Valley, *ceara* was doing remarkably well. About 75 per cent. of seeds planted germinated, and plants which were not three months old stood about $2\frac{1}{2}$ feet high, and looked absolutely healthy. At the same time at Bismarckburg, a German station on Lake Tanganyika, two days from Abercorn, two-year-old trees were 15 feet high and 12 inches

TREK WAGGON ON NYASA-TANGANYIKA ROAD.

NATIVE TELEGRAPHIST.

in diameter.   At the present moment (July 1910) nearly
400 acres of *ceara* are under cultivation in North-Eastern
Rhodesia.

Rubber in greater or lesser quantities exists practically
all over the Plateau.   The late Mr. R. C. Codrington
localised it as follows in a report addressed to the Directors
of the British South Africa Company in 1903 ; and although the possibilities of the industry have not received
very much attention since then, it is only reasonable to
believe that the forests referred to in the report have increased in size and value.   A direct and beneficial result of
Mr. Codrington's report was 'The Rubber Ordinance'
of 1904, by which trading in and export of rubber was
made illegal.

The report itself may be briefly summarised as follows :

' The Tanganyika district never contained at any time much
rubber ; but small forests, much damaged by wrongful methods of
extraction, still existed in Mporokoso's and Kalimilwa's countries.
Although Mr. Codrington was of opinion that no particular area
was worth being declared a reserve, he thought that if the whole
district were reserved, several small areas would in time become
fairly productive.   As regards the West Luangwa district, the
general altitude was too great to favour the growth of rubber,
which was only to be found on the banks of rivers running down the
Muchinga escarpment.   The North Luangwa and Awemba districts
contained several large rubber-bearing areas, of which the principal
lay around Mwaruli, the burial-ground of the Awemba kings.   Native
tradition held Mwaruli sacred, and the rubber fields were, in consequence, undisturbed.   A short time previous to the issue of the
report a considerable area known as the Mwaruli Rubber Reserve
had been proclaimed.   Small rubber forests were found on the
eastern watershed of the Luangwa Valley, on the Luapula, Luansenshi, Liposhoshi, and, indeed, most of the larger rivers flowing
to the Chambeshi and Lake Bangweolo.   Formerly considerable
amounts of rubber had been exported from these districts, and the
usual barbarous methods of extraction and digging of the roots
had done much to impoverish the resources of the country.

' In September 1902 an export duty of ninepence per lb. was
imposed ;   in February 1903 the possession of root rubber was
made illegal ;   and in May of the same year a reserve was declared
at Mwaruli ;   while in 1904 the Rubber Ordinance already referred

to came into force. These steps were consequent upon the discovery that unscrupulous traders, not content with cutting down the vines, were digging up and boiling the roots. Mr. Codrington noted as significant that of the people employed in this wanton destruction of vines, not one bore a British name, and scarcely one was a naturalised British subject.

On the whole the results seemed disappointing. But Mr. Codrington prophesied that in a few years the knowledge of the Government on the subject would be wider, and facilities for communication more extensive, while there would certainly be more indigenous rubber to justify the existence of a Forestry Department and to attract private enterprise. Some at least of these prophecies have been justified, as is shown from the following extract taken from the last Annual Report of the British South Africa Company :—

' The vast extent of Northern Rhodesia renders it impossible at present to estimate even approximately the extent of the rubber areas, but such evidence as is available points to the great prospective value of this asset. The indigenous rubber of Northern Rhodesia has been strictly protected since 1903, with the result that the number of young vines shows a great increase. This is particularly the case in North-Eastern Rhodesia, where the *landolphia*, being a natural product of the soil and very vigorous, spreads rapidly when protected. A comparatively small portion of North-Eastern Rhodesia has recently been inspected by Mr. de Josselin de Jong, an officer of the Agricultural Department, who estimates that the five rubber forests which he visited covered, in the aggregate, upwards of 21,000 acres, and that the number of existing vines was approximately 800,000. He reports that each of these five areas would make a complete estate capable of carrrying 200 vines to the acre under cultivation. Samples of Rhodesian rubber have been favourably reported upon in London, and tests are being made of the roots and stems of different varieties of the rubber-yielding plants found in Northern Rhodesia, with a view to the purchase of the most suitable machinery.'

Mr. Lyttelton Gell, a Director of the British South Africa Company, has also discussed the question of North-Eastern Rhodesia rubber in full detail. It is impossible, when dealing with a matter of such vital importance to the future of the Plateau, to refrain from digesting his report also.

'A small scientific Department of Forestry might be of great utility. Under a system of control, rubber-bearing trees would be reported upon by the Company's officials, and the Department would advise upon their value and the best methods of extraction and preparation. Encouragement could be given to the investment of capital in the systematic cultivation of rubber in reserved areas, let on terminable leases at progressive rents ; in fact, many ways could be suggested for utilising these great resources.

'There are extensive forests in North-Eastern Rhodesia capable of producing natural rubber of a high commercial value. All East African rubber, if properly prepared, is in demand in London at 2s. 6d.[1] per lb. and upwards ; inferior products fetch 1s. to 2s., and are not always saleable. On the other hand, native methods of preparation are faulty, and impair the market value.

'In the indigenous stage the rubber industry does not require any outlay upon plant or large capital. It is not speculative ; the settlement of the country diminishes the trader's risks, transport is comparatively cheap for an article so highly valuable in proportion to its bulk, and no expensive management is involved.

'The control of forest areas by native chiefs or headmen appears to be almost impracticable. To encourage careful preparation, rubber of unimpeachable quality might be accepted in payment of Hut Tax. The Lagos system, based upon a British conception of tribal property in forests, proves ineffectual, and it is questionable whether in North-Eastern Rhodesia a tribal chief possesses sufficient authority. The native who extracts the rubber is, however, the man who gives negotiable value to the Company's property, and so long as he obeys regulations he might be encouraged in every way.

'Passing to the future development of the industry, Mr. Gell summarises the more important points as follows : (1) Steady replanting of indigenous trees and preservation of shade trees in forest areas ; (2) improved methods of extraction and preparation ; (3) introduction of superior species in cultivated areas ; (4) formation of a small Forestry Department, one member of which would have a special experience in rubber ; (5) invitation of the special attention of Industrial Missions to the preparation of rubber, skilled manipulators being sent to instruct them.

He concludes with the remark that though the exploitation of wild rubber is properly a branch of Forestry Ad-

[1] Now risen to about 4s. a lb.

ministration, the cultivation of rubber stands on a different footing, being a matter for private enterprise and for the concentrated application of brains and capital.

With regard to the best species of rubber for North-Eastern Rhodesia, it must be remembered that *ceara* requires very careful handling, and often gives unexpectedly disappointing results. On page 8 of the *Annual Report of the Agricultural and Forestry Department of the Nyasa-land Protectorate*, for the year ended 31st March 1910, Mr. McCall states: ' I cannot advise planters to enter into *ceara* on a large scale, as we have little or no data regarding the life of the trees, and how they stand tapping. The experiment so far is successful when *ceara* is cultivated and planted in suitable soil, but a failure when planted in exhausted soil or left to battle against weeds without cultivation.' Speaking generally, this statement may be also applied to the Nyasa-Tanganyika Plateau, as the climate is very similar to that of Nyasaland.

It is probable that *landolphia*, planted out between trees upon which it would climb, would do best in North-Eastern Rhodesia, more especially as vines are known to flourish. A man who obtained a concession of good ground where *landolphia* vines flourished would do well, provided he had the capital to support himself for, say, five years without return.

Root rubber (so-called) is most valuable, and flourishes in many parts of the Plateau. There are good areas on the Chambeshi river alone, and plenty in the Luwingu division. In the opinion of Mr. Harger, who, until recently, was engaged in reporting upon rubber, this underground stem rubber is really *landolphia*, of which the stems, through want of suitable support and good trees, have spread laterally instead of 'aerially,' and have burrowed in the earth. The greater part of the stem can be cut, and, provided the tap root is left, will grow again. A machine is in use in the Congo Free State for extracting root rubber, and it is possible that the Guiguet machine would serve the same purpose.

Passing to the cultivation of cotton, we find that two

varieties of Egyptian, Abassi and Affifi, have been grown commercially with marked success, the quality of both varieties being very high—as much as 1s. 2d. per lb. has been realised.

The native Senga cotton is one which would pay well for cultivation, as last season a few bales of cotton grown at Mirongo were sent to England, and fetched 11d. per lb.

Nearly 1000 acres of cultivation are now under cultivation by Europeans in North-Eastern Rhodesia, mostly, however, in the South. Probably, however, cotton grown on, and exported from, the Plateau would be killed by the cost of transport—at any rate until the railway arrives.[1] With such assets in the country as the Chilubula and the Kalungwisi Falls, it should be possible to inaugurate cotton and calico mills, as is done in German East Africa. Local calico would supply a long-felt want, and could be disposed of to natives to almost any extent, and these Falls might supply motive-power for electric light.

Mr. J. Bateson, the cotton expert, whose departure on a tour of investigation through Northern Rhodesia, on behalf of the British Cotton-Growing Association, was announced to the shareholders last year, has reported very favourably upon certain districts. In accordance with his recommendations, steps have been taken to promote the cultivation of cotton on a large scale, and he has returned to Rhodesia to superintend the work. A ginnery is being established in the Kafue district, near the railway, and a plantation has been started in the same neighbourhood, at which different varieties of cotton will be tested. Mr. Bateson reports that over 1000 acres have been planted with cotton this season by white farmers. This is a very satisfactory beginning, and shows that the farmers are fully alive to the possibilities of the country in this direction. Rhodesian cotton has fetched higher prices than that grown in any other new field, except Sea Island cotton grown in the West Indies.

[1] If the proposed ginnery is erected at Karonga at the north end of Lake Nyasa, cotton could be grown, at least in the North Loangwa district, at a profit. The African Lakes Corporation quote cheap rates for ginned cotton from Karonga home, particulars of which can be obtained from their offices, 14 St. Vincent Place, Glasgow.

The *sanseviera*, a natural fibre which grows all over the country, is not at present plentiful enough to pay for working. It is proposed to augment the supply and to improve the quality by planting and cultivating.

Tobacco should, in time, come to be a feature of the country. The Senga native tobacco is well known.

Among miscellaneous agricultural products may be mentioned cassava — extensively grown through the country, but more especially in the vicinity of Lake Bangweolo—nkula or camwood, chillies and tamarinds, rice, ground-nuts, and red and white gums. Some years ago an official, who was interested in gums and resins, sent specimens of red and white gum copal to a friend who was an expert. The white, not having been properly dried, arrived in poor condition, but the red was pronounced a very fine specimen, the purity and adhesiveness indicating a most superior article, which would probably have reached about £20 per cwt. Soya beans might also prove successful.

As regards timber, the timber trees of North-Eastern Rhodesia may be roughly divided into two classes—namely, heart trees, and those of a homogeneous nature. Of the former there are very many kinds, of which *mulombwa*, *mubanga*, *kaimbe*, *mupundu*, *mukula*, *musasi*, *ndale*, and *mulebe* are a few. The heart is usually any shade of red or brown, and is always covered by an outer covering of white wood. As the heart grows thicker with the years, it seems that the outer white covering decreases somewhat in thickness. The heart is in every case both ant and borer proof, while the outer white sap covering quickly gives way to white ants, borers, and rot. These trees are always found in the inland districts away from marshy land, and make up in large part the covering of the large African forests. They need a dry soil in which to flourish. Moreover, they nearly all have the frond leaf and rugged bark, and have grown to the dimensions of timber trees in spite of the annual fires that devastate the whole country. Because of this they are not so abundant as a cursory glance at the forest would suggest.

THE CHISHIMBA FALLS NEAR KILUBULA.

F. H. Melland, phot.

The second class of trees which grow with a homogeneous nature are usually found in the *musito*—that is,
in water. One characteristic of Central African rivers
is that often in flat districts they spread their waters to
a considerable width, and it is in such places that trees
of the greatest height and girth are found. These trees
are, however, usually food for the white ants and borers,
while they do not resist decay like the heart trees of the
forests. The timber of these trees is much softer than
the heart woods—a fact which is, for one thing, due to
their more rapid growth in hot and moist places. These,
in contrast to the heart trees, are usually found with
smoother bark, and with individual leaves. There are
many kinds, of which *mupa, mwengele, luamba, musuku-
buta, musokolobe*, and *musonga* are some.

There are many other trees, and, of course, exceptions
to this rough classification, but the kinds readily fall into
these two classes.

The oak of Central Africa is undoubtedly the heart
tree *mulombwa*. It is of a dark brown colour, with an
oak grain, and is eminently suitable for furniture. When
oiled and polished the most richly figured parts are really
handsome. It is of great marketable value. The beech
is most nearly resembled by the hardwood tree *nsaninga*,
although it is much redder in colour than its British cousin.
Although this is not a heart tree, it is yet both ant and
borer proof. It is, suitable therefore, for all building
purposes.

The cedar is represented in grain by the white-wood
tree of the *musito* called *mwengele*. This is very straight-
grained and free from knots, but, being a *musito* tree, it
is one upon which white ants greedily feed. The borers
do not readily attack it ; it is very easily worked, and
is most suitable for all inside work and furniture.
Because of its grain it resembles cedar when stained.
The saplings of this tree are largely sought after by
builders for rafters, as they are very straight, easily
worked, light in weight yet strong, and usually remain
free from borers.

The wood that takes the place of deal in Central Africa is the *mupa* or *mupata* of the *musito*. Yet its grain does not resemble deal, for it is a much closer-grained wood, and of a stronger fibre. It is most useful for flooring, and for all kinds of carpentry where an ant-proof wood is not specially needed.

Of the fancy woods, such as ebony and rosewood, there are a few, but these are only occasionally met with. Mahogany of various kinds is also to be found.

For the above notes upon timber the authors are indebted to the kindness and technical knowledge of the Rev. W. Freshwater, of the Mporokoso Station of the London Missionary Society.

With regard to the question of cattle, we cannot do better than again quote from Mr. Blyth's report, written in 1905, at which time he was in charge of the Government herd at Mpanga, although he now possesses a very fine herd of his own. He speaks most highly of the prospects of the country as a cattle-raising centre, since, if the grazing being carefully selected, cattle will keep their condition all the year round. This can be accomplished by the use of hay and ensilage, both of which can be easily and cheaply made, and by growing good drought-resisting fodder, such as lucerne and hardy grasses, to carry the cattle through the dry season. But cattle need most careful attention, and if neglected or left to the care of natives they fall off in condition with surprising rapidity.

Native cattle do surprisingly well in unfavourable conditions, seeing that no care is taken as to their grazing; bulls are used to breed indiscriminately, and the heifers are bred from too young. In favourable conditions and with every care, they would quickly equal any stock now produced in South Africa. The importation of good bulls would be the quickest and surest method, but it cannot be advised, as the risks of introducing disease would be too great. There is at present no disease in the country beyond that induced by *Glossina morsitans* (except perhaps 'stiff sickness,' which usually lasts about three days), and the most important point is to prevent its introduction.

Although the German border has been closed on account of this very danger, one may perhaps be optimistic as to its being reopened in the near future. Disease has appeared and disappeared time and again in many countries, and it is well within the bounds of possibility that, without any risk whatever to the herds at present in the country, the vast resources of German East Africa—perhaps the cheapest cattle market in the world—will soon be once more available for stocking the Plateau. Had this been the case within the past two or three years, a large part of the thousands of pounds earned by North-Eastern Rhodesian natives on the southern mines would have been invested in cattle, to the lasting benefit of the country. Probably, too, more applications would be made for farms if this method of stocking were open.

The Southern Rhodesia border has, until recently, been closed against the importation of northern cattle; but this restriction has now been removed, subject to certain conditions of inspection and quarantine. With the growth of the Congo mines it is probable that in the near future the great market [for cattle will be at the Star of Congo.

The great difficulty against which cattle-owners have at present to contend is the prevalence of tsetse fly (*Glossina morsitans*), and the consequent danger of driving down herds to the southern markets. It has been suggested that—presuming the theory that fly do not bite at night to be correct—the Government should clear large spaces every ten miles or so along the route to the south. The cattle would then travel by night, and camp by day in the cleared spaces, surrounded, if necessary, by fires. There are difficulties in the plan, but it seems more feasible than either of the alternative proposals, namely, that a 100-foot track should be cut right through, or that a track should be kept free from fly by shooting down the game on either side of it.

In a recent interview the Administrator, Mr. Wallace,

made the following remarks to a representative of the *African World* :—

'Cattle are thriving in Northern Rhodesia. The herds are increasing steadily, and some imported stock has been brought in from Europe. There is an enormous tract of country waiting to be occupied. . . . It is very little use anybody going to Northern Rhodesia to take up land unless they are prepared with preliminary capital. In cases where two men have gone into partnership, and one has been able to work, they have done very well indeed with small capital—from £200 to £300; but generally speaking, if they take up stock they find themselves handicapped for want of money. The only market is in the south, across the Congo border, and at the mines.'

The rearing of native sheep and goats might be converted into an important industry. In Southern Rhodesia, in 1907, sheep fetched £1 per head, and goats 10s. ; on the Plateau they can be bought at an average of 2s., sheep and goats alike. At present the long journey down, with payment of herds and losses, both by death and by animals arriving out of condition, swallows up all profits ; but with reasonable rates upon the rail there would undoubtedly be money in such speculations for the first few months at least. After that, as breeding stock became plentiful, the prices of southern small stock would probably sink rapidly.

Some time ago a Canadian farmer, named De Clos, projected a scheme for establishing a sheep farm on Mbawala Island in Lake Bangweolo. Being surrounded by deep water, the island is free from dangerous carnivora, so that stock could be left out to graze all night, and would probably do well.

Among the miscellaneous assets of the Plateau one may quote the native cloth-weaving, which is still carried on by Chief Chinakila's *Walungu*—more for practical purposes than for adornment—and the ordinary native bark-cloth, of which many tons are now exported from Uganda and sold at a good profit.

At Sumbu, on Lake Tanganyika, excellent lime is obtainable, and there is no reason why the Alungwana coastmen

should not make this a special industry. The White
Fathers have recently made excellent cement from the
interior crust of ant-heaps, and it has proved most
successful.

No doubt, as the railways progress and the country is
opened up, so that the realisation of an outside market can
be brought before the natives, they will set to work and
improve their industries so as to bring them up to the standard demanded by European traders ; but at the present
moment nothing more is done than serves to meet their
actual needs.

With regard to the possibilities of money-making, outside those of planting and cattle-ranching already discussed,
one cannot do better than quote Mr. Pirie, who, in the
Journal of the African Society, says : ' It must be understood that in the present state of the country's progress
there are absolutely no openings for tradesmen of any kind.
. . . As regards trading, it would be well to bear in mind
that there are already powerful companies established·
against whom it would be found a very difficult matter
to compete.' This warning is still true for any one who
desires to open general trading business only ; but since
this was written several settlers have found that it pays to
run small native stores in addition to their ranches or
plantations, as has been mentioned in the preceding chapter.

Having thus discussed the main assets of the country,
it is impossible to avoid the time-honoured truism which
has been dragged in from time immemorial by every
writer upon native territories, the truism that the greatest
of such assets is the original owner of the country—the
native himself.

The natives of this country will never become a vanished
race as did the North American Indians. They teem
with vitality, they are of sturdy stock, and they are
rapidly increasing. In any discussion of the future, a
place—and that a large one—must be allotted to them.
No consideration of possible developments would be
complete without a distinct programme dealing with the
native aspect.

It has been suggested more than once in Southern papers that the superfluous population of South Africa should be transferred to Northern Rhodesia—that these territories should, in fact, be made a huge native reserve. Sober consideration of such a scheme only serves to define more clearly than before its utter impracticability. We do not want aliens north of the Zambesi ; the problems of our administration will prove quite sufficiently engrossing without complexities of this kind being added. But at the same time there is a happy mean between such a policy and its antithesis (much in favour with a certain section of the Colonial public)—that the native should be permitted to remain providing it is clearly understood that his country is to be developed entirely for the benefit of the white man. And that happy mean would seem to lie in the policy of a strongly-developed native state.

The details of such a policy are not to be lightly worked out. But, upon broad lines, such a scheme would run somewhat as follows : The native would be assisted to grow rubber, cotton, and so forth for the white man ; he would be paid in cash, and thus his wants would increase. We have a precedent for this method in Nyasaland, where cotton is bought from the natives with considerable success. Incidentally, the native—who is first and foremost an agriculturist—continues to perform the work he likes, and retains the sense of racial security, of uninterrupted possession.

Taxes should continue to be paid in money, not in kind. Taking rubber or cotton as the unit of trade, sufficient money would very quickly be earned by the native not only to adjust his liabilities to Government, but also to satisfy his demand for incidental luxuries, once he had learned that only by work, and good work at that, could such money be earned. An agricultural college could be instituted in which would be trained intelligent men, who could, later, act as travelling instructors in the art of cultivating cotton or tapping rubber. There is but little doubt that in a very short time picked natives could be trained to be good foresters. There is an Agricultural

Department attached to Kondowe, and the results have been so excellent that the Livingstonia Mission has acquired a tract of nearly thirty square miles for agricultural development.

In a recent interview the Administrator of Northern Rhodesia said : ' They (the natives) do not make much money, and we want to teach them to do so.' What better method could there be than in the establishment of a definite native industry, which would keep them employed in the dearth of local work ? Later, when planters with capital began to arrive, the assets of the country would be in a condition better calculated to yield good results. The main necessity of such a scheme is a strong Forestry Department.

The present supply of labourers for local work far exceeds the demand — except, perhaps, during the tree-cutting and fencing season, when the supply is apt to fail almost entirely. It is, indeed, this inequality in the supply which constitutes one of the prime difficulties of the situation.

The average cost of labour is, and has been for some years past, 4s. 2d. a month, including calico ration. This rate has not, so far, been affected by the high wages paid on the southern mines, nor need we fear any appreciable rise in wages at present. Thus any enterprise, such as rubber-planting, could calculate upon obtaining as much labour as it needed during ten months of the year at this rate, provided only that decent treatment were meted out to the employees.

As recruiting for the southern mines has not been long established, it is difficult to formulate a definite opinion upon what is still in the experimental stage. On the one hand there is, in some districts, a well-marked dislike to this class of work. In the beginning it was doubtless due to several reasons : firstly, the death-rate ; secondly— and no doubt more important—the distance from home and the length of the contract. The death-rate has been diminished by good diet and careful treatment ; the arrival of the railway at Ndola has put Bulawayo almost within three weeks of the most remote Plateau station. Yet the dislike remains—mostly, no doubt, as a mere matter of prejudice.

Natives are very conservative ; they like to preserve the due rotation of their days. During the early part of the dry season—that is, in April, May, and June—they have finished reaping, and have not yet commenced to lop branches for the forthcoming *vitemene*. Then they are only too eager for work. But it is a very different thing to go away for more than a year. Many of them have aged relatives dependent upon them ; who will provide these with food ? Most of them are married, and, so far, no provision has been made for the wives of mine labourers accompanying them to the south. It is only natural that they should object to leaving their wives for so long a period, with the very probable chance of finding, on their return, that the ladies have grown tired of grass-widow-hood, and have forged for themselves new chains ! More-over, the chiefs themselves do not like to see all the young labour leaving the country ; they still want their *mulasa*, or tribute labour—say, two days per able-bodied male per annum ; while more than one chief has contended that they and the older men do not profit much by the influx of wealth. The young men, when they return, have learned both selfishness and independence ; they pay their own taxes and those of some of their especial cronies, and the balance of the money goes straight into the stores. Unfortunately, also, most of the purchases are gauds and trinkets to tempt the fickle female, with the result that adultery, always the besetting sin of the Plateau, is increasing steadily. Thus the chiefs lose both the services of and authority over their people, and gain but little in exchange. This, however, is one of the inevitable results of altering the economic standards of a people—one of the prices which must be paid for the boon of civilisation.

Another obstacle to the successful recruiting of the Plateau—although it may be overcome—is that Wemba labour is the least popular of any northern labour in the southern market. The Awemba are clannish to a degree,

CEARA RUBBER (28 MONTHS) AT MIRONGO.

FRUIT AND VEGETABLES AT KILONGA MISSION.

and require careful handling. If any of their number get into trouble, the sympathies of the whole gang—who have probably all come from one little cluster of villages —are aroused, and mine and compound managers, who are not always the most complaisant of men, are apt to grow disgusted with the whole gang. It has been said that of the Awemba recently sent down, many spent a goodly proportion of their time in gaol, with the result that the deferred pay due to them on their return was considerably smaller than it would otherwise have been. This, naturally, gave rise to dissatisfaction among the delinquents themselves, and created a bad impression among their relatives at home, who were naturally not at the pains to work out the real reason for the shortage. Possibly the institution of seconding a Native Commissioner from North-Eastern Rhodesia to act as Compound Inspector in Southern Rhodesia will improve this phase of the situation.

For the rest, as has already been said, the native abhors the ticket system, which is universally followed in the south—in mine compounds, at least. And it is still a moot point whether he does not bring back with him from the mines more knowledge of vice, insolence, and general wickedness than he took down. Certainly it is a fact that the return of a gang of repatriates is usually the signal for a crop of civil and criminal cases ; but, as many of these have been accumulating during the absence of the miners, it is hardly, perhaps, a fair test.

On the other hand, there are undoubted advantages. First and foremost, although he may not like the process, the native learns what hard work really means, and it is exceedingly good for him, as he would never learn it here. Then, too, his intelligence and self-reliance are sharpened and tempered to a keener edge by intercourse with men, black like himself, but of many different tribes. He comes back, as has been said before, more of a MAN—and, by his coming, plants the seeds of ambition and adventure in the hearts of his fellows. It needs many drawbacks to counterbalance this concrete effect.

The southern mine manager, living in the daily terror of seeing his stamps ' hung up ' for want of labour, talks hotly of the indolence of ' the nigger,' his disinclination for labour, etc. This is hardly fair to the northern native. What English village would send away the bulk of its young men to a far distant foreign country—for, in the eyes of the native, Southern Rhodesia is that—without their womenkind, for a year or eighteen months ?—especially when, in the eyes of the ignorant multitude, the mine is nothing more or less than a death-trap ?

In considering the future of the country, account must, of course, be taken of Sleeping Sickness—that bugbear nowadays of all too many African administrations. This disease was first diagnosed in North-Eastern Rhodesia in 1907, and at present not more than a hundred of non-imported cases have been discovered, so that it shows no present tendency to develop into an epidemic type. Whenever a new disease attacks a country there is naturally a great outcry at first, from the fear that it may speedily become epidemic. But it seems unlikely that we shall ever upon the Plateau suffer such mortality as in Uganda, since, after all, the bulk of the population is inland, and not upon the shores of the lakes. In the older West Coast colonies, in the basin of the Senegal, the Congo, and the Niger, Sleeping Sickness has existed for over a hundred years, and where it is endemic and of long standing it is accepted as a matter of course, as, after all, the mortality is not to be compared with the enormous death-rate from cholera and plague epidemics in India. It is only the recent mortality in Uganda which has made the disease such a nightmare to the civilised world, since, except where the conditions are exceptionally favourable, Sleeping Sickness is a slow-moving malady.

There is, indeed, every reason to believe that the prompt measures which have been taken have already checked the spread of this hideous disease, and that in the course of the next decade, or even earlier, the malady itself will have been stamped out. Whether the great international waterway of Tanganyika will ever again be open to trade is still in question ; but, at any rate, the lives of those in the territory itself should be secure. And any day may witness the discovery of an effectual cure.

Hitherto we have been menaced by the proximity of the Belgian Congo, where, until recently, no precautions were taken to guard against the reinfection of this territory by prohibiting intercourse. But in July, at a Conference held at Fort Rosebery, a *modus operandi* was arrived at, and the Belgians are now exercising very much the same precautions on their side of the Luapula as are we on ours.

Financially, Sleeping Sickness has proved a heavy scourge to North-Eastern Rhodesia, and more especially to the Plateau proper. This financial strain has been enormous : segregation camps, extra medical men, road patrols, and border guards are some of the incidental expenses which have been rendered necessary ; the removal of villages wholesale from the infected area, together with the necessity of remitting the taxes of natives so removed for a year, of recompensing them for confiscated canoes, and, in many cases, of feeding them during the resulting period of shortage while their new gardens were in course of making— these are among the more direct consequences. Indirectly we have suffered from a corresponding loss of revenue ; the Congo is shut as a labour centre, and transport towards the west is almost at a standstill. Whatever the financial position of North-Eastern Rhodesia may be at the present day, it must be to her lasting credit that her Administration has not hesitated to take the steps that were considered necessary in their full completeness in the face of grave pecuniary losses. A special scientific Commission under the general direction of Dr. Aylmer May, the principal medical officer of Northern Rhodesia, has already been dispatched to the Luangwa Valley, where research work will be carried on under the superintendence of Dr. King-horn, who is a recognised authority upon Sleeping Sickness.

For the last eighteen months much has been heard of the amalgamation of the two territories of North-Western and North-Eastern Rhodesia. Already the financial side of the Administration is worked from Livingstone, while the comptroller of posts and telegraphs also supervises the mail services and postal arrangements from that place. The medical service has also been amalgamated. It is probable that before these lines are in print the civil services of the two territories will have been welded into one, which will probably be reorganised upon lines suggested by the recent Commission. The new administrative headquarters will be at Livingstone, which is no farther from most of the Plateau stations than Fort Jameson, besides being upon the Cape to Congo Railway. The present system of two distinct Administrations has proved cumbersome and unnecessarily expensive.

At the present moment the position is that an Order in Council will be shortly promulgated dealing with the amalgamation of North-Eastern and North-Western Rhodesia.[1] Mr. L. A. Wallace, C.M.G., will be the Administrator of the joint territory. It is, of course, too early to anticipate the changes which must accrue from such a development, but one cannot doubt that they will prove beneficial to the main interests of the country. Slavish uniformity will probably not be aimed at, and such matters as the game laws, import duties, hut taxes, and the like will not necessarily conform to one standard in every district.

Sooner or later the question of entering the South African Union must be considered in respect of these northern territories ; but that also is a matter which it would be premature to discuss at present.

Whether or not the Plateau can be held to be in reality a white man's country must remain largely a matter of individual opinion. From the point of view of health there is, at least, no drawback. There are, no doubt, unhealthy and malarious spots ; but they are few and far between. Such diseases as exist are frequently accompanied by an access of undesirable nervous symptoms, which are sometimes more alarming than the actual physical effect of the disease itself upon the patient. In all lonely countries there exist, in far greater degree than

[1] This Order in Council has since been promulgated, on August 17, 1911.

in crowded communities, the temptations towards drugs and drink; but these are now things of the past—a fact which is no doubt due in great measure to the presence of so many married ladies. Neurasthenia is not infrequent; the high elevation and the isolation being considered, this is not surprising. Ordinary hygienic precautions and the constant use of quinine will serve to safeguard the average individual, and the free and open-air existence tends to minimise disease.

But unfortunately other things besides mere healthy conditions are needful for successful colonisation—if such colonisation be understood to mean the permanent settlement of European families. Even in the very healthiest spots it is hardly a country for English children beyond the age of six or seven. Lack of congenial society, lack of education, lack of the ordinary interests of the average child, the difficulties of introducing white nurses or governesses, the scarcity of medical men—all these are factors— and important ones—in deciding whether or not a child should be allowed to remain in the country after a certain age. And if this is finally proved to be impossible, the situation must inevitably resemble that in which Anglo-Indians still find themselves after over a century of occupation—a situation always unfortunate, and, in this case, accentuated by the greater distance from England.

There are, it is true, good schools in Southern Rhodesia; perhaps in time one may be opened in Livingstone when numbers permit. But even then it may be doubted whether the arrangement would be a satisfactory one to most parents, and at the best it would be begging the question— the question of the permanent and complete settlement of English families.

These, then, are the main factors of the future. Lacking the gift of prophecy, it is beyond our power to do more than point to them as they exist. It lies with the capitalists of Europe to transmute what are, at present, mere shadowy possibilities into concrete facts, and the first step along the path which leads towards that goal must be the laying down of a Plateau railway. Once that has been accomplished, the results will follow in orderly sequence ; until it has been accomplished, the Plateau will remain what it is now—a land of many possibilities, peopled with contented, easy-going natives, governed by a handful of white men—a primitive, absorbing land, full of old romance, but lacking the stimulus of latter-day materialism.

Many of us would not change conditions if we could, for the peace of Lotus Land is upon us. The stress of modernity brings trouble in its train. But there are generations to follow us, and their claims must be considered. One day the Nyasa-Tanganyika Plateau may come to be a much-valued corner of the Empire ; and, with such a possibility in view, we can do no less than forego our present peace and turn to sterner matters.

INDEX